# A CINEMA OF LONELINESS

# A CINEMA OF LONELINESS

**Penn, Kubrick, Scorsese, Spielberg, Altman**

**SECOND EDITION**

Robert Phillip Kolker

New York    Oxford
Oxford University Press
1988

Oxford University Press

Oxford   New York   Toronto
Delhi   Bombay   Calcutta   Madras   Karachi
Petaling Jaya   Singapore   Hong Kong   Tokyo
Nairobi   Dar es Salaam   Cape Town
Melbourne   Auckland

and associated companies in
Beirut   Berlin   Ibadan   Nicosia

Copyright © 1980, 1988 by Oxford University Press, Inc.

Published by Oxford University Press, Inc.,
200 Madison Avenue, New York, New York 10016

Oxford is a registered trademark of Oxford University Press

Library of Congress Cataloging-in-Publication Data
Kolker, Robert Phillip.
A cinema of loneliness: Penn, Kubrick, Scorsese, Spielberg, Altman
Robert Phillip Kolker.—2nd ed.
p. cm.
Includes index.
ISBN 0-19-505389-3.
ISBN 0-19-505390-7 (pbk.)
1. Motion pictures—United States. 2. Motion picture plays—
History and criticism. I. Title.
PN1993.5.U6K57   1988
791.43′0973—dc19                           87-34945   CIP

9 8 7 6 5 4 3
Printed in the United States of America

**IN MEMORY
OF MY FATHER**

# PREFACE

American film begs us to leave it alone. From its beginnings, it has presented itself as an entertainment, as an escape; it is made to give pleasure, to excite, to offer us a surrogate reality. On occasion it offers examination of a social or political problem. But rarely has it taken itself very
seriously, and it has not, until quite recently, been taken very seriously
by its critics. In recent years many people have stopped leaving it alone.
As critical scrutiny continues, it becomes more and more clear that,
despite what most producers would like, film is not temporary, not fleeting; it has had—particularly in those years from the early twenties to
the middle fifties, when movies were the most popular form of entertainment—a cumulative effect, giving the culture a way of looking at
itself, articulating its ideology, reflecting and creating its physical
appearance and gestures, teaching and confirming its shared myths. The
questions that continue to need asking are why and how. The deeper
we probe, the more we discover about the ingenuity and the disingen-
uousness of American cinema, the ways it has used the intricacies of its
formal structure to hide that structure and present itself as an unmediated presentation of reality, even when it was offering itself as an
escape from reality. The more we look and the more we discover about
American film, the more we discover about the methods of looking,
about the ways film works upon an audience and the audience upon it.

The growth of serious critical inquiry into American cinema began as that cinema went into a decline. Beginning in the late fifties production dropped, the studios collapsed, the economic system of filmmaking degenerated into chaos. Television took over as the cultural image-maker, inheriting many of the attitudes, and few of the successes, of the major period of American filmmaking. These events permitted a space for inquiry, a convenient cleavage in cinema history. They also provided opportunities for some filmmakers to break out of the old production methods, the old assumptions of cinematic form and content, and to begin looking, along with some critics, at the nature of their medium, its history, its methods and effects. Their works began to move in more than one direction. Their films were, and are still, primarily entertainments, and the concern for making a profit determines all phases of their work. But despite, or even in the face of, this overriding and often crippling concern, some filmmakers have seriously attempted to confront and examine the form and content of what they do. They make detours into their cinematic past, they reflect upon the films that preceded them, they self-consciously call upon the formal elements at their disposal to build a narrative and control audience participation with it. There has been no direct joining of forces of critic and film-maker, but there has been an occasional paralleling of inquiry and an acknowledgment on both sides that film is a serious business: financially, formally, culturally.

Five of these filmmakers—Arthur Penn, Stanley Kubrick, Martin Scorsese, Steven Spielberg (replacing Francis Ford Coppola), and Robert Altman—are the subjects of this study. They are part of a group that has been referred to as "the new Hollywood," "the Hollywood Renaissance," the "American New Wave," phrases that suggest that they and others somehow changed or revitalized our cinema. Would that were the case. The ability of these filmmakers to function more independently than those who came before them, and their effect on filmmaking in general, has been rather compromised. The essays that follow attempt to reach an understanding of the work, the independence, the compromise, and the effect of these filmmakers on American film, and the effect of that film on the culture at large.

# PREFACE TO
# THE SECOND EDITION

American film has a peculiar, contradictory, and self-defeating dynamic. In form and content Hollywood tends to be conservative, always maintaining an ideological dead center. Economically, it tends to be adventuresome. Studios and producers spend a very great deal of money to create emotional excitement and response, the success of which is measured only by one other response—money spent by ticket buyers and then videotape renters to create enormous returns on the original investment. In hopes of these returns, great financial risks are taken. Only on the rarest of occasions, however, are they taken in favor of the imagination. Most often money (or loans or credit) is ventured on the promise that no imagination will be exercised at all, or only on already known and successful ideas. The potential of something new and intriguing being done in American cinema is always undercut by the reality that the new will, in fact, be the same as always. All novelty or originality is subsumed under the conventions informing all mass market cultural representations—film, television, journalism, politics—assurances that what is to be seen and heard is the simplest, least threatening, and most easily assimilable of what has been decided we need to know.

This cycle of self-referential affirmation is rarely broken. The first edition of *A Cinema of Loneliness* documented a period when it occasionally was, and spoke of five filmmakers who were responsible, to one degree or another, for questioning the self-affirming representations offered by film. All of those filmmakers have continued to make films since the book's publication, and indeed will have made more films by the time this edition is in press. The unhappy fact is that none of them has maintained the formal and contextual energy and inquisitiveness that marked their sixties and seventies work. Francis Ford Coppola's fall from effective filmmaking has been so great that I have replaced the chapter on his work with one on Steven Spielberg. In this failure of imagination is the trace of American cinema's fall during the late seventies and early eighties. There is no doubt that, at the moment, American cinema is moribund as a creative force. The conditions that permitted some occasional independent work in the sixties and early seventies no longer exist, or if they do, only for underfinanced, poorly distributed films (rare films like Bette Gordon's *Variety* or Jim Jarmush's *Stranger than Paradise,* both of which appeared in 1984, both of which were financed by European television).* I will elaborate more thoroughly on the dynamics of production in the Introduction. But it is important to note that, given the current means of film ownership and production, certain events are inevitable. Profitable dissemination is, as it always has been, the guiding force of all movie-making. New "delivery systems," which have expanded rapidly in the early eighties, mean that every film, long before it actually becomes a film, must be sold for videotape distribution, to cable and network television. What occurs in the elaborate deal-making processes is a sort of pre-placation, the assuring of prospective corporate clients—even before they are approached—that the film will be acceptable, accessible, and undemanding in any way. The result is a staggering uniformity and predictability of content which is generated by an invisible form that demands nothing of the spectator but an assenting gaze.

The modernist project—the questioning and revising of old forms and conventions, the denial of self-evident truths—which was a primary subject of *A Cinema of Loneliness,* is over. It was over before the first edition appeared. Kubrick's *Barry Lyndon* (1975), Altman's *Buf-*

---

*Dates are given for the first major reference to a film and reflect the year of the film's release, which is not always the year in which it was made.

*falo Bill and the Indians, or Sitting Bull's History Lesson* (1976) and *Three Women* (1977) were the last commercial films by American directors seriously to play against the conventions of cinematic story-telling. Postmodern American film has done its best to erase the traces of sixties and seventies experimentation (what little there was of it within the entire output of that period), returning with a vengeance to a linear, illusionist style.[1] That style in turn creates, or re-creates, the ready acceptance of conventional expression. Coupled with the increased ability on the part of many filmmakers to use images and narratives to manipulate response, the viewer has been subjected, more than ever, to great imaginary structures of displaced yearning, misplaced heroism, and forced amelioration in films that pose banal solutions to the wrong questions.

With very few exceptions, American film is simply no longer very interesting to someone looking for the expression of an inquisitive imagination. However, to anyone curious about how the culture is being represented in visual images, and the obverse—how visual narratives structure the images to which the culture assents—it remains fascinating and, occasionally, frightening. The new edition continues and expands the inquiry into the phenomenon of cinematic representations of the culture and brings up to date (as much as that is possible) the work of most of the directors originally discussed in the book. Despite the relative falling off of their powers, they need further evaluation and reevaluation within the changing patterns of American film. Since initial publication, Arthur Penn has made *Four Friends* (1983), *Target* (1985), and *Dead of Winter* (1987). Stanley Kubrick directed *The Shining* (1980) and *Full Metal Jacket* (1987). Martin Scorsese has made *Raging Bull* (1980), *The King of Comedy* (1983), *After Hours* (1985), and *The Color of Money* (1986). Robert Altman, despite heavy economic odds, has continued as the most prolific and most imaginative of the group with eight films: *A Perfect Couple* (1979), *Popeye* (1980), *Health* (1981), *Come Back to the Five and Dime, Jimmy Dean, Jimmy Dean,* (1982), *Streamers* (1983), *Secret Honor* (1984), *Fool for Love* (1985), and *Beyond Therapy* (1987). He has also directed material for television. The films of Penn, Kubrick, Scorsese, and Altman still stand as important markers in the history of contemporary American cinema.

Francis Ford Coppola, to whom a chapter was devoted in the first edition, has, it seems to me, proven a much less important filmmaker over the course of time. His cinematic imagination, along with his attempts to remain independent, to operate his own studio, produce or distribute other people's films, has failed. In retrospect, his films seem not to bear the amount of analysis first given them, and certainly the work he has produced since the second *Godfather (Apocalypse Now, One from the Heart, The Outsiders, Rumblefish, The Cotton Club, Peggy Sue Got Married, Gardens of Stone)* has lacked the insight and careful attention to form that marked the earlier material. While I will continue to refer to his work (*The Conversation* is still a major example of early seventies modernist practice, and *Apocalypse Now* is an important indication not only of the dissolution of formal coherence in Coppola's work but of the changing ideological patterns in recent cinema), I have substituted for him a chapter on the ideological formations of eighties film and the work of Steven Spielberg. Spielberg may be no more or less a passing phenomenon than Coppola, but the popularity and influence of his work demand some attention, and the complex of ideologically conservative films, of which his are at the lead, calls out for analysis.

The purpose of *A Cinema of Loneliness* is threefold: to examine the brief modernist movement in commercial American cinema (and in the process to examine form as meaning and the meaning of form); to investigate the ways in which cinematic images and narratives intersect with, become charged by, and represent the culture; and, at the same time, to investigate the work of certain individual filmmakers who are at one time special in their style and representative of larger cinematic movements. The first element of investigation is now historical, for the modernist period is, as I said, over. The second is an ongoing phenomenon and especially pertinent for cinema in the eighties, which became such a clear and brilliant mirror of the dominant ideology. The last element is becoming more and more problematic as the individual director has receded in importance in the filmmaking business and in the business of criticism. While it is still possible and necessary to talk of individual creators, the truth is that the brief time of the Hollywood *auteur* is gone. Producers began turning away from strong individual filmmakers—who make demands for money and time, and insist upon expressing themselves—in the late seventies. The move was climaxed by the debacle over Michael Cimino's *Heaven's Gate* (1980), a film that proved that directors who once made money (as Cimino did with *The Deer Hunter* in 1978), would not necessarily do it again, despite all their pretensions. With the exception of a moneymaker like Spielberg or a perpetual renegade and recluse like Kubrick (or a more commercially successful recluse, Woody Allen) or Robert Altman, who insists upon pursuing his interests despite the hindrances offered by the film business, the individual filmmaker has as little, or less, opportunity to work his or her individuality now than in the studio period of the thirties and forties. (This has become a special problem for women directors. With the rare exception of someone like Susan Seidelman with *Desperately Seeking Susan* (1984) and *Making Mr. Right* (1987) or Donna Deitch with *Desert Hearts* (1986)—they have had to make quite standard films, unmarked by a feminist perspective.)

Given all this, there is some small bad faith in retaining the original structure and critical point of entry in this new edition of the book. *Auteur*ism—the notion that the director is the controlling creative force in the making of the film—has been negated by the realities of production and absorbed into more complex critical theory. But in the face of these facts it seems necessary to discuss that brief period when individuals did have some opportunity to impress and express some insights and to pursue the romantic possibility that there can still be individual interventions in the homogeneity of film. By giving a certain structure to that homogeneity and noting differences through the analysis of the work of various individuals, my desire is to challenge that homogeneity of form and substance that threatens to leave American film undifferentiated and uninteresting.[2]

Therefore, with the exception of substituting a chapter on Spielberg for Coppola, and discussing the ideology of eighties cinema, the structure of the original book remains the same. Within that structure, changes have been made. I have tried to incorporate discussions of recent films within the argument rather than tacking them on at the end of a chapter. This sometimes means that, on the basis of recent work, the point of view taken on a given figure or his earlier work may have changed, requiring a somewhat different reading or conclusion.

Also, I have altered some of the grammatical stylistics of the book. A key element in the project of ideological analysis here is an attempt to understand how a film addresses its audience and its audience the film; how the viewer is made a subject of the work viewed. In so doing, my tendency was to refer to a communal "we," "our," or "us": "we see" such and such a thing. Clearly, I was attempting to account for some kind of universal response, or to posit an ideal viewer who responded for everyone. Alan Williams has noted that such usage is "wholly rhetorical" and implies a kind of transcendental subjectivity on the part of the work's imagined spectator.[3] Since my point is the denial of such transcendence, and an attempt to discover meaning and response within the interplay of film text, other texts related to it, the culture and the viewer, all of which are formed by concrete social circumstances, such an implication of rhetorical universality is counter-productive. In the end, I am not at all convinced that my substituting "the viewer" or "the audience" for "we" substantially solves the problem. The viewing subject still remains a rather diffuse and somewhat imaginary construct. But perhaps the change will be useful in pointing up the problems involved in speaking about who is addressed by a film.

Finally, and despite my complaints about the state of recent film, some effort has been made to prevent this new edition from becoming merely an angry denunciation of the state of contemporary film. While the pluralism of American cinema has become greatly reduced, I would hope that some openings for the imagination, however small and constricted, remain. Also, beneath the blandness or the violence, one can still detect the energy of American filmmaking. That this energy is greatly compromised or directed toward useless or unpleasant ends is clear; but energy has a way of expanding and finding transgressive outlets. Ed Buscombe writes:

> Hollywood has been able to produce films which present with a solidarity, concreteness and intensity no other cinema has rivalled the material of its national life. Everyone who has ever been exposed to the American cinema has not only a detailed sense of what America looks like, feels like . . . but also a vivid knowledge of the dynamism and force of its social life, represented in a style at once concrete and multi-faceted.[4]

The enthusiasm of a foreign observer may not be borne out by all the realities. Buscombe does confuse the conventions of cinematic content with the actualities of material life, and he may no longer believe that American film's style is so multifaceted. But he is quite right about the concreteness and intensity of American cinema's representations. Here is where signs of life remain. Moribund is not exactly the same as dead.

*Silver Spring, Maryland*                                        R.P.K.
*June 1987*

# ACKNOWLEDGMENTS

I wish to thank the following individuals and organizations who helped me with their time and conversation, their offer of prints to view, of research materials and permissions, of help in reading or preparing the manuscript.

Gary Arnold, Joe Balian, Stephen Bernstein, Leona Capeless, Curtis Church, Eddie Cockrell, Maria Coughlin, Wally Dauler, Linda Duchin, Don Elliott, Charles Feiner, Donna Gigliotti, Jamie Glauber, Stephanie Golden, Emily Green, Myra Hoffman, Barbara Humphrys, Margot Kernan, John Kersting, Fran Kiley, Kathy Loughney, Sheldon Meyer, Joe Miller, Clyde Norton, J. Douglas Ousley, John Pacy, David Parker, Roberta Penn, Stephen Prince, Gene Robinson, Mary Louise Rubacky, Martin Scorsese, Robert Self, John Sery, Mike Swank, Frank P. Tomasulo, Harry Ufland, Joseph Weill, Fred Whitehead, Robin Wood.

The American Film Institute, Cinecom International Films, Corinth Films, Films Incorporated, *The Journal of Popular Film,* The Library of Congress Motion Picture Section, *Sight and Sound,* Swank Motion Pictures, Oxford University Press, Twyman Films, The University of Maryland Department of Communication Arts and Theatre.

Except as noted, all stills appear courtesy of The Museum of Modern Art/Film Stills Archive.

Linda Saaty Kolker, as always, made certain that things made sense.

# CONTENTS

# A CINEMA OF LONELINESS

# INTRODUCTION

When the studios, as independent corporate bodies, fell apart in the late fifties and early sixties, assembly-line film production ended. Previously each of the major studios was a self-contained filmmaking factory with its own labor pool of producers, directors, writers, players, and technicians, turning out many films a month during the years of peak production. This self-containment and mass production created mediocrity to be sure, as well as an arrogance that comes with security of product and market. But out of the arrogance and the mediocrity came also a body of work of formal skill and contextual complexity unmatched by the cinema of any other country. If the films produced were not intended to be taken seriously as enduring examples of individual artistic worth, they often enough overcame the intent of their makers to stand as enduring examples of *filmmaking*, and all the collective energy that implies. They came as well to stand for the collectivity of film viewers; they created the images in which a culture consented to see itself.

The studios were places where support and security were offered to those who could work within their restraints, and when they fell that security and assuredness fell with them. The reasons for their fall were many and varied. Television, of course, was a major cause. In the late forties and early fifties, population patterns shifted. People moved to the suburbs and watched television rather than going out to the movies once or twice a week. Indeed, television now shares with film the major work of producing narratives for the culture. But even before the impact of television was fully felt, movie attendance began falling from its 1946 peak. Studio executives met this falling-off by tightening budgets, firing production staff (mainly in their story and publicity departments), and in general lessening the production values of their films. An attitude of self-defeat seemed to be in operation, an attitude that was reinforced by two other events that occurred between 1947 and 1949, which in fact initiated the studios' change and ultimate collapse. The hearings of the House Committee on Un-American Activities made production heads fearful and timid, uncertain as to what kind of content might be branded as subversive, what kind of creative person—director, writer, player—would be frowned upon as un-American. HUAC and Hollywood's self-imposed blacklist managed to damage irrevocably any courage the old studios might have had. The courts managed to damage their economic power. The divestiture rulings of the late forties separated the studios from the theaters they had previously owned. They could no longer count upon a guaranteed market for their films and had to seek out exhibition outlets on an individual basis. On top of this, foreign markets began placing quotas on American film. The confidence and self-sufficiency that had supported the studios since the twenties fell apart.

Uncertain as to what they could say in their films, uncertain as to whom they could say it, the studios floundered. They squandered their efforts on technical experiments—Cinerama, CinemaScope, 3D—and on overblown biblical and Roman epics. This is not to say that important films were not made in the fifties—they were, and it is a decade of films as rich in ideological contradictions as the eighties–only that the focal point of Hollywood filmmaking became diffuse, and by the end of the decade the "product," once controlled by a studio from inception to exhibition, was controlled and executed by different hands, from different sources, and for different ends.

The studios still exist, of course, but the physical means of production are no longer as centralized as they were during the decades from the twenties to the early fifties; the studios do not have their own in-house players and technicians, nor do they have strong individual identities (during the thirties and forties, each of the studios had developed a style and approach, a stock company of players, and even typical story subjects which made their films quickly recognizable). On the contrary, they are without identity and homogeneous. Whereas individuals such as Louis B. Mayer at Metro-Goldwyn-Mayer, Darryl F. Zanuck at Twentieth Century-Fox, Jack L. Warner at Warner Brothers, Harry Cohn at Columbia guided their studios with dictatorial power for years, now production executives move from one studio to another, trading past successes on recent failures and the promise of future blockbusters.

The studios through which these individuals move are no longer independent entities (perhaps "independence" is a relative term, for in their original incarnation the studios were quite dependent upon their financial officers on the East Coast and the banks who backed their films). Now they are either part of some larger, diversified corporation or owned by individuals whose function—and this is the major point of difference—is not making film, but amassing media outlets for various ideological reasons, the most important of which is the production of profit from the dissemination of news and fiction. The "product," more than before, is a means to this end. From an assembly line product made to service the mass entertainment market, film (and its reincarnation on videotape) is now part of a large structure of ownership and distribution. The studios of the past appear to be small businesses by comparison.

The effect of all this on the films that are made has already been noted. Homogeneity of production results in homogeneity of product. Filmmakers of imagination no longer have a centralized community of administrators and craftsmen who can be drawn upon to support them from production to production. Each project has first to be accepted by a corporate administrator, developed, financed, and produced as part of a major "deal." To be accepted and secured it must satisfy requirements, stated and unstated, of conventionality, easy legibility, sentimentality or brutality. Instead of the studio producer reigning over a production, the corporate executive, accountant, and talent broker have powerful control. The deal and the contract loom over the production, affecting it perhaps more perniciously than any boorish old studio head ever could.[1]

Huge amounts of money are spent (or promised) in hopes of making huge amounts of money. The shaky independence originally gained by some filmmakers when the old studio structure fell is now thoroughly compromised by the fact that many films are made as part of a complex economic structure that is created with the expectation that the individual film and its eventual appearance on videotape will spawn not only large financial returns, but offspring that will further those returns even more. The phantom promise of "artistic freedom" offered when the old Hollywood structure collapsed has turned into something of an economic nightmare where costs, salaries, profits, and reputations are juggled and manipulated, with the film itself all but disappearing in a mass of contracts and bookkeeping.

That small group of filmmakers who emerged in the late sixties and early seventies and were able to take brief advantage of the transitional state of the studios, using their talents in critical, self-conscious ways, examining the assumptions and forms of commercial narrative cinema, had a difficult task. They were without community or security. The corporate community that rapidly re-formed around them limited and compromised their small efforts, and they must now more than ever deal with the fact that without profitable returns on their work, they could not work at all. "Studio interference" has merely changed its complexion and complexity, incorporating not only economic pressures, but the individual filmmaker's own judgment and fears.

Those filmmakers have survived or succumbed to the changes in production in various ways. Robert Altman and Stanley Kubrick continue to accommodate themselves to the situation. During the seventies, Altman created his own mini-studio within which he could work with a minimum of interference. He seemed able to get backing for his films on his own terms, even though he had not had a commercial hit since *M.A.S.H.* in 1969. In 1980, after a number of his films failed commercially, Twentieth Century-Fox refused to distribute *Health*. Even though the enormous production of *Popeye* did do well, Altman decided to withdraw completely from mainstream production and sold his studio. He has since continued his career with inexpensively filmed versions of works originally written and produced for theater. Paris is now his center of operations. Kubrick divorced himself from the chaos of contemporary American production in the early sixties. He works in England, and his films have been successful enough so that he can command both money and independence. He followed his demanding and uncommercial film *Barry Lyndon* with the commercially oriented adaptation of a Stephen King novel, *The Shining*, thereby re-establishing his financial viability. Arthur Penn seemed able to work happily within the confusing bounds of post-studio production in the mid- and late sixties. His films were popular, though their popularity derived from an inherent sense of defeat that seems to have undone their creator. As a filmmaker, Penn has just barely survived into the eighties, and that survival has come with a decline in formal control and an increase in reactionary content. Martin Scorsese has survived well by making films for modest amounts of money and modest returns. Though his recent films are less formally adventurous than his seventies work, they continue (with the exception of *The Color of Money*) to be thoughtfully constructed, inquiring deeply into the nature of cinematic and cultural perception. Unlike Scorsese, Spielberg has rapidly become the master of the enormous budget and enormous project; he has formed his own production company and oversees the work of other directors. Where Coppola's imagination seemed to shrivel under the heat of large production, Spielberg's has flourished. But it is a peculiar kind of flourishing, in which imagination is put at the service of placation and manipulation. Spielberg's energy and ability to accommodate his audience make him, for the moment, the most significant figure of the "new" Hollywood and its economic demands.

But we must be careful. Dwelling upon economic realities works only to a point, after which the critic runs the risk of getting caught up in a self-defeating cycle in which the film's existence as a commodity makes serious discussion of its form and content impossible. Other realities must be attended to. In American filmmaking (and not only in American filmmaking) the economic situation is only one of many factors that determine what a film will be. The sense of defeat alluded to in regard to Arthur Penn's work is not only a problem of film finance, but of the way Penn views, and communicates his view of, American culture. The fact that his recent films have moved to the right may be the result of a confluence of personal, ideological, and economic pressure, but it is not a move dictated only by that last item. That Coppola got himself caught up in enormous projects, with a concomitant failure of narrative and structural control, while Scorsese is content with smaller, more experimental works, is as much a matter of personal inclination and emotional response as anything else. Spielberg has thrived on the big-budget, special effects film; but he is able to spend huge sums because the narrative structure and ideological energy of his films bring large audiences who are moved by them. Ideological assent generates money, not the other way around. What Spielberg has to say in *E.T.* or *The Color Purple* and Scorsese in *Taxi Driver* or *The King of Comedy* is indeed determined by the economic necessities of filmmaking, but it is determined as well by the very different ways these filmmakers perceive and respond to the culture, the ways film has delineated that culture, and the response of the culture to film.[2]

To understand this more clearly, let me repeat the fact that the initial period of transition during the late fifties and early sixties permitted a certain freedom of inquiry, which, no matter how compromised, continues to leave a small mark on most of the filmmakers who concern us here. Most of them remain, despite other problems, delighted with film and its formal properties, curious about what they can do with their medium. Their roots go back to the burst of cinematic enthusiasm and creative energy in Europe in the late fifties, where young filmmakers reexamined traditions and conventions in ways that had an enormous influence on the Americans who followed them.

The French, and Europeans in general, never had a studio system comparable to America's. At the same time, they never had an intellectual condescension toward film comparable to America's. Unlike their American counterparts, French intellectuals have not considered film a substandard form of entertainment, but rather a form of expression to be taken seriously. They have loved film, and American film in particular, both intellectually and emotionally. In the fifties, a particularly obsessed group of Frenchmen, among them Jean-Luc Godard, François Truffaut, Claude Chabrol, Eric Rohmer, and Jacques Rivette, formed a group around Henri Langlois's Paris Cinémathèque and André Bazin's journal *Cahiers du Cinéma*. They glorified American film to the detriment of French film; they perceived the ability of the individual filmmaker to rise above studio uniformity. They recognized the visual strength of American film (partly because, knowing little English and seeing unsubtitled prints, they were unencumbered by dialogue), and they recognized the strength of American film's generic patterns. They used their understanding to fashion an approach both to their own and to American cinema in a concerted critical effort. They reevaluated the role of the screenwriter and the director, they explored film genres; in short, they celebrated and analyzed film as a special narrative form with a voice, a text, and an audience deeply interrelated.[3] Their critical perceptions were passed on to American film scholars. They themselves turned to filmmaking, with an organized knowledge of what they wished to do. Their films were small, personal, and inexpensive. Early on they worked together (for *Breathless*, Truffaut supplied the story, Chabrol the technical assistance, and Godard, of course, the direction), and at least briefly after they went their own ways a sense of communal origins, and certainly a sense of commitment to cinema, continued.[4]

The influence of the French New Wave on both American film criticism and filmmaking is important and still visible, if now somewhat perfunctory (Truffaut appears as the scientist Lacombe in Spielberg's *Close Encounters of the Third Kind* and his film *Wild Child* is alluded to in *The Color Purple*; a sign in a Paris café that reads "Don't Shoot the Piano Player Anymore" is visible in Penn's *Target*). Despite the influence, no "new wave" in America occurred, no movement. That brief freedom I have been discussing was really a freedom to be alone within a structure that momentarily entertained some experimentation. The experiments that were undertaken, based upon some things the New Wave was doing, were very much on an individual basis and made within the tradition of Hollywood film. The filmmakers discussed here used those traditions and the basic patterns of American filmmaking as a point of interrogation, foregrounding them, bringing them to consciousness, attempting to determine their further usefulness as narrative tools. They tried in various ways to come to terms with narrative itself, the story and its telling, and to realize the possibilities inherent in refusing the classical American approach to film, which is to make the formal structure of a work erase itself as it creates its content. These directors, especially in their late sixties and seventies work, delighted in making the viewer aware of the act of watching a film, revealing it as an artifice, something made in special ways, to be perceived in special ways. Even Steven Spielberg, younger than the others and deeply committed to commercial narrative conventions, continues the New Wave tradition of playful allusiveness to other films within his own work.

The paradoxes and the contradictions inherent in all this are painful. Influenced by a group of French intellectuals, some American filmmakers became thoughtful about their films. But, unlike their French colleagues, the films they made rarely explored ideas and rarely explored their own larger ramifications. As delighted as they were (and in some instances still are) in the formal possibilities of their medium, as conscious as they were of the genres they emulated or attacked, they did not go very far beyond the tradition and never presented real alternatives to that tradition (in Spielberg's films, especially, the knowledge of form and structure is used to reinforce traditional response and whole hearted assent). Although their films sometimes carry on an ideological debate with the culture that breeds them, they never confront that culture with another ideology, with other ways of seeing itself, with social and political possibilities that are new or challenging. These are films made in isolation and, with few exceptions, about isolation. For without challenging the ideology many of them find abhorrent, they only perpetuate the passivity and aloneness that has become their central image.

A critical approach to these films gets caught up in the conflicts and contradictions. These filmmakers have created a body of exciting work, formally adventurous, carefully thought out, and often structurally challenging. But for all the challenge and adventure, their films speak to a continual impotence in the world, an inability to change and to create change. When they do depict action, it is invariably performed by lone heroes in an enormously destructive and anti-social manner, further affirming that actual change, collectively undertaken, is impossible. The only way to deal with them, therefore, is by examining the contradictions, keeping them present, in the foreground, confronting the films formally and contextually, aware that, no matter how much separation is made for the sake of discussion, form and content are inseparable.

To this end, this study will attempt to address the filmmakers and their works from a variety of perspectives. It will not constitute a complete history of recent American film, nor an economic survey, though both history and economics will support the discussions. There will not be a film-by-film analysis of each director's output. Not all films are of equal interest or of equal worth, and where a filmmaker's output is large it is impractical to give every film equal attention. I have attempted to avoid, wherever possible, the director's own analysis of his work. The interview, while a useful tool in film studies, seems to me too often to serve as a means of getting closer to the creator of a work rather than to the creation. My preference is to concentrate on the film itself, that organized series of images and sounds that have meaning, that exist in a carefully delimited time and space that is created when they are projected on a screen and perceived by a viewer. Films are initiated by individuals, who put the images and sounds together in specific ways, and who are influenced by their own perceptions of the world and by previous films. The films are perceived (and it is the act of perceiving that completes them) by individuals who are also influenced by their perceptions of the world and by previous films. This complex of relationships is my major subject.

The process of discussing these films will be, partly, a process of demystification (and demythification as well). There are no assumptions that what constitutes a film is merely a story with interesting and well-motivated characters that either succeeds or fails to entertain us for a few hours. On the contrary, the "story" is constituted by the formal structure of the film, which is in turn constituted by other films and the history of responses to them. Given the fact that the filmmakers under discussion already know this, one of my tasks will be to extend that knowledge further, to explain how they put it to use and how the spectator then uses it or is used by it. For this reason there will be digressions along the way, detours into the past of American cinema, discussions of its genres, some of its major directors and their influences, some of the formal attributes of film that the directors under discussion perpetuate, reflect upon, or change.

The major questions to be raised and, hopefully, answered in this study are "How?" and "Why?" How and why do filmmakers construct their works the way they do? How and why does a viewer react to them? In answering these questions I must reaffirm the fact that film, by virtue of the popularity and the immediacy of its fictions, by the nature of its means of production and consumption, is profoundly tied up with the cultural, social, and political being of the viewer. In other words, the examination of a film cannot be restricted only to the formal and thematic elements of its text or genre. Films are seen and understood (in various ways) by a great many people. They have an effect, calculated or uncalculated; the conventions and myths they have built and continue to build go beyond them and are deeply embedded in the culture.

Film is a major carrier of our ideology. To define more precisely what

I mean by this, it is necessary to back up and recover some ground. American film, from its beginnings, has attempted to hide itself, to make invisible the telling of its stories and to downplay or deny the ways in which it supports, reinforces, and even sometimes subverts the major cultural, political, and social attitudes that surround and penetrate it. Film is "only" entertainment. Film is "realistic," true to life. These contradictory statements have supported American film throughout its history, hiding some basic facts about its existence. American film, like all fiction, is a carefully crafted lie: make-believe. Film processes "reality" into the forms of fiction (or, more accurately, uses its forms to create cinematic realities) which allude to, evoke, substitute for, and alter external "reality." Film is a representation, a mediation.

This processing or representation involves the active creation of ideas, feelings, attitudes, points of view, fears, and aspirations that are formed by images, gestures, and events that the viewer either assents to or opposes. Any given film is an organization, on the level of fictional narrative, of aspects of the self and the world. That narrative substitutes for ordinary experience characters and action in a cinematically determined space and time. This organization is not innocent (not since the early part of the century, at least). Choices are made as to subject and as to the way that subject will be realized, manifested—created, ultimately—in the forms of cinema. When it is decided that those forms are to be invisible, that the act of substitution or representation will not appear to be an act of substitution or representation, that the form of the fiction will recede behind the fiction itself and therefore create the illusion that the fiction is somehow "real" and unmediated, then a very specific relationship is set up with the audience. This relationship is based upon the assumption and assertion that what is seen is "real" and cannot be questioned.[5] There are enormous implications to this phenomenon, implications that some of the filmmakers discussed here are aware of and respond to in their own work. As indicated, they have begun to take cognizance of the cinematic forms at their disposal and make that cognizance apparent. With the exception of Spielberg, they began by questioning the ideology, both formal and contextual, of their cinematic heritage, and making their questions visible.

Yet I imagine many of them would hesitate if they were told they were involved in an explicit ideological endeavor, for the term itself is fraught with connotations of manipulation, of single-mindedness, of unyielding adherence to a political point of view. In our culture, it is often demanded by critics and artists alike that art be free of any specific political attitudes. But film, of any period, by any filmmaker, speaks to an audience about specific things in specific ways. Its form and content, its fictional mode and the ways in which it is read, are part of and reflect the larger social, cultural, psychological, and political structure. That structure is itself determined by the way individuals alone or collectively perceive themselves and their existence in the world. This is what I mean by "ideology": the complex of images and ideas individuals have of themselves, the ways they assent to or deny their time, place, class, the political structure of their society. ". . .Ideology is not a slogan under which political and economic interest of a class presents itself," write Rosalind Coward and John Ellis. "It is the way in which the individual actively lives his or her role within the social totality; it therefore participates in the construction of that individual so that he or she can act." The authors quote the French philosopher Louis Althusser, who offers a definition remarkable for its use of a cinematic metaphor: "*ideologies are complex formations of montages of notions—representations—images on the one hand, and of montages of behaviours—conducts—attitudes—gestures on the other. . . .*" Elsewhere, Althusser defines ideology as "the 'lived' relation between men [and women] and their world, or a reflected form of this unconscious relation. . . ."[6] Expanding upon this, Terry Eagleton writes that ideology "is the very medium in which I 'live out' my relation to society, the realm of signs and social practices which binds me to the social structure and lends me a sense of coherent purpose and identity." He goes on to point out that ideology is "the link or nexus between discourses and power," the way an individual is represented in and to the world and the way the world represents itself to an individual. Ideology constructs the very image of the individual and his or her potency or impotence in the world.[7]

Every culture has a dominant ideology, and as far as individuals assent to it, the ideology becomes part of the means of interpreting the self in the world and is seen reflected continually in the popular media, in politics, religion, education. But an ideology is never, anywhere, monolithic. It is full of contradictions, perpetually shifting and modifying itself as struggles within the culture continue and as contradictions and conflicts develop. American film is both the carrier of the dominant ideology and a reflector, occasionally even an arbitrator, of the changes and shifts within it.[8] Film tends to support the dominant ideology when it presents itself as unmediated reality, entertaining the viewer while reinforcing accepted notions of love, heroism, domesticity, class structure, sexuality, history. During the late sixties and early seventies, some film questioned assumptions, as some directors became more independent and more in control of their work. In the eighties, American film once again became a great affirming force and, in some instances, went beyond affirmation to the active creation of ideological images and attitudes, forming discourses of power for the powerless. In the discussions that follow, I will attempt to define and account for both events.

The essential point for the analysis that follows is that narrative film is *fiction*, not reality. It substitutes images and sounds for "real" experience, and with those images and sounds communicates to us and manipulates particular feelings, ideas, and perspectives on reality. Film is not innocent, not *merely* entertainment, and most especially not divorced from the culture out of which it comes and into which it feeds. This is why I find it impossible to talk about the events and the characters of films as if they had an existence separate from the formal apparatus that creates the fiction they inhabit. While I will discuss conventional notions of motivation and character psychology, these discussions should always be seen in the context of the various structures and conventions of the cinematic fiction and the viewer's perception of them. The nature of conventional fiction is to present a clean and concentrated view of life. Even if this view is made to include ambiguities and questions, it is always neater than anything perceived in the loose and open narratives that constitute daily life. I want to return the fiction to its proper place as artifice, as something made, and to reduce the emotional aura that most American film narratives create in the viewer, in an attempt to understand the sources of that aura.

A few further things by way of methodology. Most of the films discussed here have been viewed, closely, on an editing table or VCR. I have therefore been able to look at them somewhat in the manner of reading a book, stopping, starting, going back and forth at will. This is, of course, not the way the films are generally seen by an audience. One of the many powers the film narrative exercises over the viewer is the inexorability of its telling. But because of videotape, more and more viewers are able to counter this power and re-create the privileged viewing situation once the reserve of filmmakers or critics with access to archives (though there are major problems created by the poor resolution of the videotaped image and the inaccurate rendering of screen width). To give one's self over to the controlling spell of a film narrative is now more an expression of desire rather than necessity. Some readers may wish to use this new access to material along with the book in order to discover the mechanisms of the films.

One thing that will be discovered is that, despite the greater availibility of the image, the ability to create an accurate verbal rendering of it remains elusive. At best, the descriptions may recall or allude to what exists in the film for the purposes of analysis; they may occasionally evoke; they will never take the place of the images themselves. The verbal description is always tenuous and subject to correction.

There are two textual components of film that do not receive here the attention they should. One is music; the other is film acting. The reason for their slight treatment is, frankly, a feeling of inadequacy on my part to deal with them in any but a cursory way. Film criticism has yet to develop an analytic vocabulary appropriate to the complexity of music's interaction with the narrative, or its function in helping to create the narrative. (Eisenstein made a start many years ago, but certainly the difficulties involved in learning music theory have prevented film critics from carrying his work forward.) While it is difficult to analyze the relationships between music and narrative within a particular film, one can comment on larger trends in film music: the return of the symphonic score in the late seventies; the domination of the synthesizer in the eighties. Nor is there a vocabulary adequate to an accurate and objective discussion about film acting: what it is and how it affects the film and its audience, how an individual creates a presence on the screen, what that presence is, and what the viewer's relationship is to it. Part of the problem lies in the difficulty of overcoming the Hollywood cult of personality. The serious critic may talk about the director, but the publicist and reviewer still sell the picture by the star. This phenomenon tends to pull attention away from the film itself and focus attention on the individual—who, more often than not, is a person built up by the accretion of his or her roles and publicity (Humphrey Bogart, John Wayne, Marilyn Monroe are examples)—rather than look closely at what is being created within the particular film under discussion. When critical examination is given to character in the particular film, the tendency is to fall into the trap of psychological realism I noted earlier and begin discussing the character as if he or she had an existence rather than a function within the total narrative structure. Between these extremes fall the adjectives: such and such a player gave an "edgy" or "nervous" performance, was "brilliant," was "absorbed" in the role. And, that final refuge of unexamined assumptions, was "believable."

I have few alternatives to these problems except to emphasize the fact that performance is one part of the film's structure and most interesting when integrated within the total design. I will be examining a few actors who move through more than one film under discussion: Gene Hackman appears in *Bonnie and Clyde*, *Night Moves*, *Target*, and *The Conversation*; Warren Beatty in *Mickey One*, *Bonnie and Clyde*, and *McCabe and Mrs. Miller*; Robert De Niro in *Mean Streets*, *Taxi Driver*, *New York, New York*, *Raging Bull*, and *The King of Comedy*. Discussion of the characters they play may give some indication of their style and through this some indication of the changing forms of acting styles in recent film and how the relationship between actor and director is drawn. But much work remains to be done in this area.[9]

Finally, all of the filmmakers given major attention in this study are still working. Their careers are in progress and their future films will continue to prove or deny what is said about their work to date. Because of this I have avoided anything like a grand summary or an overall evaluation of what they have done. This book is deeply opinionated, but hardly final.

## CHAPTER ONE

## BLOODY LIBERATIONS,
## BLOODY DECLINES

# Arthur Penn

The self-consciousness, the questioning of the form and content of established film genres, the realignment of the relationship between audience and film that mark the modernist project of sixties and seventies film are hardly unprecedented. To create a proper historical context for the growth of modernism, I could go back at least to Keaton's *Sherlock Jr.* (1924), in which Buster plays a projectionist who walks into the film he is showing and gets caught in its montage. *Citizen Kane* (1941) represents a major break with the conventions of realism and the seamless narrative construction that dominated film in the thirties. If I were looking for a more recent point of entry, Hitchcock's *Psycho* (1960) might be considered the first "modern" American film. The coldness and distance of its narrative structure, the unsympathetic characters, the insistence that viewers be aware of what is being done to them, and how, the film's refusal to provide a comforting and final conclusion, all are characteristics that radically alter the generally complacent and often banal narrative structure of fifties cinema. (Care must be taken, though, in generalizing about fifties film: this was the decade that produced Aldrich's *Kiss Me Deadly*, Ford's *The Searchers*, Welles's *Touch*

17

*of Evil*, and Hitchcock's *Vertigo*, each of which contains the elements that I will be defining in the works under consideration here.)

*Citizen Kane* and *Psycho* are major influences on the directors who are the subjects of this study. *Psycho* in particular is the source not only of many formal strategies but of the blood that has flowed in so much recent film. But they do remain influences rather than initiators, and they will be referred to as such throughout. What needs to be located is a contemporary filmmaker who moves out of the mainstream of American production and looks at it, even for a moment, with foreign eyes— because it is the foreign perspective on American film, the French perspective in particular, that, along with economic changes in production, influenced the major changes in sixties and seventies films. Welles, Hitchcock—perhaps even John Ford, who also figures as a major influence on the filmmakers discussed here—might have gone unnoticed by American filmmakers and film critics alike, were it not for their recognition by the French. I am not exactly suggesting that American film in the sixties and seventies is a direct result of the French New Wave of the late fifties. But the French are responsible for recognizing the complexities of American film and, by their example, enabling some filmmakers to create work that reflects upon itself and its context. They offered the intellectual means, through their criticism, and the practical means, through their films, for some Americans to stand back from their own tradition in order to re-enter it with different points of view.

With this in mind, it is still incumbent to find a place of entry, a figure who offers an example of this standing back and whose films offer a re-examination of the conventions of American cinema. John Cassavetes comes to mind as a director who very early on recognized some things that could be done in American film in response to the New Wave. In *Shadows* (1960) he attempts to create a narrative structure that parallels the improvisatory nature of early Godard; he takes a direction away from the tidily plotted narrative of heroic endeavor and melodramatic longings, so much the core of American film, toward a more loosely observed structure in which the director, his players, and his *mise-en-scène* create a process where the telling of a story becomes subordinate to the moment-to-moment insights into character and situation. Until just recently, Cassavetes followed this direction unflinchingly in most of his work, sacrificing consistent and planned narrative development to microscopic observation of his characters' attempts to articulate their pain. Precisely because of this sacrifice, I find Cassavetes's work difficult to watch and even more difficult to talk about. In a book dedicated to the study of formal strategies and the realization of expression through the structure of expression, a detailed examination of Cassavetes's films would run the risk of being more judgmental than critical. But, because the work of Scorsese and Altman would be different without his influence, and because his films so defy the dimensions of commercial American cinema, he may lurk as something of a bad conscience over what is written here.[1]

I turn to Arthur Penn as an initiating figure, but with some ambivalence. Penn came to film in the fifties from television, as did many of his colleagues (though unlike many of his colleagues, from the theater as well). His first work, *The Left-Handed Gun* (1958), was part of the cycle of fifties westerns that began reexamining and shifting some of the accepted conventions of the genre, psychologizing its hero and scrutinizing the myth of the hero itself. After that Penn moved in and out of various genres and various means of production, filming *The Miracle Worker* (1962), which he had originally directed on the stage; producing and directing *Mickey One* (1964); working for Sam Spiegel in an old-style studio production, *The Chase* (1966); finally achieving a major formal and financial success with *Bonnie and Clyde* (1967), which, indicative of the changing patterns of Hollywood production at the time, was produced by its star, Warren Beatty. These and the films that followed—*Alice's Restaurant* (1969), *Little Big Man* (1970), *Night Moves* (1975), *The Missouri Breaks* (1976), *Four Friends* (1981), *Target* (1985), and *Dead of Winter* (1987)—make up a patchwork of generic experiments, ideological reflections, guides to the culture's malaise, its best and worst fantasies. Penn's sixties films, particularly *Little Big Man* and *Alice's Restaurant*, are so acutely barometers of the moment that, the moment gone, the films have receded, becoming not so much filmic as cultural artifacts. Among his most recent work, *The Missouri Breaks* fell victim to its stars, Jack Nicholson and Marlon Brando, and it appears to have had five directors: the two actors, scriptwriter Thomas McGuane, and the United Artists production accountant, as well as Penn. While the film carries through some favorite Penn oppositions—particularly that of the individual who lives on the fringes of the legal order and confronts the guardians of that order—and while Penn introduces, for the first time and without much success, a woman of some strength and independence, it is a fairly lifeless work, unable to locate itself within a point of view or a consistent method of telling its tale. This lack of controlling point of view and consistency of structure continues to undo the succeeding films. *Four Friends*, despite its extraordinary syncretic images, is undone by an inability to deal with the contradictions of nostalgia and bitterness. *Target* signifies nothing less than an exhausted liberal filmmaker surrendering to the reigning ideology of the eighties. *Dead of Winter* is merely an exercise in gothic horror, indulging itself in the dreadful convention that proposes a woman free herself from the brutalities visited upon her by enacting even greater brutality. Clearly Penn has been unable to survive the transition out of the sixties. The cultural conflicts and cinematic experimentation that marked the decade gave a strength and urgency to his work that diminished as those conflicts diminished.

*Night Moves* was his point of turning, his last carefully structured work, a strong and bitter film, whose bitterness emerges from its anxiety and from a loneliness that exists as a given, rather than a loneliness fought against, a fight that marks most of Penn's best work. *Night Moves* is a film of impotence and despair, and it marks the end of a cycle of films. For Penn, it stands as a declaration that the ideological struggles of the sixties are over and an announcement of the withdrawal and paranoia of the seventies, which he seems to have overcome only by yielding to the conservatism of the eighties.

This may of necessity be an elegy. Penn's decline appears permanent. The final judgment on his work may be that he is not a great filmmaker, but rather an important indicator of what is happening in film, particularly in its response to immediate cultural situations. If popular enthusiasm for his work has diminished along with its own diminished structure (although *Night Moves* deserves more attention than it has received), the best of that work—particularly *The Left-Handed Gun*, *Mickey One*, *Bonnie and Clyde*, and *Night Moves*—retains its importance as a guide to the changes in American cinema in the sixties and seventies.

*Mickey One* marks the first major guidepost. For if my initial premise is valid, that French criticism and filmmaking of the late fifties and early sixties created a noticeable change in some American film, then *Mickey One* stands out, even more than *Shadows*, as being the film most influenced by the work of the New Wave, so much so that Robin Wood condemned Penn for denying his American heritage.[2] Penn himself dismisses the film as a work made in anger (he had just been fired by Burt Lancaster from *The Train* and replaced by John Frankenheimer) and in a spirit of obscurity. Fortunately, the film cannot be so dismissed. Not only is it a work of great energy and visual imagination, but it performs those operations on narrative structure that Godard and Truffaut were themselves performing in their early work. *Mickey One* undoes the closed and stable story-telling devices that American film depends upon, suppressing direct statement, clear transitions, an objective, neutral point of view, making its central character almost inaccessible. In the course of this, the film does not attempt to hide its formal devices, but rejoices in them. In sum it writes, as Alexandre Astruc instructed his French colleagues to do, with the *caméra-stylo*, inscribing the director's imagination into the film and allowing the audience to meet it actively and inquisitively.[3]

Another major operation performed by *Mickey One* is a probing into a particular genre of American film, a questioning of the conventions of that genre, its assumptions and points of view. The genre in question—and there is some controversy over whether it is in fact a genre, although I do accept it as such—is *film noir*. *Mickey One* is a film of paranoia, of a man trapped and isolated by fear, who perceives his world in the perspective of that fear. The film of entrapment, of individuals caught in a dark and foreboding world that echoes their vulnerable state of being, began in the early forties and expanded into the major dramatic style of the decade. The prevalence of its style was matched only by a lack of consciousness of that very prevalence, for it seems no one making *film noir* in the forties, and no one viewing it, was aware precisely of what was going on. The French, seeing forties American films in concentrated viewings after the war, recognized the change in form and content and brought it to critical attention.[4] Not until the late sixties, when American film critics began looking at the phenomenon in a concentrated way, and not until the early seventies, when American filmmakers began seriously to consider the applicability of *noir* to their own work, did the form come fully to the consciousness of the culture that developed it. *Mickey One* stands at a mid-point, coming some time after the initial cycle of *noir* films was over and before the *noir* revival began. An understanding of *noir* is crucial not only for Penn's film, but for so many of the films discussed here that I want to digress for a moment to discuss something of its history and implications.[5]

The move to darkness in the forties—both a visual darkness in *mise-en-scène* (the visual articulation of a film's narrative space) and a darkness in the narrative itself—was a result of cultural and technological forces operating simultaneously. At the end of the thirties, a faster film stock was developed, which meant lower light levels could be used and a greater contrast of light and dark within a shot achieved. As a result of this and other technological factors, Orson Welles and Gregg Toland could create the deeply shadowed and deeply focused space in *Citizen Kane* which became the basis of the *noir* style. They not only availed themselves of the new lighting possibilities of the time but reached back before the thirties to employ the largely dormant forms of German Expressionism and its chiaroscuro.* The result was that a decade of a particular lighting style was put to rest. The bright, even illumination and shallow focus that had prevailed in the thirties (with some major exceptions, such as the Universal horror films, which were heirs to the German style, and the films of Josef von Sternberg) gave way to a deeper focus and a deeper sense of the effect of light and shadow, just as the heroic male of the thirties gave way to a more vulnerable, anxiety-ridden character.

The formal qualities of Welles's *mise-en-scène* exist as profound manifestations of the film's narrative thrust. *Citizen Kane* is an attempt to grasp the personality of an enigma and to prove the impossibility of such an attempt. The combination of depth of field, in which many details throughout the shot, from foreground to background, are visible, and the intense darkness that encloses these details, creates a tension. The viewer sees a great deal, but wishes to see more; the surrogates for

---

*The history of film is never simple. Toland photographed *The Grapes of Wrath* and *The Long Voyage Home* for John Ford in 1940. Many of the visual strategies that would be further developed in *Kane* can be seen in them, particularly in *The Long Voyage Home*, though they stand very much apart from the content. It took Welles to integrate technology and narrative.

the viewer within the film each offer partial information about the central character, and the viewer wishes to see more still. The effect is, finally, to leave the viewer and characters within the fiction rather alone and unfulfilled, or filled with the sense of Kane's mystery and isolation.

*Citizen Kane* altered the visual and narrative conventions of American film. In the years immediately following it, the darkness of its *mise-en-scène* began to inform much of Hollywood's output, particularly those films involving detectives, gangsters, and lower-middle-class men oppressed by lust and the sexuality of destructive women. The key years were 1944 and 1945. Edward Dmytryk's *Murder My Sweet* (made at RKO, the studio of *Citizen Kane*) and Billy Wilder's *Double Indemnity* (at Paramount), the first from Raymond Chandler's *Farewell My Lovely*, the second scripted by Chandler from a James M. Cain novel, introduced the major subjects and formal structures of *film noir*, beginning a cycle that would continue through Robert Aldrich's *Kiss Me Deadly* (1956) and achieve a self-conscious conclusion, most fittingly by the man who started it, in Orson Welles's *Touch of Evil* (1958).

Throughout the forties and into the fifties, *film noir* played upon basic themes of aloneness, oppression, claustrophobia, and emotional and physical brutality, manifested in weak men, various gangsters and detectives, and devouring women who lived—or cringed—in an urban landscape that defied clear perception and safe habitation. The appearance of these figures and their landscape became so insistent that they must have been responses to some profound, if unconscious, shifts in the way the culture was seeing itself. Was *noir* merely reflecting, as many critics have suggested, a post-war depression so prevalent that the audience merely assented quietly and passively to images of its own fear? Perhaps it was a response to the deep trauma of fascism, a brutality so profound that the culture had to deal with it, in part, through representations of lesser, more knowable and contained brutalities and helplessness. Perhaps the vicious *noir* woman was somehow a response to the fears of returning soldiers that the sweethearts they left at home were busy betraying them? (*The Blue Dahlia* (1946) directly addresses these fears.) Perhaps she was a more general representation of the misogyny particularly rampant in the culture and its films after the war, or a dialectic response to this misogyny in the figure of women who would free themselves from the restraints of "normal" domesticity.[6]

None of *noir*'s forms of expression or character traits were new. The dark, brooding lighting of *noir* is present in German Expressionism. The dangerous woman has her origins in the twenties vamp and in the persona created for Marlene Dietrich by Josef von Sternberg. The *noir* male has his origins in the Peter Lorre character of Fritz Lang's *M*, Professor Rathaus in Sternberg's *The Blue Angel*, Jean Gabin's François in Carné's and Prévert's *Le Jour se lève*, as well as in the gangster films of the early thirties. The fact that these figures of the dark appear so strongly in the forties and were so readily accepted speaks strongly to the ideological shift mentioned earlier, but that shift was a temporary one. The *noir* style and themes slowly disappeared by the mid fifties. The two most self-conscious examples of the form, *Kiss Me Deadly* and *Touch of Evil*, indicate the decline by their very self-consciousness. They recognize the formal properties of *noir* in a way its earlier practitioners did not, creating brutal, exaggerated worlds which, originating in actual locations rather than studio sets, go beyond the accepted conventions of cinematic realism and become subjective visions of entrapment and threat. Their characters are bizarre to the point of madness and realize to an extraordinary pitch the hysteria inherent in most inhabitants of the *noir* universe. They are the climax of the genre, or perhaps its coda.

The suggestion has been made that the decline of black-and-white cinematography contributed to the decline of *noir*, but more likely the viability of its conventions had worn down, and further shifts in ideology demanded a change in the films that embodied it. Rather than the bourgeois man undone, a favorite theme of forties *noir*, the fifties were fond of portraying the bourgeois man at bay, threatened but triumphant. The anxieties of the fifties needed a different expression than those of the forties; reassurance and affirmation became more important than reinforcement of fears and uncertainties (a phenomenon repeated in the eighties). Anti-communism, for example, occasionally received a *noir* treatment, as in Samuel Fuller's *Pickup on South Street* (1953), but that and other cold war subjects came to be more comfortably treated in science fiction, where technology, the army, or heroic initiative could repel alien threats. Anxiety, despair, and isolation returned as fit subjects in the late sixties and early seventies, and as they did, and as young filmmakers sought native cinematic forms to explore, *noir* began to make a fitful return.

Coming as it does after the major period of *film noir*, but before the *noir* revival (of which his own *Night Moves* is a major part), Penn's *Mickey One* stands in a sort of generic limbo, foreshadowing the paranoia films of the early seventies, re-evaluating the narrative structure of the *noir* films that preceded it. Forties *noir* focused upon a world of entrapment, isolation, and moral chaos, often by observing this world from the perspective of one character. Yet despite the attempts at first-person narrative, and despite the inherent isolation of the *noir* universe, the story-telling structures of the films were traditional. The plots may have been complex (it is still difficult to figure out who committed one of the murders in *The Big Sleep*), but their form followed a basic expository style, directing the viewer through a causal series of events. *Mickey One* fractures causality, suppresses motivations, and not merely draws the viewer into an observation of the central character but forces the viewer to share his perception, a perception that is confused, paranoid in the extreme, and unable to comprehend the world in anything but a jagged, fragmented manner. The *noir* world is internalized, and is seen the way the character sees it—not *through* his eyes, but *with* his sensibility.

The story told by the narrative is in fact simpler than that of most forties *noir*: Mickey (Warren Beatty)* is a second-rate nightclub comic who gets involved with the mob in Detroit. He runs away in terror and comes to Chicago, living like a bum. He meets a girl, impresses a local nightclub impresario (Hurd Hatfield in a very bizarre role, menacing and friendly at the same time; his club, in obvious homage to Welles's *Citizen Kane*, is called the Xanadu), who auditions him. He attempts again to flee, gets viciously beaten in a fight in Chicago's tenderloin, and, unable to clarify for himself who, if anyone, is pursuing him, assumes his paranoia as a permanent condition and takes again to the stage, open, vulnerable, yet with a sense of liberation. The telling of the narrative presents this information obliquely, withholding so much in

*Names of major players, or those whose recognition is important, will be given in parentheses. For a complete list of characters for each film, see the filmography.

the way of discursive information and giving so much in the way of disconnected and grotesque images (photographed in a sharp-edged black and gray by Ghislain Cloquet and edited by Aram Avakian) that the spectator may be as affected with an opaque and fractured perception, and an attendant anxiety, as is the character in the fiction. This is not to say that the viewer "identifies" with the character in the sense of giving over emotions to that character, an experience that sometimes occurs while watching a conventional narrative. Rather, the sense of distance and confusion experienced by the viewer makes her or his perceptions somewhat analogous to the inhabitant of the fiction. The credit sequence, for example, is a seemingly disconnected series of surreal images: Mickey sits in a steam bath in a derby and overcoat with turned-up collar; behind him a group of fat men in towels look on and laugh (one wears a gun). Mickey and a girl swim under water in a pool. A girl is draped on the hood of a car, face pressed to the window as the wipers turn back and forth. Mickey and a girl make love while, in deep focus behind them, a man is beaten up. The sequence comes to a close as Mickey runs in the dark from a man yelling at him, "There's no place you can hide from them. You'll have to be an animal." There follow quick shots of Mickey burning his identification papers and sleeping on a coffin in a railroad car.

Midway through the film, in what almost amounts to a failure of nerve on Penn's part, this sequence is explained, given a context, in a flashback. Mickey tells his lover about his past; the flashback shows his former employer, Ruby Lapp (an old and puffy Franchot Tone), who explains to him his obligations to the mob. Mickey runs in panic, and there is a repeat of Ruby yelling after him, "You'll have to be an animal." This is a moment of reversion to conventional narrative procedure, in which the character's past is explained and his present—his love affair—offered in melodramatic terms (although the images in the flashback do retain a bizarre and menacing presence—Ruby's warning to Mickey is given in a meat locker, slabs of beef on hooks providing a background). Perhaps it is unfair to criticize a film that does take so many chances just because it hedges at one point. Penn, after all, is a melodramatist, a creator of large emotions through dramatic excess, and in this he is firmly within the great tradition of American film. In *Mickey One* he attempts to counter the melodramatic comfort of easy

emotions, slips back into them, and then pulls away again.[7] The romantic interlude comes almost as a relief to the jarring world that otherwise
surrounds and reflects the character (and is intended precisely as such
a sanctuary for the character himself), a world in which Mickey is implicated but also detached from what he sees.

The body of the film retains this perspective. Mickey's wanderings in
Chicago are marked by threat and provocation: in an automobile graveyard (a favorite image of Penn's, occurring again in *The Chase* and in
*Bonnie and Clyde*) he is pursued by a crane as the police demonstrate
death by car crusher. The high- and low-angle shots of the crane turn it
into a palpable and purposive menace and a reflection of Mickey's fears.
A strange Oriental figure beckons to him from the junk yard, a figure
who reappears throughout the film, finally revealing himself as an artist
who creates, out of junk, a self-destroying machine (symbolism that
would be heavy-handed in a literary form, but effective in a visual one).
Mickey goes to a derelicts' mission for shelter. The man who runs the
place can barely speak and painfully stutters words that occur over and
over throughout the film: "Is there any word from the Lord?" The
words connote a fashionable (for the time) religious angst, yet their
irony and, finally, their poignancy in relation to Mickey's loneliness and
fear are undeniable.

Loneliness and fear become manifest to Mickey in images of himself
throughout the film. One sequence in particular indicates how clearly
the world perceived by Mickey enfolds and reflects him. He flees the
automobile graveyard and, as he flees, turns to watch a car that is burst-
ing into flames. The camera is positioned behind him, and as he moves
to screen left away from the fire, the shot begins to dissolve to another
shot of Mickey, now on screen right and to the rear of the frame, walking as if through the fire, down a street toward the camera, drinking
from a bottle. These images are held together briefly so that it appears
as if Mickey were observing himself in flames. As both superimposed
shots begin to dissolve out, a third is dissolved in under them, showing
Mickey walking along a row of storefronts, his image reflected in the
windows. For a brief moment there are three—actually four—images
of Mickey on the screen at once. The entire sequence lasts only about
thirteen seconds, but long enough to indicate the fragmented and
inward nature of the character. Such cinematic bravura and directorial

self-indulgence reveal how cinematic conventions can be exploited and invigorated, renewed as elements of increased perception. The dissolve is conventionally used to indicate a change in place and/or time. But in this sequence simple transition is made subordinate to an ability to signify an entrapment of the character by himself and to make manifest to the spectator the extent to which the images of the film reflect the character's state of mind. Narrative time and space are subordinated to perception.

*Mickey One* is a self-indulgent film, and self-indulgence is not looked kindly upon in American cinema, where self-effacement is a traditional value. The breaking of the tradition has a liberating effect, on the film, on its viewers, on Penn himself. As a fiction, *Mickey One* celebrates a frightened individual who finally overcomes his fear (trite enough as a narrative premise, powerfully created through the visual structure Penn gives it), and is able to perform in a threatening and incoherent world. At the end of the film, a beaten and still paranoid Mickey goes before an audience. As he sits down at the piano to do his act, the camera pulls back to reveal him in the middle of Chicago's lakefront, exposed, vulnerable, but performing nonetheless. This is the most liberating moment in Penn's films, a rare instance when his central character does not die, become helpless, or is returned to a safe domestic enclave. And I suspect there is something allegorical in it, a reflection of the American filmmaker's allowing himself to become vulnerable and to perform counter to the cinematic conventions of the moment. Penn survived the film by abjuring it, absorbing what he learned from it, and fairly quickly realigned himself within the commercial cinema, going on in three years to create the most influential film of the decade.

The films that follow *Mickey One* owe very little to it directly. The jagged and abrupt editing of Aram Avakian is replaced by the more cohesive, though sometimes arhythmic style of Dede Allen, which depends on rapid and dynamic associations of image and movement within the image, as opposed to the dissociations that mark the editing in *Mickey One* (and which can be seen again in the film that Avakian cut for Francis Ford Coppola, *You're a Big Boy Now*, 1967—a youth movie based upon Richard Lester's *A Hard Day's Night* and *The Knack*, and which contains a sequence at a peep show almost identical to *Mickey One*). The subjective intensity of *Mickey One*, the projection of an inner fear onto the outer world which is so much responsible for the uneasy disparities of the film, is replaced by more tangible quasi-historical and political forces: southern reactionism in *The Chase*, rebellion versus societal order in *Bonnie and Clyde*, threats to middle-class order in *Alice's Restaurant*, white brutality toward the Indians in *Little Big Man*. But *Mickey One* remains an intriguing and exciting film as well as an important document. The narrative experiments of the French were inimical to traditional American cinema, and for critic and audience to accept them had to be realized more quietly, more unobtrusively than they were in Penn's film. But they were realized, and *Mickey One* acts as a kind of pointer, a direction sign for Penn and other American filmmakers to follow.

Penn's films are all marked by a tension between vitality and oppression, by a desperate need for the self to extend itself into the world, to assume a measure of control and direction, no matter how illusory and how temporary that control is. *Mickey One* expresses this tension in an oblique and suggestive form, as well as expressing a way for the tension to be resolved and the individual to endure. But in his major films, at least until *Four Friends, Target*, and *Dead of Winter*, Penn refuses to allow resolution or compromise, or even endurance. Throughout his work, he assumes the conventions of the "realist" (or perhaps pessimist) too thoroughly to allow alternatives, to allow liberation to survive, to indicate that there are political and social possibilities other than the repressive order he seems to see as inevitable. This tension exists in the form of his films as well. Although, after *Mickey One*, he turns away from open, experimental narrative forms, he cannot entirely forget the opportunities they offer, so that the conventional melodramatic structures of his films are often altered by a distancing, an attention to their existence as film and as responses to existing film genres. Like the characters in Penn's fictional worlds, the filmic construction of these worlds threatens to free itself from the conventions and authority of accepted narrative procedures, only to yield to those procedures in the end, just as his characters are forced to yield to the social order.

*Bonnie and Clyde* is the film in which all these tensions and contradictions are played out fully and to great advantage. It attempts, with varying degrees of success, to achieve a structural integrity, and becomes a social phenomenon and a major influence on many films and filmmakers who follow. Using a narrative form that appears straight-forward and "realistic" in its detail but is in fact highly manipulative, it carefully forges a relationship between viewer and central characters without hiding the fact that it is doing this. *Bonnie and Clyde* is a con-scious act of myth-making and extends this consciousness within the fiction and outside it simultaneously. The viewer is asked to feel a sym-pathy with and an admiration for its central characters, a joy in their lives and a fear for their survival, and at the same time realize they are larger than life—fictional beings in a fictional realm. The film creates a desire for emulation; the characters themselves attempt to create a ver-sion of themselves to be emulated. Like the figures of a conventional gangster film, a genre which *Bonnie and Clyde* reflects upon and updates—Rico in *Little Caesar*, Tony Camonte in *Scarface*—Bonnie and Clyde are concerned about their image, about how they look to the world. They photograph each other and send the pictures to the news-papers. Bonnie's doggerel verse about their exploits so thrills Clyde that his potency returns (the impotence motif in the film, the substitution of gun for penis, is an obvious and unexciting element, which still man-ages to work as a significant image of substitution, the establishment of masculine rule on the basis of violence rather than sexual domination). The attempts of the early film gangsters to boost themselves, to create their own legends, were observed coolly and disparagingly as another sign of their pride, which the spectator knew, even that early in the life of the genre, would lead to their fall. But in *Bonnie and Clyde* the viewer is not permitted to observe coolly and is rather asked to share the char-acters' joy in their exploits and their notoriety. Many years of gangster films modify that joy with knowledge that it will lead to their fall. Penn therefore plays with convention and revision, with expectation and desire, leading the viewer to enjoy a world he or she knows is fantastic, enviable, and doomed.

The myth-making that occurs within the narrative is doubled by the myth-making that is carried on by the narrative itself. The audience is privileged to both processes as well as its own reactions to them, a phe-nomenon Penn takes cognizance of in the film. After they commit their first murder, Bonnie and Clyde go to the movies to hide. The film they see is *Golddiggers of 1933*, and the particular sequence—in ironic parallel to their first successful bank robbery—is the number "We're in the Money." In the film they watch, people are in the audience watching the song and dance number. The audience for *Bonnie and Clyde* is therefore placed in the situation of watching a movie in which the characters watch a movie in which other people watch a song and dance number. The song and dance number comments upon events in the primary film, and was itself filmed at the time when the events in the primary film are meant to be taking place. Penn does not permit a lingering over this distancing device, for nowhere is it his intention to force his audience away from the fiction to a speculation upon the nature of film narratives, in the manner of Godard. Yet the levels of involvement are clearly marked and there to be observed. The viewer is forced, on some level, to be aware of the fact that she or he is watching a film at the same time that the film invites emotional participation. The participation is countered by a warning not to participate. Finally, as Jack Shadoian suggests, the viewer is forced into an observation of his or her own emotions.[8] The complexity of points of view within the film creates conflicts in the perception of the film and in the relationship created between the film and the viewer. Although these conflicts do not force the perception of a moral structure as they do in Hitchcock's work (on the contrary, they make the viewer question moral structures), they offer an understanding about engagement with fictions and its consequences.

The opening sequences of the film immediately provide the conflicting points of view. The credit sequence, with its old photographs and printed biographies of the characters, creates a distance, a provocation of curiosity, enforced by the sound of a camera shutter and the graphics of the titles themselves. The letters turn to red on the screen, a premonition of the violence the viewer knows is coming. (The effect of foreknowledge that was brought to the film cannot be underestimated. *Bonnie and Clyde* was a matter of such controversy upon its release that there could have been few people who went to see it without knowing, and therefore expecting, the outcome. Even without that foreknowledge, red is a fairly universal sign of danger, and a dissolving of the titles to it from a neutral color disrupts the continuity and creates discomfort.)[9] The titles set up a conflict, which is aggravated by the first shot of the film that follows: an enormous closeup of Bonnie's lips. Normally the first shot of a film is an establishing shot, situating the audience in a defined space that the characters inhabit, so that the filmmaker can begin his cutting pattern within that space. Here, as in the fragmented opening of *Mickey One,* no spatial coordinates are offered, no secure situating of the character, and, indeed, no character at all.

The closeup of Bonnie's lips (which is dissolved in over a photograph of Warren Beatty as Clyde) moves out to encompass her at her mirror. There follows a succession of abrupt shots, in which she lies on her bed, pounding on the frame and flounces about her room. The cutting is swift and arhythmical; many of the shots are terminated before the physical action contained within them is finished. In a brief time, the viewer is offered an unlocalized place and a barely determined figure. John Cawelti, in his excellent visual analysis of the film, states that the opening gives a sense of Bonnie's imprisoned sensuality, and certainly Bonnie's abrupt movements indicate frustration, a feeling of being trapped.[10] Even more, they give the viewer a sense of immediate, if confused, attachment to the character. In *Bonnie and Clyde* no time is lost and no space between viewer and characters is allowed. For, just as the viewer attempts to make sense of who and what Bonnie is, Clyde is introduced. He is seen first—by the viewer—in the street, by means of a shot inserted amid Bonnie's moving about and dressing. She immediately notices him from her window, and the next shot of him is from her point of view. When he responds to her question "Hey, boy, what you doin' with my mama's car?" he makes eye contact with her. His glance up at the window provides the shot that responds to her observation of him in a variation of a cutting format that is the basic structuring principle of American film. So basic that it deserves some comment.

Two reasons for the firm establishment of the shot/reverse shot technique have been assumed: first, it is an easy and controllable production method. The best performances of each actor can be selected and cut in; both actors need not be present for the entire filming of the sequence. Second, there was the belief that rapid cutting of a dialogue sequence (indeed, of any sequence in American film from the early sound period through the fifties, when few shots are much longer than nine to fifteen seconds) and rapid changes in point of view would prevent boredom for the viewer. Other interpretations have recently been introduced that reveal profound ideological currents. The rapid cutting of numerous separate shots into a pattern that creates an illusion of smooth continuity and links the gaze of one character to another is a way of avoiding viewer objectivity. The illusion of wholeness that is obtained (as opposed to the fragmentation created by the cutting in a film like *Mickey One*) renders the cutting invisible. The viewer is forced to attend to the events occurring within the narrative. The gaze is directed beyond the formal structure of the film and into the "story," the surrogate reality of the characters and events on the screen. The shot/ reverse shot sequence in particular does not permit the viewer to move beyond, or outside, the closed space of the characters. Their gaze is never directed outward to the camera/audience (of all conventions in fimmaking this is the strongest: no character within a film may make eye contact with the camera and with that contact announce the existence of a medium, a mechanical, optical, aesthetic structure that stands between the viewer and the people and events it creates). The viewer, therefore, is ignored, but may not ignore what is seen—a fully inhabited, articulated, closed world. Furthermore, the constant opening and closing of that world—one character looks and in the next shot the other character answers the direction of his or her gaze—seal the viewer within it. The editing structure of American film is therefore based upon an extraordinary contradiction. Many images, rapidly linked together, create a wholeness and completeness; the complexity of parts produces the illusion of an absence of parts, indeed, an absence of form. The viewer sees through the screen into a completely realized world offered as complete and valid.[11]

*Bonnie and Clyde* makes full use of the shot/reverse shot technique while reflecting upon it simultaneously. The abrupt editing of the opening sequence seems at first to deny the convention. The linking of the characters' gaze when Bonnie sees Clyde out the window embraces it fully. The film is deeply concerned with the relationship of its characters and the relationship of the viewer to those characters, while at the same time it keeps questioning those relationships, making the viewer, on some level, aware of the act of gazing. At the moment in the film when the characters make eye contact, they are immediately linked and are not separated for the rest of the film. The viewer is immediately linked to them, and rarely allowed to separate from them for the rest of the film, until violently wrenched away by their slaughter, as if being punished for being so close.

Bonnie trundles downstairs to meet Clyde, in a startling low shot which allows the viewer to look up her dress, at the same time presenting the figure in a distorting tilt. Once she is on the street, they are photographed in a two shot, and they talk and proceed to walk down a sunlit, deserted street, the camera tracking along with them, keeping them together in the shot. The camera remains close as they walk into an apparently abandoned town (the only other figure to be seen is a black man sitting in a chair, and throughout the film Penn will continually link Bonnie and Clyde to the disenfranchised). They talk, drink Cokes, Clyde does his engaging trick with a matchstick in his mouth and boasts of his outlaw prowess. Bonnie caresses his gun and urges him to "use it," pressing the connection between repressed sexuality and the need for some physical action in which to sublimate it. At this point, Penn finally offers a more or less conventional establishing shot by cutting to a long shot of the street as Clyde enters a store to rob it. This occurs a good ten to fifteen minutes into the film, and it is the first time since the credit sequence that some distance is placed between viewer and characters. But it is a contradictory distance. There is a spatial separation, but the bond between viewer and character is now so strong, curiosity as to whether Clyde will pull off the robbery so piqued that the separation is unwanted. The bravura and bantering of the two and their complete isolation have allowed the viewer no emotional room. When the camera does finally offer visual space, it comes as an intrusion. Penn, as if realizing that this new distance is unwanted, cuts immediately to Bonnie's point of view, with a shot from behind her, looking at the store Clyde has entered. He cuts from this to a closeup of her looking concerned, mirroring the emotions that all members of the audience should be feeling, and thereby reestablishing the characters' link with each other and the viewer's with them.

From this point the bond between characters and spectator is not allowed to diminish. Occasionally one or the other character becomes more sympathetic. Early in the film Bonnie taunts Clyde about his impotence, shifting sympathies to him; later on Bonnie shows her loneliness, moving sympathy to her. But in each of these instances the siding

is only temporary. Bonnie and Clyde's attachment to each other assures
the viewer's attachment to them equally. As the violence of the film
increases—and it does in a very measured progression—as the threats
to their well-being become greater, they become increasingly isolated
from their world. And it is exactly the combination of audience attachment to them and their own growing isolation that helps the film's
myth-making mechanism to operate. Their need to be free of their society's restrictions, its economic and emotional poverty, the pleasure they
take in their freedom, the tenuousness of their freedom and the sympathies and fears it has created, generate a complex of emotions that
makes the characters, finally, surrogates for some basic psychological,
social, and cultural desires and anxieties.

But herein lies the flaw of the film. The manipulation is too easily
managed; viewer response too easily gotten. The reflexive qualities,
Penn's ability make the viewer consider his or her response, is insufficiently worked out. The myth-making process, apparent as it is, is directionless; the voice that speaks the discourse of the film is unclear. Too
many questions are raised. Why should the viewer invest emotions in
these two fictional characters and make of them surrogates for his or
her own fears and desires? Why is the viewer given pleasure in their
exploits, in their vitality, only to have that pleasure brutally attacked?
Who are the enemies in the film? Why do they win? Why must the audience lose by seeing the characters violently destroyed? Heroism in
American film conventionally displays an individual who can conquer
oppressive odds and adversity; if the hero loses, the struggle of his fight
(and with the exception of some romantic melodramas it is usually a
man who struggles heroically) transcends the victory of his adversaries.
The Hollywood heroic melodrama is, of course, naive and appallingly
reductive, but in attempting to overcome it Penn and screenwriters
Robert Benton and David Newman sacrifice dialectical clarity for emotional entanglement. The adversary in *Bonnie and Clyde* is intangible.
"Society," oppressive and denying, but without detailed articulation, is
offered as the opposing force. A few details signify what this society is—
barren landscapes, the empty, dusty towns, one failed bank and one dis-
possessed farmer, some Roosevelt posters signify the Depression. But
this historical moment is not fleshed out. The connotations of death
and poverty are present, but unaccounted for. (One need only recall the

Clyde (Warren Beatty) attacked during a robbery as Bonnie (Faye Dunaway) looks on.

sequence in Ford's *The Grapes of Wrath*, where Muley rages against the injustice of losing his farm to understand how direct a definition of Depression politics and economics can be rendered, even within the Hollywood convention of personalizing the political.)

The people with whom Bonnie, Clyde, and their gang come in contact are defined only as scared, compliant, or mean. And they are usually silly or ugly. The man in the store who takes a meat cleaver to Clyde, who is only trying to steal a few groceries, is enormous and grossly unattractive. His violence is too great a response to Clyde's robbery. He scares not only Clyde but the viewer as well, who is called upon to approve Clyde's pistol-whipping him. When the teller of the Mineola bank leaps onto the window of the escaping car and gets his face shot, it is an appalling sight (such bloodied flesh had never been seen in an

American film), but the implicit comment is that, like the fat man with the cleaver, he didn't have to attack. These people who emerge from the empty, sun-baked, Depression-ridden Midwest to attack Bonnie, Clyde, Buck, Blanche, and C. W. are the ones trying to be heroes. The gang is only trying to rob banks, and banks rob the people. Bonne and Clyde don't want to hurt anyone; they are lonely people trying to escape their loneliness, their sexual dysfunction, their economic oppression. They become heroes almost despite themselves. They take pleasure in their exploits, they take part in the making of their own legend. Their stature grows from the success they have in the face of these unattractive opponents, a success that continues until these single attackers begin to join into groups and become represented by the police. This is a successful maneuver on the part of the filmmaker, for it keeps the film focused on the main characters and keeps the point of view steady. Social and political realities are present by suggestion only. Clearly something is amiss in the world, but exactly what remains unclear. The only certainty is that the film's heroes make the world come alive. The individuals who try to stop them are foolish and misdirected. When the police appear, they are as abstract and uncomprehending as the landscape.[12]

The police—seen briefly when they show Clyde's picture to the man who attacked him with the meat cleaver—first appear *en masse* as a faceless group of Keystone Kops. The initial shootout is presented as slapstick. The gang bulldoze their way out, Blanche is hysterical (which annoys not only the rest of the gang but the viewer as well, for no real threat or upset is desired, no realization that this is a desperate situation); the gang retain their control. The police are harmless until they themselves become concentrated in a single person, Texas Ranger Frank Hamer, who is humiliated by the gang. The sequence with Hamer tests and confirms devotion to the main characters. The scene is once again one of isolation. The gang's car is shown in a far shot by a lake. Another car quietly glides into the frame in front of it. The policeman, serpent-like, insinuates himself into the gang's place of rest. They jump him, they take his picture, and he is roundly taunted. The group seems to be in control, but once again Blanche's hysteria threatens the mood of triumph, provoking a reconsideration of the consequences of their actions and the viewer's own reactions. When C. W. suggests, half-seriously, that they shoot Hamer, Blanche screams a very serious "No!" And on that scream there is a quick cut to Hamer looking over at her, sizing up her weakness and her future usefulness in trapping the gang.

Even though, after the Hamer episode, the gang go on to rob success-fully and with even greater pleasure and confidence, the memory of Hamer's unblinking seriousness during his captivity, the ferocity with which he spits in Bonnie's face when she teases him, lingers and pro-vides a troubling foreshadowing for all that follows. Opposition to Bon-nie and Clyde is beginning to consolidate itself into something more serious than the Keystone Kops. The world surrounding them is not as receptive to the gang's exploits as one had thought; it is certainly not as receptive as is the spectator. When they are attacked again (an attack in which, significantly, the first bullet hits a mirror, shattering Bonnie and Clyde's reflected image, their closeness, their inviolability, and their protective isolation), blood flows: Blanche is blinded and Buck is shot in the head. The gang, in wretched shape, escape and huddle by their car. The scene dissolves to morning, and they are surrounded by a posse. The people, who with a few exceptions were friendly to Bonnie and Clyde when alone, are violent toward them when in a crowd and under the aegis of the police. But their violence is strangely impotent. The police do the serious shooting. Buck dies horribly. Bonnie and Clyde are wounded. The bystanders shoot the gang's car to pieces, whooping around it like Indians.

This is a particularly awful moment for the audience. Obviously the viewer is guaranteed a strong reaction to the violence committed upon the people to whom he or she has grown attached; but, added to this, the impotent destructiveness of the crowd is a curious punctuation. Throughout the film the relation of Bonnie and Clyde to the people sur-rounding them is tentatively good. They are attacked only twice by ordinary people (the grocery man with the cleaver and the bank teller); otherwise "folks" maintain a respectful, even cynical, distance from them. After their last robbery, Penn inserts two "interviews" with peo-ple involved, contrasting a melodramatic policeman—"There I was, staring square into the face of death"—and a bystander who prophesies their end: "They did right with me, I'm bringin' me a mess of flowers to their funeral." The people touched by Bonnie and Clyde understand them within the fiction better than the audience does outside it. Within

The Barrow gang and Frank Hamer (left to right: Michael J. Pollard, Warren Beatty, Gene Hackman, Denver Pyle).

the fiction, people are clear-headed about the gang's mythological status and do not seem to embrace them as liberated surrogates for their repressed lives. The viewer's reaction, however, is split between desire for the gang's success, the fear generated by the crowd's response, and the knowledge, enforced by other films, that the police will eventually get them. Penn, not missing a chance to play further with viewer response, and the emotional dependency he has built for his heroes, shocks the spectator with the frustrated and maddening violence of the crowd at the ambush, but then turns to give the viewer almost what had been hoped for all along. In their painful escape from the ambush, Bonnie, Clyde, and C. W. find a white car, which will finally be the place of their death. They drive all night, coming finally to an Okie camp. The crowd of poor people huddle around the car, whispering, "They famous?. . . Is that really Bonnie Parker?" A man touches Clyde. A bowl of soup is offered. The scene ends on a long shot of the car, isolated, surrounded by a group of curious, wondering people.

Like most of the bystanders with whom Bonnie and Clyde come into contact, the Okies are distant. They cannot join with the robbers; they cannot really help them, for the key to Bonnie and Clyde's success and fame is their isolation from the world in which everyone else is caught up—the people in poverty, the police in the poverty of law and order. Bonnie and Clyde are not revolutionaries, for they cannot give the people anything, save some money at a bank robbery; they offer no opportunity for people to join them. The Okies' reaction demonstrates Bonnie and Clyde's success and their failure. They gain fame, even a recognition of sorts, but they fail because people are merely in awe of them. The result of that awe is isolation. The far shot that ends the Okie sequence sums up their situation within the film; they are alone and wounded, trapped in the car, surrounded by people with a distant and wondering attitude toward them but ultimately unconcerned, for the heroes do not touch their lives. The only ones still connected to them with concern are the members of the audience, and they are forced to share the characters' isolation. Bonnie and Clyde are constructed images of vitality and escape. Ungrounded in any reality, inside or outside the fiction, that imagery is doomed to dissolve.

Note must be taken of one of the central images of the characters' isolation. The car is the place of Bonnie and Clyde's existence, of their freedom, and of their entrapment. The car functions often as part of a double frame: it encloses the characters as it itself is enclosed within the screen. Penn makes a special point of this. In the first murder, the bank teller leaps at the car, pressing his face against the window. The spectator's point of view is inside, looking through the window with the characters, and therefore the viewer is made to share the act of violence against this man. But the feeling of intrusion is shared as well. The man is attempting to violate the car, the safe place. Clyde shoots him in response to this violation. In the Frank Hamer episode there is a particularly pointed repetition of this. Clyde grabs Hamer, pins his arms, and throws him down on the back of the car, against the rear window. As he hits the glass, there is a cut to inside the car looking out the rear window as Hamer hits it. But Dede Allen, Penn's editor, chooses to break continuity slightly. Hamer hits the window in the exterior shot, hits it again when the cut is made to the interior of the car.[13] The continuity break happens quickly and is easy to miss, but has a definite function nonetheless. It emphasizes the action, of course, but emphasizes as well the outside/inside structure that the car creates. There is no one in the car when Hamer is seen from its interior. The gang is outside and in control of the intruding Texas Ranger (who Clyde, ever the good populist, insists should be looking after poor people and not chasing them). The sudden shift to a point of view from inside the car reveals a heretofore unexpected vulnerability, of which the gang themselves are as yet unaware. (Vulnerability and intrusion are suggested earlier in the film. In the clip from *Goldiggers of 1933* that Bonnie and Clyde watch, a group of men walk into the song and dance number, threatening to break it up. "Who are you?" somebody shouts in this film-within-a-film, "You'll find out," one of the intruders responds.)

The Hamer episode is the turning point of the Barrow gang's fortune. After this, the car will become a target, as in the ambush discussed earlier (which begins as the gang is huddled by their car, proceeds as they attempt an escape, driving in circles, and ends with the car being shot to pieces), and the place of their isolation, as in the Okie episode.[14] Like the film itself, which is the vehicle for the viewer's emotions, the security offered by the automobile is tenuous and it becomes the place of Bonnie and Clyde's failure. The hilarious episode with Eugene and Velma, in which the car becomes a sort of living room on wheels, filled with camaraderie and an attempt on everyone's part to convince themselves they are "just folks," ends abruptly when Eugene tells them he's an undertaker. The sequence focuses the conflict of security-vulnerability-isolation signified by the car throughout the film. The Barrow gang first surround Eugene and Velma's car, pressing their faces against the window. The point of view is from the inside, and the viewer is permitted to share the couple's anxiety and a superiority to that anxiety, for clearly the gang mean them no harm. (Compare this with the feeling of foreboding when the bank teller presses his face against the car window and is shot and when Frank Hamer is pushed against the window of the empty car.) After the gang join Eugene and Velma inside, pleasure and relaxation are mutual, until Eugene (Gene Wilder) reveals his occupation. Bonnie has the couple thrown out, and the point of view is shifted, the camera remaining with them on the outside observing the car disappear down the dark road. This is a rare moment of separation and distance from the main characters. Coming as it does after the Hamer episode and before the sentimental meeting of Bonnie with her mother and the bloody ambush, it provides a narrative pause, a space to consider feeling and response. Bonnie and Clyde are essentially alone, their vitality and their pleasures are attractive, but tentative, and the link drawn between them and the spectator puts the latter at risk of also being isolated and alone. The separation from them at this point serves as a warning.

The warning is borne out by the end of the film, when viewer perspective on the characters and the emotional relationship to them are violently shattered. Again the car plays an important role. As Frank Hamer teases information out of the blind Blanche (whom he has captured), Bonnie and Clyde sit in their white car in the rain. Bonnie reads Clyde her doggerel on their life and death, and their faces reflect the rain on the car windshield. The car is again their refuge, their place of protection, and now, at the same time, their trap. There is a cut to the outside of the car and a dissolve to Hamer, reading the poem Bonnie has sent to the papers. There follows a dissolve back to Bonnie and Clyde, sitting by their car in a sunlit field. Bonnie reads the end of her poem, its celebration of their life giving Clyde a shot of potency. As they make love, the newspapers blow across the field (significantly, and perhaps heavy-handedly, two sheets of newspaper blow apart and separate). At this point an abrupt change in the visual form of the film occurs. By means of a panning telephoto shot C. W.'s father is observed, simultaneously at a distance and in proximity, walking down a street to rendezvous with Frank Hamer and betray the heroes. Penn has placed the spectator first in the most intimate proximity with the central characters and their new-found sexuality. He then moves as far as possible from that intimacy with a shot whose focal length disrupts perspective and proximity with something analogous to the point of view of a spy. The viewer knows clearly at this point that the end is near, and knows also, finally, that, as close as she or he has been allowed to come to the characters, permission has been granted only to act as observers, helpless to avert the destruction to come.

Bonnie and Clyde's deaths occur as their car is blocked in the road by C. W.'s daddy. Clyde is outside, Bonnie in the car. Their safe place is violated. Before the bullets fly, and as the two of them realize what is occurring, there is a rapid series of shots in which each looks at the other. Since the time they first meet, Penn has attempted to keep Bonnie and Clyde closely together in the frame. Now that they are to die, he separates them physically, but at the same time associates them by the glances they exchange, glances that indicate their affection for each other and their resignation, and which climax and end the play of the gaze I discussed earlier.[15] Bonnie is ripped apart by bullets as she sits helplessly behind the wheel. Clyde is killed just outside the car. The very last shot of the film is from behind the car, observing through its window the police moving about the scene of carnage in quiet and awe. The camera almost cowers in reaction to what has happened. And what has happened is not merely the death of the characters in the film, but the destruction of the point of view that has been so carefully forged. The car violated, its inhabitants dead, the audience has no one to look at and look with; no secure and mobile isolation. The viewer is alone and lost. The bad guys have won, and the film has nothing more to tell us about the heroes. Since there is, as far as Penn is concerned, nothing more to see, the screen unceremoniously and anticlimactically goes black.

With *Bonnie and Clyde* Penn created an extreme inversion of the structure and iconography of early gangster films. There the car functioned as an instrument of protection, aggression, and ostentation, entering the mainstream of American film narrative thereafter (how many dramatic films do not contain at least one major dialogue sequence in a car?).[16] But no gangster used the car as a surrogate world the way Bonnie and Clyde do. Penn has changed the gangster environment. The gangster film, in its beginnings and through its metamorphosis into *film noir* in the forties, was radically urban in its setting. Gangsters were creatures of the city, which provided them with protection for as long as possible.[17] Bonnie and Clyde are country gangsters (a type that offers relatively little cinematic tradition—Nicholas Ray's *They Live by Night* and Joseph H. Lewis's *Gun Crazy*, both 1949; perhaps also Fritz Lang's *You Only Live Once*, 1937)—and as such they require the mobility of a car and, more important, protection from the openness, the vulnerability that is paradoxically created by the sunlight. With *Bonnie and Clyde* Penn is, in a way, extending the investigation of *film noir* that he began in *Mickey One*. But it is an extension by contrast, placing the hunted characters in the open daylight rather than in an enclosing urban darkness. They are as vulnerable and ultimately as trapped as their *noir* relatives, but it is a vulnerability and entrapment countered by an openness and innocence signified by the country. In American film, as in the classical pastoral poem, the country is conventionally a place whose inhabitants are untouched by corruption, a place that offers security and comfort.*

This is of course another of the film's paradoxes. I have pointed out that the world Bonnie and Clyde inhabit is insecure, barren, and lifeless; they give it life by their activity. Unlike their thirties and forties progenitors, these two gangsters have nothing mean-spirited about them. They do not share the attractive repulsiveness of their thirties ancestors nor the depressed paranoia of their *noir* cousins, and the audience does not share the mixed feelings toward them that are experienced toward Rico in *Little Caesar* or Tony Camonte in *Scarface* or even Tommy Powers in *Public Enemy*. The morality of the thirties gangster films does not permit a whole-hearted endorsement of their heroes. The brutality and stupidity of the inhabitants of these films always stand in the way of an unmodified admiration of the small men who made it big. The viewer must actively separate the gross charm of these characters from their sordid urban background, their viciousness, the ugly people who surround them, and the morally platitudinous police who always look for a way to get them. When the gangster film was transformed into *film noir*, the characters became even more unreachable; they became small, mean figures scurrying about in the dark. Nicholas Ray attempted to redeem the gangster in *They Live by Night* but only managed to create a passive couple trapped by circumstance, and their own innocence. The attraction of Bonnie and Clyde is that they are neither passive nor innocent. They are active and know perfectly what they are doing. They are attractive to us—as are their thirties forebears—precisely because

---

*Noir gangster films such as Jacques Tourneur's *Out of the Past* (1947) and John Huston's *The Asphalt Jungle* (1950) clearly present the conventional contrast of city and country and the frustrated desire of their gangster heroes to find comfort in the pastoral world.

of their energy and the way they give life to their barren world. The very isolation that undoes them is part of their attraction. Unlike most other movie robbers and gangsters, Bonnie and Clyde are without any peers to pressure them or threaten them. The only people they have to overcome, other than the police, are themselves. To be sure, Blanche and her hysteria help give them away, but Blanche is a sort of negative force. Her failing is that she does not share the vitality and joy of her companions.

Bonnie and Clyde are self-made crooks. This is a basic trait of movie gangsters, to be sure. Admiration of them is rooted in the ideology of the individual who succeeds by dint of personal effort, the man who distinguishes himself by energetically circumventing normal societal patterns (only a man, whether a gangster or in other business, the figure of admiration is male; if a woman circumvents normal patterns, she is looked upon as strange or threatening). The thirties movie gangster embodied this ideology to curious ends. He started as a member of the lumpenproletariat, an economically disenfranchised individual who began working his way up in an urban "business" organization. As he did so, he gathered to himself the tangible properties of a man of means: a fancy lady, clothes, cars, a penthouse, hangers-on, and a reputation. The gangster is a parody of the bourgeois on the make, every working man's dream of leaving his class and getting to the top. The working man had, after all, always been told he could get there—at least that he had the opportunity to—but with matters of class, education, and economic situation never recognized, it was not apparent how that opportunity could be realized. The myth of the gangster provided a reasonable surrogate (all myths are surrogates) for his own desires. It also provided a built-in caution. If a poor man violently works his way to the top and remains unregenerate when he gets there, he will be destroyed.

*Bonnie and Clyde* reworks this ideology for the sixties, generalizes it and depoliticizes it even more than did the early gangster films, appealing to the cultural discomfort growing at the time, the ripening of a rebelliousness that was just beginning to find the Vietnamese war an object for rebellion. Penn sketches in a world that is unhappy and repressive, just enough to make the spectator uncomfortable with it, but not enough to provide the details of that repression. The viewer is therefore left free to generalize, to make it analogous to the repression many people were experiencing in the sixties. Penn makes his heroes young, appealing, and oddly classless (though, in the traditional style of Hollywood heroes, very classy, for Warren Beatty takes on the appearance of Robert Kennedy more than once in the film, and Faye Dunaway's Bonnie looks more like a woman's magazine model than a poor southwestern bank robber; in fact the film did create some fashion fads for a brief time). Officially, the characters, like their ancestors, are "lower class," Bonnie is a waitress, Clyde a petty thief. But they have no essential class accouterments and do not seem to want them. Only a bit of glamour and recognition. Their robberies seem to advance their status not one whit; they gain no power, and they gain no things. What they do gain is a certain tentative freedom and happiness, self-esteem, and each other's love, qualities more immediately attractive to a young mid-sixties audience.

Romantic love plays almost no part in the early gangster genre, whereas *Bonnie and Clyde* can be read, on one level, as being mainly about romantic love. Clyde is a powerful and dominating figure. He tells Bonnie how to wear her hair; he offers her an exciting life. He can't make love, but somehow that is made to appear more Bonnie's fault than Clyde's. Early in the film she is portrayed as being too demanding and too insulting of Clyde's impotence. Clyde's self-deprecating acceptance of his problem makes the audience sympathize with him. Besides, clearly he is a man, because of his gun and his readiness to use it. Clyde's substitute phallus serves for Bonnie until the end of the film, at which point they have reached a closeness with each other that gives Clyde back his sexual potency. That they die soon after this gives the film a perfect melodramatic structure. Try as he may, Penn cannot bring himself to reverse certain fundamental cultural themes that are imbedded in American cinema and the ideology that informs it. One of the most fundamental of these is that love is not simple and triumphs only by great sacrifice. Sacrifice is the key element of melodrama, and Penn makes it a structural principle of this film, and most of the films that follow it. Only in the simplicities of domestic closeness portrayed in *Target* is love uncomplicated, although even there it must be proved by action.

Love is never free. Neither, Penn would lead us to believe, is freedom. Bonnie and Clyde are shot down, as was every gangster in every film before them, and most films after. Very rarely can American filmmakers break the convention of the criminal paying for his crimes. Even if he does not die, he suffers morally and spiritually (the figure of Michael in the second *Godfather* film is the perfect example). The very mythologizing process of *Bonnie and Clyde* demands that the characters, whose point of view is so closely shared by the viewer, be sacrificed so that they may transcend themselves. In that sense, Penn moves far from his generic starting point. The death of the thirties gangster had, of course, a moral necessity.[18] If such an individual survived, societal order would have little meaning; and, according to Hollywood, everyone must suffer for their sins. But Penn is not merely creating gangsters who go against the social order—all gangsters, by generic definition, do—he is using them to make the viewer uncomfortable with that order. By their ability to enjoy their criminal life, by their camaraderie, by the ease with which the viewer is permitted to share their point of view and therefore share their momentary triumph over the desolation that surrounds them, Penn allows Bonnie and Clyde to generate themselves as figures of freedom. As they proceed, they suffer loneliness and an awareness of their fate, and fear for them grows. But they are unyielding; they do not wish to change, nor does the viewer wish them to. At the same time, the understanding is that they will not prevail, and this makes the spectator angry with the society that she or he knows will undo them.

Finally, the subjectivity of the viewer must come to terms with the subjectivity of the characters and the relationship between viewer and character that is fostered and denied by the film. For the first part of the film that relationship seems sound, as the viewer is asked to support and enjoy Bonnie and Clyde's activities. When their fortune changes and it is clear that they will die, the relationship is strengthened; the viewer wishes their survival but begins to fear for his or her own reactions if they do not survive. When they are destroyed, the relationship is cut off, the intersubjectivity so carefully fostered is broken and the viewer is left, as it were, alone. The structure of the film is ruptured, and there is nowhere to turn except back inward. The crucial element of *Bonnie and Clyde* is its final sequence. The punishment the viewer receives by watching the grotesque, slow-motion, bullet-punctured destruction of the two characters is immense. Immediate and unanswerable questions are raised. Do these terrible images deny the admiration the preceding body of the text has insisted upon? Is the narrative suddenly proclaiming its heroes were wrong? If they were wrong, if these fictional characters are to be disapproved of, then surely such pains to create the admiration for them should not have been taken. Were they too free? Were they having too much fun? Is Penn assuming the melodramatic directive that everyone must pay for his or her pleasures? Is the viewer being asked to share the death agonies? If he or she has been asked, indeed commanded, to share the main characters' perspectives and, by sharing, to admire them and feel for them, then perhaps the demand is also made to share the agonies of their deaths.

But of course a screen death cannot be shared. And as the attack begins, a great distance is created between viewer and characters, not only by means of camera placement, but because of the use of slow motion and the very horror of the sequence. Agony and dying are represented; the viewer must contend with reactions to the representations—a situation basic to most movie viewing. The representation of violent death stimulates a complex response of fear, revulsion, attraction, and desire, to see that which ordinarily cannot be seen, in the safe context of knowing that what is seen is not really seen. But in this particular instance, no such representation is desired; the viewer simply wants the characters alive and the conflict is therefore all the more intense. Benton and Newman's original script called for Bonnie and Clyde's death to be swift and indeed only alluded to, using stills to replace action. But Penn felt that a drawn-out, slow-motion death would enlarge the characters, seal them in the viewer's memories, enforce their mythic dimensions.[19] That intention is successful. I do not think the film would have entered our contemporary mythology or have had the influence on American film it had without the characters dying the way they do.

The end of the film makes manifest its inherent contradictions. In order to mythologize his characters, Penn makes the audience love them, share the intimacy of their gaze, and then severs the tie violently. The result is that the film leaves the viewer desolate, shattered, and alone, as if witness to the assassination of a public figure. The viewer is punished for enjoying the characters and their exploits too much. As I said, it is the nature of melodrama to deny unalloyed pleasure and freedom: the form regards them as attractive sins for which penance must be paid. *Bonnie and Clyde* merely extends this pleasure-pain, profit-and-loss phenomenon further than it had been extended before. The real changes it makes in the conventions of melodrama involve the extent of the suffering the viewing subject must endure and the extent of the violence that provokes that suffering, both the viewer's and the characters'.

With *Bonnie and Clyde*, Penn breaks for good and all a major cinematic contract between viewer and filmmaker which held that violent death on the screen would be swift and relatively clean. A bloodstain was permissible, a recoil from the force of the bullet, perhaps; but little more. He solidifies the convention begun in *Psycho*. Violent death is now to have an immediacy and to create a physical reverberation; it is to have a sense of anatomical detail. No doubt this new element resulted from certain historical anxieties. The Kennedy assassination (which Penn alludes to not only in *Bonnie and Clyde*, but in *The Chase* and *Four Friends*) and the Vietnamese war, two of the American traumas of the sixties, made the culture acutely aware of the details of physical suffering and placed those details within a profoundly emotional context.

Penn is concerned in all his films with examining that context and the complex responses to violence and its representations. He begins the examination early in his career. In *The Chase* (written by Lillian Hellman), a liberal sheriff (Marlon Brando) of a Texas town is beaten to a pulp by the bored, bigoted, frightened petit-bourgeoisie of the town because of their resentment of him. This same awful bunch, a kind of liberal's nightmare of contemporary southern reactionary degeneracy, assassinate the town's free spirit (Robert Redford), who has escaped from prison and whose return aggravates their repression and frustration. The film is a sort of miniaturized and overheated allegory of the Kennedy assassination, speaking of a violence born of hate, jealousy, ennui, and emotional impotence. No one is ennobled in the film. The middle class is seen as vulgar and destructive; its opponents, the sheriff and the escaped convict, capable only of helpless rebellion. The entire situation is repeated in a somewhat different register in *Four Friends*. Again the violence explodes out of repression and anger. The main character of the film, Danilo, plans to marry the daughter of a rich man; there is the suggestion of incest between daughter and father. At the wedding, the father shoots his daughter and himself in a sequence so structured, and so carefully placed within the film—which is, among other things, a history of the sixties—that it becomes, like the violence in *The Chase*, disturbingly analogous to the political assassinations of the decade.

The only possible response to the violence in these films is helplessness, for the massiveness of the perpetrators' bigotry in *The Chase* and their madness in *Four Friends* seems insuperable. Earlier, in *The Left-Handed Gun*, Penn attempted a different balance. Billy the Kid kills out of revenge, a sense of loyalty to a man who befriended him and was, in turn, shot down. But Billy is larger than his revenge. He is portrayed as a force, as the young vitality of the West; his high spirits puzzle him as much as they threaten the society around him. Penn deals differently with viewer attitudes toward Billy than with those developed toward Bonnie and Clyde. Billy is a creature, ironically, of the fifties, rather than of the old West, just as Bonnie and Clyde are of the sixties, rather than the Depression thirties. He is the misunderstood, misunderstanding adolescent, and Paul Newman's portrayal is closely related to James Dean in *Rebel Without a Cause*, here an orphan with two surrogate fathers. One is murdered; the other is Pat Garrett, who murders Billy because he believes the anarchic sense must be contained. The distortion of oedipal relationships, two fathers demanding two opposing kinds of action and order, finally destroy the suffering subject.

When Billy kills, it is out of a sense of righteousness and occasionally regret. The violence has an extraordinary (for the fifties) deliberateness. If violence in *The Chase* is overwhelming and revolting, in *The Left-Handed Gun* it is stylized and exaggerated. Measured images of violence are offered, more detailed and analytic than had usually been presented in American film, and intended to demonstrate both the suffering and the banality of the violence up to then taken so much for granted. One sequence in the film foreshadows the ritualized violence that the Italian westerns of the late sixties (particularly those of Sergio Leone) would develop almost as a parodic response to the intensity of violence by that time rampant in American film. Billy and his friend Tom confront a deputy, one of the people Billy needs to kill to finish his revenge. The space they inhabit is expanded and strained: they are forward and on the left of the frame, while the deputy, in deep focus, is across the western street. The deputy in an hysterical attempt to get help rings a triangle. Billy almost relents, and another friend does the shooting. As the deputy is hit, there is a cut to a shot looking out from a room behind him, and he falls with his face pressed against the glass, smudging the window as he slides to the street (the face on the glass is a favorite image of Penn's; it occurs in *Mickey One*, in the murder of the bank teller, as well as the various faces that press in on car windows in *Bonnie and Clyde*, and in a variation—a murdered man sliding down a glass door smeared with his blood—in *Target*). There is a sense of pain in these sequences, of suffering. When Billy's friend is shot in an ambush he cries, "I feel my blood." Penn is inquiring into the physicality of shootings and beatings and the ways that physicality can be expressed on the screen, experienced by his characters, and understood by his audience. In *The Left-Handed Gun*, Penn's concern is with a boy whose feelings are too large and too primitive, who suffers and causes suffering despite his attempts to do otherwise. In *The Chase*, suffering is a result of meanness and cruelty and a repressive intolerance. In *Bonnie and Clyde*, a sort of combination and transformation is achieved. Billy the Kid and Bubber Reeves of *The Chase* become the Barrow gang, though the gang lacks the psychological motivation of the earlier characters. The townspeople of *The Chase* become the generalized and oppressive authority that must destroy the gang.

The violence increases throughout these films as the oppressive forces and those attempting to liberate themselves from them become stronger; and it begins to get out of hand. *The Left-Handed Gun* inquires into the ways violence is depicted. *The Chase* portrays the cruelty of violence blindly and fearfully directed at those who only want to avoid it. (Between these two films, *The Miracle Worker* deals with violence as a therapeutic instrument, as a way of demonstrating how, by emotional and physical strength, a determined woman deals with the primitive, blind child she attempts to civilize; the violence of *Mickey One*—in particular the vicious beating of Mickey—grows out of the bizarre and perceptually distorted world the character dwells in.) In *Bonnie and Clyde*, Penn begins to show signs of enjoying the presentation of violent events for their own sake and playing with the attraction-repulsion the audience feels with respect to these events, leading them to bloodshed and then punishing them when they get there. This is another contradiction that emerges from the film. The violent activities committed by Bonnie and Clyde have a liberating effect; the violence done to them disrupts viewer pleasure, creating a shocking and brutalizing effect. This violent play upon emotions begins to reveal a certain amount of cynicism, which becomes fully realized in *Target*, where CIA agents and Eastern European spies chase and shoot each other with an obligatory regularity partly dictated by the genre, partly by Penn's refusal, in this particular film, to examine the purpose of the activity he creates. It is climaxed in *Dead of Winter*, whose genre requires unmeasured amounts of sadism and bloodletting (at one point in the film, the heroine has a finger cut off).

The cynical employment of film violence that developed in the films of Penn and other filmmakers in the sixties did not go undetected and unexploited. Violence is an easy way to command emotional response under the pretence of "realism." Penn showed the way. *Bonnie and Clyde* opened the bloodgates, and our cinema has barely stopped bleeding since. One filmmaker most responsible for the flow was Sam Peckinpah, and it is of interest to consider him in relation to Penn in order to see how the violence of *Bonnie and Clyde* became distorted and mismanaged, and how Penn's attempt to understand the relation of that violence to the moral situation of the audience (however uncertain or cynical that understanding is) becomes the tool of a rather vicious sensibility. If Penn's films, at least until *Night Moves*, are concerned with the losing battle of freedom against oppression, then Peckinpah's films see the battle as always already lost. Peckinpah could only elegize over a fantasy time when men enjoyed each other's companionship in an open frontier, before politics and civilization and order turned them into enemies. He indulges in a curious populism that excludes everyone but rugged men who laugh at women and abuse them and who embrace death as the final proof of their lives' worth. *The Wild Bunch* (1969), his best film, works on the level of its fascination with the body exploding in blood and falling in slow motion. But "works" is a terribly neutral verb. The anatomical and balletic spectacle of the film is undeniable, its celebration of death surprising, if nothing else. It remains a film to admire and to despise simultaneously. Were *The Wild Bunch* the only one of its kind, it would stand as an important example of one way cinema deals with physicality, one way it can create representations of the violent end of life. But it does not stand alone: Peckinpah (and others) have gone on endlessly repeating variations on the theme of male identity and male bonding (but never with an insight into its fragility or its homosexual subtext) in narratives that require more and more exploding flesh to prove that this male bond cannot succeed past its repressions.

An excellent contrast with Penn is offered by *Pat Garrett and Billy the Kid* (1973), Peckinpah's version of the Billy the Kid myth. In *The Left-Handed Gun*, Penn examines the construction of the myth and how it creates violent tensions between its subject and those that surround him. Peckinpah assumes the given of the myth and allows his

The violent end of life: Peckinpah's *The Wild Bunch*. Thornton (Robert Ryan) gazes at the bodies of Bishop (William Holden) and Dutch (Ernest Borgnine).

narrative to encompass its demise. His Billy (Kris Kristofferson) is a tired remnant in a world that can no longer contain him and whose politics need a corrupt law and order rather than the anarchy Billy represents. And so his friend Pat (James Coburn) is sent out to kill him. This—the transition of the frontier into civilization—is an important part of the culture's mythology, and one that John Ford handled, in *The Searchers* and *The Man Who Shot Liberty Valance*, with a great deal of passion and sensitivity (though, unfortunately, with a great deal of racism as well). Peckinpah handles it with a smugness that debases any power the subject might have and so flattens the moral landscape of his narrative that violence becomes the only way to give it shape.

There is a sequence in both *The Left-Handed Gun* and *Pat Garrett and Billy the Kid* in which Billy escapes prison by shooting his jailor. Penn treats it, as he does the film's other violent sequences, in a stately, almost ceremonial fashion. Billy is up on the roof of the jail; the jailor, Ollinger (Denver Pyle, who will become Frank Hamer in *Bonnie and Clyde*), is in the street, looking up. There is a rapid switch of point-of-view shots, from Ollinger to Billy, out of focus against the sun, and the reverse, from Billy down to Ollinger. Billy aims his gun. Before he shoots, Ollinger begins falling back. Billy fires and there is a cut to a slow-motion shot of Ollinger continuing his fall. This early use of slow motion for violent death introduces a major element into contemporary cinema, a specifically cinematic code that, over the years, will come to signify not only the pain and finality of dying, but the viewer's desire to assume a distanced and pleasurable gaze at the represented act. From this slow-motion fall, there is a cut to a lower shot of Ollinger hitting the ground at normal speed. The sequence ends with a far shot of the body and a boot lying next to it. The man has been blown out of his shoe. A child enters and laughs at this peculiar juxtaposition, and gets slapped by its mother.

The film is an obvious influence on Peckinpah, for the use of slow-motion violence is an element that he adopted and made his own. But the shot of the child laughing at the death tableau may very well have helped form a central Peckinpah motif, one which informs the opening images of many of his films, which involve images of children and death. The laughing child in *Left-Handed Gun* is analogous of the surprise Penn intends the viewer to have in the face of sudden violence:

amazement at the enormity of Billy's action, at the fact that a child can laugh at such a grotesque tableau, and at the same time a somewhat distanced awareness of that very grotesqueness. A multiple perspective is achieved. Before he allows things to get out of hand in *Bonnie and Clyde*, Penn is concerned with the contradictions inherent in the representation of violence. The physical destruction of one human being by another is traumatic and always amazing, repellent, and attractive. For Peckinpah, however, violence is reduced to an attractive necessity. Children are not merely drawn to it, they learn it early. Knowledge of death and mutilation is part of their nature and, Peckinpah suggests, grows with them. When Peckinpah repeats the murder of the jailor in *Pat Garrett and Billy the Kid*, the child does not laugh with innocent incomprehension at the body; an adult has to restrain the child's eagerness to run out to it. The killing itself shows the juicy expansion of bloodiness that so many years of cinematic violence have allowed. The set-up is the same: Billy on the roof, the sheriff on the street. Their recognition of each other is done not merely through a series of reverse shots, but through cross-cut zooms. The stately sense of surprise and awe which Penn prepares for the violence in *The Left-Handed Gun* is replaced by movements of anticipation and eagerness. A zoom forward moves perception forward, directing viewer to action. And the action itself, in good Peckinpah fashion, is thrown at the audience. Billy's rifle blasts at the camera; the jailor, who has been made into an unsympathetic religious fanatic, explodes in blood. Like the child who runs out to greet the spectacle, the viewer is excited by it. The required reaction is very simple.

Bloodiness is part of the material texture of Peckinpah's cinematic world. His violence is not "realistic." The notion that late sixties cinematic killing is "real" is real nonsense. Most people have not and never will see a person blown apart by a shotgun, and if seen, not in slow-motion. What is seen so often on the screen since *Bonnie and Clyde* has become, as I noted, one more cinematic convention, which is accepted, through repetition, as a norm. Therefore, to say violence is a given for Peckinpah is to say that in his cinematic universe, and in the response of some viewers, it is a given, but not a necessary reflection of some cultural or psychological need. His violence permits one to be excited by dynamic movement and offers, to use some old-fashioned language, a vicarious thrill. There is, as I mentioned, pleasure, an effect of the safe viewing of a transgressive act. More than the violence itself, the *image* is important, the fact that one is permitted to see the unseeable. But the thrill is short-lived. Peckinpah's narratives become repetitive spectacles of independence and individuality lost. They give no real indication of why these qualities are lost or why they should be lamented; his male-centered, female-hating, trial-by-blood situations become finally only hymns to death. There is something, as many have noted, vaguely fascistic about them. They are oppressive and humiliating.*

The violence that spread through American cinema from the late sixties on indicates the extent of the miscalculation made by Penn in *Bonnie and Clyde*. Despite his effort to create a special context for the slaughter, to understand it and attempt to make the viewer consider it

---

*Many years ago, in "Oranges, Dogs, and Ultra-Violence" (*Journal of Popular Film* (Summer 1972)), I argued that Peckinpah, in *Straw Dogs*, was condemning the violence of his characters and the audience's positive reaction to it. I was dead wrong. If he reflects upon his work at all, it is only manifested in the grossest kind of confusion. *Cross of Iron* (1977) is a celebration of the death spirit of war, focusing on a battalion of Nazi soldiers on the Russian front. There are the "good" German soldiers and a martinet. (The Russian soldiers are never personalized, except for a battalion of women who are degraded.) At the end of the film, as the two German antagonists go off laughing together, accepting each other's faults, Peckinpah suddenly launches into a montage of stills depicting war atrocities, ending with an extraordinary epilogue from Bertolt Brecht about the end of Hitler: "Don't rejoice in his defeat, you men. For though the world stood up and stopped him, the bitch that bore him is in heat again." I expect that Peckinpah meant this ironically to reverse everything he had developed in the film. But since the narrative proper has more weight than the epilogue, the effect is shock and disbelief over his almost schizophrenic attempt to dissociate himself from his film and inject the notion that war can be admired for what it does to men's characters, but hated for what it does to other people. *Cross of Iron* is the dead end to which Peckinpah's death hymns lead.

A similar, if less grotesque confusion occurs in *The Wild Bunch*. Bishop and his gang aid the brutish Federale troops, yet admire Villa's revolutionaries. Peckinpah treats the revolutionaries with romantic awe and allows Sykes (a member of the original Bunch) and Thornton (Bishop's past friend who has become his enemy) to join them after the Bunch are destroyed in their suicidal attack on Mapache. But his sympathies remain with the self-centered group of men whose vitality only embraces death.

His last film, *The Osterman Weekend* (1983), is a peculiar meditation on betrayal and marital angst, an attack upon the CIA and media manipulation (the script was by Alan Sharp, who wrote Penn's *Night Moves*, from a Robert Ludlum novel). Peckinpah cannot avoid interrupting his meditation with gun and cross-bow fights, battles with baseball bats, all slow motion and all betraying an exhausted imagination.

as well as react to it, the obvious pleasure it created was taken by filmmakers as a signal that audiences wanted and would pay for more
extended killings. The intensity and detail of the violence in *Bonnie and
Clyde*, though tame in retrospect, were at the time unlike anything that
had been done before. The various and conflicting messages Penn had
hoped to generate—the radical fracture of audience point of view; the
massive overreaction of authority to individuals who try to defy it; the
impossibility of vitality and freedom; the glorification in death of two
martyrs to that vitality and freedom—are lost in the spectacle of characters who, having earned affection and admiration, are slowly shot to
pieces. Form took precedence over meaning, and the formal trend of
violence started by *Bonnie and Clyde* has been irresistible. American
filmmakers in the last twenty years have been ready to leap for the veins
more quickly and easily than for the intellect. The general blood-letting
in American film, whether caused by repressive authority or by an individual seeking revenge, speaks not only to the desire to gaze at the forbidden scene, but to some immediate needs and fantasies which grow
out of fear or a desire to see enemies easily disposed of—a purpose not
intended by Penn.

Even the filmmakers under discussion in this book, as conscious as
they are of the forms they use and the problems they deal with, find it
difficult to distance themselves from received ideas and cultural clichés.
Although they are less likely than Peckinpah to fall into the foolish and
violent clichés of masculine camaraderie, and unwilling to assume, like
Sylvester Stallone, that an audience will accept a fearless, sub-literate
individual who can correct a perceived foreign injustice by invulnerable
force, they will yield often enough to elements that are guaranteed a
ready-made response. Violence is an integral part of all their work and
it is often difficult to separate it as an element of audience exploitation
from its other function as a means of demonstrating or analyzing
important cinematic or cultural phenomena.


After *Bonnie and Clyde*, Penn tones down the violence in his own films.
It still appears, but briefly and pointedly (until *Target* and *Dead of Winter*, where it has no point at all). The destructiveness of fear and anxiety
remains his most pertinent subject, realized in the hopeless cycle of lib-

erty gained at the price of failure. Like his earlier films, *Alice's Restaurant* plays the disenfranchised against the established order of society. This film goes a bit further, though, in its depiction of part of this order, embodied in Alice and Ray, who attempt to embrace the communal yearnings of free-spirited teenagers. The film was made at the high point of the antiwar movement, when many of a left-liberal frame of mind had visions of a sharing communal world withdrawn, somehow, from the larger, repressive society. Arlo Guthrie, son of the old freedom singer, was one of the many spokespersons of this group, and his narrative song, "Alice's Restaurant," about a Thanksgiving dinner that ended in jail when he was caught dumping garbage in an empty lot, and about the army's refusal to draft him because he had a prison record as a litterer, became something of a rallying point. Penn attempts to flesh out the song, give it a setting and a larger narrative. The result is a fantasy of communal life fraught with the frictions of jealousies and sexual tensions of the bourgeois world.

Unlike his procedure in *Bonnie and Clyde*, Penn keeps a distance from his characters in *Alice's Restaurant*, examining their attitudes, his own, and the viewer's. In the first part of the film, as Arlo moves in the straight world, he is often observed through a window, separated from the viewer's immediate gaze. The sexual insecurity that was at that time aroused by long hair on males is turned upon the spectator. As Arlo is forced to be the butt of many jokes about his hair and his sex so, in a fashion, is the viewer. In the first scene at the draft board an offscreen, masculine voice questions Arlo. When the speaker appears, the voice turns out to belong to a woman clerk. Later, at Arlo's school, a female voice is heard talking to him. When connected to a figure, it turns out to be a male guidance counselor. Penn mocks the audience's inability to comprehend and accept otherness, contrasting continually the gentle, unassuming Arlo with the bullying people around him. But the gap is breached. Arlo, running away from college, stops at a diner. He is taunted by local rednecks and hurled through a window. This is the only violent scene in the film, and it quite literally breaks the distance and pushes Arlo into the audience's sympathies.

The film works wholeheartedly on Arlo's side, though less than wholeheartedly for Alice and Ray, surrogate parents to the commune. They are self-conscious about their role as protectors of hippiedom, mediators between the straight, middle-class world and their young communards. They are caught up in the old codes of behavior, of male supremacy and sexual exclusiveness. By the end, Alice is isolated, emotionally and physically, from her surroundings, as was Arlo at the beginning. Unlike the earlier films, no one wins at the end of *Alice's Restaurant*—not oppressive authority, not the liberated hippies. The commune breaks up, and Alice is left alone. A film that wishes, with all its heart, to celebrate community ends by observing isolation. The last shot is a long, complicated track and zoom around Alice, approaching her and retreating at the same time, expressing movement and stasis and, finally, uncertainty.

That uncertainty was turned to irony and near hostility in Penn's 1983 film about the sixties, *Four Friends*. Here the decade is looked back upon as a foolish and undirected time, a moment of distraction from private concerns and the necessary settling of individual affairs. The film suffers a significant breach in its structure. Written by Steve Tesich, it is his loose autobiography of an immigrant's journeys through America, his relations with an implacable father, and a somewhat tedious narration of the young man's love for, fascination, and inability to get along with one of his childhood friends, Georgia. Penn's talent does not appear in his control of the narration, and definitely not in his direction of his actors (he is unable to elaborate the character of a free-spirited woman, and Georgia turns out to be foolish and weak, rather than strong with a measure of self-direction). The strength of the film lies in his embellishment and re-creation of the narrative, his ability to fashion images that concentrate events and phenomena of the sixties and early seventies into concentrated tableaux, rich in ideological and historical portent, which are to a degree reflected through a foreigner's eye (an inconsistency in point of view is one of the film's damaging structural problems).

In a sequence that takes place in 1961, Danilo, the central character, interrupts a high school employment program by raging at the fact that the school is being used to feed recruits to army and industry. Later, at a beach party, a ball with John and Jacqueline Kennedy's picture is thrown in slow motion through the air, the dominant icons of that period becoming part of the play of teenagers. The Kennedys' image—people who existed mainly as image—is treated nonchalantly by the characters in the narrative who, of course, have no idea how much power the image will collect to itself as the decade proceeds. A racial incident with a black member of their group occurs at the party, which, like the disruption of the high school assembly, portends the greater conflicts to emerge during the decade. Later still, on the road, Danilo sees this black friend in a bus traveling to Mississippi. The friend calls to him to follow, but Danilo, wrapped up in his personal anxieties, will not join the freedom riders. The car and bus fork away from each other on the highway. After the wedding sequence in which Danilo's fiancée is shot by her father, and Danilo himself wounded in the eye, he leaves the hospital. His face is partially bandaged—like Blanche in *Bonnie and Clyde*. Later he will wear glasses with a dulled lens, reminiscent of Clyde's glasses with one black lens. Before he leaves, the music of the national anthem can be heard on a radio. Entering the street, an electric guitar sounds; traffic noise is heard; a black man with a headband walks by; a stoned girl stands on the street. The late sixties teems on the sidewalk, a moment of noise, chaos, and by inescapable association with the hospital, of violence, pain, and sickness. No sweetness of hippiedom exists as it does in *Alice's Restaurant*, no doomed promise of revolt as in *Bonnie and Clyde*. Looking back, Penn sees the time in images of slightly crazed freaks, flag burners, and appalling Greenwich Village "happenings." A time of waste and, the film suggests, the dissipation of subjective energy.

The beginning of the decade is full of portent, broken by the conflicts between social necessity, self indulgence, and personal need. The end of the sixties is a time of bitter and foolish contradictions. Danilo spends the night at the home of one of his old friends, who was in Vietnam, where he married, and brought home a Vietnamese woman. He awakens to see the friend's Vietnamese children staring at him. On television, the astronaut's walk on the moon is taking place. The sound of someone attempting to start up a lawnmower is heard, and Danilo steps to the window, where he sees his friend's wife bent over the lawn mower, trying to work it. The television pictures of the moon, the Vietnamese woman at the lawn mower, with her long hair and native dress, merge into a somewhat terrifying representation of power and banality, of overblown heroism and of the violence committed in the name of preserving the very suburban landscape which the Vietnamese woman now inhabits, itself a representation of complacency and anxiety. This is one of Penn's most inventive set of images; more than image, a semiology of the late sixties, signs of a culture in which the profound and the mundane are so placed together that profundity is muted by the ordinary with the profound indication that nothing of value has been understood from history.

But finally Penn cannot manage the pressure of his own discovery. His unhappiness with the sixties cannot overcome his apparent willingness to assume the desperate assurances of the harmony and well being of the eighties. *Alice's Restaurant* ended with the image of unbreachable solitude. The retrospective images of the sixties in *Four Friends*, the accumulative montage of despair and emptiness, end with the illusion of happiness. The four friends of the title finally overcome history and personality and get together, sitting around the fire on a beach, a happy, isolated community, removed, for the moment, from the demands of the world.

In retrospect, *Alice's Restaurant* is a melodramatic dirge to the youth culture that Penn had a part in creating with *Bonnie and Clyde*. *Four Friends* is a soured re-encounter with that same culture, bitter enough to be a denial of many things he had suggested about it earlier. But *Bonnie and Clyde* was itself already a dirge to the impossible spirit of the rebellion that it celebrates. Unable to offer alternatives to the rebellion-repression cycle of American culture, Penn can merely create various manifestations of it, and by so doing sets a trap for himself. The seeds for the despair and the desire for retreat that grows in the later work are present in the earlier films. From the myth-making of *Bonnie and Clyde* to the withdrawal and uncertainties of *Alice's Restaurant* to the positive demythifications of *Little Big Man*, Penn can be seen tracing a pattern of uncertainty and disillusion just slightly ahead of what is occurring in the culture at large.

*Little Big Man* does attempt to forestall the disillusion. Penn moves back into history, or more accurately into the myth of history created by film, in order to account for the origins of the rebellion-repression cycle. The film, first, acts to undo the conventions of the western by exposing them as pompous frauds and inhuman gestures. It refutes Peckinpah's bloody lamentations over the loss of simple times and simple camaraderie by ignoring such lies and showing the West as merely another arena for the establishment of personal and political advantage. The only inhabitants of the West who offer a stable, ordered culture are the Indians, the "human beings," as they refer to themselves. And here a second revision of convention occurs.

The western has taught that the white man brought civilization to a savage land. Penn tells the opposite: the white man was the active destroyer of a culture that was established, passive, benevolent, that wished only to pursue a very human and life-promoting civilization. He is also presenting a variation on his own usual narrative structure. The admirable figures here are not, as in *Bonnie and Clyde*, active and rebellious, but quiet and conservative. The opposition to them is not an established order, but an *establishing* order. The gentle old chief, Old Lodge Skins, is placed against the blustering egomaniac, General Custer. Between them and their worlds is the narrative voice of the film, Jack Crabb (Dustin Hoffman), who lives out the conflicts of both worlds and clearly marks the hypocrisy of one and the stability and honesty of the other.

Once again a trap is sprung. The initial anger that informs the film slowly changes to nostalgia and special pleading. Penn's Indians are irresistible (it is important to note that the film was made at the time when a new guilty consciousness was developing with respect to the Indians and what had been done to them), but, like all his irresistible characters, they are doomed. No hope is offered, except a lesson to be learned from the Indian way of life—an unlikely prospect, and not too trustworthy: there is a gay Indian portrayed in the film as fully stereotyped as any other film homosexual and indicative that these Indians are simply figures of a white, middle-class, homophobic imagination. Indeed the Indians of *Little Big Man* suddenly become part of a myth older than those created by the western, the myth of the noble savage. They are installed within Penn's pantheon of lost causes and destroyed lives.

Robert Altman, with *Buffalo Bill and the Indians* (1976), attempts to come to terms with this aspect of the western myth without reverting to sentimentality and nostalgia. But at the turn of the seventies, Penn seemed to be unable to deal with his culture in any other way. For whatever reasons, he withdrew from filmmaking for five years, contributing only a documentary on pole-vaulting to a film on the Munich Olympics. He returned with a bleak and despairing film.

*Night Moves* returns to the *noir* world of *Mickey One*, yet without that film's energy and delight in its exploits and its offer of liberation in the face of anxiety. To situate it properly, it is necessary to return to the discussion of *film noir* begun earlier. In 1964, the *noir* cycle over, Penn could elaborate upon it, reinvestigate its milieu and characters and its relationship to the audience. By the mid-seventies, something of a *noir* revival was taking place. Altman's *The Long Goodbye*, Coppola's two *Godfather* films, Scorsese's *Mean Streets* and *Taxi Driver* (and to a certain extent Roman Polanski and Robert Towne's *Chinatown*) were investigating again the dark, barren, angst-ridden world that had enveloped crooks, detectives, and simple men of the middle class in the forties.

The reassertion of the *noir* spirit is not strange, given the new filmmakers' consciousness of cinematic history, coupled with the historical and cultural events of the sixties. The first appearance of *noir* in the mid-forties can be explained, as I mentioned, by the war and an almost dialectic response to victory. The genre reflected an anxiety attendant upon the expansion of power away from home, the separation of families, the new economic status of women, and, perhaps, a knowledge that the culture (and the country) was not as secure and as innocent as had been thought. Indeed, with the memory of fascism and the knowledge of nuclear power, it seems obvious that images of strength would be countered and even conquered by images of anxiety and fear. The fifties shifted the anxiety, making it a response to the communist myth. By convincing the culture that communism was the root source of evil and terror, and that its discourse could and would be expunged, a tentative feeling of control returned, along with a reactionary and protective innocence about the world at large. Representations of domestic strength, of women subdued to subordinate positions, of alien visitors destroyed, countered the anxiety which continued to appear in film from time to time. In the sixties domestic upheaval, assassinations, an unexplained and inexplicable war, a rebellion within the middle class of its children, the collapse of that rebellion; in the seventies, some understanding of how corrupt the political and economic institutions that went unquestioned in the fifties were, changed the images once again. In response, the culture went into something like a depressive reaction, a helpless withdrawal from political and social difficulties as they pressed more urgently. Before the conservative regrouping of the eighties, when depression turned into an aggressive denial of realities needing attention, the feelings of powerlessness became realized in film images and themes of paranoia and isolation stronger than forties *film noir* could have managed.[20]

These images and themes took various forms. There were Peckinpah's male death songs, the revenge and vigilante films, such as Peckinpah's *Straw Dogs*, Michael Winner's *Death Wish*, Phil Karlson's *Walking Tall*, Don Siegel's *Dirty Harry* and its sequels, and a long list of black exploitation films, all employing the Hollywood convention of the lone hero who takes upon himself the task of cleansing corruption. The revenge film implies potency, an ability to act and to correct oppressive situations, but it implies it on a local level only; the society is unchanged when the hero is finished "blowing away" a few villains. As this genre moved into the eighties, the lone hero began working on a more global level. Rambo begins his imitation of life destroying a small town because the local sheriff doesn't like him (a potentially interesting point that his first act of revenge is self-protection rather than protection of others, and that the future protector of American interests is, like Arlo in *Alice's Restaurant*, told to get a bath and haircut by the constabulary). In his sequel, Rambo takes on Vietnam and the Russians. Victory unattainable by organized warfare is won by a determined loner.

The reverse side of the heroic venture manifested itself in the paranoia film, such as Sidney Pollack's *Three Days of the Condor*, Alan J. Pakula's *The Parallax View* and *All the President's Men*, Stanley Kramer's *The Domino Principle*, Paul Schrader's *Blue Collar*, Coppola's *The Conversation*, films spawned by assassinations, the Vietnam war, and Watergate, films whose images reinforced fears of lost control over political and economic institutions, whose discourse insisted that no matter what efforts are made, an unknowable presence—governmental, corporate, both—will have its way and exert its ineluctable power. These films exemplified impotence and despair and signaled disaster, a breakdown of community and trust so thorough that it left the viewer with images of lonely individuals, trapped, in the dark, completely isolated. But, in fact, whether the films offered the myth of a violent hero or spoke of no heroes available to conquer the threat, they affirmed passivity and by reiteration soothed and comforted it. The eighties revenge films, the films in which lone heroes once again conquered, or groups of children (child-like heroes in the case of Indiana Jones) asserted control via supernatural or extraterrestial means did not change the basic ideological position. They merely shifted the discourse along the same ground, still without images of collective action, and certainly not rational action. The films diverted impotence by permitting a fantasy of power.

Not all of the films of the seventies cycle of despair fit comfortably within the *noir* category. Some, like the vigilante films, are urban westerns, others are chase thrillers. But many of them are informed with a *noir* sensibility, and when that sensibility overtakes the entire film, the sense of desolation is tremendous. *Night Moves* is such a film. Like many of its forties predecessors, it has as its subject a detective, a film figure who has continually responded to changing cultural attitudes about control and authority, potency, and success. During the Depression the urbane William Powell held the Thin Man series together, operating with the ease of the dilettante, detached and disinterested, so much in control that detection became another upper-class amusement, a pursuit only momentarily dangerous and barely serious. There was little sense, in these films, of being in touch with the danger they hinted at, and it took the entrance into film of Dashiell Hammett's and Raymond Chandler's hard-boiled fiction, and the simultaneous development of *film noir*, to establish the detective as a lower-middle-class working man, morally committed to his work, willing to enter a dark, amoral world to find reasons and answers. Humphrey Bogart, as Sam Spade in *The Maltese Falcon* and as Philip Marlowe in *The Big Sleep*, became the archetype against whom all succeeding film detectives were measured. The sense of assurance, the willingness to descend into the dark world and return, sullied perhaps but with morality intact and order seemingly restored, turned the Bogart persona into the image of calm strength and persistence that would yield success. (The fact that this persona also manifested the opposite qualities—a dis-ease and insecurity, a control that was always tenuous at best and non-existent at worst—is something I will examine further when discussing Altman and *The Long Goodbye*.)

*Night Moves* consciously plays against the idea of the forties Bogart detective by retaining the world he inhabited, brought up to date in the seventies but still filled with the dark streets, the fancy homes, and the labyrinthine plotting that marked the *noir* world of Spade and Marlowe. The difference lies in the detective himself. Gene Hackman's Harry Moseby is a figure of contemporary anxiety, with none of the wit and bluff that Bogart brought to his roles, none of the security in self-preservation, indeed, none of the sense of self and its endurance that allowed the forties detective to survive. I said he was the subject of the film, but in fact his subjectivity is on the point of dissolution. Harry is not the self-protective neurasthenic that Elliott Gould's Marlowe is in Altman's *The Long Goodbye*; quite the contrary, he feels very deeply and sees in a limited way the world around him. What he does see, however, fills him with an almost paralyzing unhappiness, an inability to move in a way that will make things clear and give them order. "Who's winning?" asks Harry's wife as he watches a football game on television. "Nobody," he answers. "One side's just losing slower than the other."

Detective films are about seeing, about perceiving and discerning. The success of the detection depends upon how clearly things are seen and how secure the point of view of the perceiver is. Harry sees, but he has no point of view, no moral position from which to act upon what he sees. Images in the film are continually reflected, often by distorting surfaces; Harry is observed, or observes, through screens and windows. Much of the central part of the film, Harry's visit to Florida, where he attempts to find and return his client's runaway daughter, Delly, and discovers a complex smuggling operation, is filmed in darkness and empty spaces. The cutting of the film does not permit sequences to complete themselves. A new scene may be entered with the dialogue of the previous one carried over, so that no comfortable continuity between narrative units is allowed. The viewer is given no more security of structure, no fuller sense of subjective certainty, no more certain sense of clear perception than is the character (a strategy similar to what Penn does in *Mickey One*).

However, the form does not function merely to make the viewer share Harry's darkness and despair, but to indicate the difficulties of seeing and knowing clearly anything about anyone. This perceptual murkiness extends to the character's insights about himself and the viewer's understanding of him. At one point a psychological explanation for Harry's anomie seems to be offered. His father ran away when Harry was young and Harry felt the need to find him. He tells his wife that he tracked his father down once, found him on a park bench in Baltimore and walked away. This information could offer a touching bit of understanding for the character and a typical screen-writing ploy—when in doubt, explain the character's personality by giving him or her trouble with parents. But here it serves a different function. What appears to be psychological explanation is not. No explanation is given for Harry's refusal to greet his long-sought-for father. It is offered as the expression of one more emotional dead end, one more provocation of anxiety and hopelessness. The oedipal structure is itself repressed, offering no promise for the subject to emerge into knowledge and order. In *Night Moves*, interior and exterior states are the same: fearful and insoluble. The act of detection creates an anxiety in Harry that does not permit him to bring the act to an end. Or perhaps the ending and the possibility of revelation that endings bring are too painful, or simply impossible. The question, and it saturates the film, is that, if the end of the search is painful, how much more so can it be than the search itself, which proceeds as a series of stumblings and humiliations, deaths and personal agonies? Penn raises this question again in *Four Friends*, and although that film ends with an affirmation of community—however small and delimited—the journey of its hero, like that of Harry, is lonely and despairing.

Impotent anger, impotent actions, impotent anxiety permeate *Night Moves*. Sexuality is a thing of loathing and a weapon. Harry follows his wife and discovers his own cuckolding. When he confronts the man, a physical cripple (complementing Harry's emotional state), he is insulted with his own movie origins. "C'mon, take a swing at me, Harry, the way Sam Spade would." And when he confronts his wife, he can only let out his rage by grinding a glass down the disposal. The child Delly, one of the objects of Harry's search, is promiscuous to the point of destruction of herself and others. She sleeps with everyone, including her stepfather. "She's pretty liberated, isn't she?" asks Harry. "When we all get liberated like Delly," he is told, "there'll be fighting in the streets." The reorganization of sexual politics—one of the few major cultural achievements of the seventies—is here turned to another dismaying, oppressive image. Paula, the woman Harry meets during his

*Night Moves:* darkness, empty spaces and screens. Harry Moseby (Gene Hackman), Delly (Melanie Griffith), Paula (Jennifer Warren).

PAULA

Florida quest and who joylessly makes love to him, and betrays him, is saddened by her sexuality. In *Bonnie and Clyde*, sexuality is displaced into violence and its momentary triumph over that violence becomes a prelude to death. In *Alice's Restaurant* it is a source of jealousy and conflict. In *Little Big Man* it is reduced to sniggering chauvinism. In *Four Friends* it is a major cause of Danilo's pain and Georgia's self-destructive activities. Penn is never very comfortable with it (but then none of the filmmakers discussed here are), and in *Night Moves* it is manifested as one more weight upon his characters' spirits, a depressing activity good only for betrayal and for further anxiety.

The emotional paralysis and moral corruption that permeate the film suppress any clear manifestation of plot and render any attention to it useless. Partly in the tradition of the *noir* detective film, the complica-

"C'mon, take a swing at me, Harry, the way Sam Spade would." Marty Heller (Harris Yulin) and Harry Moseby.

tions arising from the entanglements of the film's characters with each other indicate the difficulties of detection and the almost impossible labyrinths the detective must follow. Ultimately, the plotting becomes lost in the searching itself, which is a contest between the moral strength of the detective and the potently amoral state of the world he encounters. This strength is vitiated in *Night Moves* by the fact that Harry has himself no moral center and no faith in discovering one. As his "case" widens; as the search for Delly expands to a search for a ring of antique smugglers, and this ring widens to include his friends and, though it is never stated, his wife (who works in an antique store); as the deaths build up; and as clues are missed or aborted, the possibilities for success disappear. Harry's job becomes not so much detecting as confirming the existence of a moral swamp, an unclear, liquid state of feelings and rela-

*HARRY No moral center No faith in Discovering one*

tions in which the drowning of the spirit is perpetual. Paula tells Harry how the films of the Kennedy assassination appear to have been taken under water, and this metaphor for the opaqueness of the general political and cultural condition spreads over the film, literally—in the vague, swimming quality of the films Harry views showing Delly's death, of the scene of the discovery in Florida of an airplane under water, its pilot's corpse eaten by fishes, and of the climactic sequence of the film.[21]

At the end of his quest Harry goes out on a boat named, with perfect irony, the *Point of View*. As Paula dives in an attempt to discover the contraband that is the source of everyone's machinations, we see Harry from her point of view, looking through the glass bottom of the boat, out of reach and out of touch. A plane buzzes Harry and shoots him in the leg. A Mexican antique surfaces on the water, an ugly statue similar to one Harry was looking at in a friend's office earlier in the film. Paula comes up, only to be hit by the plane, which goes under in its attempt to destroy them all. Through the glass bottom, Harry sees the drowning

The destruction of the *Point of View*.

*[handwritten margin notes: DROWNING of the SPIRIT / Kennedy / opaqueness / WATER / Fishes / CHINATOWN / CONTRABAND]*

pilot, a friend from L.A., a stunt man whose only implication heretofore *[friend from L.A.]* was his involvement in the "accident" that killed Delly. Each looks helplessly at the other through the water. Finally the camera withdraws, dissociating itself from anybody's point of view. It assumes the high, downward angle that Hitchcock loves to take when a character is in moral or physical danger. The spectator, removed from any certain understanding of events, left only with a response of shock, helplessly observes Harry, crippled in the *Point of View*, going around and around in the water.

*Night Moves* seems almost inevitable in Penn's career. In film after film he has attempted to maneuver the spirit of life against the repressive order and laws of society that bring death to those who move against them. He has contented himself not with an attempt to understand the peculiarly American variety of the politics of repression and the attempts to struggle against it, but with the emotional power of the struggle itself, and has reaped from his audience the emotional profit that seems always to come from being witness to the death of vitality, from the reaffirmation that we are lost and helpless. But in *Night Moves* *[Harry Moseby emotionally dead from beginning]* the profit of loss seems to have run out. Harry Moseby is emotionally dead from the beginning. He does not so much entangle himself in the oppression of others as merely sink deeper into his own and their moral vacuum. There is not even the external force of authority to fight against as there is in the earlier films. As in *Mickey One*, the outside is a reflection of the inside, but in *Night Moves* there is no triumph, and both interior and exterior worlds remain squalid and empty. The destroyers seem to have won; they have become us

Penn trapped himself within the cycle of advance and retreat, liberation and inevitable repression, that has marked all his films. His attempt to break out of it in *The Missouri Breaks* is unconvincing. When Jack Nicholson's Tom Logan cuts Brando's throat, thereby destroying the landowner's hired gun, it is only a local act of revenge (it is also little more than Nicholson "killing" Brando, which may be the oedipal act of a young actor transcending an older one but not of one character or situation transcending another). Logan kills the landowner as well, but not ownership; and while the film offers another response to the myth of the western frontier, it has little of the political and emotional insight into its lies that Altman's *McCabe and Mrs. Miller* has, or even Penn's own *Little Big Man*.

Indeed, Penn seemed to catch himself in a double trap, one the ideological bind of his own making, the other the bind of any filmmaker in Hollywood who can only do what he or she gets the financing to do. Neither *Night Moves* nor *Missouri Breaks* was very successful commercially, and Penn did not make another film until *Four Friends* in 1981. There, as I noted, he turned upon the sixties with some anger and disappointment. His next film, *Target*, is so different in point of view from anything else he made that it can be accounted for either as an act of commercial necessity or as an indication that the ideological turmoil expressed in the earlier work had simply been resolved by a decided turn to the right. The conflicts, contradictions, and despair that developed through *Night Moves* are here settled by violent action that affirms rather than destroys, and a secure closure that presumes to offer comfort in place of unsettling questions.

The oedipal material suggested and suppressed in *Night Moves* emerges in *Target* fully formed and so well worked out that father, son, and even mother are united in the image of the resurrected family. Gene Hackman reappears not as the crushed and dissolved subject of a dark and corrupt world, but as a father with an exciting past that at first needs to be repressed and then reactivated and settled when the family is in danger. His wife is kidnapped; his son needs a role model for adulthood. Conflict between father and son turns into a harmony resulting from the activity of men aiding distressed women. This abstraction of the film seems to offer some ground for speculation, a suggestion that Penn may be once again questioning the effects of violence and the platitudes of domesticity. Such is not the case. Both the narration and the material narrated—the plot and its characters—are banal beyond all reason.

Hackman's character is "Duke" Lloyd, a former CIA man, who left the organization after a critical spy mission, taking up a new life with wife and son (Chris, played by Matt Dillon, one of the many sullen, arrogant adolescent figures to emerge in Hollywood since the late seventies). In the early sequences of the film, before the character's past is revealed, Penn creates quiet images of the ordinary man. Hackman

operates a lumber yard in suburban Texas. On the dashboard of his car
are samples of wood mouldings, an unobtrusive sign of an unobtrusive,
somewhat boring man, restrained and subdued. He eats in his car; he
attempts to make contact with his distant and independent son. His
wife goes to Paris, both she and Chris believing his father is too passive
and retiring to join them. When she is kidnapped by an East German
agent, who believes Duke was responsible for the murder of his family
(it turns out that Duke's CIA chief was responsible for the destruction
of the agent's family and the betrayal of Duke), he goes back into action,
his son at his side.

Structurally, the film is made of alternating sequences of dialogue and
action. Most of the former is flat and without much purpose other than
exposition of plot. Some of the latter shows only traces of the hard,
often oblique cutting that marked the earlier films. There, Dede Allen
often provided an arhythmic montage that tended to fragment conventional continuity and charge action sequences with rapid and disturbing
shifts of point of view. (Dede Allen was the sole editor on *Bonnie and
Clyde*, *Alice's Restaurant*, and *Little Big Man*, one of two editors on
*Night Moves* and one of three on *Missouri Breaks*, after which she did
not cut for Penn. The lack of vitality of the later films may be due to
her absence.) Whether because of indifferent editing or simply indiffer-
ence, *Target* is uninflected by anything disturbing in its form or substance. No questions are raised about perception, purpose, or place in
the world. No interrogation is made upon the spy genre that controls
the film; only the portrayal of Schroeder, the East German agent whose
family was murdered, offers a point of interest. The only visually meaningful sequence, after the opening of the film, is the confrontation of
"Duke" and Schroeder, at the latter's home, in the mist, by the graves
of Schroeder's family, where the narrative offers sympathy to the individual formerly thought to be evil. (The sympathetic enemy agent is
hardly new to the genre, however; the decent man among evil forces is
an important method by which cold war fiction prevents itself from falling between the edges of an impossible Manichaeism or into the paralysis of complete despair.) Finally, an unquestioning satisfaction is generated by this film which seems only to respond to its makers' inability
or unwillingness to confront contradiction and discomfort.

Beyond the spy apparatus, the concept of family is the film's major

Family melodrama/family harmony. *(Top)* Four Friends: Danilo (Craig Wasson) and his parents (Miklos Simon, Elizabeth Lawrence). *(Bottom)* publicity still for *Target* (Matt Dillon, Gayle Hunnicutt, Gene Hackman).

subject. Referred to obsessively in dialogue, plot, and visual structure, it becomes almost a thing of worship. Certainly the family has concerned Penn before—a number of families are involved in the desperate movements of *The Chase*; Clyde, Bonnie, Buck, Blanche, and C.W. form a small, often bickering family in *Bonnie and Clyde*; questions of alternate family structures are raised in *Alice's Restaurant*; and comforting families are finally formed at the end of *Four Friends*. But none of these films accept and assent to the traditional image of family so unquestioningly as does *Target*, with all the appropriated ideological accouterments of the controlled domestic structure, in which women are appointed a static place, the children appropriately acculturated according to gender, and the father emerging as protective hero. Such a structure is central to the conservative ideology of the eighties, of course, and we shall see many images of it in the course of this study. But rarely, even in Spielberg's work, does it appear so unadorned in its ideological certitude as here, and never has Penn created such unquestioning, stereotypic images. By film's end they become almost parody; yet a deadly seriousness refuses to permit them or the viewer to raise questions about their validity.

Schroeder, the East German spy who thinks Duke murdered his family, holds Duke's wife captive in a warehouse, where he has her gagged and trussed in an airplane seat. She is wired with explosives, raised and spotlit, as if she were simultaneously a religious icon and a slightly pornographic image of woman in bondage. As Duke tries to undo her without blowing her up, his former CIA boss appears and his complicity in the affair is exposed. Schroeder, maddened by the loss of his family, anxious to get revenge, is pleased to find the true culprit and orders Duke, his son, and Duke's now unbound but still gagged wife out. "Take your family and get out," he yells, the word "family" now echoing throughout the film with the excess of repetition. Duke's old boss is placed in the wired seat. The family runs out of the warehouse just as Schroeder and the CIA man go up in a burst of flames. "Are we o.k.?" cries the wife, when Duke finally removes the gag from her mouth. His enthusiastic response, the prolonged hugging and loving looks between the three characters in front of the burning building, affirms that they are not merely "o.k.," but reintegrated as the perfect domestic enclave, each member in their appropriate role. The bad "family"—the CIA with its twisted relationships—has been destroyed, as far as its evil influence on Duke is concerned; Schroeder's wronged family has been avenged; and, set against the burning building, signifying the violence that would be done against them, the American nuclear family emerges transcendent.

At the end of *Four Friends*, Danilo, Georgia, their old friends and children, sit rejoicing around a camp fire. Despite its sentimentality, the sequence creates a necessary linkage and pause for these characters who have been struggling with each other and with the decade for so long. In the midst of that struggle, Penn had created the most despairing scenes of domestic collapse, resulting from the shooting of Danilo's fiancée and the suicide of the murderer, her father. After recovering from his wounds in the hospital, Danilo visits the widow. He knows that her husband and daughter are dead; he discovers now that her son—his old college friend—has died as well. "The excess of all this is a little staggering," she says, her self-consciousness undercutting the melodrama of the sequence. She is composed alone amidst the rooms of her mansion, in black, with dark glasses, one of the loneliest figures to appear in recent film. "For thirty years I've been a wife," she says, "and for over twenty I've been a mother. Now those words are taken away from me. I'm now a woman. I don't know what to do with that word." She literally howls in her isolation. Penn and Tesich momentarily enter the heart of dread, of a woman seeking to redefine the very language of her life. The little community of families at the end of the film is an almost necessary closure to this image of emptiness and incapacity, a confession of the inability to confront the enormous task of restructuring social relationships that can create such solitude. The final images of *Target* offer no such confession because the narrative has posed no such problems. The female figure is simply bound and gagged in place, literally, figuratively, culturally; her husband and son have done their patriarchal duty and liberated her back into the familial trinity. The world exploding behind them is of no consequence; they are now "safe."

And so, in effect, is Penn. With no more questions to raise about the culture and its images, he is liberated into the ordinary structures of Hollywood filmmaking, where action and suspense, signifying the total passivity of the spectator, are substituted for inquiry and speculation. Early in *Night Moves*, Harry Moseby's wife asks him if he wants to see an Eric Rohmer film. "I saw a Rohmer film once," Harry answers. "It was kinda like watching paint dry." Early in *Target*, Duke and Chris sit in a Parisian café. A sign on the wall reads, "Ne Tirez Plus Sur Le Pianiste"—"Don't Shoot the Piano Player Anymore."

The reference to Rohmer is to a filmmaker of delicate dialogue and witty, ironic situations, who, in films like *My Night at Maud's* and *Pauline at the Beach*, eschews physicality and violence for sequences built upon two people talking to each other within a carefully defined and visually simple—but acute—setting. The talk that goes on involves moral problems, choices, feelings, and thoughts, and the appropriateness of those feelings and thoughts; the intricate decisions about how and why one person acts toward him or herself and others. People lose in Rohmer's films; they make mistakes and wrong judgments; but they do not suffer inordinately, and they all have a strength that enables them to continue thinking. Rohmer's films are inimical to the conventions of American cinema. For a Penn character, quite possibly for Penn himself, such films would indeed be like watching paint dry.

The second reference is to François Truffaut (who in 1960 made a film entitled *Shoot the Piano Player*). Legend is that Truffaut was one of the people Benton and Newman originally considered as director for *Bonnie and Clyde*. The mixture of genres, the intersection of comedy and seriousness that Penn achieved in the film owes much to Truffaut. And I would guess that Penn must have envied Truffaut's ability to create popular entertainments that connoted seriousness of intent. The piano player is dead. The film culture that supported Truffaut's work and others like it is no longer supported by a business now less than willing to accommodate minority taste. Penn has no doubt discovered that the accommodating is now completely the job of the filmmaker. *Target* or *Dead of Winter* may not quite stand as the obituary for the *auteur*, but certainly as signs of the forced or chosen demise of inquisitive filmmaking intelligence.

## CHAPTER TWO

## TECTONICS OF THE MECHANICAL MAN

# Stanley Kubrick

If some of Arthur Penn's problems as a filmmaker can be attributed to his desire to embrace the form and content of commercial American cinema, and thereby getting caught up in its contradictions in the process, Stanley Kubrick's success can be attributed to his total divorce from these contradictions. Of all American filmmakers, he works in the most non-American fashion. He has eschewed American production methods; he has in fact eschewed America. Only four of his ten films—*Fear and Desire* (1953), *Killer's Kiss* (1955), *The Killing* (1956), and *Spartacus* (1960)—have been made in the United States (one of the distracting delights of *Lolita* (1961) and *Dr. Strangelove* (1963) is seeing how British exteriors are made to stand for American and, in *Full Metal Jacket* (1987), how they are made to stand for American *and* Vietnam locations). Kubrick himself has lived in a kind of isolation in England, traveling little and immersing himself in his projects. He is close to the European standard of the film *auteur*, in complete control of his work, overseeing it from beginning to end.

But with this control and his almost total independence, one contradiction does arise. Instead of creating "personal" and "difficult" works, of the kind European filmmakers are supposed to make, Kubrick seemed destined to be recognized as a great popularizer.[1] The films of his trilogy—*Dr. Strangelove, 2001: A Space Odyssey* (1968), *A Clockwork Orange* (1971)—were commercially successful and demonstrated an unerring ability to seize upon major cultural concerns and obsessions—the cold war, space travel, the ambiguities of violence—and represent them in images and narratives so powerful and appropriate that they became touchstones, reference points for these concerns: myths. *2001* is not only a narrative of space travel but a way of seeing what space travel *should* look like. The film is a design for our imagination and a notion of modernity, creating the lineaments of a modern environment and enunciating the metamorphosis of human into machine. His cinema became the image of what we think this and other worlds should look like; the space apparatus of *2001* forms the basis for the *Star Wars* trilogy and for *Close Encounters of the Third Kind. Dr. Strangelove* is the complete text of politics as a deadly joke, a text that has become more and more accurate in the years since its first appearance. *A Clockwork Orange* holds in suspension, in the cold light of its cinematography, the outrageous contradictions of freedom and repression, libido and superego, the death of the other in the name of liberation of the self.

These films offer insight while giving immediate pleasure; they are beautiful to watch, funny, and spectacular. The "youth culture" of the late sixties and early seventies embraced *2001* and *A Clockwork Orange* for reasons of their immediacy and their spectacle. Kubrick was in danger of being seen as the panderer of contemporary film. Until he did something rather amazing. After three films that structured a mechanics of the modern age, he made a costume drama. *Barry Lyndon* (1975), based on a largely unread Thackeray novel published in 1844, about an eighteenth-century rogue, was the most unlikely and proved to be the most uncommercial film that an artist who had seemed so able to gauge the needs of his audience could have made. Had Kubrick abandoned his audience? After a decade of successful filmmaking, was he becoming self-indulgent or losing his judgment? Or was he not as calculating and cold about filmmaking as some critics have thought? It is well known that Kubrick plans his films by computer and solves production problems as if he were playing chess with a machine. There is a notion that this is perhaps somehow responsible for the popular success of the trilogy—that Kubrick calculates his narrative and its effects, perhaps even viewer response. But now the great calculator, the independent popularizer, had erred.

Or had he? Kubrick's films have far outlived their popularity of the moment. His best films—*Paths of Glory* (1957), *Dr. Strangelove*, *2001*, and the unpopular *Barry Lyndon*—yield up more and more information on each viewing, revealing themselves as meticulously made and carefully considered. Kubrick *is* very much a calculator, his films are cold and have strong designs upon their audience—emotional, intellectual, and commercial. He has proven that the last does not cancel out the first two, and it is a happy coincidence when all three are offered to and met by the filmgoer. One can speculate that with *Barry Lyndon* it was not Kubrick who failed but his audience. The film is an advanced experiment in cinematic narrative structure and design and attests both to the strength of Kubrick's commercial position (no other director could have received the backing for such a project) and to the intensity of his interest in cinematic structures.

He followed *Barry Lyndon* with *The Shining* (1980), an adaptation of a Stephen King novel (such as were proving popular at the time), a film which, on first sight, seems to confirm Kubrick's ability to calculate his intent and his effects. A broad, loud, perfectly unsubtle film, it is more a parody of the horror genre than a film seriously intent upon giving its audience a fright. Even beyond parody, it first appears as a mockery of its audience, almost an insult in its broadness to those who would not attend to the subtleties of *Barry Lyndon*. But like all of his mature work, *The Shining* reveals more on subsequent viewing. Without doubt a parody of the horror genre, it is also—as are many recent representatives of the genre—an examination of the family, in this instance a discovery of the madness of the patriarchal domestic unit and a prophecy of its collapse.[2] Prophecy, satire, and a carefully controlled narrative and visual structure place it in an interesting relationship to the rest of Kubrick's work.

*Full Metal Jacket*, the most recent film to appear as of this writing, seems less certain in that relationship. A film about Vietnam, it generates many of the uncertainties and ambivalences of all other films of its kind. As a work by Kubrick, it seems less assured, less structured, less clear about its own point of view than do the preceding films. Because it is a war film, I will treat it in relationship with *Paths of Glory*, hoping that such a context will reveal both its successes and its flaws.*

In the following chapter, I want to concentrate on *Paths of Glory, Dr. Strangelove, 2001, A Clockwork Orange*, and *Barry Lyndon*, along with some thoughts about how *The Shining* clarifies Kubrick's attitude toward sexual politics in the other films. This means the earlier works will be slighted. They make up an interesting body of generic experiment and indicate something of the direction in which Kubrick was to move.[3] *Killer's Kiss* and *The Killing* are gangster films in the *noir* tradition. The sense of entrapment and isolation they offer is visually acute, and the hard black-and-white photography, the glaring lights, and a sense of exaggerated, even distorted space were to be developed and refined until Kubrick became a master of organizing large and expressive cinematic spaces. The nightmare sequence in *Killer's Kiss*, in which the camera rushes through a claustrophobic city street, photographed in negative, is a source for all the major tracking shots in the films to come, shots which integrate a subjective point of view within an environment that encloses and determines the character who inhabits it. The structure of *The Killing*, in which Sterling Hayden's Johnny Clay attempts to organize a foolproof racetrack robbery, only to be undone by a dismal accident, creates a concatenation of events that points the way to the typical situation of the Kubrick character, entangled and destroyed in systems of his own creation, systems that turn upon him and take him over.[4] These two films provide a base for the future work, which are not as generically oriented as they were.

Unlike the other directors discussed here, and with the major exceptions of *The Shining* and *Full Metal Jacket*, Kubrick became essentially uninterested in the subtle interplay of convention and response, the interplay of expectation and satisfaction that tinkering with generic patterns allows. His sources are mostly literary rather than cinematic. The complexities of *2001*, for example, are much closer to science fiction

---

*\*Full Metal Jacket* was released just as this book was about to go to press. My experience has been that Kubrick's films tend to gain in resonance and yield more meaning after a passage of time. Necessity, therefore, makes the commentary on this film somewhat tentative.

literature than to the science fiction films of the fifties (even though it is necessary to consider those films in order to understand fully what Kubrick is doing). And by literary sources I mean two things: that most of his films come from pre-existing literary works, and that they have an intellectual complexity associated more with the literature of words than with that of film. The second of these characteristics is of greatest interest. Rather than Kubrick's use of literary sources, his translations from verbal to visual and aural text, what I find of most value in his work is his ability to generate ideas from the organization of a complex spatial realm that encloses his characters and expresses their state of being. For in Kubrick's films we learn more about a character from the way that character inhabits a particular space than (with the exception of *Dr. Strangelove*) from what that character says. Kubrick's is a cinema of habitations and rituals, of overwhelming spaces and intricate maneuvers, of the loss of human control, of defeat.

But before entering these spaces, I want to approach them from various other directions. Kubrick's influences emerge from the work of two seemingly opposite filmmakers, Orson Welles and John Ford. Every filmmaker of the last twenty-five years, American or European, will admit to the influence of *Citizen Kane*, but very few, perhaps only Kubrick and Bernardo Bertolucci, have indicated an ability to put into practice the *mise-en-scène* Welles developed in *Kane* and his subsequent films. The Wellesian cinema is a cinema of space and spatial relationships. The camera, for Welles and for Kubrick, is an inscriber of a deep and complex visual field. Working within the design of the set, it creates an intricate space which it then begins to investigate, building a labyrinthine narrative structure that is a reflection of its investigations.[5] *Kane* is a study of the inviolability of personality, an inviolability proven when other people attempt to break it. A newspaper reporter provokes four people to re-create the character of Charles Foster Kane. The narrative that results is made up of the interlocking points of view of these people, points of view that create various spatial relationships between perceiver and perceived and between the audience and its perception of the narrative. The camera functions as creator and mediator of the entire structure, and the result is an extreme formal and thematic complexity. For all the discussion of Wellesian deep focus, moving camera, and long takes, and how these cinematic elements allow great freedom to observe spatial relationships, not many observers have noted that the more one sees in Welles's films, the more opaque and intractable what is seen becomes. For so intricate are these relationships, so complete and closed the world they create, that they become tenuous and abstract. The Wellesian *mise-en-scène*, especially in his later films—in *Touch of Evil* and *The Trial* (1962)—creates a space so radically dislocated that it becomes a mental landscape. Knowable structures and the spatial relationships between human figures and those structures are distorted by lighting and camera placement to the point of straining the perceptions of the audience. Until *Chimes at Midnight* (*Falstaff*, 1966), the Wellesian *mise-en-scène* becomes more and more complex, overwhelming, and subjective.

Kubrick assumes many of Welles's attitudes toward the articulation of cinematic space. His composition in depth is almost as extreme—although he depends more upon the distorting qualities of the wide angle lens than Welles did—as is his use of the moving camera. But where Welles tends to move his camera to investigate the intractability

Wellesian space (Tony Perkins in *The Trial*).

of the space he is creating, Kubrick most often uses it to traverse that space, to control it and understand it. He is much more inclined to use the moving camera as a surrogate or parallel for the point of view of a character than is Welles. Compare the fleeing backward-moving camera retreating in front of Joseph K. in *The Trial* with the stately backward-moving camera that tracks Alex's walk into the record boutique in *A Clockwork Orange*. In the first instance the camera shares K.'s panic, it emphasizes his entrapment, and by retreating through a corridor of extreme dark and light it combines the need to escape with an indication of the impossibility of ever really emerging from the psycho-political cage K. inhabits. For Welles the moving camera often describes a double perspective, that of the character and that of the environment, and the two are almost always at odds. By contrast the sequence quoted from *A Clockwork Orange* links the viewer to the character in a different way. His movement, the camera's, the synthesized version of the march from the fourth movement of Beethoven's Ninth Symphony, the bright metallic colors, the assuredness of the entire structure indicate total control: Alex's control of the situation and viewer pleasure in acknowledging that control. Much the same can be said for the celebrated tracking shot of Commander Poole in the centrifugal hall of the spaceship *Discovery* in *2001*—another rare shot indicative of peace and comfort with the character's surroundings.

But this is greatly oversimplified. The comfort Kubrick affords his characters is always ironic. The control Alex manifests in the sequence referred to is temporary. And while the spectator may marvel at the nonchalance of the inhabitants of the spaceship, she may marvel as well at how they can be so nonchalant in such a strange and overwhelming place. In *The Shining* there is a sequence in which Wendy comes into the great hall of the hotel where her husband, Jack, is supposed to be writing. He is not at his desk, and she looks at his papers, discovering that what he has been writing, obsessively, over and over, in every conceivable pattern on the pages, is "All work and no play make Jack a dull boy." There is a cut to a camera position behind a pillar in back of Wendy. The camera begins to track to the left, a movement coded in horror films to indicate the approach of the monster, often signifying the point of view of the monster itself. But here, as the camera ends its movement on Wendy, who is standing stunned over the desk, Jack's silhouette moves into the frame from the right, and he asks, "How do you like it?"

A curious sense of false comfort is initially created by this movement. Jack's madness and the danger he threatens have been well established by this point—indeed Wendy enters the hall carrying a baseball bat to protect her from his violence. Within the generic expectations set by the horror film, confirmed by the specific shock of discovery of Jack's manuscript, the camera movement is an assurance for the audience that the mad husband will attack; it is the bearer of his threatening gaze. But Jack's appearance at the opposite side of the camera's trajectory is a surprise and suggests that the moving camera signified another point of view altogether (a suspicion confirmed by Kubrick's not very successful attempt to suggest that the hotel has some strange life of its own that controls Jack himself).

The central sequence of the sniper in *Full Metal Jacket* keeps the viewer close to the Marines and their terror and suffering. At three points, Kubrick breaks this proximity, cutting unexpectedly to the point of view of the sniper within the burning building. In each instance, the camera, without yet revealing the sniper's identity (a very young Vietnamese woman), moves by craning or zooming forward to the next victim of the attack. Rather than a supernatural presence, the moving camera here represents an unknown, dangerous, and very immediate perspective. Each cut to this point of view removes the viewer from a space of chaos and pain to the place where the chaos and pain originate, outside the control of the characters and the viewer's own gaze.

The moving camera, finally, represents Kubrick's own control over the *mise-en-scène*. Like Welles, he creates a double perspective with his moving camera. The difference lies in the fact that, where Welles investigates the enormity and fearsomeness of the space he creates, Kubrick is superior to it. He can permit the viewer to share a character's point of view and then remove the viewer from it, or allow the viewer to join it briefly enough to create discomfort, thereby defining point of view in many ways simultaneously. Where Welles implicates the viewer in his spatial labyrinths, Kubrick permits greater room to observe and judge his characters' situation and the viewer's own perception of the situation as well.

Colonel Dax's march through the trenches in *Paths of Glory* is an excellent example. As a tracking shot, a technical accomplishment, it is powerful and assured; as a point-of-view shot, communicating Dax's control of his situation and what that control must lead to, his sending his men out to be slaughtered, it becomes more complicated. The physical space and the emotional space comment upon each other. As observer, the viewer is presented with rapid, assured movement, but that movement is contained by the trenches, their filth and smoke, and their purpose, to hold the soldiers until they leave for the battlefield and death. Later in the film, as the three soldiers condemned to die march to their place of execution, the camera both observes them and assumes their point of view, tracks toward the sandbags, past onlookers (a photographer, the generals responsible for their deaths). In this case, the characters are not in control of their space; quite the contrary, they are controlled by it, surrounded and impelled by the mechanism of their destruction. When Dax is located in this sequence it is by means of a cutaway to him in the crowd, photographed through a telephoto lens, isolating him, demonstrating his impotence, and in fact answering the seeming assurance of movement and control ironically expressed in his earlier walk through the trenches. All through the film, the camera creates and then observes a world in which the characters manipulate and are manipulated, depending on who and where they are.

This act of description, here and in all of Kubrick's films, is done on a cooler and calmer level than in Welles's films. There is a level of hysteria in Welles that Kubrick avoids. Even *Dr. Strangelove*, a film about hysteria, observes that hysteria from a distance that makes it all the more odious and horrifying. Welles pulls, distorts, amplifies space; Kubrick distances himself from it, observes it, peoples it often with wretched human beings, but refuses to become involved with their wretchedness. (Only in *Full Metal Jacket* does Kubrick permit some direct communication of hysteria and pain.) The penultimate sequence of *2001*, astronaut Bowman in the Jupiter room, the human cage, offers an example in contrast. Welles would diminish the human figure and indicate his inferior position. The space would be deeply sculpted in light and shadow. But Kubrick chooses to create this environment in bright, clean lines. The gaze at the character is that of the intelligence that has "captured" him. At the same time, the viewer shares Bowman's own detachment and curiosity about himself. As he passes the stages of his age and youth (having entered the whirlpool), the camera gazes over his shoulder as he sees himself at different points in his life (this is a rare time in his later films when Kubrick uses the over-the-shoulder shot; but its use here is most unconventional, since Bowman sees not another, but himself—and, of course, there is no true reverse shot possible, for there is no one looking at him). Like Welles, Kubrick creates a visual realm and proceeds to explore it. But unlike Welles's worlds, his is mysterious not because of its intricacy and darkness but because of its clarity and apparent simplicity, a simplicity that belies the complexities it contains.

Both filmmakers are concerned with the ways humans inhabit environments, and both use cinematic structures to observe this. Welles is a humanist, one of the last in the classic sense of the word. He is deeply aware of the power, the inviolability, and the fragility of the human subject and seeks to affirm its centrality and control. The spatial fractures and distortions he inflicts on his characters, the extremes of light and dark through which he sees them, the narratives of power and impotence, gain and loss in which he sets them, all attest to the moral battles of mortal men and women, whose worlds reflect their struggle. Kubrick is an anti-humanist. He sees men (with the exception of *The Shining* his films are rarely concerned with women, except in a peripheral and usually unpleasant way) mechanistically, as determined by their world, sometimes by their passions (as is Humbert Humbert in *Lolita*), always by the rituals and structures they set up for themselves. Forgetting that they have set these structures up and have control over them, they allow the structures to control them. Like William Blake, Kubrick perceives individuals and groups assuming a helpless and inferior position with respect to an order they themselves have created. They undo their own subjectivity. But Kubrick does not go beyond anti-humanism to embrace another social or philosophical order, for he does not see the possibility of men or women regaining control over their selves and their culture. He sees rather a dwindling of humanity and its destruction, apocalyptically in *Dr. Strangelove*, through a transformation at the mercy of other-wordly intelligences in *2001*, through the destructiveness of domestic politics in *Barry Lyndon* and *The Shining*, through the utter defeat offered by war in *Full Metal Jacket*.

As complex as the design and the spatial manipulations in Kubrick's films may be, their narrative structure (with the exception of *The Killing* and *Barry Lyndon*) is usually very simple and direct. This marks another difference between Kubrick and Welles, whose narratives are as complex as the visual realm in which they are articulated. In this simplicity, Kubrick is allied with John Ford, though it is a strange and perverse alliance, and one that must be approached via Welles. One of the most tantalizing statements by a filmmaker about his work and his influences was made by Welles early in his film career: "John Ford," said Welles, "was my teacher. My own style has nothing to do with his, but *Stagecoach* was my movie textbook. I ran it over forty times."[6] Ford's *Stagecoach* (1939) in fact does contain some stylistic elements that Welles expanded upon: some deep-focus cinematography, low-angled shots that take in a room's ceilings, an occasional capturing of light and dust, textures that Welles would find attractive. Just a few months before working on *Kane*, Gregg Toland, Welles's cinematographer, photographed *The Long Voyage Home* for Ford. The chiaroscuro in this film was expanded upon in *Kane,* and, as I noted in the discussion of *film noir*, it is possible to see these two films, with Toland as mediator, profoundly influencing the photographic style of forties cinema. But besides these visual attributes, which Ford pretty much abandoned in the later forties when he did more exterior shooting and worked in color, but which Welles went on to refine and expand, there is apparently little that Ford and Welles have in common. What I think we find in Welles's statement is a wish, a desire, not to have emulated Ford, but somehow to have absorbed his narrative facility. The characters, events, and surroundings in Ford's films have a connection one to the other, an integration that allows his narratives to move with immense ease. Ford's films are about communities, families, or a group of men or women who survive by resorting to an integral strength among themselves (or the memory of such strength, should the community die or be proved false).[7] The thematics and the formal structuring of these communities in Ford's films work in a harmony of cause and effect, action and reaction that goes beyond the normal narrative felicity of Hollywood's classical period. Ford hides his methods, but not their effects. His compositions are bold and rich in information, his editing precise, and the dramatic confrontations of his characters open and direct. Yet in his best work all is contained in a simplicity of structure that is full of tension.

Welles's films are about individuals in decline. Families and other groups barely exist in his work, or if they do, as in *The Magnificent Ambersons*, they exist to show their decay. The narrative structure of Ford's films, with its tight, seamless, closed construction, the perfect congruity of its parts, embodies his concern with the relationship of people in a closed unit. Welles's complex, jarred, and fragmented narratives reflect the struggle and defeat of his characters. His admiration of Ford is the admiration of an opposite, a desire to attain what he knows he is incapable of attaining because the nature of his insight and his own cinematic necessities for realizing that insight render the attainment impossible. The moral struggles of Welles's characters are shattering; those of Ford's are healing. Welles's fictions are created by a pessimistic liberal-humanist intelligence; Ford's by a conservative intelligence that slowly loses its optimism over the course of time.

If the relation of Welles and Ford is dialectical, the relationship of Kubrick and Ford is diabolical. Kubrick, on his own terms, attempts to pursue the narrative linearity that Ford developed to perfection. But his narratives achieve an intellectual richness Ford could not and would not aspire to. What occurs, then, in Kubrick's work is an articulation of cinematic space directly influenced by Welles, a narrative structure that is close to Ford's, and a narrative content that responds to Ford's by denying its insights and the myths it draws upon and re-creates. Kubrick, like Ford, is concerned with individuals in groups; but his groups are almost always antagonistic or exclusionary. The Kubrick community is cold, as cold as Kubrick's own observation of it. There is rarely any feeling expressed, other than antagonism, and certainly no integration (the camaraderie tentatively suggested in parts of *Full Metal Jacket* is an anomaly and suggests either that Kubrick is momentarily assenting to the conventions of the war film or—more likely—is provoking the painful irony of men joining in groups only to kill or be killed).

An interesting example in comparison occurs between Ford's *Fort Apache* (1948) and Kubrick's *Paths of Glory*. Ford's film concerns the antagonism between an Indian-beleaguered cavalry outpost and a martinet commander, Lt. Col. Owen Thursday (Henry Fonda). Thursday is presented as an intrusion into the composed and ordered community of the men at the fort. He hates his assignment and acts out his hatred by demanding a strictness of military procedure that the men have never found necessary. Their order is one of fellowship and gentleness, and they integrate their family with their military lives. As a result, Thursday is an irritant and in his attempt to intrude upon them he is isolated from them.*

The result of the conflict is the massacre of Thursday and his men by the Apache that results from Thursday's inability to recognize the Indians as men to whom understanding and courtesy must be given. The violent differences in situation and attitude are presented in the visual configurations of the battle with the Indians. They are seen situated within hills and rocks, secure and inhabiting an enclosed space. Thursday and his soldiers are isolated on the plains, vulnerable and open. The spaces Ford's characters inhabit and the way they comport themselves within them are, as in Kubrick's films, a key to their emotional state. Thursday is always removed and isolated, first from his own men, then from an understanding of his opponents in battle. His separation and his inability to resolve the tensions between self-sufficiency and community, rules of order and emotional freedom lead to his fall and the fall of his men. But these tensions also lead to the terrible ambiguity of the film as a whole. In the body of the film Thursday is roundly condemned; his inability to yield leads to catastrophe. In the epilogue, however, John Wayne's Captain York insists that the catastrophe and its cause must be ignored. Thursday has been celebrated in the press as a hero, and York (and by implication Ford) upholds this myth. The army must be accepted as the advance guard of American civilization, and as a harmonious community in its own right. The society at large must

---

*On his arrival at the fort, Thursday interrupts a dance, that primary Fordian sign of civilized community. (In *Paths of Glory*, the dance is a sign of a rigid and heartless community.) He is stiff and alone compared with the ease and movement of the men and their wives. The central conflict occurs between Thursday and Capt. Kirby York (John Wayne), who emerges not quite as the mediator between Thursday and his men (that role is taken on by Thursday's daughter, who provides the domesticating softness absent from her father), but more as a leader whose sensitivity provides a practical contrast to Thursday's unyielding behavior.

believe that Thursday and his men worked together for a common good. At this point in his career, Ford had to perform an act of conservative rehabilitation on a narrative that threatened the notion of a flawless American military.

*Fort Apache* suffers a major conflict between some truths of human behavior and the need for historical myth. The myth-making possibilities of the narrative seem to stop working when forced to deal with a character it cannot contain, and so Ford adds a coda convincing the spectator everything is all right after all. *Paths of Glory* makes no pretense of examining legends. Rather, it dissolves the Fordian notion of community and replaces it with a radical isolation of individuals who, though they are part of a large organization, are forced to be alone. Their desolation is created, in part, by the form of the narrative itself. Earlier I said that Kubrick was in the Fordian narrative tradition in that he usually employs a simple linear structure. This observation must be modified by noting that, though linear, the narratives are often foreshortened and condensed. A great deal of information is presented in a short period of time. In his early work—predating the French New Wave experiments in narrative discontinuity—Kubrick leaves out transitional elements and linking passages. Ford worked to perfection the Hollywood tradition of seamless story construction. His narratives have a kind of centripetal action, drawing all their elements into a relationship with one another and finally (with the possible exception of *Fort Apache*) into a stable center.* Kubrick's narratives work centrifugally. Parts of the whole are delineated and then set outside a center never seen or defined, and therefore non-existent. Kubrick's narratives are about the lack of cohesion, center, community, about people caught up in a process that has become so rigidified that it can be neither escaped nor mitigated.

*Paths of Glory* is precisely about such a process, or rather the processes that make up military organization, an organization formed of ritual, predetermined, and so absolutely exclusionary that each human

*It can be argued that some of Ford's later films, like *The Searchers* and *The Man Who Shot Liberty Valance*, demonstrate a marked lack of stability and security within the old myths. But even these films, like *Fort Apache*, seek amelioration, an accommodation with order and certainty, which, in the case of *The Searchers*, compromises the work.

element within it is separated from the next. The matter is not, as in *Fort Apache*, of one misguided individual disrupting an established community, but of antagonistic individuals, each out for his own aggrandizement or protection. The essential struggle in the film is, as Alexander Walker and others have pointed out, between classes—the aristocratic leaders of the French army in World War I on one side and the proletarian troops, the scum, or the "children," as the general staff calls them, on the other.[8] In the middle is Colonel Dax (Kirk Douglas), loyal soldier, bad attorney, self-righteous, and trapped within the military organization. Three entwined and opposing forces—the general staff, Dax, the troops—are set within two related but opposing spaces, two areas of activity which, knitted together, provide the narrative structure and rhythm of the film. The "story" is made by the way events occur within and are defined by these spaces. The generals inhabit a chateau of enormous rooms, flooding sunlight, and walls hung with the late seventeenth- and early eighteenth-century paintings that so obsess Kubrick that they appear in one form or another in every film (except *Dr. Strangelove*) from *Paths of Glory* until *Barry Lyndon* (which in a sense becomes those paintings). Such a chateau, with all its accouterments, is itself an image of elegance and rigid formal structures. By emphasizing the spaces of the chateau, Kubrick demands the viewer understand and account for its associations and connotations, particularly within the given context. In this cold and elegant, inhumanly scaled habitation, the generals play a brutal and elegant game. "I wish I had your taste in carpets and pictures," says General Broulard (Adolf Menjou) to General Mireau (George Macready) when he first greets him, intending to cajole and bribe him to lead his troops to disaster.

The second space consists of the habitations of the troops: the dark and squalid trenches, the battlefield that looks like the surface of the moon turned into a garbage heap, the prison that holds the three men assigned to die for cowardice. The narrative moves between these spaces, climaxing at the firing squad (an extension of the chateau) and the cabaret (an extension of the trenches). There is no indication that anywhere else in the world exists. Unlike *Fort Apache*, where the fort, situated in the midst of the wilderness, is seen as its embattled but self-sufficient focus, there is no indication of any physical connection

between the front and the chateau, or between both places and anywhere else. Kubrick is creating a closed world, or rather closed worlds,
since they are isolated from each other. Mireau visits the trenches, and
Dax the chateau, but each is out of place in the other's realm. When
Mireau and Broulard first meet in the chateau, they start as antagonists
but end as happy and comfortable conspirators, circling about the great
hall, the camera moving with them, building rhythms of deceit and
death. But Mireau in the trenches is completely out of place. When he
inspects and brutalizes the troops, the camera flees in front of him, making dynamic the viewer's revulsion at his mechanical "Hello there, soldier, ready to kill more Germans?" Dax's walk through the trenches, as
pointed out earlier, is comfortable and assured; the camera not only
precedes him, but shares his point of view. In the chateau, Dax is either
isolated or enclosed in the discomfort of its spaces.

But just here a question is raised. Dax is comfortable with his men
and uncomfortable with, indeed antagonistic to, the general staff. Does
that mean that his is the mediating and ameliorating voice of the film,
speaking of humanity in the midst of the terrifying brutality that occurs
around him, speaking reason as does the John Wayne character in *Fort
Apache*? He clearly does not accommodate himself to the space of the
generals, but his comfort with his men proves to be an illusion. He
sends them to battle, knowing most will be killed; and though he joins
them, he remains separate. In the complex tracking shot that accompanies the attack, the camera continually zooms in on Dax, picking him
out, showing him with the men, but separate from them. For Dax is
finally not the man of the trenches one would perhaps like him to be,
upholder of the rights of the scorned and misused. He is a powerless
creature of the high command. When the men retreat, and immediately
after a closeup of a raving Mireau "If those little sweethearts won't
face German bullets, they'll face French ones"—the film cuts back to
the chateau. Two soldiers are seen moving a large painting, expending
energy shifting signs of a worn-out elegance. Dax, Mireau, and Broulard
meet on the fate of the troops. Mireau is framed against a large, bright
window, Dax and Broulard, the mean and cunning general who first
ordered the attack, are framed together, beneath paintings—an odd
pairing, but indicative of Dax's manipulated, used status. The three bar-

gain over the men's lives, Broulard ordering that three be chosen, tried, and executed. Dax will defend the men in the trial, whose outcome is preordained.

In this sequence, as in others, Dax appears to reflect or incorporate the viewer's anger at the generals and sympathy for the troops. He seems to be the voice of reason against their cunning brutality. But he is not, and could not be if he wanted to. Kubrick is playing as cruel a game with viewer expectation as the generals' play with their troops in the fiction. Throughout the film every expectation holds that Dax will get the men off; conventional narrative patterns have coded this situation with such certainty. The good and helpless, in film fiction, are not permitted to die (particularly in 1957, before a certain cynicism had taken over such dependable conventions). Here the codes do not work. When Dax gives his impotent defense summary at the courts martial, stating, fatuously, that he can't believe compassion, "the noblest impulse in man," is dead, the camera tracks him from a low angle, behind the guards, who are situated behind the prisoners. Dax is trapped between the men and the judges, walking back and forth, seen through the legs of the guards. He is completely enclosed. The track is lateral, in contrast to the swift forward motion of his earlier walk through the trenches. The composition is sufficient to show that he is as imprisoned as the men he uselessly defends.[9] In a curious way, Dax has become Ford's Lieutenant Colonel Thursday—upholding rigid procedure, but here in the face of an even more rigid procedure. Unlike Thursday, Dax has no humane alternatives. He is trapped and doomed.

Kubrick refuses to see a way out and cannot find any justification for the presence of "noble impulses." After the firing squad, Dax is reduced to name-calling. In his last confrontation with Broulard in the chateau, he calls him "a degenerate, sadistic old man." And as Broulard comes to understand that in defending the men Dax was not acting out of a desire for a promotion he calls him an idealist and says, "I pity you as I would the village idiot." He proclaims his own proper behavior in the whole affair and asks where he went wrong (he is pleased with himself for having ordered a court of inquiry to investigate Mireau for ordering fire on his own men). Dax answers, "Because you don't know the answer to that question, I pity you." Mutual sarcasm and hatred, and a thorough impasse. Kubrick should have ended the film there, with two duty- and ritual-bound antagonists in impotent confrontation. Instead, like Ford in *Fort Apache*, he chooses to add a coda that might have a softening effect. Dax passes an inn where some of his troops are relaxing. A German girl sings to them. First they boo her, then sing along, weeping. Outside, Dax allows them "a few minutes more" to indulge themselves.

This bit of sentimentality runs against the grain of the film. What had been a close and tight structure of brutality, false hope, and greater brutality now seems to be diminished by a conventional means to move an audience, communal tears. In fact what Kubrick does here is the opposite of what Ford did. The coda to *Fort Apache* is very much military stiff upper lip: the army has its problems, but they all work out for the greater good. Kubrick creates an easier structure of meaning: the man who cries has feelings and is therefore somehow aware of his lot. Tears permit the audience to release pity and understanding, easing somewhat the moral frustrations suffered during the course of the film. The coda distances the viewer from what has happened, but in the wrong direction. It seems to deny the narrative by presenting conventional material much easier to accept than what preceded. Possibly, the last sequence needs to be read ironically, concluding that these wretched souls only find relief weeping over another wretched soul on the stage, and that even this relief is short-lived, since they must return to the prison of the trenches. But even were this the intent it is done too quickly and too easily. Nothing before has given much of a sense of the troops' individuality. The three men chosen for execution are little more than types. Now Kubrick demands recognition that the men have the emotions the generals do not.

If this sequence works, it does so by restating the entrapped condition of everyone concerned. The generals are trapped by their adherence to a military ritual of patriotism, place-gaining, and self-aggrandizement; the men are trapped by their inferior status and total passivity. (The only officer who actively attempts to save his men's lives does so passively. Lieutenant Roget, a drunken coward who caused a man's death on a night mission, refuses, out of fear, to send his troops out of the trenches to assault the Ant Hill.) Indeed Dax, caught between his duty to the military and allegiance to his men, is himself passive. He makes no move to take his case outside the military cage. No world exists

*[handwritten margin notes: CODA GERMAN SINGING / FOR KOLKER DOESN'T WORK]*

beyond the trenches and the chateau; all behavior is dictated by the unyielding rules and rituals that belong to them. There is no indication that mutiny or an appeal to other powers is possible. Determination of behavior is complete.

When Kubrick returns again to the subject of war in the trenches, the idea of behavioral determination is unchanged, though somewhat mitigated. Like *Paths of Glory*, *Full Metal Jacket* takes place in well-defined and related spaces, presented sequentially rather than intercut: the barracks and fields of Parris Island training camp; the streets, Marine camp, and the office of *Stars and Stripes* in Da Nang; the burning ruins of Hue. Unlike *Paths of Glory*, these spaces do not form a complex of class and ideological contradictions and tensions. Little is seen or heard of the military high command (one fatuous colonel appears and speaks some hysterical nonsense, claiming, for example, that "inside every gook there is an American trying to get out"), and there is no character equal to Col. Dax to present even the illusion of moral order.

More strongly than in *Paths of Glory*, the determining order is the necessity to kill, passed on to the Marines from their first moment in training camp by means of the monotone, hysterical, and vulgar drone of the Drill Instructor (often presented in steady, uninflected tracking shots which precede him through the barracks or on training marches; tracking shots signifying a deadening repetition, a used-up energy of military ritual). "Here you are all equally worthless," he tells his men. The very first shots of the film show the recruits' hair being shaved off, their individuating characteristics removed (indeed the film's two major figures, Joker and Cowboy, look almost identical to one another). And as training continues, this dehumanized raw material is moulded into "the phoney tough and the crazy brave," men whose function is to kill or die for the "beloved corps."

Through it all, Kubrick attempts to chart an uneven dynamic of character action and viewer response. The early scenes of the boot camp sequence seem to offer a misguided patriotism, that element often found in military films in which the tough but fair sergeant bullies his troops into shape for their own good. But this direction is changed drastically when the most ill-treated of the recruits, Pyle, goes mad and shoots both the Drill Instructor and himself. Early camaraderie seems to form between the men, particularly as Joker attempts to help Pyle through his difficulties. This initial sense of community is shockingly broken when, after the sergeant punishes the men for Pyle's mistakes, they beat Pyle terribly in the night, Joker delivering the most devastating blows. Camaraderie threatens to break out again in the latter sequences of the film, during the sniper attack on the troops in the burning city. But viewer response is again redirected. After three men die, Joker discovers the sniper and attempts to kill her (the irony of a woman inflicting such damage on men trained in an atmosphere of obscene sexism is suggested without commentary). His rifle jams, and before he can use his pistol, another soldier shoots her. She lies wounded, begging to be killed. Joker stares, his face held in long close-up, and he finally pulls the trigger. His comrades congratulate him. One calls him "hard core." He is pleased with himself. He marches off with his troops and in voice-over ruminates on how pleased he is to be alive, even in a world full of shit. Into the night, against the burning buildings, the troops march, singing the Mickey Mouse theme song.

*IRONY END of JACKET*

The troops sing at the end of *Paths of Glory*, and it is only slightly less banal than these hard-core killers chanting "M-I-C-K-E-Y M-O-U-S-E." The soldiers in the earlier film were forced into combat by their officers. Here they seem to go willingly and with a desire to prove themselves. There is no threat of a firing squad, but rather the willing acceptance of duty and the need to prove one's worth. Joker's act is not so much a mercy killing of the young Vietnamese, but an act of mercy for himself, something that realizes and actuates his training, that validates his military life. If he can't kill a real, live enemy, he can kill a dying one. He is caught—as he himself says, referring to the "Born to Kill" motto on his helmet and the peace button on his jacket—between two conflicting forces.

And so, in effect, is Kubrick. I said that the dynamic of character action and viewer response in *Full Metal Jacket* is uneven and, I might add, erratic. As in the cabaret sequence of *Paths of Glory*, there is here the threat of sentimentality, of the rather vicious illusion that, whatever monstrous things war does, it at least brings men together into a community. And although Kubrick never indulges this sentimentality as strongly as Oliver Stone does in *Platoon* (1986), it still lurks in the aura of this film. No other Vietnam film, with the possible exception of *Apocalypse Now* (but without that film's hallucinatory and mythic preten-

*OLIVER STONE'S PLATOON*

sions), so expresses the hopelessness of that war, its sense of already and always being lost by the United States ("I'll be Custer," a soldier says; "who'll be the Indians?" he's asked; "We'll let the gooks be the Indians"). But *Full Metal Jacket* cannot seem to avoid the generic imperatives of the war film and the ideological determinism that still drives any recall of Vietnam. Somehow, all Vietnam war films suggest that American innocence and fellowship *should* have prevailed; somehow the wrong side won, but it was not quite anybody's fault—except perhaps a sneaky and vicious enemy. The anger that informs *Paths of Glory* is gone, but not replaced with any firm perspective. War is depicted still as a violent and painful event, but there is no clear sense of who is responsible for it or where it is likely to lead.

In the case of both *Paths and Glory* and *Full Metal Jacket*, one almost wishes another film had been made, one in which either Dax or the troops took some active role in saving themselves, some opportunity to indicate there might be an alternative to being manipulated or brutalized, or some awareness on the part of the troops in the last film of who they are and what they might be doing. But Kubrick is not a revolutionary filmmaker. Quite the contrary. The force of his films grows out of their sense of frustrating inevitability, of men almost willfully submitting themselves to an ineluctable order of events. When, in the film following *Paths of Glory*, Kubrick tried to create a revolutionary figure—transforming, through the person of Kirk Douglas, the impotent Dax into the heroic Spartacus—the result was considerable failure. And I am not sure that the failure of *Spartacus* is the result only of a bad script and of Kubrick's inability to exercise complete control over the production (he was called into the production by Douglas to replace its first director). Part of the film's problem may result from the fact that a human being attempting to escape or to correct an intolerable situation does not fire Kubrick's imagination as does an individual trapped in an intolerable situation. If Arthur Penn celebrates the attempt to overcome oppression, no matter how much he believes such attempts are doomed, then Kubrick mourns the doom that follows upon *no* attempt to overcome. Those wonderful tracking shots in his films lead, finally, to the grave. There is for him no revolutionary spirit nor even a simple Fordian spirit of communal energy or sacrifice for the greater vitality of the community. His characters merely die or dwindle, isolated and trapped.

Kubrick's ideas seem responsive to the decade in which he began his creative work, and *Paths of Glory* is indeed a film of the fifties, as *Full Metal Jacket* is of the eighties: periods in our history when passivity was looked upon as a virtue and opposition condemned and barely heard. In that light, they are deeply conflicted films. To have taken as strong a stand against military order as *Paths of Glory* does was itself remarkable for 1957—so remarkable that the film was banned in France for years. To have created such an unrelenting narrative (with no sexual or romantic interest), structured in such stark and demanding images, was, for the time, more remarkable still. But with these images to have created a narrative that stops with a revelation of lives trapped and not go on to suggest how they might be freed is itself an intellectual gambit typical of the decade. This was the period of "the end of ideology," a political dead center which declared useless, if not treasonous, any political-cultural structure other than the status quo. As a critical tool, this ideology against ideology prescribed analysis without judgment, understanding without a declared point of view. *Paths of Glory* suffers from the end of ideology paralysis because it seems to attack an ideological stance—assumptions of hierarchical rule and the fitness of a given order—and then backs off. Revealing the ugliness of a situation and its propensity to destroy men, demonstrating how a moral stance against the immorality of such a rigid structure turns to impotent self-righteousness, it provokes great anger at a ruthlessness that appears unassailable. But finally the anger is, like Dax's, useless. Offering no possibility of altering the situation portrayed, it leaves the viewer only to wallow in the self-pity of the men in the café, weeping at cruelty and at our seemingly natural and helpless passivity in its face.

Full Metal Jacket leaves an enormous, uninformed distance between the viewer and the men singing the Mickey Mouse song at the end. Into that space are thrown questions of their stupidity, bravery, foolishness, banality, their child-like nature (the troops are referred to as "children" in *Paths of Glory*), their function as tools. The questions float with no promise of being attached to adequate answers or even interesting speculation. True to the ideological formation of the eighties, the film

Military spaces: Mireau (George Macready) and Dax (Kirk Douglas) in the chateau of *Paths of Glory; (opposite)* Thursday (Henry Fonda) and York (John Wayne) in *Fort Apache.*

GOOD political ANALysis
ON PAths of GLORy,
full metAl JAcket

deflects speculation or political opinion into an evocation of the recent past—complete with the inevitable sixties rock-music sound track. An illusion of what may have been threatens to substitute for an analytic reading of history, and the realities of history are continually voided in the spaces of despair.[10]

The response to both films is frustration, something that John Ford, for one, would never permit. Perhaps because of his conservatism, his allegiance to the rightness of military and domestic order, and because of the clarity with which he sees the relationship of individual and group, Ford insists upon a harmonious reaffirmation of a healing order. The rule-bound, mean-minded Lieutenant Colonel Thursday of *Fort Apache* is an anomaly who, no matter what damage he causes, must be understood and absorbed, recuperated into a larger historical myth. Passivity is never a problem for a Fordian character. When such a character can no longer act, he withdraws into heroic isolation from the

*[handwritten marginalia: Both Films Response frustration vs. FORD / Recuperated into a larger Historical myth / PASSIVITY is NEVER A PROBLEM FOR A FORDIAN CHARACTER]*

group he once aided. Ford's characters are supremely secure in their place and, with the exception of Ethan Edwards in *The Searchers*, are, or become, actively engaged in promoting concord within that place. The conflicts they suffer are the result not of ideological turmoil but of ideological certainty. Ford is secure in the belief that the American democracy he celebrates is the best of all social-political orders, and his characters act out narratives that confirm the fitness and security of that order. For Kubrick, fitness and security become traps to destroy his characters, traps from which they cannot extricate themselves. In Kubrick's fictions Fordian stability becomes a prison house and his characters are both—and often simultaneously—inmates and jailers. They do not lunge against the physical, emotional, and ideological spaces they inhabit, as do Welles's characters; they are not comfortable in them, as are Ford's. They are caught, they sometimes struggle, and they almost always lose. Not the soldiers singing in the café or in the ruins of Hue, but the frozen figure of Jack Torrance, trapped in a (literal) labyrinth, face contorted in a scream, at the end of *The Shining*, stands as a summary image of Kubrick's ineluctable pessimism.[11]

Kubrick realized the error he made in *Paths of Glory*, the error of permitting his own anger and frustration to intermingle with those of a character in the fiction, thereby inviting the audience to assume a point of identification and ultimately be frustrated. Sentimentality—except for its uncertain appearance in *Full Metal Jacket*—and melodrama quickly vanish from his work. While he never moves far beyond the entrapment, impotence, and despair figured in *Paths of Glory* (and foreshadowed in *The Killing*), his narratives and their cinematic structures become more distant and abstract, and his characters less the psychologically motivated creations we are used to seeing in American film and instead more obsessive, maniacal ideas released in human form, expressions of aberrations in the human personality. More than in *Paths of Glory* they are functions of the spaces they inhabit, spaces that themselves create closed and inflexible worlds, predetermined and unalterable, even, in *2001* and *The Shining*, supernatural.

Discounting *Spartacus*—as do, with good reason, most commentators on Kubrick's work—*Lolita* is the last film in which he attempts the study of a character who demonstrates at least some awareness of who he is and what he does, even though, as always, that character has no control over himself or others. This is also Kubrick's last film, until *Full Metal Jacket*, in which the human figure is foregrounded and observed against, rather than within, the space he inhabits. James Mason's Humbert Humbert attempts a quizzical posture before the bizarre characters and places he meets and journeys through, and the long takes with which Kubrick observes this figure decaying under the force of his sexual obsession serve to bring him uncomfortably close to pathos. Through it all, Kubrick is fascinated by the characters he is creating (particularly with Peter Sellers's Quilty), but apparently uncomfortable at the same time. *Lolita* does not achieve an identity. Part adaptation of a celebrated book, part event (both novel and film received much publicity due to their content), part character study, part attempt to make England look like America, it remains a curiosity piece. In regard to the elements of Kubrick's work I am discussing here, it demonstrates his need to withdraw even further from the world he creates, to integrate his characters more fully with the total design of the film, to demonstrate how a world is formed by a personality and then re-forms and destroys the personality who made it. This is a process and a method that become fully realized in what may be Kubrick's best work: *Dr. Strangelove: Or, How I Learned To Stop Worrying and Love the Bomb.*

*Dr. Strangelove* is an unusual film that serves the function of prophecy. In the early sixties, Kubrick perceived in the dominant political ideology certain modes of speech, figures of thought, and images of America's imagined place in the world that allowed him to set up a narrative of events so logical and unavoidable that the only possible result (in the fiction made up by the narrative) was the end of the world. The narrative, in its turn, has created a structure of explanation for political behavior that becomes more valid and more chilling the longer that behavior continues. The term "Strangelovian" has entered the vocabulary, and our history in the years since *Dr. Strangelove* has tended to imitate the film as much as the film, at the time of its making, imitated history.

A number of elements work toward making the film a complex text of ideas and reflections and predictions. Not the least of these is the extreme simplicity of its narrative structure. There are (not counting a brief sequence in Buck Turgidson's bedroom) only three areas of action: the war room, an enormous black space ringed by fluorescent light, a dark version of the chateau in *Paths of Glory*, computerized maps replacing the paintings; the cockpit, control room, and bomb bay of a B-52; and the offices and exterior of Burpelson Air Force Base. There is no interrelationship between these locations, no communication.[12] Each operates on its own. Even within these areas, no one speaks to another, only to himself. No one listens, no one responds. Words are interchanged, but the words are, in the war room, only clichés; at the base, lunatic ravings; and in the plane, military jargon. These three areas of activity are intercut to form the narrative. The activities that occur in each area are caused by what goes on in the others and are independent of the others at the same time. A mad general declares an alert and seals off his base; SAC bombers, which are in the air all the time, proceed to their target, cutting themselves off from communication; the war room coordinates plans to cut off the attack by aiding Russian defense, by means of a hysterical American president talking on the telephone to a hysterical Russian premier. Everyone talks, or tries to talk, on the phone. The first line of dialogue in the film is delivered by General Ripper (Sterling Hayden) on the phone to his chief aide, Mandrake (Peter Sellers), asking, significantly, "Do you recognize my voice?" Everyone does indeed recognize everyone else's voice. No one understands a word that is being said.

*Dr. Strangelove* is that rarity among American film in which verbal language plays a major role. In fact it is a film about language that creates its own destruction, its own death, and the death of the world. In a film that delineates a love of destruction and death, a *Merkwürdigliebe* (Strangelove's German name), everything done and everything said manifests this love and hastens its consummation. What Kubrick, Terry Southern, and Peter George do in their script and what Kubrick does in his direction is create a series of linguistic and visual reductions and give the characters utterances which defeat meaning. Like the auto-destruct mechanism on the SAC bomber's radio, the characters' words undo and destroy themselves. The bomber, for example, is introduced by a very serious voice-over narration explaining the SAC system. When the film cuts to the interior of the plane, Major Kong

(Slim Pickens) is reading *Playboy* and the communications officer playing with a deck of cards, images which immediately undercut the seriousness of the introduction. When the attack plan is confirmed, drums and trumpets begin playing "When Johnny Comes Marching Home," music that will accompany all the sequences in the bomber, creating a music-image complex that ultimately contradicts itself. No one comes marching home from this battle.

Major Kong prepares for "nuclear combat, toe to toe with the Russkies." He pulls out a cowboy hat, which he wears through the rest of the flight. He tells his men, "I reckon you wouldn't even be human beings if you didn't have some pretty strong personal feelings about nuclear combat. . . . If this thing turns out to be half as important as I figure it just might be, I'd say that you're all in line for some important promotions and personal citations when this thing's over with. And that goes for every last one of you, regardless of your race, color, and your creed. . . ." Both image and words clash with the seriousness of purpose expected from the situation: a bomber about to start Armageddon. The words in particular reduce meaning to a level of banality and cliché. Roland Barthes, speaking of linguistic structure in the works of Sade, writes that "he juxtaposes heterogeneous fragments belonging to spheres of language that are ordinarily kept separate by socio-moral taboo."[13] Kubrick's characters in *Dr. Strangelove* do precisely the same thing. The socio-moral taboos they break are those which keep expressions of serious connotation apart from those that are banal. A drawling cowboy ought not be associated with the commander of an aircraft carrying a nuclear bomb. When this cowboy begins speaking, one does not wish to hear grammar-school commonplaces and locker-room psychologisms. When this is precisely what is heard, it is very funny because of the surprise, and very frightening, because of the gap between the utterance and the context, which demands other language. The serious is made light of and the ridiculous is made serious. The language circles upon itself, it has no subject or object, no detachable meaning. The meaning is the utterance itself and its own perfectly logical irrelevance and banality. Of course "human beings" have "strong personal feelings" about "nuclear combat" (does the topic arouse impersonal feelings in something other than "human beings"?). These men, however,

Linguistic subversion: Major Kong (Slim Pickens) on the bomb (a production still from *Dr. Strangelove*).

seem to have no feelings about anything. They use language to express the obvious, the reductive, and the redundant, utterances that speak about feelings in ways that indicate their absence.*

This linguistic subversion continues throughout *Strangelove*, destroying meaning whenever it threatens to emerge. When the Russians discover the Americans are entering their air space, says General Buck Turgidson, clutching his book, *World Targets in Megadeaths*, "they are gonna go absolutely ape. . . ." Turgidson (George C. Scott) is particularly apt at laundering language of meaning, substituting jargon for information (hopes to recall the SAC bombers are "reduced to a very low order of probability") and speaking about the end of the world in the terms of a businessman ("I'm not saying we wouldn't get our hair mussed. But I do say no more than ten to twenty million killed. Tops. Depending on the breaks"). And the president himself, Merkin Muffley (Peter Sellers), a fussy little liberal with a vulgar name, well-meaning and unable to comprehend the mechanisms set in operation, delivers himself of a line that encapsulates the refusal of these men to understand their actions or the distance between these actions and the words they use to describe them. To Turgidson and the Russian ambassador, wrestling over a spy camera, he says, "Gentlemen, you can't fight here, this is the war room."

At the center of this is Jack D. Ripper, the mad general ("he went a little funny in the head—you know, a little funny," says the President to Premier Kissoff on the hotline) who put all the mechanisms of doom into operation. In his confusion of language, the psychotic ease with which he amputates and reconstructs meanings, he permits the entire structure of death to be erected, or, more appropriately, permits the structure, already erected, to work itself out to completion. He is a fundamentalist anti-communist, filled with all the clichés that go with that aspect of the culture's dominant ideology. He is also rather confused sexually, believing that post-coital relaxation and depression are really a loss of vitality (he is not, as many critics say, impotent; his radical

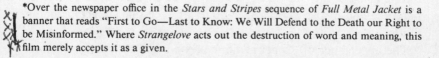

*Over the newspaper office in the *Stars and Stripes* sequence of *Full Metal Jacket* is a banner that reads "First to Go—Last to Know: We Will Defend to the Death our Right to be Misinformed." Where *Strangelove* acts out the destruction of word and meaning, this film merely accepts it as a given.

misunderstanding of normal psycho-sexual reactions is much more horrifying than mere sexual dysfunction and is part of the transfer and
breakdown of meaning that informs the film).

I said Ripper is at the center of this, but that is an inaccurate metaphor for the film. *Dr. Strangelove* is about the lack of center; it is about
a multitude of tangents glancing off non-concentric circles. That Ripper
sets the mechanisms in operation is a convenience of plot and evi-
dences, perhaps, some need on Kubrick's part to present a "human factor" in the proceedings. The inhumanity of the cold war and its destructive potentials are somehow mitigated if one can point to an individual
who is mad and triggers those potentials into action. Happily, in the
following films, Kubrick tries with some success to eliminate this essentially humanist desire to account for the world through the melodrama
of the individual. However, Ripper is the most radical example in *Dr.
Strangelove* of the dislocation of word and meaning, form and substance. His great speech is a concentrated collapse from the somewhat
shared clichés of reactionary discourse into the crazed, subjective discourse of someone who is creating his own meanings. "Mandrake," he
asks his barely comprehending aide, "do you recall what Clemenceau
once said about war?"

> He said war was too important to be left to the generals. . . . But
> today war is too important to be left to the politicians. They have
> neither the time, the training, nor the inclination for strategic
> thought. I can no longer sit back and allow communist
> infiltration, communist indoctrination, communist subversion
> and the International Communist Conspiracy to sap and impurify
> all of our precious bodily fluids.

There is a perfectly logical movement to these words, just as there is
perfectly logical movement to the mechanism of defense and retaliation
that makes up the war machine. But the logic of both is internal only.
The forms are correct, but what the forms signify is illogical and
destructive. Ripper's speech ends in bathos, in perfect nonsense. The
mechanisms of the war machine end with a different kind of anti-cli-
max: the end of the world, the sapping of everyone's precious bodily
fluids.

The appearance of Ripper as he makes his speech is a fine example
of the way Kubrick creates an image that objectively comments on

character and situation. The general is composed in closeup, from a low angle, his face brightly lit from below, against a black background. He is smoking a long cigar. This is the image of a man isolated in his own madness, yet protruding from his entrapment, threatening the viewer's space (which is represented, in this sequence, by Mandrake, who attempts a façade of calm and sanity in the face of Ripper's ravings). This appearance of Ripper is similar to a shot of Norman Bates in Hitchcock's *Psycho*. At one point Norman leans over the camera, his face emerging from the dark in an unexpected, and unsettling, angle. These two closeups of madness are similar in effect, but lead in different directions. The madness of Norman Bates is significant of a momentary, unknown, unpredictable terror, always lurking, seldom perceived. The madness of Ripper is the madness of the body politic, which should be easily perceived and perfectly predictable, for it results when individuals create a mock rationality based on language and gesture that appears logical and is in fact dead and deadly. Only the universality of his discourse makes it invisible. Norman's madness is local, the momentary eruption of violence in an unexpecting world. Ripper's madness is global. He is the disseminater of violence, the patriarch of a political and ideological structure whose purpose is to prepare the world for death.

*Dr. Strangelove* is a discourse of death. Its language and images, the movement of its narrative bespeak the confusion of life and death and the desire to see the one in terms of the other. The persistent sexual metaphor of the film emphasizes the reversal. From the copulating bomber that opens the film, to Ripper's confusion of sexual release with a subversive draining away of vitality, to the planned storage of sexually active men and women in mine shafts to await dissipation of the doomsday shroud, to Major Kong's riding his great, phallic H-bomb into the apocalyptic orgasm and the death of the earth, sexuality in the film is turned to necrophilia, which in turn is part of a greater mechanism of destruction over which the individuals in the film are power-less.[14] The rage to create a controlling order undoes potency; the attempt to erect a structure of power results in the collapse of all structure. The patriarchy erects a world whose function is auto-castration.

If Jack D. Ripper is the mad father of this structure, Dr. Strangelove is the holy ghost, the spirit and mover of destruction. He is also the fascist machine, aroused by the word "slaughter," drawing life from death, becoming fully activated just as the apocalypse occurs. When the men in the war room think that the bombers have been recalled, Turgidson says a prayer: "Lord! We have heard the wings of the Angel of Death fluttering over our heads from the Valley of Fear. You have seen fit to deliver us from the forces of evil." On the words "Valley of Fear," Kubrick cuts to Strangelove sitting in his wheelchair, apart from the others, shrouded and crouching in darkness. The words of the prayer, like all the other words in the film, are undone, the image cancels their denotation, for everyone has been delivered into the Valley of Fear; and the Angel of Death becomes the figure around which all the others will cluster.

Through the creation of Dr. Strangelove, Kubrick comes to an important insight. At the peak of the last cold war, at a time when the great, grim myth of communist subversion was (as it still is) the operative force in America's ideology, Kubrick suggests that fascism is operating as the ghost in the machine. The glorification and celebration of power and death that feed politics and form the urge for domination define the fascist spirit. In the film it is resurrected in the body of Strangelove just at the point when death dominates the world. This is a chilling idea and perhaps difficult to comprehend for those who tend to look at fascism as a momentary historical aberration that died with Hitler. Kubrick is suggesting that death was its disguise and that strength was drawn from its ability to hide in the guise of anti-communism and the cold war. This was a brave insight for the time. Its validity remains undiminished.

I have been talking very seriously about a film that is, of course, very funny. Part of the complexity of *Dr. Strangelove* is that it presents its prophecy as comedy, provoking laughter and fear, observing with bemused condescension a situation that reveals to an audience its own powerlessness and potential destruction. Kubrick manages this situation by applying, in this work of contemporary cinema, the specifically literary form of eighteenth-century satire. To understand how comfortable he is with this form, it is helpful to compare *Dr. Strangelove* with another film released in the same year and by the same studio (Columbia), Sidney Lumet's *Fail-Safe*. The subject of both films is essentially

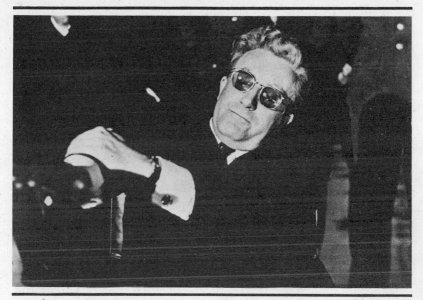

The fascist machine (Peter Sellers as Dr. Strangelove).

the same, except that the bombers in *Fail-Safe* are sent to their targets by a mechanical error and, rather than ending the world, an even score is achieved. To make up for U.S. planes bombing Moscow, the president (played by the American movie icon of presidents, Henry Fonda) sends a plane to bomb New York. The difference in the telling, however, is important. Lumet's film is straightforward melodrama. All the characters are given psychological motivation for their actions, and the narrative is developed out of basic cinematic conventions of human conflict. The film demonstrates Lumet's skill in developing overwrought situations through a tightly controlled *mise-en-scène* and cutting that emphasizes conflict and tension.*

Lumet, in *Fail-Safe*, sees the cold war as an arena in which various temperaments and the occasional neurosis are played out and fudges

*A partial list of Lumet's works from the late fifties through the eighties—*Twelve Angry Men, The Pawnbroker, The Group, Bye Bye, Braverman, The Seagull, Serpico, Murder on the Orient Express, Dog Day Afternoon, Network, Equus, The Verdict, Garbo Talks, Power, The Morning After*—indicates a craftsman at work on a variety of genres, linked by a strong sense of the arrangement of conflicts among people in extreme situations.

the political issue by blaming destruction on mechanical failure. Kubrick presents the cold war as a massive breakdown of temperament and control, growing out of an intemperate desire for control, a surrender of inquiry and insight to monolithic modes of thinking and acting that, once put into motion, cannot be stopped. Mechanical failure or even "human error" are not the causes of Kubrick's apocalypse, but human activity imitating and surrendering itself to the mechanical. These different approaches to the same situation are therefore rendered in different forms. Where Lumet finds melodrama the best structuring mode for conflict, Kubrick finds satire the best mode for structuring a narrative of the mechanical man and the death of language.[15] Satire gives him the distance needed to observe the process by removing the illusory wholeness of character created by psychological realism and its need for character "motivation." He is left free to draw abstractions and manipulate his figures into appropriate patterns of action and response.

"Two things . . . are essential to satire," writes Northrop Frye: "one is wit or humor founded on fantasy or a sense of the grotesque or absurd, the other is an object of attack. . . . For effective attack we must reach some kind of impersonal level, and that commits the attacker, if only by implication, to a moral standard."[16] The world as portrayed in *Dr. Strangelove* does not exist beyond the film. It is, rather, a grotesque amalgam of various elements, various ways of thinking and seeing, a discourse created from the variety of babbling voices that make up our political structure. The characters of Jack D. Ripper and Buck Turgidson are constructs, types of the right-wing general, or the nightmare vision of what the archetypal right-wing general would look and sound like. Strangelove is more than a parody of Edward Teller and Werner von Braun (with a dash of Henry Kissinger); he is a terrifying fantasy of resurrected fascism. And he is funny. All the characters in the film are funny, because they are exaggerated. But they are only funny to the spectator. No one in the film ever laughs.* Not only do the exaggeration of character and their absurd slaughter of language make them funny; the maniacal seriousness of their activities and their inability to perceive how wretchedly hilarious they are make them funnier still.

---

*After a number of viewings, if you look closely, you will see Peter Bull, who plays the Russian ambassador, smile at Peter Sellers's Strangelovian antics; but this is one actor uncontrollably reacting to another's talent and is not meant to be noticed.

This demands a considerable separation, on the viewer's part, from what is occurring within the world of the fiction. The satirical mode requires observation and judgment rather than identification; as I said, the conventions of psychological realism and character motivation are removed. One need not understand, in the conventional sense, why the characters are behaving the way they do. Rather, as Frye says, the observer must reach an impersonal level, where he or she is guided by a moral "voice" who develops the discourse that addresses and instructs the spectator. In classical satire, this voice is often heard directly, setting out ideas of normative behavior against which the aberrations of the characters can be judged. In *Dr. Strangelove* that voice is not so much heard as it is insinuated through the viewer's reaction to the discourse (the closest thing to this voice in the film is Mandrake, who attempts to remain calm and rational amidst the lunacy). The discourse is funny because the viewer understands, with Kubrick, that it is monstrous; it is appalling because, with Kubrick, the viewer has assumed a moral stand against it and has become part of another, more rational discourse. Rational rarely means optimistic. Should the viewer be terrified by Strangelove's emergence from his wheelchair as a fully organized body of death, then, with Kubrick, she or he assumes what is often the final perspective of the satirist, a depressive pessimism, a certainty that what is seen and revealed as stupidity and arrogance is unstoppable. Indeed, *Dr. Strangelove* owes so much of its vision and power to earlier literary modes that it can be seen through them and as part of them. It shares the anger and despair, as well as the energy, of Jonathan Swift and Alexander Pope (the link is recognized: the target of the SAC bomber is Laputa, one of the kingdoms visited by Gulliver in his travels, a world of scientists so inward-looking that they must employ people to hit them on the head to bring them to consciousness of the external world). And the last lines of Alexander Pope's *Dunciad*, which sees the powers of dullness and rigidity and the death of the mind conquer the world, are, despite their old and elegent language, quite applicable to the film:

> Lo! thy dread Empire, Chaos! is restor'd;
> Light dies before thy uncreating word:
> Thy hand, great Anarch! lets the curtain fall;
> And Universal Darkness buries All.

Film (along with the other arts) has largely forgotten satire (or replaced it with parody or lampoon). Moral righteousness is unacceptable, and the holding of a complex moral or political opinion is considered too often a personal fault and a liability in a creator. That Kubrick was able to rediscover the validity of satire and, more than that, make it work in a way that contemporary writers and filmmakers have not is important. Satire is an intensely social-political form which requires a close engagement with the world rare in American filmmaking, and its presence in Kubrick's work is indicative of a commitment not ordinarily found.

*Dr. Strangelove* is the only film Kubrick has made that so strictly follows the satiric model. The films that follow are more speculative and open. They do not offer the audience a determined response. The images with which they build their narratives achieve a great complexity and demand the viewer confront them with intelligence. But in so doing the force of anger that is present in *Paths of Glory* and *Dr. Strangelove* is diminished. The films remain cautionary in their response to the mechanization of human behavior, but Kubrick seems more willing to stand away and observe the spaces in which his mechanical men operate, less willing to condemn them, and perhaps, with *Full Metal Jacket*, ready to sentimentalize them. Never a filmmaker to suggest alternatives to the world he creates, he structures his later films with a high level of uncertainty, allowing a latitude of interpretation that often, and particularly in the case of *A Clockwork Orange*, creates confusion and dissatisfaction.

But *2001* and *A Clockwork Orange* do continue Kubrick's engagement with immediate cultural and ideological problems. They are intimately tied to the time at which they appeared; and *2001* was influential not only on other films of the same genre but on basic cultural perceptions about what the design of future technology might look like. The film also constitutes Kubrick's most radical break with film narrative tradition, at least until *Barry Lyndon*. His early work was marked by conciseness and immediacy. *Paths of Glory* and *Dr. Strangelove* have a sharply rhythmical structure of sequences occurring in rapid progression. The progression and the relationship of parts are clear. The films are closed narrative forms; at their end all action is concluded; all loose ends, all the events started within the narrative, are tied and explained.

The narratives may be rich in connotation, but their denotative realm, the immediate meanings of what is seen and heard, is precise and accessible. In *2001* denotation is at a minimum and often withheld. The narrative structure refuses to explain itself through conventional means. Actions and events are not immediately motivated, while transitions are startling and spare. There is little dialogue, and much of what exists is deliberately banal. The film has an open structure in which the viewer plays an operative role. Denied a stance of passive observation in front of a predetermined set of meanings, he or she is asked instead to be engaged with the forms and images, and the text as a whole, and from that engagement work through a continual process of meaning, connotation, and suggestion. *2001* has drawn so much commentary because it is, to use Peter Wollen's words on the theory of open narrative construction, "the factory where thought is at work, rather than the transport system which conveys the finished product."[17]

This kind of openness is alien to American film, which traditionally operates according to conventions of narrative completeness, securing a viewing subject within the fictional world (a process I have described working in *Bonnie and Clyde*).[18] Even among the filmmakers discussed in this book, each of whom is aware of the formal possibilities of his medium, we rarely find a work practicing the kind of open-endedness present in Kubrick's film. We have seen it in Penn's *Mickey One* and will see it in some of Altman's films, particularly *Three Women*. The process of open-endedness is not necessarily synonymous with ambiguity, an effect which offers uncertainty instead of plurality of meaning. Ambiguity presents no demands on the viewer. Quite the contrary, it relieves him or her of any real responsibility of decision or understanding. Ambiguity can mean nothing more than a freedom from concern about what is seen, for it is presented as indefinite, unrealizable, unknowable. Ambiguity provokes passivity, affirms the viewer's secure subjectivity by assuring her or him that meaning need not upset assumptions or endanger tranquility.

Openness demands activity and integration, a release of subjectivity into numerous positions, a denial of identification and other conventional ploys by means of which the text erases its formal existence. Rather than linking the viewer firmly to a fictive world, the open text demands recognition of the processes of formal mediation, formal *cre-*

*ation* of meaning. The conventional, closed text provides for the viewer. The open text provokes, indeed demands participation, questioning, working with the film's visual and aural structures. Often this is brought about by emotionally distancing the viewer from the narrative. Closed narrative, invisible form, emotional identification force entry into the work's predetermined structure. The less immediate and apparent the narrative links and meanings, and the more immediate and apparent the formal elements of the work, the more options are permitted. These options include ignoring the work altogether or confronting it intellectually and emotionally in an ongoing process.

Kubrick does slip into ambiguity at some crucial points in *2001*, almost entirely in *A Clockwork Orange*, and to an uncomfortable extent in *Full Metal Jacket*. *2001* does not play with temporal structure as much as modernist European and Third World film did in the sixties. Although it covers a span of time from pre-history to infinity, its structure is perfectly linear. There are great gaps in its temporal field, but no overlappings, no flashbacks or simultaneous actions (with two exceptions: as the ape "learns" how to use the bone as a weapon, there is an insert of the monolith, indicating his "thinking" about it and its influence on him; and as he begins using the bone, there is an insert of a felled animal). But the film's very linearity, its almost obsessive trajectory through time, with nothing but visual clues, and minimal clues at that, as to how parts of the trajectory are linked, helps create its open and inquisitive structure. The paucity of narrative information and explanation, the precision of its visual detail and the complexity of the images provide a wide-ranging field for inquiry. They also provide a field for no inquiry whatsoever. The narrative of *2001* is so sparse, its images so overwhelming, its theme of human submission to a higher force so insistent that it runs the risk of rendering rational engagement with it impossible.[19] Much of the initial, positive reaction to the film, particularly on the part of young people was a result of its enormous images and anti-rational stance. It became, in the late sixties and early seventies, a "drug" movie and was promoted as such ("the ultimate trip," the advertisements proclaimed).

In this light it is easy to see the film as a mindless bit of visual stimulation, and rather than grandly theorize about its narrative experimentation, decide that its structure is merely vague and therefore entirely undemanding. In short, the film may be as inducive to passivity and *←THIS PASSIVITY READING NO lonGER ACCepTed* yielding acquiescence as any forties melodrama, and as such seen as preparing the way for the science fiction films of Lucas and Spielberg, which are even more overwhelming in their imagery and anti-rational in form and substance. John Russell Taylor saw the film as indicative of a shift in sensibility, a change in audience demands and expectations that signaled a willingness, even a desire, to accept minimal story, in the conventional sense, and maximum sensation. He believes that Kubrick sensed this shift and exploited it, creating an undemanding, because unarticulated, work.[20] In other words, because *2001* met with an uncritical response from many viewers, and because this response is made possible by its non-discursive form, it is possible to dismiss the film as a work that panders to the immediate needs of an undemanding and uncritical audience. *NON-DISCURSIVE form*

The problem as to whether the film is a complex experiment or a cheap thrill can be solved Solomon fashion. *2001* is two films. One is a work for its moment, a technological fantasy, and a bombardment of visual stimuli that can accentuate a high or cause one. The other (particularly when seen in a 35mm anamorphic print rather than the more overwhelming 70mm), is a speculative, pessimistic inquiry into the forms of the immediate future.* The film continues and enlarges upon Kubrick's attempt to observe the way men occupy space (both literally and figuratively), how that space is articulated, how it both reflects and imposes upon human behavior. Seen this way, *2001* is an extension of *Dr. Strangelove*, a prophecy of things to come in light of things as they now are. But more than *Dr. Strangelove*, *2001* is concerned with the appearance of things to come and the reaction to such appearances by the inhabitants and the observers of the fiction. On an important level, *2001 IS 2 films (Solomon fashion?)*

---

*All theatrical film, since the early sixties, has been exhibited in one version of wide screen or another. The anamorphic process (of which there are many, CinemaScope and, now, Panavision being the main ones) squeezes the image onto the 35mm frame. When it is unsqueezed by the projector lens it yields a wide image of approximately 2.35:1. Standard wide screen is in a ratio of 1.85 or 1.66 to 1. (The standard ratio of film before the advent of wide screen was 1.33 to 1, or 4 x 3.) While the anamorphic image is wide, it is less overwhelming than the 70-mm format in which *2001* was originally released. Note must be taken that, when any anamorphic film is transferred to videotape, almost two-thirds of the image is lost at all times.

*2/3 RDS LOST ON VIDEOTAPE*

it is a film about design—about size, texture, and light, about the ways that objects within a cinematic space are delineated, ordered, shaped, and colored, and about how human figures interact with those objects.

Earlier I said it would not be fruitful to talk about *2001* in generic terms, in its relation to other science fiction films. But one area of that relationship is important, namely the way Kubrick's film changes the genre's conventions about how the future will look. In the fifties—and earlier, if we wish to go back to William Cameron Menzies's *Things to Come* (1936)—the conventions that inform the cinematic design of the future, or of "advanced" extra-terrestrial civilizations, are cleanliness, spareness, and order. These codes are visually manifested in straight lines and severe geometric forms. The materials of the future world are metal, glass, and plastic. Wood is never seen. Clothing is uniform, smooth, close-fitting. Human habitations are never crowded: figures occupy areas in a neat and orderly arrangement, and always in bright light. Except for the vastness of outer space, darkness does not exist (this aspect of the convention is turned into a stylistic trait by Steven Spielberg, for whom hard, almost blinding light becomes a key signifier of a frightening, but finally friendly, extra-terrestrial presence). Certainly all this is partially the result of literary influences. Utopian literature, from Plato's *Republic* on, represents its perfect world as the model of clean, rational order. But it is curious that in our century, when that model has been broken by the anti-utopian literature of Orwell and Huxley, it has persisted in film. (Though not without some important, almost dialectical responses. The above-ground city of the elite in Fritz Lang's *Metropolis* (1927) is an early design of the clean and streamlined future, but the workers' underground city is crowded, dark, and noisome. More recently, Richard Fleischer's *Soylent Green* (1973) and Ridley Scott's *Blade Runner* (1982)—a complex meditation on power and ownership set in a *film noir* future—depict earth as foul and overcrowded, an inner-city slum extended and magnified. Scott's earlier *Alien* (1979) offers another response to *2001*, *Star Wars*, and *Close Encounters* with a spacecraft that is not a white, fluorescent lit, antiseptic space, but a slightly worn interstellar warehouse.)

The persistence of the convention can be explained by the phenomenon of convention itself, which exists as a repeated form, generating a positive response in audiences who accept its representations as valid and, pleased by their response, desire more and respond to more of the same. For viewer and filmmaker alike, repetition becomes easier than invention. Obviously the repetition of this particular set of signifiers is responsive to a profound need to mark progress by images of tidiness and cleanliness. An uncluttered, linear environment is better. The question, "Better than what?" is hardly even implied; "better" is simply what is signified by this complex of meaning. The future means greater efficiency, more done with less effort. The future is progress, easy movement forward with no physical or emotional barriers. Neatness and spareness are its signs.

These equations do yield contradictions, particularly throughout fifties science fiction. In Robert Wise's *The Day the Earth Stood Still* (1951), a streamlined messenger from space and his smooth-skinned robot come to warn the earth that its nuclear bombs threaten the universe. The visitor is clearly an admirable figure, but his rationality and calm are supported with an enormous power that will destroy the earth if it does not heed him. Fred M. Wilcox's *Forbidden Planet* (1956) shows the world of the Krel as the epitome of order, efficiency, and intellectual strength. Unfortunately, the Krel forgot about their unconscious drives, which became personified and destroyed them. The clean, ordered, and rational future was to be feared as well as desired. In Don Siegel's *Invasion of the Body Snatchers* (1956), the calm rationality achieved by those who have been taken over and subverted by the aliens seems to themselves desirable; to those not yet taken over it is horrifying.

Such contradictions are troublesome because they go unquestioned. Images of order and spareness and light mean "future." The future is inevitable, often good, but sometimes threatening. Too much order and too much dependence upon rationality threaten the spontaneity of the human spirit. But whether good or threatening, the images are basically the same. The creators of science fiction film seem for the most part unable to see a future that looks otherwise. It may only be created with extreme images. Kubrick, in *2001*, looks closely at the conventions, at the assumptions about the look of the future, and considers their ramifications. The future and its automatic connotations of efficiency and progress are questioned by exaggerating the very extremity of conventional images.

In *Dr. Strangelove,* the womb-like war room, with its halo of fluorescent light, its computerized wall maps, its faceless, unsmiling inhabitants, and the SAC bomber, with its multitude of neatly arranged buttons and switches and equally unsmiling inhabitants, are images of efficiency and progress that lead to a breakdown of control and reason. The efficient structures of progress become efficient structures of death. In *2001* the principal images of the future present in so many science fiction films are extended much further than they are in *Dr. Srangelove,* so far in fact that they acquire new meaning. *2001* is as much about science fiction, or at least our reading of the conventions and meaning systems of science fiction film, as it is about the search for some extraterrestrial force. The design of the film combines the traditional components of linearity, cleanliness, and severe geometrical forms with an extraordinary sense of detail. The exteriors and interiors of Kubrick's spaceships seem to suffer from a *horror vacui.* Surfaces are intricately textured and articulated; interiors are filled with screens and buttons that do not merely flash, but flash complex verbal, mathematical, and graphic messages. At times the screen the audience watches is filled with other screens, themselves filled with information (one of the most dramatic episodes in the film, the computer HAL's murder of the hibernating astronauts, is done through words and graphs on a computer screen, flashing the stages of the astronauts' decline, ending with "Life Functions Terminated," a cold, mechanical machine message of death).* Reviewers at the time of the film's release commented upon the minimal dialogue in the film, but they failed to point out just how much language, via print, computer graphics, mathematical formulas and configurations, does in fact appear. Visually these words and graphics are themselves clean and linear, presented (as are the credits of the film) in a typeface called Helvetica, a bold, uniform, sans-serif type introduced in 1952 and ever since used on posters, in road and building signs, and for other directional devices. Helvetica has been the favorite typeface for advertising and corporate communications. It is, in short,

*There are other important machine communications: the viewer learns some of the details of the Jupiter mission from a television program viewed by Poole and Bowman in the space ship. Bowman learns the final detail, the need to discover the source of the monoliths, from a videotape that is played just as he finishes dismantling HAL.

the typeface of the modern age and has achieved the status of having a
meaning beyond what the words formed by it have to say. Helvetica,
writes Leslie Savan, means "sanitized, neutralized, and authorized."
"You see Helvetica," writes one designer, "and you perceive order."
Form becomes an ideological event.[21]

*2001* is a Helvetica film. Not merely the verbal and mathematical
images flashed on screens, but the total design of the film predicates a
clean authority, an order of total mechanical, electronic perfection. But,
as I said, Kubrick is not merely assuming the equation clean equals
future equals better. He is examining the assumption and returning a
verdict. That verdict is implicit in much utopian literature, explicit in
anti-utopian fantasies of the twentieth century, and the cause of conflict
in much American science fiction film: the future equals emotional and
intellectual death. Perfect order and perfect function decrease the need
for human inquisitiveness and control. A perfectly clean world is clean
of human interference. But *2001* is no humanist's outcry against the
diminution of the spirit, nor does it share the hysterical (and hilarious)

*Handwritten margin notes: FORM BECOMES AN Ideological EVENT; Instrument vs Critical Reasoning; 2001 IS A Helvetica film*

A Helvetica world *(2001)*.

equation of alien mind control with the International Communist Conspiracy implicit in many fifties science fiction films. There is not even the anger over human surrender explicit in its predecessor, *Dr. Strangelove.* The film exists as a leisurely, distanced contemplation of technological advance and human retreat, the design of man accommodated to and owned by his machines, neat, ritualized, without awe, without response. Gene Youngblood tries to make a case for Kubrick's prophesying a new consciousness in his bland, non-reacting scientists and astronauts, a sort of reverse nostalgia in which the future is reverie, "melancholy and nostalgia, not for the past, but for our inability to become integral with the present"[22]—for loneliness in the face of progress. This, however, is wishful thinking; more appropriately, late nineteen-sixties wishful thinking, when passivity and withdrawal were regarded as one possible response to the irrationality of the corporate, technological State. Youngblood is right that Kubrick is presenting the human being as an outsider but wrong in implying that this is a psychological or metaphysical position. Kubrick's men are on the outside like the buttons and "read-outs" of their machines; which is to say they are not outside at all, but perfectly integrated into corporate technology, part of the circuitry. Everything—except, finally, the machine itself— works in perfect harmony. This is not humanity out in space, it is Pan Am, Conrad Hilton, ITT, Howard Johnson, Seabrook Frozen Foods

Screens and buttons *(2001).*

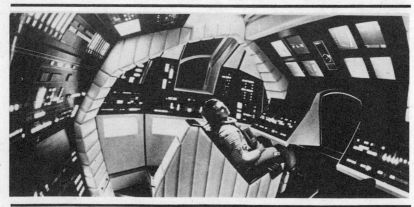

(the corporate names that adorn the space station and spaceship), computers and their men and women. The people in the film lack expression and reaction not because they are wearing masks to cover a deep and forbidding anguish, as would be the case in a film by the French director Robert Bresson, for example. They are merely incorporated into a "mission" and are only barely distinguishable from the other components. They are sans-serif figures.

*Robert Bresson*

*SANS-serif figures*

What then of the film's premise, the notion that the history of man has been guided by unknown, extra-terrestrial forces, represented by a dark version of a Helvetica character, the black, featureless monolith? Here the openness of the film is so great that there is a danger of falling through it. The only helpful way of dealing with it is in a dialectical fashion, seeing its contradictions clearly. History, one possible reading of the film would have it, is at the mercy of a god-like controlling power. The transmitters of this power, the monoliths, teach the use of weapons to kill; they lure humankind into technological perfection; they carry humanity to a transcendent stage of rebirth. Men, therefore, have a reason to be passive, for they are the servants of a higher order, slaves of a predetermined plan so precisely calculated that only a precise calculator, the HAL 9000 computer, realizes its full meaning and gets, quite literally, emotional about it and goes crazy (I don't mean to underplay this; I find the confrontation of HAL and Bowman, the latter undoing the computer's thought patterns while it cries "I can feel it," to be one of the most powerful and ironic sequences in the film—an agon between a man and a construction with a human voice in which the latter wins the viewer's sympathies).

*Not mine*
*" "*

*HAL + BOWMAN confrontation*

*An Agon ?*

But suppose the monoliths do not literally represent an existent higher intelligence? They may be read allegorically, as imaginary markers of humanity's evolution, dark and featureless because one of the valid connotations of the future is the unknown, a blindness to possibilities. Extending this further, the monolith becomes not a precipitator, but an obstacle to full development. After all, the first result of contact with it is killing. The ape touches it and learns to use a bone as a weapon. The wide-screen closeup of the ape's arm crashing down his new-found club is a prophecy of human savagery to come. The weapon

*✓*

*OR A VISUAL Representation of the ineluctible qualtative GAP THAT TURNS INSTRUMENTAL THOUGHT into CRITICAL thinking (SUPERMAN)*

may be a tool to control nature, indicated by the shot of a beast being
felled; but it is also used to hold territory and to slay others. Kubrick
attempts to present many mitigating situations. The apes are being
attacked; they need to defend themselves. But they also take an undeniable pleasure in the kill. Brutality is aligned with pleasure, and the
bone weapon is a mark of progress. In one of the most celebrated bits
of editing in the history of American film, the bone, hurled into the air,
becomes a spaceship. But this leap forward is no great leap at all.
Kubrick's vision of space travel is spectacular, but deadly. The ape
showed a manic joy in its discovery; the space travelers show neither
joy nor sorrow; they are mere receivers of the data flashed on the various screens that surround them. The territory they conquer seems to
offer no excitement, no danger to them (until one of the tools revolts).
The ape used the tool, fashioned it into a weapon; now the tools and
the men are hardly distinguishable.

When the bland Dr. Heywood Floyd touches the monolith discovered on the moon, the movement of his hand echoes that of the ape.
The monolith emits a signal, and in the next shot shows the *Discovery*
mournfully making its way toward Jupiter. The music, the deliberate
track through the spaceship's centrifugal main hall, the quiet passivity
of the astronauts give this sequence the air of a ceremonial, a detached,
sad, and lonely aura. This is the end of man, alone in space, surrounded
by the frozen, half-dead bodies of the other crewmen, and finally locked
in combat with a machine of his own making. The isolation is complete,
though Bowman and Poole take no cognizance of it. The situation is
not unlike that in *Dr. Strangelove*. There the mechanisms of isolation
were ideological. Here the ideology is not as apparent, but must be
sought out in the deadpan faces and automatic reactions of the astronauts, the seductive perfection of the technology, in the red eye of HAL
that watches over the proceedings and takes charge. As in *Dr. Strangelove*, the end of human subjectivity is prelude to the death of the person;
but here Kubrick allows a further step, an indication of rebirth, of
change. The old Bowman in his bed in the Jupiter room, looking up at
the monolith, calls to mind a statement by William Blake: "If the doors
of perception were cleansed, everything would appear to man as it is,
infinite." The point-of-view shot from Bowman's position looking at
the tablet presents it as an impenetrable mass, both promising some-

thing beyond it and enclosing that something at the same time. Once *THE monolith AS obstacle to Be transcended* again, the monolith can be seen to signify an obstacle, a perceptual block that must be transcended.

This places the spectator, of course, on the brink of the metaphysical, a place the film begs us to enter and a place I would like to avoid. Any critical remarks on *2001* must note the suggestion of rebirth, how it moves from the dawn of man through his senescence and back to before the dawn. The enormously evocative images that constitute the film's final sequences point to possibilities of renewed intelligence, a return to a sense of curiosity. The fetus moving through space is the only image in the film of a human being unencumbered by things and, curiously, undiminished by surroundings. But it is, at the same time, an image of enormous solitude and powerlessness. Why is it there? Who is guiding events? The initial dilemma returns: either there is assent to the power of the images and to sensation, or to the suggestion of the narrative that *OR AN eternal return, determinism* some super-intelligence is guiding our destiny. In either case, assent is acquired, and the openness of the film is suddenly threatened. The final *OR, films can Be Read in a different way* sequences of *2001* are the most disturbing, for they are at once beautiful and overwhelming, vague and ambiguous, and suggestive of human impotence in the face of a higher authority. These images and their *Not as Reflection of an ideological position that tries to real-ize it)* implications lead to some difficult and unpleasant conclusions.

The uncertainty and suggestiveness proved too difficult for Hollywood to leave be. Almost fifteen years later, Peter Hyams wrote and directed a "sequel" to the film for its original studio, MGM. *2010* (1984) constitutes the reverse shot of Kubrick's film. As if the openness of the original needed other images to respond and close it, give it manageable and unthreatening meaning while resituating the viewer in a secure and knowable space, Hyams reduces Kubrick's design and narrative structure to a set of simple and—within the context of the science fiction genre—reasonable answers. He replaces the non-discursive power of Kubrick's imagery with dialogue that attempts to account for everything. While their countries prepare for war over Central America, Russian and United States scientists join forces in space to save the original *Discovery* rocket ship, reanimate HAL, and find the meaning of the monoliths. HAL turns out to be quite reasonable after all, and the monoliths signal the birth of a new sun and world, caused by an intelligence that promises peace as long as it remains undisturbed. Dr. Floyd

*2010 !!! ug...
(1984)!*

(played by Roy Scheider, who inflects his role with conventional character traits in a film where the human figures are foregrounded rather
than integrated into the *mise-en-scène* as they are in *2001*) suggests that
in this new universe humans will take a second place. "You can tell
your children," he writes to his son as he returns from his mission, "of
the day when everyone looked up and realized that we were only ten-
ants of this world. We have been given a new lease—and a warning—
from the landlord." The revelation of a new intelligence only confirms
the old language of ownership and subordination.

The narrative of *2010* settles back into the classic model of *The Day
the Earth Stood Still*, where superior powers will permit Earth to live in
peace, unless its "petty squabbles" threaten the universe. Then it would
be destroyed by super-human powers. *2010* is not so blatantly totalitarian; in fact its attack on the American government (clearly depicted as
being right-wing in the film) and call for U.S.-Russian cooperation place
it among the very few liberal films to appear in the eighties. But a great
paradox of American science fiction film is that, no matter how pro-
gressive it attempts to be on a superficial level, there is an apparently
inevitable reversion to a reactionary base. "Superior forces" are either
authoritarian, patriarchal, and therefore threatening, ultimately
destructive powers or, in Spielberg's science fiction, not authoritarian
or threatening, but still patriarchal. The rationality and orderliness
predicated for a "higher intelligence" always turns out to be repressive,
especially when presented as salvific.

In attempting to conclude the difficult openness of Kubrick's film,
Hyams only compounds the unpleasant conclusions that can be drawn
from it. Both films, and many others beside, structure enormous
images, and place the human figure in a passive role, creating narratives
that implicitly or explicitly indicate an inescapable human destiny at
the mercy of some super-human force. They always run the risk of
structuring themselves upon a totalitarian, quasi-fascist model. Susan
Sontag writes:

> Fascist aesthetics . . . flow from (and justify) a preoccupation with
> situations of control, submissive behavior, and extravagant effort:
> they exalt two seemingly opposite states, egomania and servitude.
> The relations of domination and enslavement take the form of a
> characteristic pageantry: the massing of groups of people; the

turning of people into things; the multiplication of things and grouping of people/things around an all-powerful, hypnotic leader figure or force. The fascist dramaturgy centers on the orgiastic transaction between mighty forces and their puppets. Its choreography alternates between ceaseless motion and a congealed, static, "virile" posing. Fascist art glorifies surrender, it exalts mindlessness: it glamorizes death.[23]

*VIDEODROME 9?*

She includes *2001* as a representative work.

I do not agree completely with her assessment, for the very reason that formally *2001* does not create the kind of insistence, the rhythmical structuring of assent that is part of the fascist model. Perhaps, as I have indicated, the options offered by *2001* are what save it from falling into this trap. Certainly, it reveals the condition of people turned into things, but, as in *Dr. Strangelove*, does so from a cautionary perspective. Rather than glamorize death, it points toward (a rather fantastical) rebirth. Yet, undeniably, the film points toward surrender to a hypnotic force and suggests that this surrender is inevitable.

The film toys dangerously with images of assent and surrender. If it manages to escape total commitment to a vision of human impotence and enslavement it does so through narrative openness and the speculative nature of its images.[24] Yet the fact that *2001* dallies with these issues, offering the possibility of audience surrender to its spectacle, and turns that surrender into a theme, is indicative of a definite and troubling strain in American film since the late sixties. In content and form, often both, a number of American films have indeed submitted to a quasi-fascist aesthetic, and it is necessary to digress a moment to see where Kubrick stands in relation to this movement.

*MORE OF THE PASSIVITY DISCOURSE ''.*

In the early seventies, responding to the ideology of the Nixon regime, there was a cycle of reactionary revenge films, in which Don Siegel's *Dirty Harry* (1971) and Michael Winner's *Death Wish* (1974) were key entries. Imbued with the law-and-order fantasies of the time, these films present a strong-armed cop or an aroused bourgeois (sometimes a small-town sheriff, as in the *Walking Tall* series) who battles not only criminals but a caricatured liberal authority which seems to thwart his every move with irritating laws. In the eighties, moving on a global scale in response to the openly aggressive images inherent in the ideology of the Reagan years (I will examine this ideology and the films

*EARLY 1970's REACTIONARY REVENGE films  
DIRTY HARRY (1971)  
DEATH WISH (1974)  
LAW+ORDER FANTASIES*

that grew out of it in more detail in Chapter Four), the revenger took on terrorists, or the Vietnamese, or the Russians themselves. A caricatured liberal authority was sometimes transformed into a caricatured bureaucratic authority that still was unresponsive to desires for the rapid and complete righting of assumed wrongs. The Rambo films were the most prominent examples of these variations, and all of them, whatever small changes they work upon their conservative base, carry forward the cinematic tradition of a powerful individual avenging a largely passive society. They speak to a strong societal frustration and a desire for expedient action, and are obsessed with the idea that a super-hero can do what the society as a whole cannot. They encourage passivity by presenting fantasies of a virile and aggressive leader who will emerge to save the society. They all glorify death and murder with an almost transcendent mindlessness.

More disconcerting than these is a small group of films that not only suggest a quasi-fascist solution to societal problems but create a formal pattern of assent and submission in their very structure. The paradigm for this is, of course, Leni Riefenstahl's famous documentary of Nazi Germany, *Triumph of the Will* (1935), a work whose images and rhythm demand total involvement (or total divorcement). Fortunately unable to hypnotize anyone, its intent is still clear: to create a longing in the audience to partake in the faceless geometric mass of happy people, eyes upward, worshipping Hitler. Formally it not only points the way to the ideology, it is the ideology in action. And what *Triumph of the Will* now fails to do, such apparently diverse (and unequally creative) films as William Friedkin's *The Exorcist* (1973), John Milius's *Conan the Barbarian* (1983), Steven Spielberg's *Close Encounters of the Third Kind* (1977), Tony Scott's *Top Gun* (1986, a film whose "virile posing" and militarist pageantry, whose fantasies of the powers of flying, connected to adolescent sexuality and rock music, make it a model for the banalities of fascist form), the majority of "slasher" films in which men murder women, and a large number of children's television cartoons whose central figures are mechanical super-heroes, succeed in doing. These films were not consciously made in the service of a greater political movement, to be sure; but they succeed, on a smaller scale, in inducing a state of irrationality, enveloping and absorbing the

viewer, permitting no distance and no discrimination. They communicate power and terror simultaneously, resulting in a state of passivity
that restrains a desire for unrestricted, destructive activity. Consider the
"Ride of the Valkyries" sequence in Coppola's *Apocalypse Now* (1979),
where the camera assumes the point of view of the attacking helicopter
gun ship, providing a murderous elation and superiority for the viewer,
countered by the reverse shots of the Vietnamese village and its inhabitants who are destroyed. What choices are presented between power
and helplessness? The film manipulates the viewer into a subordinate
position of awe and hopelessness.

   *Close Encounters* provides the most immediate comparison to *2001*,
and a fascinating example of fascist form. Spielberg creates a revision
of the basic fifties science fiction subject, the invasion of the earth by
aliens. Fifties xenophobia and fear of communism rarely permitted
films to present the aliens as friendly and never allowed passive acceptance of them. But by the seventies there seemed in the culture to be
greater openness to—perhaps more need for—giving over to some
greater protective and benevolent force (this is one of Spielberg's major
preoccupations, and in Chapter Four I will examine it in more detail).
Therefore, Spielberg's spacemen are welcomed and revered. They are
not a threat, but they are overwhelming and inescapable. As in fifties
science fiction, the army still figures as the authoritative force. But
where, in the fifties, it impotently attacks the aliens, now it is prepared
to greet them and, indeed, employs a massive cover-up operation to do
so, a cover-up infiltrated only by a few civilians who, controlled by the
spacemen, fight their way to be present at their epiphanic appearance.

   The structure of *Close Encounters* is such that the viewer is allowed
as little free will as the characters in the film. Extremes of dark and light,
a predominance of low angle shots and rapid dollies toward figures and
objects, the incredible size of the space paraphernalia (the "size" of the
sound track itself) continually reduce the spectator to an accepting position. The film provides no place to move emotionally, and no place to
think. Subordinate to lights in the sky, to the army, and finally to an
elephantine spacecraft, so overwhelming and so intriguing, the viewer,
like the characters in the film, has no choice but to yield to its presence.
I submit that the strategies employed by Spielberg are precisely analo-

The awe-struck gaze at the descent of the spaceship in *Close Encounters of the Third Kind.*

*Close Encounters Strategies Analogous to Riefenstahls Triumph of The Will*

gous to those employed by Riefenstahl in *Triumph of the Will.* The descent of Hitler from the clouds to an adoring populace dwarfed by his presence and their own monumental, geometric configuration is echoed in *Close Encounters.* Here humans are dwarfed by their loneliness in the inhabited night-time sky, by lights, by obsessive geometric figures (the characters contacted by the aliens have implanted in their minds the shape of a mountain where the aliens will land); and finally by the enormous ship that descends from the clouds and reduces them to open-mouthed awe. *Close Encounters* is a fantasy, it may be argued (to which, I will argue later, that such fantasies represent and respond to major currents in the culture), a work of the imagination that should not be submitted to ideological scrutiny. Spielberg could not have consciously intended such a structure, and, besides, what other reaction is possible but awe and submission to such awesome forces?

As I have insisted throughout, no work of cinema, or any other imaginative form, is ideologically innocent, and Spielberg is responsible for the formal construction of his film, whether or not he is aware of its parallels and heritage.* Spielberg, like most commercial filmmakers, is working, it can be argued, in the mainstream of American film, developing forms of audience involvement, giving a thrill, creating emotion. Alfred Hitchcock has said, "I feel it's tremendously satisfying for us to be able to use the cinematic art to achieve something of a mass emotion."[26] Hitchcock, though, always shows his hand, always gives the audience means to step back and observe what is being done to them and why. Hollywood film, at least before the late sixties, often attempted to demonstrate some respect for its audience. Although it worked through an invisible style and thereby insisted that the audience perceives its characters and their actions as if they were an unmediated presence; although it played out fantasies of melodrama, and induced passivity to a great degree, rarely did it dehumanize or attempt to reduce the audience to a function of the sound and images confronting them. Kubrick, in *2001*, retains this respect. Spielberg (and not only Spielberg) does not. Where *Close Encounters* seals the viewer inside its structure from the opening shot—a blast of light and sound from out of the darkness—and keeps him or her submissive for its duration, *2001* demands above all viewer attentiveness and is open, where *Close Encounters* is closed; speculative, where *Close Encounters* is predetermined; filled with detailed images, where those in Spielberg's film are merely overwhelming. *2001* is, among other things, about the terror of dehumanization; *Close Encounters* is about the yearning to yield to something more exciting than the merely human that will relieve us of responsibility. And where *2001* is often ironic and always (with the exception of the "Stargate" sequence) calm, *Close Encounters* is sentimental and hyper-emotional. If Kubrick dallies with the notion of predetermination and ultimate control by a super-intelligence, his speculation is part of the film's larger inquiry and design. Ultimately this is not a very palatable speculation; but the film offers at least an open nar-

*Was George Lucas aware of what a number of critics have seen: that the final sequence of *Star Wars* is patterned directly after a sequence in *Triumph of the Will*? The formal imitation is too perfect for it not to have been conscious. Here, then, is a genuine case of ideological confusion. The plot of *Star Wars* involves a red army in revolt against the black fascist forces of "The Empire." When the red army wins, it celebrates in a Nazi rally! As I noted, most American science fiction, for a variety of reasons, is inherently reactionary.[25]

*[handwritten margin notes:]*
HITCHCOCK CINEMATIC ART V MASS, emotion BUT ALWAYS SHOWS HIS HAND

2001, IS ABOUT THE TERROR OF DEHUMANIZ OFTEN IRONIC CALM,

STAR WARS FINAL SEQUENCE //'S
TRIUMPH OF THE WILL?

COULD this NOT BE A CRITIQUE OF MODERNISM?
ASSUMPTION that PRODUCTION WORK OF ART SIGNIFIES ASSENT to its REPRESENTATION ("PASSIVE AVOIDANCE")

rative and an intellectual space in which the viewer may consider what is going on.

The concept of the open narrative is an attractive one because it places a task on the viewer, forcing him or her to be actively engaged in creating a meaning system from the film. But there is a danger. The form runs the risk of removing responsibility from the film's creator, which can result—as I noted earlier—in ambiguity rather than a provocative openness. *2001* demonstrates this danger when Kubrick's very acute observations of human passivity and ennui are mitigated by suggestions that this ennui is part of humanity's ineluctable service to a master race. The danger is even greater in *A Clockwork Orange*, where Kubrick seemingly gets himself stuck in a thematic quandary: is the only alternative to passivity an individuality so brutal that many must suffer for one person to be free? Is the political future merely one of self-serving manipulations for power? Is the delight in viewing violence a reflection of a perverse need for it, at least in a safe and distanced form?

If *Dr. Strangelove* is satirical and *2001* contemplative, *A Clockwork Orange* is cynical. There are no responsible answers to the problems it poses. Though rhythmically dynamic and carefully structured in a perfectly symmetrical form, the film is formally not as interesting as *Dr. Strangelove* and *2001*. Rather than attempt to create an integrated *mise-en-scène*, its images move toward mere spectacle, and they, along with the editing pattern, easily fit Sontag's description of a "choreography [that] alternates between ceaseless motion and a congealed, static, 'virile' posing." *A Clockwork Orange* seems to be the one film in which Kubrick makes easy choices and easy set-ups. Yet, for all its problems, it attempts at times to follow some of the patterns suggested in the preceding films and sporadically seems to deny the understandable reaction of some critics that it is a hollow pandering to audience desires for more and more violence.

In its design, *A Clockwork Orange* is the dialectic to *2001*. The clean lines and intricate detail of that film are here replaced by clutter and occasional squalor. Only Mr. Alexander's house reflects the sterility of *2001*; but where the cold, clean space tools were fascinating in their detail, the writer's home is only arid and pretentious. The Korova Milkbar, where Alex (Malcolm McDowell) and his droogs get high, bears a resemblance to the Hilton space station in color and furnishings, but it

has the added features of erotic sculpture and very un-Helvetica print-
ing on the walls, advertising the various "moloko plus" drugs that Alex
uses. In *2001*, decoration is at a functional minimum; on earth it has
assumed an erotic obviousness and cheapness.[27] The sexuality that was
repressed in *Strangelove* and disappeared in *2001* emerges in the world
of *A Clockwork Orange* in graffiti, paintings, and sculptures and in the
brutality of Alex and his comrades. Sexuality has become the mundane
in art, an expression of violence in human behavior. And it is precisely
the mundane and the brutal that inform the world created in the film.
Passivity and a lack of human, communal integrity resulted in global
destruction in *Strangelove* and the suggestion of slavery to super-human
forces in *2001*. Here it results in a mindless brutality, a violence of one
individual against another, and the state against all. The love, order,
and gentleness that are announced by the humanist tradition as the
goals of every individual, Kubrick observes as fantasies. Hate, manipulation, and cruelty are the dialectic to these fantasies, and the life of
the mind and spirit becomes the caricatured target of the vitality of the
libido and the club. The Cat Lady (whose home is festooned with animals and grotesque erotic art) does battle with Alex by wielding a bust
of his beloved Ludwig van Beethoven (to whose music Alex has grotesque and violent fantasies), while he does her in with a bloated, white,
sculpted penis.

When *2001* makes its transition from the ape's bone floating in the
air to the spaceship, something important is left out: what happened to
the violence, indeed the joy of violence that the bone represented? *2001*
indicates it has been drained from humans and placed in their mechanical surrogates. HAL cleanly kills off all but one of the crewmen on the
ship. *A Clockwork Orange* returns to examine the ape's heritage. The
beating scenes are choreographed like the ape sequences in the earlier
film. When Alex and his droogs beat up the hobo and Billy Boy's gang
they use their clubs as did the ape when he killed the leader of the
opposing tribe. When Alex beats up his own gang, his slow-motion
antics are similar to those of the ape with his bone. The dawn of man
has become the senility of man. Violence prophesied by the ape's discovery of a murdering weapon has become violence realized and ritualized, a force no longer to be examined or understood but to be used,
either anarchically or under the control of the state. Kubrick seems to

offer no other alternative to the aggression that he sees as an inherent component of human behavior (he is a great fan of Robert Ardrey and his "territorial imperative" ideas about human aggression); violence must manifest itself in some form, controlled or uncontrolled. In *2001*, humans have delegated their responsibilities to their machines, and the machines become the aggressors. In *A Clockwork Orange* responsibility is not so much delegated as dissipated. Life is lived at such a low level of vulgarity that the only expression it seems able to achieve is destruction (a state of things repeated, though in another context, in *Full Metal Jacket*). The state of humankind is hopeless.

At the end of *2001*, old humankind is catapulted by some force back into the cosmos as a wandering fetus, presumably ready to start anew. Toward the end of *A Clockwork Orange*, Alex catapults himself out of a window, driven to attempt suicide by his nemesis, Mr. Alexander, the liberal writer brought to madness by Alex's destruction of his wife. He tortures Alex with the music of Beethoven, to which Alex has been conditioned to react with horror. Like Bowman, Alex is sealed in a bare room. Though not the room of sanitized rococo splendor, the last plastic gasp of human civilization that marked man's end in *2001*, it provides a similar enclosed and observed isolation, with this ironic difference: it does not constitute a way station to another form of existence. When Alex leaps to his death, he is indeed reborn, but only to his former violent self.

*A Clockwork Orange* is a dismally cyclic vision which seems unable to do anything but celebrate the violence it portrays, because it portrays only that as being alive. The death of feeling and response Kubrick depicted in the preceding films comes alive as its own opposite. Life only responds to death; love becomes the attraction to brutality. It is no longer a strange love. One may feel superior to the characters of *Dr. Strangelove* because they are grotesque and ridiculous; their monomania is obvious. There may be a similar reaction to the characters of *2001*, because they are insensitive to the wonder of their world. But Alex is admirable. One cannot help but be fond of his vitality and verbal dexterity, and Kubrick manipulates viewer response accordingly. The narrative moves from a bravura celebration of Alex and his atrocities, observed with horror and excitement, to restrained observation of Alex's arrest and imprisonment, when he is treated so badly the viewer can hardly avoid sympathy. The Ludovico treatment that subdues him is presented subjectively (to be accurate, the point of view throughout the film belongs to Alex: he narrates, there is hardly a scene in which he is not present, and the spectator therefore shares his perspective and attitudes). With the stage performance that demonstrates the success of the treatment, Alex's humiliation and the spectator's sympathies for him are complete. After his humiliation, the narrative duplicates the first part of the film almost incident by incident, only with Alex as the butt of the events (the hobo whom Alex beat up returns with his hobo friends to beat Alex up; Alex's parents take in a boarder who kicks Alex out; Alex's droogs have become policemen and turn on him; and of course the mad Mr. Alexander tries to send Alex to his death as earlier Alex sent Mrs. Alexander to hers). By the time Alex is reborn to his former self, response is so thoroughly on his side that it is hard to tell whether Kubrick is amused at his own powers of manipulation or agreeing with the admirability and good fortune of his character.

Is Alex's way of life to be admired? Is his animal aggression more admirable than the deviousness of the Minister of the Interior and the state? Or is everyone to be condemned, as in *Dr. Strangelove?* One clue to Kubrick's position is the association made between three of the characters. Two of them share similar names: Alex and Frank Alexander, the writer whose wife Alex rapes. Along with Fred, the Minister of the Interior, they make a strange trio. It is as if the three—the loony liberal, Frank Alexander, first cold and sterile, then all chattering grimaces; Alex DeLarge, the violent child, virile killer, magnificent wielder of club, penis, and language, and pathetic victim; and Fred, the devious law-and-order politician, who first uses Alex to show how he can get crime off the streets and then uses him to get it back on the streets when it is politically advantageous to do so—are aspects of the same personality. (In his novel, Anthony Burgess makes the connection between Alex and Mr. Alexander explicit. "F. Alexander. Good Bog, I thought, he is another Alex." In the film, when Alex rings Mr. Alexander's doorbell, it sounds the opening of Beethoven's Fifth Symphony, beloved of Alex.)[28] In the manner of William Blake, Kubrick divides up components of human behavior and places them in separate bodies. The joke, therefore, if joke it is, lies in placing these three social/emotional/political abstractions within the flesh of separate characters, playing them off against each other, and convincing the viewer that they offer real alternatives, when in fact they represent aspects of the human personality that should be integrated. If Alex triumphs in sympathy over the others, it is because vitality is more attractive than deviousness and hypocrisy, even if that vitality is misdirected and distorted. This reading is indeed hard to come by, and it takes some strength of conviction to believe that Kubrick is laughing at both his characters and at his audience for refusing to see his joke (though this ability to scorn his audience is evident again in *The Shining*). The film gives every indication that the audience must admire Alex and admire him with little hesitation. If this is so, the film becomes exploitative of its audience in the worst way. If Kubrick has a satirical intent in artificially dividing components of the human personality into separate types but then builds for one of these types—Alex—a narrative that makes him so attractive and sympathetic that one loses sight of the schematic pattern, then the text becomes skewed and the audience used. The viewer is given little option but to sympathize with a vicious character.

Things are further complicated by the character of the chaplain in the film, whose speech on the necessity of free will seems to be a thesis statement. Even in the formal satirical structure of *Dr. Strangelove*, Kubrick did not make a direct statement of position, allowing the audience to assume its own moral and rational perspective. But in creating a serious religious character, who proceeds to talk seriously and with feeling about an irresistible idea, the narrative and spectator attachment to it are further skewed toward a sympathy with poor Alex.* Coming as it does at the point of Alex's greatest humiliation and focusing attention on what seems to be a central theme of the film, this speech offers no choice but to assent to the chaplain's words. Kubrick's films are all to some extent concerned with failure of will, with a giving up of active participation in events and allowing those events to take control. *A Clockwork Orange* goes beyond this to indicate the threat of a direct

---

*In *Paths of Glory*, the priest is depicted as powerless and hypocritical. The unpleasantness of his character is pointed up by that fact that he is played by Emile Meyer, a singularly ugly individual most often associated in fifties film with roles of brutal, corrupt New York policemen. In *Barry Lyndon*, Murray Melvin's Reverend Runt is a priggish character who cannot be taken seriously.

manipulation of the will of one individual by others (no super-human powers here, only the state). But seen objectively, Alex has a will that needs manipulation. He is a killer, with no rationale for his acts but the general decadence of the society he lives in. We are faced, finally, with an old problem. No alternatives are offered. If a society exists in which humans are reduced to passive, quasi-erotic squalor, if the state exists only to manipulate the wills of its semi-conscious members, then certainly anyone with initiative and some vitality, even if that vitality is directed toward death, must be appreciated. The viewer can only be trapped by the cyclic nature of the film as much as its characters are.

*A Clockwork Orange* is, finally, a confused work. As an act of provocation, as a film that reveals how easily a spectator can submit and be made to react favorably to images of violence, it is of major importance. "It's funny," says Alex, as he speaks of his feelings during the Ludovico treatment, during which he is conditioned by watching violent images, "how the colors of the real world only seem really real when you viddy them on the screen." Kubrick seems to ask for assent to the ramifications of this statement. Whatever he may be saying about the brutality of "civilization," he seems at the same time to want to demonstrate everyone's willingness to accept and even enjoy the representations of that brutality which are more powerfully "real" than anything seen in the "real" world. And so a paradox emerges, one that I have already noted in Peckinpah's *The Wild Bunch*. The thematic confusion of the film is transcended by the kinetic delight the viewer may take in Alex's exploits, delight forced by the narrative's drive and construction of the character which makes these exploits appear to be representations of life rather than death. Judgment is rendered difficult, and the film, finally, can be seen as a cynical manipulation of its audience—a cynicism that indicates Kubrick had become ready to allow his audience to wallow in its own worst instincts, or that he simply did not have an adequate understanding of the problem. Or that he didn't care.[29]

Which brings me back to where I started, to the notion that Kubrick is a clever calculator of audience desires and able to satisfy those desires in slick and glossy images. As much as *A Clockwork Orange* indicates a struggle to justify those images and provide them with a narrative context, it does not allow the viewer to escape their initial power and attraction, their essential deviousness. As if in reaction to this problem and confusion, Kubrick made *Barry Lyndon*, a film that insists its audience remain distant and contemplative, observant and barely involved. *Barry Lyndon* is more open than *2001*. Slow, almost static, its images are of such painterly beauty that they seem to call for admiration as composed objects, apart from their narrative function. These images are peopled with characters whose actions and motives appear irrelevant to contemporary concerns. There is none of the kinetic frenzy and modernity of *A Clockwork Orange*, no invitation to admire individuals or assent to specific acts. The film demands only attentiveness and cooperation from the viewer, demands it more than any of Kubrick's preceding films. More, indeed, than almost any film by an American director one can think of.

Popular critics were incapable of dealing with the film, for it denied so many of the filmic conventions they could securely respond to. "Story" or "plot" is minimal; the emotional reactions it calls forth are small and unclear; the characters do not exist as psychological entities. But it is pretty; more than one critic offered the comment that its images belonged in a museum (tantamount to saying the film was dead). The popular audience fared little better. Because of critical response the film got poor distribution, and many of those who did see it were no doubt bored or baffled.

In attempting to account for popular critical response to a film we often learn more about audience expectations than we do about the film itself. The reaction to *Barry Lyndon* was a reaction less to what that film is than to what it is not. Because it does not meet demands for action, clear motivation of characters, straightforward development of story in simple, dramatic terms and with a functional, unobtrusive style, it sets itself at odds with the traditions of American commercial filmmaking. Certainly *2001* suffers from these same "faults"—it has, in fact, a less dramatic structure than *Barry Lyndon*—yet it had a considerable popular success. The difference, of course, lies in the immediacy of its images, their technical fascination, and, finally, the awe created by its attractive mystical connotations. *2001* is a celebration of technology and an elegy to the end of man, but an elegy mitigated by the suggestion of rebirth that ends the film. *Barry Lyndon* is an elegy that is unmitigated, and rather than fantasize a future, it only evokes a past. The only technology it celebrates is that which makes its own cinematic construction possible: the refined use of the zoom lens, the candlelight cinematography. But the joy and skill of the film's construction are played against the sadness and loss to which the film is addressed. Kubrick structures a decline of vitality and a loss of individual power more severe and final than that seen in any of his other films. At the end of *Barry Lyndon* a date is observed on a check: 1789, the year of the French Revolution. But there is no suggestion that a change in society, a change in the rituals of social behavior, is possible. Kubrick leaves the viewer with an impression of permanent passivity and entrapment. In a peculiar way, *Barry Lyndon* can be seen as Kubrick's first film, setting up historical patterns of obsession and impotence, ritual and retreat that inform all his other work. It is a ceremony of loneliness, and I wonder if the sadness it evokes was as responsible for its unpopularity as its unconventional form.

The pictorial aspect of that form continually calls for admiration. But the admiration is tempered by the reminders that its beauty is cold and the characters who dwell within the images are suffering from the coldness and the very perfection of form and formality that is, visually, so admirable. Formal beauty should give pleasure; Kubrick makes it communicate sadness. The film's images become charged with feelings of loss, an effect enhanced by the dirge-like quality of much of its music. The more the viewer tries to come to terms with what is seen and felt, the more distance and isolation is forced upon her or him.[30]

This dialectic of attraction and distance is carefully structured by the way the images are composed and the way the narrative progresses. By creating compositions that entice and then distance the viewer, Kubrick generates a frustration and a longing that parallels the experience of the character of Barry Lyndon (Ryan O'Neal) himself, who wishes to enter the world of grand society and is rendered impotent by its formal rituals, rituals which are unable to accommodate his vitality. A major compositional strategy in the first part of the film exemplifies this process. Kubrick will begin with a fairly close shot of one or more individuals and then very slowly zoom back until these individuals become part of a much larger composition, engulfed by the natural world that surrounds them. This achieves a number of results. The repetition of the slow reverse zoom creates a steady, somber rhythm. Visually, it tends to reduce the importance of individuals by placing them within a greater natural design.[31] By doing this within the boundaries of a single shot, rather than by cutting, Kubrick achieves an effect of continual change of perspective, of point of view, and of subjectivity. A shot that begins close to human figures who, by all the rights of cinematic and cultural convention, should be observed and attended to, and then moves from them, forcing a realignment of the viewing subject and the subject viewed, disturbs balance and relationship. Alan Spiegel writes:

> ... the motion of the camera begins in drama and ends in spectacle, starts off with an action and finishes with a design, converts human value to aesthetic value and a utilitarian image into a self-reflexive image. ... Characters and situations are taken away from us even in the midst of their happening; the camera withdraws from that to which we would cleave close—and in this respect, our sorrow is collateral to Barry's: we too can never get what we want or keep what we get, and the motion of the camera is a measure of our bereavement.[32]

This reading may be a bit too literal. A viewer cannot identify with a camera movement any more than he or she can with Barry himself. One can, however, be provoked into observing and, perhaps, responding to correspondences, to the frustration experienced when the film refuses to yield what is expected and to Barry's frustration (and destruction) in a world which refuses to yield to his desires. The film's continual play with subjectivity and positioning of the viewing subject provokes unease. The viewer is removed from proximity to the figure. The figure is denied proximity to his own satisfaction. On all levels, desire is squelched.

Another sequence of shots in the film fulfills in a different manner the same function as the reverse zoom. These shots are static and they take place indoors. I refer to those sequences lit only by candlelight, which are at first very warm and intimate: Barry and Captain Grogan, the only friend he will ever have, talk in a dark candlelit tent about Barry's mother and about the ruse played upon him in the duel with Captain Quinn; Barry and the German girl he meets after his desertion talk of their love in a dark farmhouse made intimate by the golden yellow candlelight and the girl's baby, prominent in the composition and foreshadowing Barry's own child whom he will love to his own destruction. But the candlelit sequences soon begin to embrace larger numbers of people, in gambling halls and at banquets, where the yellow light and hideous make-up create a vision of the dead come to life. With the exception of one late sequence, in which Barry, his mother, and his son Bryan share a moment of intimacy and warmth, the candlelit shots diminish the human figure as they progress. They replace intimacy with distance, the human with the inhuman, or, more disturbing in these images, with the human made to look like death.

The candlelit sequences and the reverse zoom shots are only two of the compositional and structural devices used throughout the film that draw attention to themselves and force a reconsideration of the conventional proximity of viewing and narrative subjects. To an even greater extent than in his previous films, Kubrick structures both images and narrative with deliberateness and certainty, leaving the viewer much space to observe and contemplate, but at the same time guiding this observation, commenting on what is seen, forcing attention to how things are seen. By means of cutting, for example, and by playing on proximity and distance through montage, Kubrick can indicate Bar-

The human figure made to look like death: a candlelit scene in *Barry Lyndon*. Reverend Runt (Murray Melvin), Lady Lyndon (Marisa Berenson).

ry's precise social and emotional situation at a given moment. When Barry's banishment from polite society is complete, he is observed in a closeup with Bryan, reading—a quiet, domestic, and tranquil shot. Immediately Kubrick cuts to an extreme long shot of the same scene so that the two figures appear dwarfed under a painting in an enormous room, isolated and barren. The effect is more striking than would have been achieved by zooming back from the figures to show their isolation in a large space. The rapid change isolates them and isolates the viewer from them, reasserting the refusal, throughout the film, to permit any intimacy with the characters, to give any hope that isolation can be overcome.

In a potentially touching sequence, where Barry attempts a reconciliation with his wife, Kubrick takes pains to minimize emotional content. Lady Lyndon (Marisa Berenson) sits almost naked in a tub, one of those curious, upright affairs, similar to the tub in which Marat sits in David's painting. As Barry stands over her, behind and between them can be seen a painting of a man kneeling before a lady. As the sequence continues Barry apologizes to Lady Lyndon for his indiscretions and assumes a kneeling position just like the man in the painting. There follows a closeup of the two kissing, which is immediately followed by a long shot of the castle in which they live (variations of this shot occur frequently in the latter part of the film, acting as punctuation, reinforcing the fractures of continuity suffered by the character and the perception of him). Everything in the sequence, the strange appearance of Lady Lyndon, naked in the tub, the action of the characters echoed in the painting, the cutting into the embrace by the shot of the castle, forbids closeness but assures attention and an awareness of the rigidity of the characters' lives.

Paintings are a primary means by which Kubrick creates these structures. Paintings appear throughout the film, and the film as a whole is made of painterly compositions. This phenomenon climaxes an almost obsessive concern throughout Kubrick's major work. Late seventeenth- and early eighteenth-century paintings decorate the chateau in *Paths of Glory*. Humbert Humbert shoots Quilty through an eighteenth-century portrait in *Lolita*. A rococo landscape hangs over the interior of the derelict casino where two gangs fight in *A Clockwork Orange*, and a tapestry hangs over Mr. Alexander and his friends when they torment Alex later in the film. In each instance, the camera focuses on the painting and then moves down to pick up the action, the first one violent, the second sadistic (in the first instance, the painting appears immediately after one violent act and before another). The Jupiter room in *2001* is decorated with art similar to that in *Paths of Glory* and is, in fact, a fluorescent-lit, antiseptic parody of the chateau in the earlier film. A curious combination of both appears in *Barry Lyndon* in the enormous chamber in which Barry discovers the Chevalier of Balibari (Patrick Magee). Just as Bowman had been observed in the earlier film, the Chevalier is seen from behind, at a table, eating in grand solitude, in an enormous rococo room. A reverse shot reveals his grotesque made-up face.[33]

In all instances, Kubrick uses paintings for ironic juxtaposition. The quiet, civilized artifice of late seventeenth- and early eighteenth-century French art embodies a code of polite behavior in sharp contradiction to the brutal codes of military order and justice played out in *Paths of Glory*. The pastoral landscape in *A Clockwork Orange* is in complete contrast to the rubble in which the gangs fight. The elegant seventeenth-century chamber—cum-motel room cum-fishtank—in which Bowman moves from youth to old age in *2001* is a parody of images of "civilization" that might be drawn from the humdrum mind of an astronaut. The dream of order and politeness, the reality of brutality and manipulation and death: these antinomies plague Kubrick to the point where in *Barry Lyndon* he attempts to enter the paintings themselves and, rather than merely use them as ironic visual counterpoint, pierce these ritual signs of order and civility to discover other rituals, to discover the dynamics of a civilization whose rigid façade on canvas reveals other rigid and brutal façades when these canvases are set in motion.

Kubrick is not making paintings come alive (like those opening sequences of certain films in which a sketch or painting under the credits proceeds to dissolve into the "real" scene as the film begins). He is using a painterly aesthetic to set his characters within a design, to re-create the forms and formalities—the rituals—of the past *as* rituals and to keep the viewer continually aware of the external and internal rigidities of the images. "Each image," writes Alan Spiegel, "seals off direct access to its content by converting content into an object of formal admiration; the formalism, that is, insures the image as both visual enticement and proof against further intimacy."[34] I would modify this in one important way: the images do not convert content into form— form always precedes content. Rather, the images in *Barry Lyndon*, these forms of light and color, human figures, natural landscapes, architectural surroundings, resist yielding a content. They point more to themselves than they do to any expected narrative event. Kubrick is not making paintings come alive; he is playing the viewer's perceptual expectations of painting against those of cinema. One comes to painting to observe static design. One comes to film prepared to see motion, drama, and narrative. *Barry Lyndon* continually threatens to deny drama and narrative by emphasizing rigid composition and then threatens rigid composition with movement and narrative. In all instances expectations are stymied. The conventions of eighteenth-century painting are reversed: instead of order and politeness, there are ugliness and brutality. The conventions of contemporary American cinema are reversed: instead of action and a clever story, there are static, painterly images that require as much or more attention than any story they might be telling. Once again, the viewer is not permitted complete satisfaction of aesthetic or emotional desire. And, as if this were not enough, Kubrick adds yet another element which prevents easy access to the characters and their world, a narrator whose words cannot be trusted.

Kubrick has always favored voice-over narration. The temporal jigsaw puzzle of *The Killing* is fitted together by a narrator. Humbert Humbert narrates *Lolita*, and a narrator gives the historical setting at the beginning of *Paths of Glory*. In *Dr. Strangelove* a voice tells us about the doomsday machine and explains the SAC system. *2001* replaces narration with titles at the beginning of each section (as does *The Shining*, where the titles give days and times in such minute profusion that they become parodic and cease referring to any usable meaning within the narrative). In *A Clockwork Orange*, Alex's voice reflects upon what is being seen and what he is feeling. Joker comments sporadically on events and his reactions in *Full Metal Jacket*. In most instances, the voice-over is a device of convenience, a neutral point in the discourse useful to keep the plot from diverting attention from *mise-en-scène*. The voice-over creates a mock serious tone in *Dr. Strangelove* and a mock-tough, sometimes sentimental one in *Full Metal Jacket*, but only in *A*

*Clockwork Orange* is this voice an integral part of the discourse, helping to form it and mould the viewer's attitude toward the central character, to whom the voice belongs. Alex's voice, with its verbal vitality, its delight in its speaker's exploits, its self-pity and final triumph, both seals viewer sympathies and causes fright at the same time. The narrator in *Barry Lyndon* is a friendly, somewhat detached, always calm and completely anonymous voice (though it is, of course, the voice of Michael Hordern, immediately recognizable to anyone familiar with British film) that provides a variety of services. Discussing what has happened and what will happen, it speaks also of what is happening and what the characters are feeling, often talking of things not seen that would remain unknown had the narrator not mentioned them. In short, the narrator of *Barry Lyndon* is part of another discourse, the teller of another tale, often parallel to the narrative seen on the screen, though as often denying what is seen or telling a great deal more that contradicts what is seen.

Sometimes, particularly in the battle sequences, the narrator will provide a moral and political perspective absent from the visual and dramatic narrative. He may merely be sadly cynical: "Though this encounter is not recorded in any history books," he says of the absurd and suicidal march of British troops into stationary French lines, "it was memorable enough to those who took part." Memorable indeed, for in this battle Barry loses his friend, Captain Grogan. As we see the troops marching by a burning building, and as Barry, carrying a goat, walks into a closeup, the narrator, leaping far beyond the immediate implications of the scene, states, "Gentlemen may talk of the Age of Chivalry, but remember the plowmen, poachers, and pickpockets whom they lead. It is with these sad instruments that your great warriors and kings have been doing their murderous work in the world." There is a cut to a shot of Barry carrying a milk pail, at which point the narrator comments on Barry's low circumstances, though he assures us that he is fated for greater things. Just prior to his dissertation on warriors and kings, the narrator, over a shot of Barry standing by a fire, has commented upon Barry's desire to escape the army. This brief series of images and voice-over comments manages to create three different narrative directions, one in the visuals, two in the narration. On the screen are images of Barry thoughtful by the fire and in the voice-over there is offered something presumably close to his thoughts—he wants to desert. The images then show him involved in the low, hum-drum life of a soldier, at which point the narrator takes off on his own speculations about the politics and meanness of war, comments almost more appropriate to *Paths of Glory* than to what is going on here (clearly Barry is not a plowman, poacher, or pickpocket, those "sad instruments" who the narrator says fight the wars). The visual content remains the same until, having disburdened himself of his sadness over war's inhumanity, the narrator comments on Barry's particular state and assures us it will change, due to accidental circumstances. In the next sequence, Barry steals the uniform of one of the two homosexual soldiers bathing in the river (two characters, who, despite demonstrating some stereotypes of movie homosexuals, express a devotion to each other unlike any of the "straight" characters in the film) and is off to the better things the narrator has promised. Barry's life as a soldier and his unhappiness with it; the narrator's philosophy of war; the narrator's assurance that Barry will go on to other things—none of these elements are contradictory. They simply provide the viewer with more information than is seen or heard within the film itself at this point. Most of all, they remove any immediate uncertainties as to where the narrative is going. Barry will get away from the army (though, as it turns out, only temporarily) and will do well in life (but again only temporarily).

The narrator can present material that contradicts the visual narrative. He undercuts Barry's love affair with the German peasant girl by explaining, in elegant and humorous language, that she is little more than a whore. He tells of the horrible recruitment of children by the Prussian army and how Frederick the Great stoops to kidnapping "to keep supplied those brilliant regiments of his with food for powder." The visuals accompanying this condemnation show only young soldiers marching. As he talks of the deplorable sadism, mutilation, and murder that go on among the ranks, Barry is merely seen leading a soldier through the gauntlet—unpleasant enough, but hardly the visual equal to the words. As Barry marches with Prussian troops, the narrator says: "Thus Barry fell into the very worst of courses and company, and was soon very far advanced in the science of every kind of misconduct." In the following scenes, Barry engages in battle, saves the life of General Potzdorf (who first discovers his desertion and later becomes his protector). Except for the brief gauntlet scene, there is no visual evidence of Barry being anything but a proper soldier. Perhaps, as one writer suggests, Kubrick was so sensitive to the criticism of violence in *A Clockwork Orange* that he did not film sequences that would bear out the narrator's words. Perhaps such scenes would have been opposed to the film's design. The violence that is shown—the boxing match, the battles, the various duels—is ceremonial and distanced.[35] The one major explosion of violence, Barry's attack on Bullingdon, and the one time Barry is the subject of violence, in the duel with Bullingdon, are startling and effective because they are unusual in their immediacy and their expression of emotional and physical pain.

The distance between the narrative offered in voice-over and the narrative offered in the visuals is as specifically determined as the differences in perspective offered by the zoom shots. The viewer is forced to take a double view—in this case of Barry the vicious wretch spoken about by the narrator and Barry the sad, incompetent man of feeling seen in the main narrative. The result is a film somewhat reminiscent of *Citizen Kane*. In Welles's film, different perspectives, different points of view of an individual, some friendly, some adverse, conflict with the viewer's own perception of a powerful man racked with loneliness and an inability to express his passion appropriately. *Kane* confronts the viewer with at least five distinct personalities whose points of view interlock to create the narrative. In *Barry Lyndon* there is only the viewer's perception, fractured and variously redirected by the structure of the film. The contradictions set up by the narrator and the obstacles to emotional involvement set up by the composition and design of the images keep, curiously, forcing attention away from the film and into a confrontation with the perceptions and attitudes themselves. Kubrick is not playing the games he played in *A Clockwork Orange*, where the viewer is requested to identify with a brutal killer. If Barry is vicious and dissolute, there is only someone's word for it; no visual proof is offered. Indeed no proof is offered that validates any of Barry's suffering. He is unpleasant to his wife for a time: riding in a coach, she asks him not to smoke. He responds by blowing smoke in her face. The narrator comments that Lady Lyndon occupied a place "not very much more important than the elegant carpets and pictures which would form the pleasant background of [Barry's] existence." Later Lady Lyndon sees him kissing Bryan's nurse. But Barry makes up with his wife, and the narrator never mentions whether his behavior is any different from that of any other male member of the society Barry wants to be part of, or whether his parvenu status makes his behavior the more odious. Once more there is no satisfactory accounting, within the visual narrative of the film, for the contradictory and condemnatory information given by the narrator. The ceremonials the film is about and the ceremony that the film *is* prevent full assent to anything said and to many things shown.

The result of all of this, as I said earlier, is to make a viewer's emotional situation vis-à-vis the film parallel to the emotional situation of Barry Lyndon, who cannot enter the rich, decaying world he so craves and whose moments of emotional satisfaction are undone even before they are finished. After Barry, provoked beyond endurance, beats Bullingdon in front of a proper gathering of gentlefolk and is properly ostracized from their proper company, there are gentle scenes of Barry and Bryan playing—polite but happy family scenes. Over these are the sad melody of the Handel *Sarabande* and the voice of the narrator:

> Barry had his faults [a more moderate statement than the earlier
> reference to his viciousness and depravity], but no man could say
> of him that he was not a good and tender father. He loved his son
> with a blind partiality. He denied him nothing. It is impossible to
> convey what high hope he had for the boy and how he indulged
> in a thousand fond anticipations as to his future success and
> figure in the world. But fate had determined that he should leave
> none of his race behind him, and that he should finish his life
> poor, lonely, and childless.

The narrator undercuts the content of the visuals (the images of domestic pleasure) and removes any doubt about the outcome of the narrative. Only the details of narrative closure are needed. Bryan dies from a fall from his horse, the horse Barry gave him and which the child rode with an enthusiasm that proved to be his undoing, as did Barry's own enthusiasm in his undertakings. Bryan's deathbed sequence is the most sentimental thing Kubrick has ever filmed; it momentarily breaks the film's distance and, because its sentimentality so jars with the rest, viewing it is uncomfortable. Alan Spiegel condemns Kubrick for the conventionality of this sequence, as others have condemned him for not having more sequences like it in his films.[36] But the sequence does work within the structure of fragmented points of view I have been discussing. Suddenly the viewer is permitted direct emotional engagement, in the conventional form of melodramatic representation, and just as suddenly the rigid formal structure of the film returns. Once again easy emotional access or unquestioning identification with the character is disallowed.

Soon after Bryan's death comes the duel between Barry and Bullingdon, a violent sequence that is at the same time restrained and so structured as to deny access to its highly emotional content. The sequence is set within an abandoned building (possibly a church), the characters isolated against walls (Bullingdon is composed so that the walls are clearly defined behind him; Barry is shot with a telephoto lens, similar to the way Dax is photographed during the execution sequence in *Paths of Glory*, so that he is slightly removed from the action, isolated both in it and from it). The sequence emphasizes Barry's aloneness more than any other in the film, trapping him in a final, perfectly ordered, unimpassioned ritual of proper, murderous conduct. Barry, as always, tries to bring some humanity to it, refusing to kill Bullingdon by firing into the ground. But, as in every other instance when Barry attempts to humanize his world, he suffers for it. Bullingdon may be a revolting coward, but when given his chance, he shoots his stepfather, takes advantage of weakness, and triumphs.*

No matter what Barry attempts, he loses and is isolated. No matter what attempts the viewer makes to join emotional ranks with the film, he or she loses and is isolated, forced into a contemplative stance before images and actions which permit only observation; settings and characters which are culturally distant; and an aura of sadness, painful to confront in the character of Barry Lyndon, more painful to confront in oneself.

This may be the formal triumph of the film, but it raises a question

---

*Early in the film, Barry duels with the cowardly Captain Quinn. Not knowing the duel is faked, Barry thinks he has shot Quinn and is sent from his home. In this sequence he duels with his cowardly and vicious stepson, whom he does not shoot, but is shot himself and sent from his home. It should be noted that in the first of those happy family scenes referred to earlier, Barry and Bryan play at dueling, thereby foreshadowing the serious duel with Bullingdon.[37]

about *Barry Lyndon* and about Kubrick's work in general. As much as the formal structures of his films force a coming to terms with perceptions and engage the viewer in an active role determining narrative development and meaning, the result of the work is a reinforcement of the audience's own passivity and impotence. Let me put it another way: struggling to emerge from the discussions of *Barry Lyndon*, and, to a lesser degree, of *Dr. Strangelove* and *2001*, is the adjective "Brechtian." The confrontation these films provoke between their structure and meaning and the viewer's perception of them, the way they insist upon a reconsideration of how one understands and responds to cinematic narratives and, subsequently, to what those narratives relate, the way they inhibit stock emotional responses, would seem to indicate a working out of the Brechtian principles of distancing, of substituting intellectual for emotional response, of turning narrative into a process involving understanding, rather than a product demanding a predetermined reaction. Films like *Paths of Glory, Dr. Strangelove, 2001, A Clockwork Orange* separate the viewer from ideological assumptions and represent, with some objectivity, the forms and images of our culture that are usually taken for granted. The corporate names that adorn the space station in *2001* and that film's entire treatment of technology offer discomfort with an unquestioning attitude toward the myth of progress and the ideological given of scientific and corporate hegemony (no matter that the corporate names most likely represent contributors to the financing of *2001*, their presence in the new realm remains a source of unease). *A Clockwork Orange*, as uncertain as it seems to be of its own center, still questions certain attitudes toward violence, both of the cinematic and the day-to-day variety, offering visually enticing images of violence while exposing the ease with which those images entice the viewer. More profoundly than *A Clockwork Orange, Barry Lyndon* examines the easy clichés of "individual freedom" and societal necessities. Barry, somewhat like Alex, suffers from an attempt to exert his own vitality within a social structure too rigid to support it.[38] *Barry Lyndon*, however, extends less cynicism and more sad contemplation. One of Kubrick's most anti-Fordian films, it represents the domestic unit as a composition not of security and comfort but of rigid economic ceremony, between whose members checks pass rather than affection.[39]

Once again conventional narrative propositions—the family in this instance—are questioned, distanced, given a material context.

The collapse of affection and the turning of the domestic unit into a threat is the subject of the film that follows *Barry Lyndon*. *The Shining*, like the previous films, and perhaps more deviously, insists again upon a somewhat distanced contemplation of complex ideas about societal and psychological structures. But here the Brechtian analogy becomes strained in many places. As a horror film, it invites profound viewer engagement while, as a parody of the genre and a transference of attention from the family in horrific circumstances to the horror of the family, it denies or at least threatens that engagement at the same time. I suggested earlier that *The Shining* exists on a number of levels. Loud, broad, and—on an immediate level at least—quite explicit, it stands as a response to the meditative solemnity of *Barry Lyndon* (much as the dynamic, violent *Clockwork Orange* stands over and against the contemplative *2001*). The film assaults the audience with image and sound, as if mocking that audience's unwillingness to respond to the previous work. In fact one can read an author/audience allegory within *The Shining*, seeing the character of Wendy as the audience itself and Jack Torrance as the filmmaker, violently assaulting her because she will not respond as he wants her to. With this reading, Kubrick can be discovered distancing himself from his own Brechtian role, denying the rational composure he usually creates and instead battering his audience with image and sound to make its members react—a position he assumes again, with even greater uncertainty, in *Full Metal Jacket*.

Audience reaction is, of course, a primary signifier of the horror genre. The most valid "meaning" of a horror film is the amount of controlled fright that can be generated in its spectators. To this end, Kubrick exaggerates his usual stylistics. The wide-angle lens and the moving camera (made even more fluid here by means of the Steadycam device) are used more broadly than in the previous films. Distortion of *mise-en-scène*, the purposive, almost obsessive movements through the corridors of the Overlook Hotel, suggest—as such stylistic devices do in many horror films—the point of view of an Other, of some monstrous, destructive force that reigns and, in Jack's case, takes over the characters. Shock cuts, inserts of bizarre characters and events meant to represent Danny's visions and Jack's own hallucinations of horrible occurrences past, present, and future, build elements of fear and expectation. But these devices operate reflexively, forcing recognition of them as parts of horror film's stylistic baggage.

In the final analysis, Kubrick refuses, as always, to allow the viewer an unmediated fall into the fictive world he creates. The film provokes no real terror, there is no manipulation of audience into an irrational reaction to irrational events. Precisely because the structure of the film is so broad as to be almost parodic, and the acting of Jack Nicholson and Shelley Duvall exaggerated to the point where they threaten to become abstract commentaries on the conventional figures of the horror film psychotic and his intended victim, the whole text keeps moving beyond the expectations it sets up. But, were it only a parody of the genre, it would rank as a minor effort on Kubrick's part (although certainly the best of the many Stephen King adaptations that appeared during the early eighties). Because it does finally go beyond its own parody to an investigation of the madness and violence of the family, *The Shining* becomes not only an important part of Kubrick's work but a major extension of some of his ideas.

In the vastnesses of their fears and obsessions, Kubrick's male characters extend the effects of their oppression and repression to everything and everyone they contact. Their inability to act upon the world they create, the world that finally destroys them, forces them to enact violence upon each other and very often, as in *Lolita*, *A Clockwork Orange*, to an extent in *Barry Lyndon*, and, though the circumstances are extreme, in *Full Metal Jacket*, upon women. *The Shining* concentrates upon this particular kind of violence and examines some of its larger ideological ramifications (an examination avoided in *Full Metal Jacket*, where the structures of order are hidden, and women figure as sexual objects, references of ridicule, and the mysterious, finally pitiable, embodiment of the unknowable enemy). Perhaps because a woman (Diane Johnson) co-scripted the film with Kubrick, *The Shining* goes further than the other work in foregrounding the function of patriarchy in Kubrick's structure of defeat, defining it within the context of the family and the explosion of violence inherent within the repression that so often constitutes the family unit. The film, finally, is indeed a horror show about possession, breakdown, and madness, but not of the super-

natural kind. Jack Torrance is possessed by his own terror and hatred
of the inhibitions placed on him by patriarchal imperatives. His domesticating restraints break down, and he attempts to live out a male fantasy of the destruction of the wife and child he is supposed to love and
protect.

Like all of Kubrick's men, Jack is trapped. Within the generic elements of the film's plot, he is trapped by the hotel and the supernatural
remnants of its past (a former caretaker killed his own wife and family).
Within the hermeneutic of the text, he is trapped by an obligation to be
father and husband that he finds untenable. He imprisons himself and
his family in the hotel for a winter, a space so huge and labyrinthine
that it engulfs them all while intensifying their already unbearable proximity. Unable to break out, like all of Kubrick's characters, he seals the
trap so tightly that it collapses and destroys him.

He desperately attempts to retain his dominance, screaming and curs-
ing at his wife, demanding isolation from her and his child with the
excuse that he must be left alone to write. He attempts to maintain control by the very power of the patriarchal gaze. Wendy and Danny walk
through the enormous hedge maze outside the hotel. The camera follows them, finally tracking in behind them in a threatening gesture. At
the end of this movement the shot dissolves to the back of Jack who,
instead of writing, is playing handball against the walls of the great
room. Over these two scenes a section of Bartók's *Music for Strings,
Percussion, and Celesta* is playing. In one of his more spectacular
matches of music and image, Kubrick times Jack's stroke of the handball against the wall to coincide precisely with a loud chord in the Bartók piece. The effect is startling, demanding attention not only to the
scene, but to the very mechanics of how visuals and sound are matched
together to create it. Jack stops playing his game and goes over to a
model of the hedge maze in the room. As he looks, the camera assumes
his point of view almost ninety degrees over the model, zooming down
slowly into it. Wendy's and Danny's voices are heard and their figures
suddenly become visible in the maze's center. The two spaces—the
model and the actual maze—merge under the controlling gaze of the
father, who attempts to exercise godlike power over his family until that
power makes him mad.[40]

In effect, Jack himself is the subject of that gaze, for it turns inward

Jack shares words of wisdom with Lloyd the bartender (*The Shining:* Jack Nicholson, Joseph Turkel).

and he becomes its victim. In the process, he runs through other masculine roles. At one point, after he has turned violent, Wendy protects herself and her child by beating Jack with a baseball bat and locking him in a storeroom. To gain her sympathy, he whines like a small child needing his mother's protection: "Wendy, baby, I think you hurt my head real bad. I'm dizzy. I need a doctor. . .Honey, don't leave me in here." Before his death, he comes back as a demonic parody of the dutiful husband. Released from the storeroom (by the ghost of the previous caretaker who had killed his family), Jack bashes down the door to the family's living quarters with an axe, looks through the wreckage and announces with murderous glee the words every wife (according to the movies) wants to hear: "Wendy, I'm home!"

At other times, Jack plays out a role that synthesizes all the others, the long suffering, woman-hating male, the clichéd figure of the slob at the bar, complaining of how his wife does not understand him. This scene is quite literal, as Jack is entertained by the ghost of the hotel's barman (acted by Joseph Turkel, last seen in a Kubrick film as one of the convicted soldiers in *Paths of Glory*). "White man's burden," Jack complains to Lloyd about his wife—the banality of the language equal to that of *Dr. Strangelove* in exposing its own deadness while implicating Jack in the entire complex of repressiveness.* "Nothing serious, just a little problem with the old sperm bank upstairs," he says. "Women," replies Lloyd the barman, with the full satisfaction of someone newly discovering a useless cliché, "can't live with 'em, can't live without 'em." Jack finds this irresistible: "Words of wisdom, Lloyd. Words of wisdom." And he drinks his phantom drink to this phantom truth. As every besieged husband must, he looks for an affair. Entering the mysterious, forbidden hotel room where his son was just assaulted, he discovers a naked lady in the bath. She comes to him, they embrace, and in his arms she turns into a scabrous, laughing old crone. Facing all the turns of domestic unhappiness and madness, Jack is undone and unforgiven. The isolation he has sought for himself and his family drives him further into the isolation of his own ideological position. None of the promised masculine pleasures are available to him and he finds patriarchal power untenable, unendurable. "All work and no play make Jack a dull boy." The deeper he falls into his isolation, the more he feels—like that other Jack and his precious bodily fluids in *Dr. Strangelove*—his freedom and vitality drained away. In *Dr. Strangelove*, Kubrick could not resist extrapolating the effects of repression on the entire world. By the time of *The Shining*, the body politic is reduced to the body of the family and then further to the body of the individual.

Jack fails at all his intended tasks. Even his wife, the very figure he attempts to subdue permanently, turns on him and gets the upper hand. On the generic level, Wendy is a stereotyped horror film character, both the instigator and the object of the monster's rage.[41] But she transcends her generic role—like the Sigourney Weaver character in *Alien*, who

---

*The only victim—beside his family and himself—of Jack's rage and madness is a black man, the hotel cook who returns to help Danny, with whom he shares extra-sensory powers.

protects herself and destroys the monster. Wendy assumes the "masculine" role in a wonderful symbolic gesture. Just before the scene in which she discovers Jack's bizarre manuscript, she sits with Danny watching Road Runner cartoons (Jack is doubtlessly meant to be associated with the hapless Wiley Coyote). Getting up to go to Jack, she moves to the rear of the frame and silently, so far back in the composition that it takes some attention to notice it, picks up a baseball bat, with which she will beat down her violent husband. The figure oppressed by the phallus steals it in order to control it. Later, when Jack attempts to smash his way into the bathroom where Wendy and Danny are hiding, she stabs his hand with a large knife, an act of displaced castration that further reduces Jack's potency and threat. The patriarch is hurt with his own weapons, diminished by an acting out upon him of his own worst fears of losing the symbol of his power.

But, as we have seen, Kubrick is not a filmmaker who will offer final triumph to anyone, male or—especially—female. During her last run through the hotel, as Jack is pursuing Danny, Wendy is subject to some supernatural apparitions. She sees through a partially open door a bare-assed man in a pig costume apparently engaging in oral sex with a man in a tuxedo. This homosexual intrusion—appearing as a frightening specter—supplies a final inflection upon the film's meditation on domestic angst and patriarchal collapse, suggesting that all sexuality is a thing to be feared and loathed. Jack sees women as threatening objects. To fight him and protect herself and her son, Wendy has to acquire phallic authority and power. The result is that all social-sexual structures collapse, not to be re-formed into a new, liberating order, but to the destruction of everyone. The son Jack tries to kill and Wendy protect withdraws into a schizophrenic world of visions and fears. Wendy, first confronted by a psychotic, possessed husband and then by a vision of homosexuality that by popular definition is a denial of ordinary domestic structures, disappears into the snow along with her son, safe from Jack but still not freed from the subordinate position of despised object. Jack is reduced to a howling beast and finally a frozen corpse in the maze, trapped by the very son he wanted to kill and who proved—like everyone else—cleverer than he (and, for good measure, able to conquer Oedipus). Only misogyny and misanthropy survive. The image at the very end of the film, a photo on the hotel wall sug-

gesting Jack had always been there, that this scene of madness and violence is forever acted and reenacted, confirms the notion of an eternity
of despair, of oppressive systems created by people who allow those systems to destroy them.

And this is the reason, finally, that Kubrick's work cannot comfortably be labeled as Brechtian. Brecht believed that the work of imagination could activate an audience's political response and insisted that
the contemplative distance created by the formal structure of the work
of art be only a prelude to the active seeking of cultural and social
change. The distancing structures of Kubrick's films offer only a powerful reaffirmation of the inability to go beyond the repressive objects
and rituals men and women have erected for themselves. Brecht would
use the imagination to reassert subjectivity into active, collective political structures. Kubrick uses his imagination to show that subjectivity
is forever destroyed by monolithic, unchanging, dehumanized
structures.

In discussing the troubling passivity inherent in *Paths of Glory* and
the nascent sentimentality and avoidance of history in *Full Metal
Jacket*, I said that Kubrick was hardly a revolutionary filmmaker. It
would be misguided to demand of him that his work affirm viable possibilities of action, engagement, and change since these do not seem to
be part of his artistic/political sensibility. More important, when these
possibilities are offered in American film they almost invariably appear
in melodramatic, heroic fantasies, the very forms Kubrick eschews. Nor
can the critic demand that Kubrick investigate the culture in the manner of, say, Jean-Luc Godard. Kubrick, despite his geographical distance, is too much an American filmmaker. Godard is a true Brechtian
and an ironist whose restrained, self-interrogating films allow his characters and the cultural paraphernalia that surround them to do intellectual battle with each other, with an open invitation for the spectator to
join. Kubrick is an ironist whose films are both controlled and open,
inviting emotional more than intellectual engagement (even though
they are intellectually more rigorous than the work of any other American filmmaker). They are considerably more declarative than are the
films of Godard, stating more than they question. Even though they
offer room to observe and draw conclusions while attacking the core
ideological structures of the culture, the conclusions drawn are always

the same. The viewer is invited to watch the spectacle of the characters losing and perhaps consider some ramifications of the loss, but little more. His powerful spectacles and intriguing, intricate formal structures open a cavern of mirrors which reflect either our own worst fears of ourselves or our most passive inclinations to remain as we are.

CHAPTER THREE

## EXPRESSIONS OF THE STREETS

---

# Martin Scorsese

*"I'm God's lonely man."*

Travis Bickle

Arthur Penn and Stanley Kubrick stand as the first generation of contemporary American cinema's small avant-garde. Both of them began their filmmaking careers in the fifties, just before the French New Wave helped initiate a break in Hollywood's classical style. Martin Scorsese is part of the next group of directors, which include Steven Spielberg, Francis Ford Coppola, George Lucas, John Milius, Brian DePalma, and Paul Schrader, who came to filmmaking maturity after the French left their mark.[1] That mark contains some complex tracings. Like Godard, Truffaut, Rohmer, Chabrol, and Rivette, the American filmmakers studied film carefully, both formally and informally. Like the French, they spent a great deal of their youth watching film; but instead of turning to critical writing about their subject before actually making films, many of them attended film school, an extraordinary event in the history of American filmmaking.

In most cases, the older generations of American filmmakers learned their craft in the business, and for most of them that learning was intuitive. They watched and they followed, by and large directing films the way everyone else did. The occasional stylistic and personal inflections that appeared in some of their work grew out of the freedom offered by the studio system, where the volume of films made permitted some little room for individuals to vary the basic patterns. There were exceptions, of course. Foreign directors in Hollywood brought with them some different approaches, though most of these were quickly absorbed into the mainstream. The American triumvirate—Ford, Hitchcock, Welles—articulated major variations and modifications on the classical style. Ford's were mostly to be noted in certain repeated compositional groupings and the extended thematic of community; Hitchcock's in a redesigning of the perceptual space of film and viewer, as well as an obsessive concern with the fragility of bourgeois order; Welles's in a revision of thirties *mise-en-scène*, a remodeling of compositional depth, renewed attention to the shot itself, and a career-long obsession with the thematics of power. Each of them gave conscious thought to the construction of film narratives. The new filmmakers learned about the history of film and the techniques of its construction outside of the production system, a process which offered the possibility of a less intuitive and more analytic approach then that of their predecessors. They combined a love of film with the desire to understand it. One of them started from a scholarly perspective: Paul Schrader wrote a book on Robert Bresson, Carl-Theodor Dreyer, and Yasujiro Ozu and an important essay on *film noir*. Martin Scorsese taught film at his alma mater, New York University.

This analytic perspective was modified by a number of things, most important of which was the desire of these young filmmakers not to be independents, but to join the mainstream of Hollywood production. Many of them, including Scorsese, Copolla, and Milius, the director Peter Bogdanovich (who, though not often associated with the group, also began as a cinephile), Joe Dante (the director of *Gremlins*), cinematographer Laszlo Kovacs, actors Bruce Dern and Jack Nicholson, began their commercial filmmaking work under the guidance of an important individual in the recent history of Hollywood. Roger Corman, under the aegis of American International Pictures, an organization that was devoted to low-budget movies, offered an entry into the film business and simultaneously something to escape from. AIP produced horror, science fiction, beach-party, and bike films, and there is only so much room in these genres to move around and test out talent (as Dennis Hopper and Peter Fonda discovered when they attempted to turn the AIP bike film into a grand generational statement in *Easy*

*Rider* (1969)). If Corman taught his pupils to work quickly and cheaply, he also taught them the necessity of finding a situation that provided more leisure and more room for imaginative growth. Coppola, for example, filmed the low budget horror film, *Dementia 13*, for Corman in 1963. Within a few years, he was beginning to write and direct features for the major studios.

Whether they moved through AIP, or went from film school directly to features, or, in the case of Spielberg, to television, the imaginative growth of these individuals was hardly equal. Following his enormous financial success with *American Graffiti* (1973, steered through production by Coppola) and *Star Wars*, Lucas withdrew from directing to become producer of his films, content to initiate and guide rather than to make images. After a demonstration of great narrative skill in the two *Godfather* films and *The Conversation*, Coppola substituted grand spectacle and barren technology for imaginative visions of power and loss. He wished to be more than a producer and director, but a mogul in the old Hollywood sense. None of his desires were satisfied. John Milius has never transcended his ideological restraints. A self-proclaimed fascist, his work (*Conan the Barbarian* and *Red Dawn* (1984), for example) is overblown with portent and violence, full of the racism, misogyny, meanness, and vulgarity that go with his ideology. Brian DePalma has made a career of the most superficial imitations of the most superficial aspects of Hitchcock's style, worked through a mysogyny and violence that manifest a contempt for the audience exploited by his films (though in *Scarface* (1983) and *The Untouchables* (1987) he has shown a talent for a somewhat more grandiloquent allusiveness). Paul Schrader started as a script writer (he wrote *Obsession* (1976), which was Brian DePalma's imitation of *Vertigo*, the AIP produced *Rolling Thunder* (1977), as well as *Taxi Driver*), and has directed films of his screenplays that demonstrate varying degrees of competence and reaction—*Blue Collar* (1978), *Hardcore* and *American Gigolo* (1979), *Cat People* (1982); an intricate examination of politics, psychology, and aesthetics, *Mishima* (1985), and a curious film about working-class family life and rock and roll, *Light of Day* (1986). Spielberg most successfully merged a love of film with an understanding of commercial necessity that has given him the most power and freedom of the group. I will examine what he has done with it shortly.

Martin Scorsese has certainly not been the most commercially successful of this generation of filmmakers. Until very recently, with *The Color of Money* (1986), he has not made a "blockbuster," and even his best attended films prior to *The Color of Money—Alice Doesn't Live Here Anymore* (1974), *Taxi Driver* (1976), *Raging Bull* (1980)—do not approach the profits of Spielberg or the Coppola of the *Godfather* years. This has created some benefits. Scorsese has so far not had to compete with himself, making each successive film bigger and more spectacular in order to top the profits of the preceding works. More important, by working with moderate budgets, and expecting moderate, rational returns, he has been able to keep up a certain level of experimentation and inquiry in his work. Of all the young, post-New Wave filmmakers, he has retained his excitement about the narrative possibilities of cinema, his curiousity about cutting and camera movement, and his delight in toying with the conventions of the classical form. The construction of his films is never completely at the service of the viewer or of the story it is creating. There is an unashamed self-consciousness and a kinetic energy in his films that sometimes threatens to overtake both viewer and story, but always provides a commentary upon the viewer's experience, preventing him or her from easily slipping into plot. He creates an allusiveness, a celebration of cinema through references to other works, that has its equal only in the films of Godard, Bertolucci, and Wim Wenders. Whether his "star vehicle," the film structured for the presence of Paul Newman, Tom Cruise, and the comfortable gaze of the spectator at admired figures, changes this and marks Scorsese's capitulation to the conventions of the zero-degree style remains to be seen. Perhaps *The Color of Money* is merely another cinematic allusion, proving that Scorsese can make as ordinary a film as any other filmmaker.

Scorsese does not create stately compositions in the manner of Kubrick or monumental structures like Speilberg's. His work does not have the intellectual distance and rigor of Kubrick's or perform the radical experiments in cinematic space and genre of Robert Altman. He is, of the directors discussed here, closest to Arthur Penn, especially the Penn of *Mickey One* and *Bonnie and Clyde*. Like Penn at his best, Scorsese is interested in the psychological manifestations of individuals who are representative either of a class or of a certain ideological grouping; he is concerned with their relationships to each other or to an antagonistic environment. Scorsese's films all involve antagonism and struggle, and constant movement, even if that movement is within a tightly circumscribed area that has no exit. His work is like Penn's (and like that of most of the other filmmakers discussed here) in that there is no triumph for his characters. With the exception of Alice Hyatt in *Alice Doesn't Live Here Anymore*, Paul Newman's Eddie in *The Color of Money*, or, more fantastically, Rupert Pupkin in *The King of Comedy* (1983), all of his characters lose to their isolation or their antagonism (Paul Hackett in *After Hours* (1985) survives his ordeal, but like Travis Bickle his survival is hardly a triumph). Unlike Penn's, Scorsese's work shows a degree of stylization which eschews, for the most part, the sixties conventions of realism, defined primarily by location shooting and natural acting styles. In *New York, New York* (1977), he moves indoors entirely, depending on studio sets to achieve an expressive artificiality. *Raging Bull* is photographed on locations, but in black and white, a process by now so unconventional (although becoming less so since it has been adopted as a style for rock videos) that it creates a distance and stylization heightened by the film's narrative contours and the construction of its fight sequences. In all his films, there is a sense that the place inhabited by the characters is structured by their own, slightly crazed perceptions, and by the way the viewer is made to see and understand those perceptions.

This brings me back to a central concern of this study, the problem of point of view, of how and why a filmmaker allows viewer entry into the fiction, and where the viewer is permitted to stand and observe. In Kubrick's work, there is always the sense that the entire *mise-en-scène* is commentative, representing not a dwelling, a habitation, but what an observer ought to think or feel about that habitation. Kubrick does not so much construct places for his characters to live as he does an idea about how and why those characters live. Penn will often depict characters as emerging from or being formed by an environment that barely contains them: the Depression South in *Bonnie and Clyde* seems to call forth a rebellion against its barrenness; the dark, fragmented Chicago of *Mickey One* threatens its hero by echoing his state of mind. Spielberg often creates a masterful *mise-en-scène* of middle-class suburbia, which is then made both strange and attractive by the entry of a foreign force.

In quite classical fashion, his films are composed and cut so that the viewer is made complicit with the events and firmly joined to the characters, responding to their ordinariness and the threat or comfort offered by the intrusive phenomenon. The point of view manufactured by Spielberg is finally that of the dominant cultural discourse, to which his films securely attach the viewer. Robert Altman, on the other hand, radically fragments *mise-en-scène* and perceptual location, demanding the viewer pay attention to its various parts, refusing the comfort of conventional placement.

Scorsese's *mise-en-scène* does something quite different. Though not as fragmented as Altman's, it is never accommodating. His characters do not have homes that reflect comfort or security. The spaces they inhabit are places of transition, of momentary situation. But these places are not Kubrick's abstract ideas of places. The Manhattan of *Taxi Driver* or *After Hours*, the Little Italy of *Mean Streets* (1973), even the Southwest of *Alice* are perfectly recognizable, almost too much so. The *mise-en-scène* of *Mean Streets*, *Taxi Driver*, *Raging Bull*, and *After Hours* represents more than New York, a place of tough people, crowded streets, fights, and whores. They represent, to borrow a notion of Roland Barthes's, a New York-*ness*, a shared image and collective signifier of New York which has little to do with the city itself, but rather expresses what everyone, including many who live there, have decided New York should look like (and much different from the New York created by Woody Allen, whose streets and apartments are comfortable habitations for walking and conversation). At the same time— and this is where the difference with Kubrick occurs—the New York of *Mean Streets*, *Taxi Driver*, *Raging Bull*, *After Hours* is reflective of the energy of the characters, in the first; the anomie of Travis Bickle, in the second; the confused violence of Jake La Motta in the third; the paranoia of Paul Hackett in the last. And these qualities are communicated to the viewer by means of the ways Scorsese allows his or her entry into the *mise-en-scène*. Through composition, lighting, camera movement, and cutting he provides the viewer a primary perceptual pattern, a point of view, which is then joined with another point of view created within the narrative, that of the central character. Edward Branigan writes that one aspect of point of view is a "condition of consciousness. . .which is

*represented. . . ."*[2] Scorsese represents states of mind and guides viewer
response to them with great care and through a complex organisation
of visual and aural elements.

The complexity is heightened by the fact that, in most of his films,
Scorsese creates a tension between two opposing cinematic conventions, the documentary and the fictional. The documentary, by means
of a free moving, often hand-held camera that records people on the
streets or talking informally in what appear to be actual rooms, offers
an illusion of objective observation of characters, places, and events
which might exist before and after the filming of them. The fictional, as
noted above, creates a subjective point of view, coded so that the viewer
understands that what is being seen has been created for the fictional
moment, a controlled artifice. No matter how conventionally "realistic"
a fiction is, there is the tacit understanding that it has no material reference outside of itself. Scorsese's work contains such a severe *anti*-real-
istic element that the world he creates often becomes expressionistic, a
closed space that reflects a particular, often stressed, state of mind.[3] But,
like Jean-Luc Godard (who, with Bernardo Bertolucci, is a strong influence on his work), he understands the arbitrary nature of the documen-
tary/fiction conventions, and freely mixes them. In much of his work
there is the sense of capturing a "reality" of places and events that might
exist even without his presence. Until *Taxi Driver*, he employs the
hand-held camera and the rapid, oblique editing which have become
associated with a "documentary" and improvisational style. In all of
the films set in New York, the street imagery, no matter how colored
by the characters' perspective, allude to a material presence, a factual
existence. His actors (particularly Robert De Niro and Harvey Keitel)
create their characters with an off-handedness, immediacy, and unpredictable violence that give the impression of un-premeditated existence
(as opposed to the carefully studied character-making obvious in the
way Kubrick directs his players). When these qualities are interwoven
with the subjective impressions of the world that is communicated by
the ways the characters see their environment and themselves, and
when Scorsese modifies location shooting (which, by the mid-seventies,
was taken for granted in contemporary film) with artificial sets, stylized
lighting, and slow motion photography, a self-contradictory perceptual

structure is created. "Realism" and expressionism work against each
other, creating a strong perceptual tension that can be felt throughout
his work.*

Scorsese started his commercial career with a film strongly influenced
by the New Wave. *Who's That Knocking at My Door?* (1969)—a finger
exercise for *Mean Streets*—is inscribed in the hand-held, jump-cut,
non-transitional style that many filmmakers took from the surface of
the French films of the early sixties. Its *mise-en-scène* is partly neo-real-
ist, partly documentary, mixed with the subjectivity of perception and
allusiveness that marks *Breathless* and *The Four Hundred Blows*.[4]
*Who's That Knocking?* is an "experimental" film in all senses. Formally, it begins trying out the camera strategies, the restless, foreboding
movement, that will become one of Scorsese's major formal devices.
Contextually, it prepares the way for *Mean Streets*, J. R. (Harvey Keitel)
being an early version of Charlie in the later film—more of an
oppressed Catholic than his later incarnation, less rooted in his environment, standing over and against New York rather than being
enclosed within it as Charlie is.

Scorsese has not yet found in this early film a method of integrating
the character with the space he occupies so that the two become reflections of each other in a mutually defining *mise-en-scène*. Nor has he yet
discovered a way of incorporating his love of film, manifested through
allusion, within the narrative. Here the allusions stand out irrepressibly;
the central character speaks Scorsese's obsession with his cinematic
inheritance. J. R. and his girl friend (Zina Bethune) have a long discussion about westerns, John Wayne, and Ford's *The Searchers* (along with
*Citizen Kane* and *Psycho* a key film for all of Scorsese's generation of
filmmakers). At a party, when a man shoots up a shelf of liquor bottles,
there is a cut to a photograph of Wayne with a gun and a montage of
stills from Hawks's *Rio Bravo*. This allusiveness will remain in Scorsese's later work, becoming more thoroughly woven into the pattern of

---

*Scorsese has made some more or less conventional documentaries: a film about his fam-
ily, *Italianamerican* (1974); one on a friend, *American Boy* (1978); and a big theatrical rock
film, a documentary on the last performance of The Band, *The Last Waltz* (1978). This
last film, photographed in 35mm by some of the best cinematographers working in American film, contains sequences shot in a studio, with The Band playing on a set reminiscent
of *New York, New York*.

his films, until *Taxi Driver* becomes a version of *The Searchers* and *Psycho.*

*Who's That Knocking at My Door?* stands as a document of Scorsese's beginnings. Something like Kubrick's early films, it is less an impersonal generic exercise than an inquiry into the possibilities of subjective cinematic expression. But unlike Kubrick, Scorsese needed the technical facility and formal restraints of commercial production to develop his style. He never falls into the zero-degree style and simple generic repetitions that those restraints can cultivate, but, like other strong American filmmakers, uses them as a base to build upon, as a tradition to recognize and overcome. This base was provided by Roger Corman and American International Pictures.

*Boxcar Bertha*—the film he made for AIP—is a work completely unlike its predecessor, *Who's That Knocking at My Door?* or its successor, *Mean Streets.* Yet it sets itself up as a link between them, if only by smoothing out the stylistic quirks apparent in the former and preparing for the consistent and assured approach of the latter. A violent work, much a part of a group of period evocation films influenced by *Bonnie and Clyde* and popular in the seventies, it is a short, direct narrative which does little more than prepare for an enormous gunfight at the end and a rather repulsive series of images in which David Carradine is nailed to the side of a freight car which pulls out, camera mounted on its top, looking down at the crucified body as a distraught Bertha (Barbara Hershey) runs after. The only inherent contextual interest of the film is its mild pro-union, pro-left stand (the nominal subject is a radical union organizer of the railroads in the thirties). This is, I am certain, the work of its screenwriters, Joyce H. and John William Corrington, for it is a subject Scorsese otherwise shows no interest in. What Scorsese adds to the film is a further indication of his talent with the moving camera. Scattered throughout are shots in which the camera booms down upon a character or arcs around two people talking to each other, investing them with an energy and tension that will be developed more fully in the films to follow. *Boxcar Bertha* is an important work not so much *by* Scorsese as *for* him; it permits him to work within the basic patterns of early seventies film, its violence and its urgency, and to understand how those patterns can be worked together with the looser, more self-conscious and subjective elements of *Who's That Knocking?*

The integration occurs in *Mean Streets*, a film which can be seen as "documentary" in the form of a carefully structured narrative fiction of four young men growing up on the fringes of society in New York's Little Italy, or as a subjective fiction of incomplete lives and sporadic violence in the form of a documentary of four young men in New York's Little Italy. I do not mean to be overly ingenious, but *Mean Streets* does keep altering its perspective on itself, combining what appears to be a spontaneous capturing of its characters' lives with carefully considered, formal arrangements of *mise-en-scène* and character point of view. This is not a confused or confusing alteration. On the contrary, Scorsese carefully integrates a double perspective in the film, a free-flowing observation and a carefully structured point of view both of and from a central character. As opposed to the contained, highly structured lives of middle-class Italians developed by Francis Ford Coppola in the carefully made narratives of the two *Godfather* films, Scorsese investigates the almost incoherent street ramblings of disenfranchised men whose lives are defined by disorder, threatened by their own impulses, and, though confined by narrow geographical boundaries, paradoxically liberated by the turmoil of the bars, tenements, and streets that make up their confines. The central character of the film, Charlie (Harvey Keitel, who here and in *Who's That Knocking?* becomes a kind of alter ego for Scorsese, even sounding like him) is a further development of the character of J. R. in the earlier film. Less guilt-ridden than J. R., Charlie attempts to come to terms with his Catholicism, his future as a petty mafioso, and his odd, violent friend Johnny Boy. This character, played by Robert De Niro, in the first of five films he has made with Scorsese, is a saintly idiot, a figure with no center, who destroys himself with his own inarticulate desire to be a free spirit.

But then none of the characters in the film, with the possible exception of Tony, the barkeeper, has the center or sense of direction that one expects from characters in conventional film fictions, and it is the purpose of the film to observe them in their randomness and as part of an unpredictable flow of events. When Charlie is on the streets, no matter how central he may be to the narrative moment, he is composed in the frame as one figure among many, standing off-center, next to a building, other people moving by him. Johnny Boy is continually "caught" in randomness. When first seen in the narrative proper (his name, like those of the other characters who are introduced at the beginning, flashed on the screen, in imitation of the way David and Albert Maysles introduce the characters in their documentaries), he is at the end of a street. He pauses by a mailbox, throws something in it, runs up the street, looking back as the box explodes. In another sequence, he is up on a roof, shooting a gun at the Empire State Building uptown. Elsewhere he walks down the street, the camera rapidly tracking him from behind. A kid bumps into him, whom he proceeds to beat up. Little violences, sporadic shootings, fistfights punctuate the film as if they were parts of ongoing events, or as if they were moving toward some greater violence, which in fact they are. The end of the film is an explosion of gunfire and blood. The exasperated loan shark Michael pursues Johnny Boy, Charlie, and Charlie's girl friend, Teresa, in a car chase through rainy streets. Michael's henchman (played by Scorsese) shoots them up, horribly wounding Johnny Boy in the neck (as De Niro's Travis Bickle will be shot in the neck in *Taxi Driver*).

This random, violent flow of events is fed by the persistent uncertainty of Charlie's perception of them; his attempts to test his Catholicism; his attempts to justify his life: "You don't make up for your sins in church; you do it in the streets; you do it at home. The rest is bullshit, and you know it." These are the first words heard in the film, and they are spoken over a dark screen. At their conclusion, the first shot is one of movement: the camera moving into Charlie as he rises quickly from his bed. The rhythm of the whole film is established by the fact that Charlie is seen not at rest and then getting up, but in motion as the shot begins. A hand-held camera follows him to a mirror on the opposite wall; a crucifix is prominent behind him. A police siren is heard outside. Charlie goes back to bed, and as he lies down there are three rapid cuts, each one closer to his head. (Scorsese commented that he had seen this triple cut in Truffaut's *Shoot the Piano Player* and used a variation of it in all his films.[5] He also would have seen it in Hitchcock's *The Birds*.) On the second cut, a loud rock song begins on the track. Without preparation or explanation, this carefully executed sequence generates a nervous and purposeless energy that continues throughout the film. It also creates an immediate intensity and initial engagement, which is supplied by the kinetic closeup of Charlie's face. ". . . The simplest closeup is also the most moving," wrote Godard; it can "make us anxious about things."[6] And complex closeups, like those which open *Mean Streets*, the intensity of which is magnified by hearing the vocal component first, both voice and face unlocated temporally and spatially, forces viewer attention, makes us uneasy, and does not permit rest. A few of the films under discussion here—*Bonnie and Clyde*, *A Clockwork Orange*, as well as *Godfather I*—use a similar method of entry, beginning on a closeup, without the conventional establishing shot. The face demands attention; its lack of location causes some discomfort. The act of locating it, which is partially the job of the film, partially the job of the viewer perceiving the film, creates a tension between the viewer's expectations and desires to be comfortably situated within the narrative and—in the case of *Mean Streets*—the stubborn refusal of the narrative to meet those expectations and desires.

This stubbornness is apparent in Scorsese's refusal to allow his narrative to begin just yet. The jump cuts to Charlie's face are followed by, of all things, a shot of an eight-millimeter movie projector, which throws on a small screen scenes from the street, scenes of Charlie and Johnny Boy, flashing lights in the night, a church which suddenly fills the screen, giving way to shots of the San Gennaro Festival, which will provide visual and aural background throughout the film. The scenes from the projector provide background for the credits and provide as well an active expression of the fiction/documentary tension I spoke of earlier. (Home movies will provide another kind of punctuation, as well as color footage in a film otherwise made in black and white, for *Raging Bull*, another Scorsese street film about Italians.) The immediacy and proximity of the opening shots are momentarily undercut by the projector, the home movies, the typewritten credits. Is the film we are about to see a version of Charlie's home movies? Are they somehow subjective projections of his memories? The *cinematic* reality of *Mean Streets* is stressed throughout as Scorsese intercuts scenes from his favorite films, integrating cinematic allusions into the narrative in a way he was unable to do in *Who's That Knocking?* Charlie and his friends go to see *The Searchers*, the film discussed at length by J. R. and his girl friend, the film that will have a perverse influence on *Taxi Driver*. Charlie and Johnny Boy go to see Roger Corman's *The Tomb of Ligeia*. Outside the theater Charlie stands under a poster for John

Boorman's *Point Blank* with Lee Marvin's gun pointing, forebodingly, at Johnny Boy's head. In the middle of the sequence in which Charlie and Johnny Boy are gunned down, the image of Glenn Ford standing over his wife's body in the blown-up car of Fritz Lang's *The Big Heat* suddenly appears (it turns out to be a movie on television watched by Charlie's Mafia uncle, who is oblivious to what is happening to his nephew, but oddly close to it through the image on the screen). These intrusions and allusions, like a poet's allusions to other poems within his or her work, or a jazz musician's quotations from other melodies within the piece he or she is playing, serve a double or triple function. They constitute a celebration of the medium, an indication of a cinematic community; they enrich the work by opening it out, making it responsive to other works and making others responsive to it; and they point to the nature of the film's own existence. The viewer is urged to observe the film's relation not to "reality" but to the reality of films and their influence upon each other. *Mean Streets* is a film, and by playing upon the various signs of its existence as film, it becomes a documentary not only of fictive events, but of itself.

The eight-millimeter projector is part of that self-documentation, showing fragments of Charlie's world that *Mean Streets* as a whole shows in only a slightly less fragmented way. It alludes to the way Charlie sees himself in his world, and *Mean Streets* is a documentary of how its characters, Charlie in particular, see themselves. After the credit sequence, those characters are introduced and the narrative returns to Charlie, observed in church, the church observed from his point of view as he prays and comments upon his unworthiness. The camera tracks around him as he announces his desire to do penance for his sins. He talks about the pain of hell and puts his finger over a candle flame. "You don't fuck around with the infinite. There's no way you do that. . . ." "The pain in hell has two sides," he says, "the kind you can touch with your hand; the kind you can feel with your heart. . . . You know, the worst of the two is the spiritual." And with these words there is loud rock music and a cut to a slow-motion tracking shot down the glowing red bar that is the focal point of the group's activities.

The expectations created by montage might lead one to believe that the cut on these words from Charlie and the church candles to the drifting point of view in a fiery red bar, replete with go-go dancer, indicates that this place is Charlie's hell. But unless Scorsese is adopting a literal Sartrean position, it is not hell, but merely the place where Charlie hangs out. The redness, the slow motion, the disrupting arcs around Charlie when he talks with the loan shark Michael about Johnny Boy are all disturbing and portentous. More than anything else they indicate Charlie's uncertainty of himself, an existential uncertainty of who he is and how he should act. They communicate the nascent violence of this and every situation Charlie is in (through the movement, the lack of rest, the lack of a stable eye-level gaze, the fistfight that breaks out behind Charlie between two people who have nothing to do with him). If this is hell, it is eagerly embraced by Charlie, as a place to work out his conflicts, perhaps even a place to die in, but not as a place of suffering or torture. This is, rather, a place of great vitality, even of hilarity. The relationship of all concerned is loose and joking. The joke goes very sour at the end, and serious strains in Charlie's life keep emerging. But an apparent good-naturedness is kept up most of the way. When Johnny Boy comes into the bar, Charlie says to himself, in mock piety, "We talk about penance and you send this through the door. Well, we play by your rules, don't we? Well, don't we?" The camera booms into him and cuts to his point of view of Johnny Boy, walking down the bar in slow motion as the Rolling Stones sing "Jumping Jack Flash." Charlie's guilt, his burden, is a screwy kid whom he protects and who gets them both shot up. Charlie talks about suffering and about penance, but these are deeply internalized, only a few profound signs of his suffering are seen until it emerges directly from the barrel of a gun.

A film that does not have emotional turmoil as its subject but merely as a referent, and chooses instead to make its own action its subject, is some distance from the conventional narrative that focuses on a few characters working through a defined set of problems. *Mean Streets* is not about what motivates Charlie and Johnny Boy, not about what they think and feel (although these are present), but about how they see, how Charlie perceives his world and Johnny Boy reacts to it. In none of his films will Scorsese opt for the psychological realism of explained actions, defined motivations, or identifiable characters. If his often-commented-upon Catholicism does appear in his work, it is in the form of a purgatorial sense of his characters' serving in the world, not looking for grace (if they do, they never, with the possible exception of Alice and Eddie, find it), but attempting survival and barely making it. The world they inhabit is violent in the extreme, but it is a violence that is created by the characters' very attempts to make peace with it. From the point of view of the characters in *Mean Streets*, their world is perfectly ordinary, and Scorsese reflects this through the documentary nature of many of the images. But at the same time, there is the perception of a heightened sense of reality, a stylized, expressive presence most evident in the bar sequences, in the restless, moving camera, in the fragmentary, off-center editing.

Vitality and tension are apparent not only in the images, but in the dialogue (written by Scorsese and Mardik Martin) as well. Everyone in *Mean Streets* is a compulsive talker—not obsessive, like Cassavetes's characters, who appear, at least in his early films, driven to reveal themselves through their words at all moments and always on the brink of, or deeply in, hysteria—but using words as an extension of themselves, a sign of their vitality. Their language is rooted in New York working-class usage, profoundly obscene and charged with movement.[7] The slow, self-conscious, and reflective speech of Coppola's middle-class mafiosi in *The Godfather* is here replaced by an expressive thrust of endless words. In a great set piece of the film, Johnny Boy is attempting to explain to Charlie why he does not have the money to pay off Michael (the need to pay this debt is one of the few things that provides something like a conventional "plot," though it is less like a plot than a motif). In a simple set-up located in the back room of the bar, against dark walls, punctuated by a bare light bulb hanging over Charlie, a sequence cut in simple shot/reverse shot, over-the-shoulder continuity, with an occasional far shot of the two men, De Niro tells the following story, whose telling serves to create the character who tells it:

> You don't know what happened to me. I'm so depressed about other things I can't worry about payments, ya know what I mean? I come home last Tuesday, I had my money, in cash, ya know . . . blah, blah, bing, bing, I'm comin' home, I ran into Jimmy Sparks. I owe Jimmy Sparks seven hundred, like for four months. I gotta pay the guy, he lives in my building, he hangs out across the street, I gotta pay the guy, right? So what happened? I had to give some to my mother, then I wound up with twenty-five at the end of the week. And then what happened? Today, you ain't gonna

believe, this is incredible, I can't believe it myself . . . I was in a
game, I was ahead like six, seven hundred dollars, right?
*Charlie:* You gotta be kiddin'.
*Johnny Boy:* Yeah, on Hester Street. You know Joey Clams?
*Charlie:* Yeah.
*Johnny Boy:* Joey Scalla, yeah.
*Charlie:* I know him too, yeah.
*Johnny Boy:* Yeah, no, Joey Scalla is Joey Clams.
*Charlie:* Right.
*Johnny Boy:* Right.
*Charlie:* They're the same person (*smiles*).
*Johnny Boy:* Yeah!
*Charlie:* Hey!

The dialogue between Johnny Boy (Robert De Niro) and Charlie
(Harvey Keitel) in *Mean Streets*.

*Johnny Boy:* Hey! So I was in there playing Bankers and Brokers. All of a sudden I'm ahead like six, seven hundred dollars. I'm really winnin'. All of a sudden some kid walks in and the kid yells that the bulls are comin', right? Yells that the cops are comin'. Everyone runs away, I grab all the money, I go in, it's an excuse, like, to get away . . . Ya know, and I give everybody the money back later, and that way I get out, I don't have to go into the game and get a losin' streak and all that. What happens? I come out in the yard. I don't know this buildin'. I don't know nothin', I couldn't get out, it was like a box, big, like this (*makes the shape of a box with his hands*). So I gotta go back in. Not only do I go back in, but this kid says it's a false alarm. Can you imagine that? I wanted to kill this fuckin' kid. I wanted . . . (*bites fingers in mock rage*). I was so crazy, man, I wanted to kill this kid. Meanwhile I gotta get back in the game, bing, bing, bing, I lose four hundred dollars. Meanwhile Frankie Bones is over there, Frankie Bones, I owe him thirteen hundred for like seven, eight months already. He's after me, I can't even walk on Hester Street without duckin' that guy. He's, he's like waitin' for me, like I can't move, ya know, and he sees that I'm losin', right, so like he's waitin' for me here, so he's tappin' me on the shoulder (*taps Charlie*), he says, "Hey," tappin' me like this, like a hawk, "hey, ah, get it up, you're losin', now give me some money." I says, "Hey, Frankie, come on, ya know, ya know, give me a break over here, let me win some back, ya know, I got debts, I mean I'm in the big O." He says, "Never mind, give me the money." I says, "O.K. Frankie," so I give him two hundred dollars. Meanwhile I lose the deal, I go outside, I'm a little depressed . . . anyway I wanna cut this story short, 'cause I know you don't wanna hear all this, and I know, I know, I know. But . . . (*Charlie protests that it's all right*) to make a long story short, anyway, I went to Al Kaplan, gotta new tie, I got this shirt . . . like this shirt? . . . it's nice . . . This tie. . . .

De Niro's Johnny Boy is all nervous energy and self-delight, the opposite of the serious, unsmiling, self-contained Vito Corleone whom he creates for Coppola in the second *Godfather*. The character makes himself from moment to moment, almost speaks himself into being (as opposed to the characters played by Sylvester Stallone, the eighties icon of the simple hero, whose inarticulateness uncreates his character continuously). The result is that his language and that of the other characters play a game with the viewer similar to that played by the film's images: it seems spontaneous, emerging from the moment—indeed a great deal of improvisation must have occurred in the creation of it. Yet it manifests rhythm and energy and concentration greater than could be expected were it merely made up and "overheard" on the spot (the notion of improvisation, introduced by Godard and brought into American narrative film by Cassavetes, Altman, and Scorsese, is one of the trickier problems in modern cinema, giving an effect of immediacy and spontaneity that is in fact created with craft and planning, the demands of shooting being too precise to allow for many on-the-spot changes and surprises). Like Abraham Polonsky, who in his 1948 film *Force of Evil* heightened to a poetic rhythm the diction and cadences of New York dialect, Scorsese, his co-writer, and his actors take the forms of the everyday language of a particular ethnic group, concentrate it and make it artificial, the artificiality creating the effect of the overheard and the immediate.

The language of *Mean Streets* becomes a means of self- and group-definition, speaking of an unrooted life yet at the same time attempting to root that life in a community of shared rhythms and expressions. Of course the expressions themselves can be used as weapons against this community. Early in the film Michael, the loan shark, tells Charlie that Johnny Boy is a "jerk-off," a phrase that brings Charlie immediately to his friend's defense. At the film's end, Johnny Boy throws the same phrase back at Michael, which, with the empty gun he waves at him, puts Michael in a killing rage. Words which communicate not meaning but feelings are dangerous; but they are at least alive (compare the language of Kubrick's characters, which communicates rigid, unalterable ideas and is deadening). This tension of a dangerous vitality, friendships that become provocations, a restlessness that can't be satisfied, makes up the structure of the film.

*Mean Streets* does not, finally, define itself as any one thing. Although the film depicts the activities of a group of disenfranchised urban ethnics, it does not attempt to comment on a social and economic class. A film about volatile emotions, it seems uninterested in analyzing emotions or baring souls. Although it deals with gangsters, it does not reflect upon or examine the generic tensions of the gangster film, as do *Breathless, Bonnie and Clyde*, Kubrick's early films, or the *Godfather* films.[8] What it does reflect is Scorsese's (and hopefully the viewer's) delight in

The violent climax of *Mean Streets* (the hand holding the gun is Scorsese's).

the film's capacity to capture a moment of communication, of interaction, and out of a series of such moments to fashion a sense of place and movement, energy and violence. *Mean Streets* reflects Scorsese's growing control of point of view, his ability to shift from objective to subjective observation, often intermingling the two, until, in *Taxi Driver* and *Raging Bull*, they become inextricable.

Like *Mean Streets*, the subjects of *Raging Bull* are working-class Italians in New York, and the film shares a number of elements with its predecessor. The relationship between Jake La Motta (Robert De Niro) and his brother, Joey, echoes that of Johnny Boy and Charlie. There is the nascent—and in the boxing ring quite gruesome—violence, the neighborhood tough guys, and the stylized imitation of New York, working-class speech (the film was co-scripted by Mardik Martin and Paul Schrader). And there is again the desire not to define a motivated, understandable character who dwells within a traditional narrative design. *Mean Streets*, although it contains some elements of the gangster film and of *film noir* (even, perhaps, of the thirties Warner Brothers Dead End Kids cycle), does not build itself on a firm generic base. *Raging Bull*, by the nature of its subject, is immediately associated with the sub-genre of the boxing film, and Scorsese has therefore to confront certain conventions, such as the revelation of a sensitive soul beneath the fighter's hardened exterior. The film does toy with some of the sub-genre's characteristics. Jake La Motta finds his prestige, his means of impressing himself on the world, in the boxing ring, the only safe outlet for his aggressiveness. La Motta naively desires to succeed in the sport on his own, and must confront those inevitable elements of the boxing film—the mob and their demand that he throw a fight. But these generic prerequisites, rather than reining the film into a conventional pattern, serve only to point up its eccentric structure and Scorsese's refusal to make his character and narrative conform. One need only compare *Raging Bull* with any of the *Rocky* series to see how far Scorsese moves his text outside of the pattern that elaborates the boxing ring as a successful stage for the working-class hero, or a stage for any heroics at all.[9]

Yet out of the denial of generic elements and the refusal to create a simple narrative and comfortable character continuity, Scorsese comes as close as he can to a psychological study—much closer than he does in *The Color of Money*, where actions, reactions, and motivations are more conventionally rendered than they are in the other films. *Raging Bull* is the inscription of sado-masochism onto the body of an individual who punishes himself and others because he cannot understand or control either. Like so many of Scorsese's characters, La Motta is a subject without subjectivity, without a firm comprehension of self or its location. More than the characters of *Mean Streets* or even Travis Bickle in *Taxi Driver*, La Motta exists without cultural, ideological, or even class moorings. He is a function of his vocation, his physical size (with which he must do as great battle as with any opponent), his incomprehension, and his monolithic jealousy. The characters of *Mean Streets* at least had the comfort, however uneasy, of their community. La Motta has no comfort, only the pull of his inarticulable aggression, his self-destructiveness, and his need for recognition. The narrative lurches him from one violent or demeaning situation to another. On the stage of a cheap nightclub, in the ring, or in a domestic space, La Motta gives or receives abuse.

The film opens in 1964, where an enormously fat La Motta rehearses his nightclub routine, reciting the lines that contain the film's title— "Just gimme a stage where this bull here can rage"—demeaning even his violent nickname. As he ends his act with the cliché "That's entertainment," a phrase that levels all public activity into a low level of banality, Scorsese cuts to a mid-closeup and a superimposed title, "Jake La Motta, 1964" (such identifying titles tag the film with certain documentary conventions, as they do in *Mean Streets*). A second cut shows a young, lean La Motta in the ring, poised with fists up. The title reads 1941. On the soundtrack, the La Motta of 1964 repeats "That's entertainment," and his younger incarnation gets punched violently in the face.

"Entertainment" is punishment and sacrifice, or sacrament, a means to escape from the body by using the body to give or receive pain, or as a public demonstration of the private need to inflict damage (public and private merge in a group of scenes in which Scorsese cuts from La Motta and his wife-to-be Vickie leaving the room to make love, to La Motta fighting Sugar Ray Robinson, and then back to another scene of love making).[10] The ring is where La Motta's person and personality are constituted and dissolved and the boxing matches are created as a kind of interior landscape, an arena of violent despair and terror, a dark space punctuated by photographer's flash bulbs and fights breaking out in the audience. This strange, vicious world is articulated by disembodied moans and shrieks (the soundtrack is the most carefully articulated in any of Scorsese's films), of fragmentary, slow motion shots of fists and faces receiving them with a frightful sound and explosive splatterings of sweat and blood. The point of view within the ring is of a kind of semi-consciousness and a dissolving of the self—an expression of La Motta's interiority. Outside of the ring, where events are observed somewhat more neutrally, with much of the quasi-documentary presence of streets and tenements that marks *Mean Streets*, La Motta's dislocation and lack of center are indicated by another visual signifier of weakened consciousness. When La Motta looks at his wife with the jealousy that—except for violence—is the only expression of his feelings for her, he sees her and the people she is with in slow motion, moving as if unconnected with the world, another projection of his own confusion.

An enormously fat Jake La Motta, doing his nightclub routine. Robert De Niro, *Raging Bull*.

An interesting point of contrast occurs here. In *The Color of Money*, Scorsese's other film about sports, he abjures almost all the perceptual experimentation present in *Raging Bull* and his other films. Eddie and Vincent, the two pool players, one cool, persistent—even genial—in his search for a comeback and wish to promote his younger colleague for his own profit, the other arrogant, unrestrained, rebelling against the older man's using of him, exhibit none of the alienation, anger, and violence that bulge up in Jake La Motta. The streets, motel rooms, and pool halls through which they move are more neutral, less charged with energy than similar locations in the other films, for here there is no vital or aberrant personality for them to reflect. The struggle between characters inside the film and star personalities who are creating the characters absorbs a great deal of energy. The characters that are finally created are themselves more calculating and self-aware than Jake La Motta or indeed any other figure in Scorsese's work (and demonstrate none of the moral urgency present in the characters of Robert Rossen's 1961 film, *The Hustler*, to which *The Color of Money* is something of a sequel). The pool sequences show some of the invention of the boxing matches in *Raging Bull*—explosions of virtuoso camera movement, image and sound editing—but they often seem to grow out of a directorial uncertainty or discomfort rather than the necessity of *mise-en-scène* and character. More than anything else, they signify attempts to make Scorsesian cinema out of the minimally dynamic movements of the ball on the pool table. They erupt out of the otherwise flat and inexpressive ground of over-the-shoulder shots of Eddie and Vincent talking to each other and represent Scorsese's own energy breaking through the self—or commercially—imposed restrictions of form that oppress the film.

*The Color of Money* is, one can hope, an anomaly in Scorsese's work, whereas *Raging Bull* continues the line of inquiry into inarticulateness and ideological abandonment that was begun in *Mean Streets*. In both films the characters are unassimilated into the dominant discourse of the culture, and must talk or—in the case of Jake La Motta—fight their way into a temporary presence, which vanishes when they do. This futile attempt to establish the self, to constitute subjectivity within a disinterested world is a constant thematic of Scorsese's films, pursued in a variety of contexts and with many variations of the documentary/expressionist approach. And if *Raging Bull* is an extension of *Mean Streets*, it is also a reconsideration of the ideas Scorsese developed in *Taxi Driver*, which is the centerpiece of his work and the one that best represents the control of *mise-en-scène* and the play of perceptions within it. *Taxi Driver* also is the film that most violently and ironically works through the problem of the dislocated subject.

Like *Raging Bull*, *Taxi Driver* is an extension of *Mean Streets*. But where the earlier film examines a small, isolated urban sub-community and the later one an individual, sadomasochistic individual who finds some outlet in a larger community of organized sports, *Taxi Driver* focuses on one isolated urban sub-individual who has difficulty making any contact with the external world. Where *Mean Streets* presents its characters in tenuous control of their environment, at home in their surroundings, and *Raging Bull* a character whose emotional environment is the battleground of his own body, *Taxi Driver* presents its character trapped by his environment, swallowed and imprisoned. More accurately, the objective-subjective points of view of *Mean Streets* and *Raging Bull*, which permit the viewer to look both at and with the characters, is replaced by a subjective point of view that forces the viewer continually to see as the character sees, creating a *mise-en-scène* that expresses, above all, the obsessive vision of a madman. Finally, where *Mean Streets* celebrates urban life in its violence and its community, and *Raging Bull* points to violence as the formal, even sanctioned means of an individual's expression of self, *Taxi Driver* rigorously structures a path to violence that is separate from community, separate from the exigencies of any "normal" life, separate from any rational comprehension and need, but only the explosion of an individual attempting to escape from a self-made prison. An individual who, in his madness, attempts to act the role of a movie hero.

*Mean Streets* is a diffuse *film noir*, its dark, enclosed, violent urban world recalling many of the *noir* conventions. But, despite its violent end, it escapes the total bleakness of *noir* precisely because of its sense of community. Even though its characters *are* trapped, they do not evidence the loneliness, dread, and anxiety manifested in *film noir* (nor does Jake La Motta, whose absence of a defined self is also an absence of self-consciousness). Again, despite the cruelty that ends the film, the bulk of it emphasizes a friendship—albeit unstable—among its characters. *Taxi Driver,* however, renders the conventions of *film noir* in an immediate, frightening manner. The film's central character lives completely enclosed in a city of dreadful night, so removed and alone that everything he sees becomes a reflection of his own distorted perceptions. Travis Bickle (De Niro again, in a performance that matches the one in *Raging Bull* for the degree of its obsessiveness) is the last *noir* man in the ultimate *noir* world: closed and dark, a paranoid universe of perversion, obsession, and violence. In the creation of this world, Scorsese goes to the roots of *film noir*, to certain tenets of German Expressionism that call for "a selective and creative distortion" of the world by means of which the creator of a work can represent "the complexity of the psyche" through a visual style that exposes the "object's internal life, the expression of its soul."[11] Scorsese does want to "expose" the inner life of his character, but not to explain it. As with Jake La Motta, the internal life of Travis Bickle remains an enigma throughout the film. The subject without subjectivity cannot be explained, even through the most dreadful violence, and a major concern of the film is to frustrate viewer attempts at understanding that mind. But, as always, Scorsese is very interested in communicating the way a world looks as it is perceived by such a mind, and he uses "a selective and creative distortion" of perception in extraordinary ways, more formally coherent and extensive than he will in his later films.

I want the focus of my analysis to continue examining the ways Scorsese creates his expressionist, *noir mise-en-scène*, and how he asks the viewer to observe and even enter it. But before proceeding with that analysis, it is necessary to inquire briefly into the role of Paul Schrader, who wrote the script for the film and who has received some attention from its critics. Schrader—whose work I briefly discussed earlier—is an articulate screenwriter and director, whose essay on *film noir* remains the best on the subject and offers pertinent ideas for an understanding of *Taxi Driver*. However, most critics have chosen to look at his book, *Transcendental Style in Film: Ozu, Bresson, Dreyer*, to help explain *Taxi Driver* and the apparent disparity between what Schrader might have intended and what Scorsese executes. Many of these critics wanted to see in the film a study of Travis Bickle as a lost and insular but coherent and self-contained individual, in the manner of a Robert Bresson character who achieves a spiritual grace by the almost negative persistence of his activities (the kind of character Schrader attempts to create in his own *American Gigolo* and, to a certain extent, in *Mishima*, though here the matter is rendered difficult because the original figure on whom the character is based was a fascist, and Schrader is not quite able to deal with the political aspects of the personality).

Certainly, if this was Schrader's intent, Scorsese has perverted it.[12]

For Scorsese's character starts and ends without grace, persists in unmotivated fits and starts, and lives in a world so much his own creation—or, better, his own perception—that no salvation is possible, for there is no one to save and no one to do the saving. If Schrader intended *Taxi Driver* to be an inquiry into spiritual isolation and redemption, the loneliness and transcendence of the outcast, the film presents no such transcendental material, for this is not the way Scorsese sees individuals inhabiting their world. He has rooted his film in the very earthbound context of the madness of a lonely, barely coherent individual who cannot make sane associations between the distorted fragments of his perceptions. The "salvation" he receives, the recognition he gains for gunning down a mafioso and freeing a young runaway from a brothel, is simply ironic, the result of other people's distorted perceptions, and in no way changes the central character or his inability to understand himself or his world. If anything, it aggravates it, for there is an indication at the film's end that Travis Bickle has some glimmering and fleeting recognition of his madness, but only enough to make him turn away from that recognition.

One problem does arise in the film when elements that attempt to give Travis more character and "motivation" than Scorsese wishes him to have seem to intrude. The problem appears in the diary—Schrader's invention and borrowed from Bresson's *Diary of a Country Priest*—that the character keeps and which he reads in voice-over throughout the film. In discussing the use of voice-over commentary in the films of Bresson, Schrader writes that the "narration does not give the viewer any new information or feelings, but only reiterates what he already knows. . . ; it only doubles his perception of the event. Consequently, there is a schizoid reaction; one, there is the sense of meticulous detail which is a part of the everyday, and two, because the detail is doubled there is an emotional queasiness, a growing suspicion of the seemingly 'realistic' rationale behind the everyday."[13] Schrader and Scorsese follow this Bressonian principle only sporadically. For example, Travis is observed in his cab and, from his point of view, street after dismal street is seen, populated solely by hookers. His voice comments: "All the animals come out at night, whores, skunk pussies, buggers, queens, fairies, dopers, junkies." Here the voice-over does strongly double the viewer's perceptions of Travis's one-dimensional view, emphasizing, along with

the visuals, the selectiveness of his point of view that makes the viewer
"queasy" and "suspicious" over the relationship between Travis's
"reality" and any that is likely to be experienced outside his gaze. But
when, later, Travis suddenly uses words like "sick" and "venal" to
describe the world he has chosen to see, or says of himself, "All my life
needed was a sense of someplace to go. . . . I don't believe that one
should devote his life to morbid self-attention. I believe that someone
should become a person like other people," the voice-over comes per-
ilously close to the old convention of psychological motivation. Travis,
in words quite above the diction level he usually uses (early in the film,
talking to the manager of the cab company, he did not even know what
"moonlighting" meant), is suddenly offering reasons for his behavior.
Schrader and Scorsese are allowing the entry of language that gives an
analytic cast to the character, unsupported by what is seen of or by him.
This is language that offers possibilities that motivation and rationale,
of a conventional kind, will allow the viewer to "understand" and
account for the character, and perhaps dismiss him as yet another tortured soul.

   While Travis is speaking of himself in the words just quoted, the
images and music track lead in quite different directions. For this
sequence Bernard Herrmann provides a thudding sound almost like a
heartbeat.* Travis is lying expressionless in bed. His face is expressionless, but the camera, craning over and down to him, provides a commentary more eloquent than the words. Travis is a paralyzed being;
what feelings he has come in abrupt, disconnected spurts. The movement of the camera is almost a lunge toward him, which expresses both
an attempt to approach him (to carry the gaze close to a figure we feel
we must understand) and a repulsion from him, for the angle of
approach to the figure is too disorienting; no one could ever "normally"
see a figure from this angle and with this approach. And it is just this
tension of attraction and repulsion that the film depends upon to keep
the viewer at an appropriate distance from the character and to with-
hold an explanation of who or why Travis Bickle is. His voice-over

-----

*I wish it were possible to describe, in other than imprecise, impressionistic language, the
facets of Herrmann's score for this film and the ways it models the various sequences. The
score is his last, and ranks just after his music for *Citizen Kane*, *Vertigo*, and *Psycho*.

commentary at this point, as at others, is a distraction and a false clue to an enigma.

Perhaps it would be fairer to the film and to Schrader and Scorsese to disregard the obviously abortive Bressonian influences (or simply to acknowledge their presence and how they do and do not work) and look rather at Schrader's concepts of the *noir* hero in order to understand Schrader's contribution to the creation of Travis Bickle and his perverse universe. "The ... final phase of *film noir*," Schrader writes of the period 1949-53,

> was the period of psychotic action and suicidal impulse. The *noir* hero, seemingly under the weight of ... years of despair, started to go bananas. The psychotic killer, who had in the first period been a subject worthy of study ... now became the active protagonist. ... *Film noir*'s final phase was the most aesthetically and sociologically piercing. After ten years of steadily shedding romantic conventions, the later *noir* films finally got down to the root causes of the period: the loss of public honor, heroic conventions, personal integrity, and, finally, psychic stability. The third phase films were painfully self-aware; they seemed to know they stood at the end of a long tradition based on despair and distintegration and did not shy away from that fact. ... Because *film noir* was first of all a style, because it worked out its conflicts visually rather than thematically, because it was aware of its own identity, it was able to create artistic solutions to sociological problems.[14]

Certainly *Taxi Driver* is aware of its own formal identity, more so than the films of the period Schrader discusses precisely because it comes after them. The film defines its central character not in terms of social problems (though it does suggest these) nor by any *a priori* ideas of noble suffering and transcendent madness, but by the ways the character is perceived and perceives himself and his surroundings. He is the climactic *noir* figure, much more isolated and very much madder than his forebears. No cause is given for him, no understanding allowed; he stands formed by his own loneliness and trapped by his own isolation, his actions and reactions explicable only through those actions and reactions. I do not mean to be enigmatic, only to indicate that Scorsese has made a film that not only expresses insularity and psychosis, but is insular itself. In the tradition of *film noir,* the world created by *Taxi*

*Driver* exists only within its own space, a space which is itself formed by the state of mind of its central character, in that strange double perception in which the viewer sees the world the way the character sees it and sees the character himself, thereby permitting both proximity and separation.

*Taxi Driver* does suffer somewhat from a split between its screenwriting and its director's intentions. But it is an important and still valid premise of the *auteur* theory that the director absorbs, or, better, re-creates the script into something else—the film itself, which is more than the script. If we assume that Schrader's notions of the formal integrity of *film noir* are valid, we can forget about Bresson—whose very *lack* of expressiveness and whose insistence upon suppressing the internal and subjective makes his work inapplicable to Scorsese's film—and proceed to a close examination of this film about the "despair and disintegration" of a psychotic killer who is its active protagonist. In its very first shot are found the methods of presentation that will be at work throughout.

The shot is of the front end of a Checker cab emerging from smoke, and is immediately recognizable. The streets of New York often have steam pouring from their manhole covers, and such a sight, at night, illuminated by headlamps, is quite striking. Scorsese therefore begins with an image familiar to anyone who knows New York. But at the same time he instantly defamiliarizes it, makes it strange.* The smoke is yellowish, and the taxi that emerges from it is not so much moving as looming, viewed from a low angle and traveling at a speed too slow and regular for it to be an "actual" cab on the street. The music which accompanies this presence is percussive and slowly accelerates in tempo and loudness, not unlike a car engine starting in slow motion. The shot dissolves to a tight closeup of a pair of eyes, first tinted red, then normal in color, then red and white. The eyes move back and forth, scanning, blankly, something as yet unseen by the viewer. A dissolve to the reverse shot (what the eyes are seeing) shows the world outside the cab

---

*The notion of defamiliarization, "making strange," was developed by the Russian formalist Viktor Shklovsky. He applied it to aesthetic creation and perception in general, but it seems particularly apt in accounting for the way the viewer is forced to see things in a work like *Taxi Driver*.[15]

through a wet and blurred windshield. The people and traffic seen through the windshield are hard-edged, but their movements are multiplied and extended so that they leave trails of light and traces of their forms (this is, of course, a special effect, and therefore calls attention to itself as a specific filmic device as well as a perceptual aberration). The shot dissolves again to people going by on the streets, tinted red and blue, and moving through the smoke in slow motion; there is a dissolve back to the eyes looking left to right and then to the smoke with which the sequence opened.

Some critics have referred to this sequence, and the opening shot in particular, as an emergence from hell. This is an evocative analogy, but misses the point. It is precisely the lack of definition, the lack of knowable space, which has about it just the hint of the recognizable and the everyday that makes it so disturbing. The defamiliarizing of the familiar; the introduction of the blankly moving eyes (again, cinematic convention connects the title of the film, the shot of the cab, and the eyes, so that the viewer assumes they are the eyes of the driver; cinematic history refers the eyes and the flashing light to the opening sequence of Bernardo Bertolucci's *The Conformist* (1970), another film about aberrant perception and personality, whose opening is itself influenced by the credit sequence of Nicholas Ray's *In A Lonely Place* (1950); the strange movement of the people on the street (which recalls the slow-motion crowd in the bar sequence in *Mean Streets*, which indicated Charlie's detachment from what he sees, and anticipates the slow-motion point of view shots given to La Motta in *Raging Bull*); the gaze both at and from this foreboding car and its occupant moves the viewer into a realm of distortion and threat in which he or she remains throughout the film. This credit sequence is also outside the narrative proper (in the sequence following this, Travis goes to a cab company to ask for a job driving) and is therefore out of time, a kind of perpetual state of mind that diffuses itself over the film.

As the smoke clears, Travis, viewed from behind, enters the cab company to ask for work. His movement is accompanied by the crescendo of the main musical theme. As an exposition of plot, the ensuing sequence is simple. The antagonism between the cab owner and Travis offers a direct expression of anger that envelops the film as a whole, and their dialogue supplies some minimal information about the character:

he can't sleep at night; he goes to porn movies; he was in the Marines. But more than what is said and done, what is seen in this sequence and the way it is seen continue to provoke, almost subliminally, discomfort and perceptual dislocation. The camera observes Travis from behind as he stands over the cab owner. Opposite him, through an opening in the wall, two men are arguing. Barely heard, they play no direct role in the sequence (on second viewing one of the arguing men is recognized as Wizard (Peter Boyle), who will be one of Travis's cronies at the all-night cafeteria, and to whom Travis will attempt to disburden himself—"I got some bad ideas in my head"); but they form a focus of attention in the shot and literally reflect Travis, the angry, inarticulate man. The reverse of this shot, the look at Travis, places him low in the frame, too low and off-center, so that behind him a man seated on a stool seems too large for the perspective of the shot. A bit later, when asked about his license, Travis answers that it's clean, "real clean, just like my conscience." The cab owner blows up at him, and the camera booms up and forward, bringing Travis too close. The placement of the character in both of these shots and the movement toward him in the second is too portentous for the narrative function at the moment. The portent is greater than the immediate action and that skews the reaction that one might have to a coventional expository dialogue sequence. The placing of a character in unexpected parts of the frame, particularly in closeups that are off-center or off-angle, is a device that Scorsese is here borrowing from Hitchcock, from whom he has learned the ability to load viewer perceptions, offering something more than is expected, and preparing the viewer, almost unconsciously, for events to come.

When Travis leaves the dispatcher's office, the camera follows him to the cab garage, but leaves him to pan across its dark space, following a totally peripheral character (Wizard, again), picking up Travis as he walks back into the frame and out to the street. At first look, this seems a perfectly ordinary way to get a character from one point to another without cutting. But the question arises as to why the camera doesn't stay with him all the way rather than abandon him for an anonymous character. It is a curious shot, and is related to an even more curious shot later in the film. Following Travis's disastrous date with Betsy (Cybill Shepherd), during which he takes her to a porn movie only to have her walk out on him in outrage, he calls her from a public phone in an office building. Travis is observed at a distance, off-center, talking on the phone. His face is turned away. He is solicitous to Betsy and agonizingly simple-minded, concerned that she has the flu, wondering if she got the flowers he sent her (she says she didn't, and in the next sequence we see his room filled with dead flowers). Suddenly, the camera begins to move away from Travis, tracking to the right and coming to rest before a corridor that leads out to the street. It stays there as, off-screen now, Travis finishes the conversation. As he begins a voice-over comment on how Betsy refused to come to the phone on subsequent calls, he walks into the frame and down the corridor.

The compositional structure of the film resituates the viewer, forcing her or him to share the spatial dislocations of a character who is radically displaced from his environment, and who perceives that environment empty of any "normal" articulations and filled rather with his own aberrations. The camera observes him in unconventional and uncomfortable placements within the frame, even removing him from the frame entirely when the camera indicates, unexpectedly and disconcertingly, the spaces around him—the neutral spaces of the taxi garage or the barren space of an office hallway, the highly significant spaces of his room, with its cracked walls, dead flowers, boxes of junk food. Scorsese also explores the expressive possibilities of temporal distortion. I noted that the narrative is encased within the timeless drift of the cab through the distorted streets, a drift that opens and closes the film and punctuates it throughout. There is the slow-motion movement of the people on those streets and the visual multiplication of their movements. And there is also this odd occurrence after Travis leaves the taxi garage in the sequence discussed earlier. The camera picks him up in a far shot walking up the street. Sunlight brightens the buildings behind him, but he is in shadow. There is, quite unexpectedly, a lap dissolve. But rather than moving to another place and time, which is the conventional meaning of this device, it merely moves Travis a little closer forward in the shot and shows him taking a drink from a bottle in a paper bag. The effect here is produced not by any new expository information, turn in the plot, or by a dramatic interchange, but simply by a cinematic device that works against expectations and is therefore disturbing, setting up a complicated relationship with the character.

The lap dissolve, as I said, is conventionally used to signify a lapse of time and/or a change of place. Here the effect is rather of a momentary lapse of consciousness, or of a drifting unbound by time, a perception by us of the character's state of mind. Scorsese will repeat the device during the "You talkin' to me?" sequence, as Travis accelerates his psychotic preparations for murder (and repeat it again with somewhat diminished effect in *After Hours*, when Paul Hackett mounts the steps to the Soho loft where his strange evening will begin; by the time of *The Color of Money*, the device ceases to be an expression of perception, and returns to its conventional role as signifier of time passing). In all instances it forces the viewer to look at the character and disturbs that look at the same time. As with the other acts of visual displacement, the gaze is dislocated, disrupted, and the viewer is permitted neither proximity to the central character, sympathy with him, nor comfortable distance.* Within this context the shifts in diction between Travis's speech and his voice-over diary entries, which I earlier criticized, might be understood: they become further acts of dislocation, further denials of coherency in the character.

The viewer, made to gaze *at* the character in particularly discomforting ways, is made as well to gaze *with* the character himself, to see the world as he sees it. This is done immediately in the credit sequence through the appearance of the people in the street, and more forcefully, because more subtly, in the observation of the men arguing in the cab owner's office. His gaze is joined whenever he drives in his cab. Whores and gangs inhabit every street, whores and their clients, and would-be murderers are his fares. "Did you ever see what a forty-four magnum pistol can do to a woman's face?" asks a passenger (played by Scorsese) as he forces Travis to pull over to the curb and look with him at an apartment where, he says, his wife is having an affair with a black man (the gaze of two psychotics, one the function of the other, join, doubling the viewer's distressed perceptions). "I mean, it'll fuckin' destroy her.

*Scorsese may have gotten the idea for the dissolve that plays against temporal and spatial expectations from Bernardo Bertolucci, who creates a similar effect in *Before the Revolution* (1964) and *The Spider's Stratagem* (1970). In the latter film, two characters have a conversation which is continually interrupted by fades to black—a transitional device similar to, though more emphatic than, the dissolve. But the fades do not actually interrupt anything, for each time the scene returns the conversation continues with no indication of a major change in time.

Just blow her right apart. . . . Now did you ever see what it can do to a
woman's pussy? That you should see. . . . I know you must think I'm
pretty sick. . . . I'm paying for the ride. You don't have to answer." And
through it all, Travis remains impassive. He never looks at his passen-
gers except through his rear-view mirror. He never reacts when his cab
is spattered by a water hydrant or by garbage. A man walking down the
street with his shirt pulled over his head or another yelling down the
street over and over again, "I'll kill her, I'll kill her," brings no reaction
from him.

Neither coincidence nor a reflection of "reality" explains why the
only people Travis sees are the mad and the disenfranchised, why the

only streets he sees are the stews of the city, why the cafeteria frequented late at night by him and his cronies is populated only by pimps and nodding drug addicts. These are the only people and the only places of which Travis is aware. They constitute the only things he perceives, and, since the viewer's perceptions in the film are so restricted to his own, the only things the viewer is permitted to perceive as well. The camera, therefore, does not, as Diane Jacobs suggests, appear "helpless to avert its gaze from the horrors that walk in its path," nor does it revel "secretly in the filth and the suffocation."[16] Rather it takes a very active role in transmitting a point of view which may itself be helpless to avert its gaze from filth and ugliness. Travis is prey to his own isolated and

God's lonely man *(opposite, below)*: Travis Bickle (Robert De Niro) in *Taxi Driver*.

isolating gaze (a gaze that is infected with the myth of New York as a foul sewer—the "New York-ness" mentioned earlier), and the viewer, in turn, is prey to it. *Taxi Driver* is not a documentary of the squalor of New York City but the documentation of a squalid mind driven mad by its perception.

*Taxi Driver* is the portrait of an obsessive, a passive obsessive, so oppressed by his isolation that when he does act, it is only upon the dark and disconnected impulses triggered by his perceptions. There is, as I have noted, no analysis of, nor reasons given for, his behavior— none, at least, that make a great deal of rational sense. He can, perhaps, be viewed as a radically alienated urban castoff, a mutant produced by the incalculable dehumanization of post-industrial society (the news continually makes us aware of the random murderers who keep appearing and disappearing in our culture). But the film withholds any political, social, or even psychological analysis. (The presence of a presidential candidate who becomes Travis's aborted target is used only to point out how terribly distant vulgar politics is from "the people" it professes to address.) However, after saying this, I must point out that the film does not neglect an analysis of the cultural aberrations that afflict Travis, and, by extension, viewers of the film. Scorsese quietly, even hilariously, suggests one possible motivation for, or result of, Travis's psychosis. The more deeply he withdraws, the more he comes to believe in the American movie myths of purity and heroism, love and selflessness, and to actuate them as the grotesque parodies of human behavior they are. Travis Bickle is the legitimate child of John Wayne and Norman Bates: pure, self-righteous, violent ego and grinning, homicidal lunatic; each the obverse of the other; each equally dangerous. Together they create a persona so out of touch with ordinary human experience that the world he inhabits and perceives becomes an expressionist *noir* nightmare, an airless and dark trap that its inhabitant escapes only by drawing everything into it with him. The final irony occurs when Travis's act of slaughter, which he believes is an act of liberation and purification, is taken as such by everyone else, and the viewer finds him or herself potentially caught by the same aberrations as he; the double perspective offered by the film fuses, and the lunatic is momentarily accepted as hero.

In fact the closeness forged between spectator and character point of view, and the gap in understanding or comprehension of that character, create a confusion that finally makes it difficult to see just how tightly the movements to destruction are drawn and how those movements are shaped by the various myths and ideological distortions that play upon the little that remains of the character's mind. Travis gets involved with two women, each not a character as much as a further creation of his aberrant sensibility. Betsy, the campaign worker for the clichéd liberal candidate, Charles Palantine, is, by Travis's own admission, a dream girl. She is a fantasy figure from a fifties movie, appearing to him as a woman in white who comes "like an angel" out of the "filthy mass" he sees himself living in. "They cannot touch her," he says, emphasizing each word (further emphasized by the camera's panning across the words written in Travis's diary). As Travis spies on her from outside campaign headquarters, the viewer is given a privileged look at her, unmediated by Travis, with her fellow workers, and she turns out to be a perfectly mediocre personality involved in mindless conversation. Her ordinariness is played against Travis's stare, his impassive observation punctuated by strong camera movements which destabilize the space he occupies and make his presence a threat. When Travis invades Betsy's office, he speaks to her in the words of a movie hero. He says she's the most beautiful woman he has ever met; he thinks she is lonely, that she needs a friend. He projects his own feelings on her in such sentimental terms that she can hardly help but react to them. (But why would a sane woman react at all to a weird man who has been staring at her and then greets her with a line out of a rotten movie? Is she fooled by his charm? Is it because this is really Robert De Niro talking to Cybill Shepherd? Is it, as Patricia Patterson and Manny Farber suppose, just bad scripting and improbable motivation and reaction?[17] Or is Scorsese allowing Travis's fantasy—and the viewer's—to play out a while? One of the things movies tell us is that it is not impossible for the most improbable boy to win the beautiful girl.)

Scorsese is not entirely disinterested in the character of Betsy. He allows her to play with Travis, to indulge a kind of preppy curiosity about the freakish and the threatening. Once they begin talking—in a cafeteria sequence which is edited so that Betsy often appears in a shot over Travis's shoulder, but he almost always in a shot alone—it is clear how separate they are. Betsy says he reminds her of a song by Kris Kristofferson. "Who's that?" asks Travis. Betsy quotes from the song: "He's a prophet and a pusher, partly truth, partly fiction, a walking contradiction." This is perfectly meaningless to Travis. "You saying that about me? . . . I'm no pusher." "Just the part about the contradictions. You are that," says Betsy, who might as well be talking to no one. In the next sequence Travis is seen buying the Kristofferson record, or more accurately, part of him is seen, his arm, with a military patch that says "King Kong Company," through the window of the record store. Betsy is wrong. He is not a contradiction, but a thing of disconnected parts, any one of which can take momentary precedence until another disconnected part jars momentarily into place. The shuffling Andy Hardy romancer takes his white angel to a porn movie, and when she flees, condemns her to hell and says she is cold like all women. Cold "like a union," he says, drawing on a notion of people in groups, a notion totally repellent to this lonely man.

The second woman, or girl rather, is a twelve-year-old prostitute, who tries to get into Travis's cab and is pulled out by her pimp, who throws Travis a twenty-dollar bill. The event occurs midway between his first meeting with Betsy and his taking her to the porn movie, and just after he has picked up the candidate Betsy works for. This is a marvelously contrived series of coincidences (as most any movie plot is), and serves to echo the random, fragmentary nature of Travis himself. Betsy will put Travis over the edge; candidate Palantine will be his first object of violence; Iris (Jodie Foster), the baby whore, will catalyze the explosion. There is no real connection between them, except that they are all clichés, all the reflections of a junk-food mind to which women are either white angels or poor girls in distress, and presidential candidates clean, dashing men who, being clean, will clean up the mess that Travis is obsessed with. "The president should clean up this whole mess here," he tells a slightly astonished Palantine, "should flush it down the fuckin' toilet." If Palantine can salvage Travis's world, then Travis can save Iris from hers. Or, if no one can cleanse Travis's world, then he at least can save one person from it. Never mind that Iris is too stoned to know what Travis is talking about and is living in circumstances similar to those of her would-be savior. Living, that is, under the oppression of clichés. In one of the few sequences of the film which does not encompass Travis's point of view, Iris and her pimp, Sport (played with outrageous menace and unctuousness by Harvey Keitel), are alone in the red-orange light of their room. Sport plays out a strange ritual of seduction and ownership, holding Iris to him (she comes up to his chest) and dancing her about the room. "I depend on you," he says. "When you're close to me like this I feel so good. I only wish every man could know what it's like to be loved by you.... It's only you that keeps me together."

Iris is torn between two sets of platitudes, the concerned protective language of Travis and the cheap sentiment of Sport, whose words to her are like the junk food Travis is always eating, superficially filling but empty and finally destructive. Like junk food they are addictive, and therefore imprisoning. Hearing these words and seeing Iris's situation outside of Travis's perception set up a peculiar tension: either Travis, in all his madness, is correct in wanting to "save" Iris from her situation because it is repulsive and inhuman, or he is blind to the ludicrousness of the situation of a little girl secure within a grotesque parody of affection stronger than he can know, and therefore his desire to help her is meaningless because she neither desires nor needs any help. Throughout the film, the world is perceived as Travis perceives it; now, briefly, it is seen without him, and it appears hopeless, outrageously hopeless, yet carrying a suggestion that the loneliness that Travis sees and experiences everywhere can be mitigated. The mitigation is cruel and fraudulent, but it is something compared with nothing. The destructive solitude of the family, to which Iris is returned after she is "freed" by Travis, a solitude we hear about through the droning voice of her father, reading a letter he has written to Travis, may be cleaner and more moral, but no less oppressive and sentimental.

It would be foolish to imply that the film is advocating teenage prostitution; that is not the question at hand. Scorsese is examining aspects of an ugly world, a non-bourgeois world that has adopted the other's clichés and revealed them as destructive. Travis is slowly destroyed by those clichés until, becoming the demonic parody of the avenging hero, he becomes a destroyer. In his dealings with Iris, he becomes nothing less than a parody of John Wayne's Ethan Edwards in Ford's 1956 film *The Searchers* (the film that obsesses Scorsese's alter ego, J. R., in *Who's That Knocking at My Door?* and which Charlie goes to see in *Mean Streets*). Ethan is himself a figure of neurotic obsession, who wants to rescue his niece from the Indians because of his hatred of miscegenation and his desire to purify her and bring her back to white civilization. (Certainly Sport, in his hippie gear, is meant to be a version of Ethan Edwards's rival, Chief Scar, even though it is Travis who wears the Mohawk haircut.) The equation—Travis Bickle as Wayne's Ethan; Iris as Natalie Wood's Debbie; and Sport as the Chief—is perfect. Like Debbie, who becomes accommodated to the Indians before Ethan rescues her, Iris has accommodated to her world; it is an ugly accommodation, but it works on its own terms. Like Chief Scar, Sport attempts to protect his people, and like Ethan, Travis will overcome all odds, will risk his life, to save what is left of Iris's innocence. Travis believes in the rightness of his plan, as does his filmic forebear. What he does not see is that his whole notion of saving people is based on a movie cliché of heroic activity (which Ford himself questioned), a cliché that his madness seems to make valid. Iris passively submits to the clichés of squalid sentimentality; Travis submits to the clichés of violent action. (Betsy believes movie clichés, too; she is fooled by them until Travis attempts to draw her directly into his world, at which point she flees; the angel in white cannot exist in the dark hole of a porno house.) The different reactions of Iris and Travis to their predicament are presented in a strong montage that follows upon the sequence between Sport and Iris. As the pimp dances his whore away with loving words, shots are heard on the sound track. There is a cut to Travis, isolated in the square opening of a shooting gallery. As he shoots, the square leaps forward, persistence, threat, single-mindedness, madness directly confronting the viewer.

The violence that Travis commits in his attempt to "save" Iris (or, more accurately, the violence that Scorsese creates on the screen) is the most problematic aspect of *Taxi Driver*. It is so enormous that it seems, on first viewing, to rupture an otherwise carefully restrained and thoughtfully constructed film, finally obviating that restraint by overwhelming it. At the time, and on one viewing, the sequence could be considered one of the more cynical moments in contemporary American film. This needs a context. By 1976 the simulation of violence had reached a level of mindlessness and predictability that left only three alternatives: exaggerate it to more insane proportions in order to elicit a thrill from an audience dulled by endlessly exploding hemoglobin bags and men careening backward from the force of a shotgun blast; show an actual death; or forget the whole set of conventions, retire the various forms of brutality and consider some other manifestations of human behavior. By 1978, that current of film violence had largely run its course, only to be revived again in the horror, slasher, and revenge films of the early and mid-eighties. But in 1976, there was some indication that the second alternative, the filming of an actual death, could be conceivable. The rumor and brief public appearance of "snuff" films (one of them was called *Snuff* and purported to show the "actual" dismemberment of a woman) threatened to overturn the conventional relationships between film and its subjects by inverting the conventions of narrative art.[18] Were the "snuff" films "real," the contract of narrative film that states that what we see on the screen is a lie (does not *really* happen) would have to be rewritten. All distance between what is seen and what is understood by what is seen would be lost. The question would no longer involve a viewer becoming prisoner to an illusion of reality—or of attending a documentation of reality— but being guilty of assenting to the actual event of murder. The only real meaning of such films would emerge from the moral choice of attending them or not.

The snuff films were probably lies (I did not see them, and I say they were lies out of a certain need for self-assurance and protection); they failed to gain an audience (surely a sign that we do need the protection of fiction); but it is impossible to downplay the significance of their appearance at the time, or their reappearance in modified form in the *Faces of Death* videotapes which were among the highest renters at local video shops during the mid-eighties. The documentation or representation of violence and death must respond to a deep need for mastery on the part of many viewers, and no doubt an equally deep need to see represented the aggressiveness that is embedded in the general ideology but repressed in reality. Certainly they respond to an irrepressible desire for exploitation on the part of filmmakers and distributors.

Scorsese cannot be entirely absolved of exploitative intent. He is a commercial filmmaker and violence of some kind has always been part of his *mise-en-scène*, part of the way in which he understands the world. That is its only possible defense. The violence in *Taxi Driver* grows and develops out of the entire structure of the film and is, finally, so stylized that it provides commentary on the whole perceptual complex of violence in film. At the same time it is enormous and insistent enough to create a very real nausea. Travis prepares to shoot down candidate Palantine at a rally. "My whole life has been pointed in one direction," he comments. "There never has been any choice for me." The obsessive decides that there is an object for his obsessiveness. Packed with weapons, his hair shaved like an Indian, he attends the rally, is spotted, and runs. (It is of interest to note that "freeing" Iris by violence is not the first act Travis considers. Killing is his major impulse, and that urge connects itself to Iris only after the attempted assassination fails.) He returns home, drinks beer, and takes aspirin. At night he goes to Sport's apartment building in the East Village, where, after taunting Sport (who throws a lit cigarette butt at him), he shoots him in the stomach and goes off down the street to sit on a stoop. He returns to the building and enters, the dark interior appearing somewhat like the set of a German Expressionist film. The camera tracks through the corridors. An avuncular old man, who was earlier seen as the money collector for Sport's brothel, pursues Travis, who turns and shoots fingers off the old man's hand (close up and in slow motion—reminiscent of the scene in *McCabe and Mrs. Miller* where the Reverend's hand is shot off by the gunman, Butler). Sport reappears and shoots Travis in the neck. Travis shoots Sport some more. The camera assumes a position above the stairs; we hear the sound of blood trickling, and there is a momentary calm, broken by Travis shooting more bullets into Sport and shooting and beating the old man, who starts running after him, yelling maniacally, "You crazy son of a bitch . . . I'll kill you. I'll kill you. I'll kill you."

At this point, in slow motion, a customer opens the door of Iris's room. There is a cut to a shot of Travis being pursued by the old man, and a return to Iris's customer, who shoots Travis in the arm. The maniacal catapult that Travis has built to hold one of his guns and deliver it to his hand pops out and allows him to shoot the customer in the face (as De Niro's Vito Corleone shoots Fanucci in *Godfather II*). The old man, still yelling "I'll kill you," grabs Travis from behind as they enter Iris's room. They fight on the floor; Travis gets a knife he has concealed around his ankle, stabs the old man in the hand (the one that was not shot earlier), and then blows the old man's brains out, spattering the wall with blood (through all this, Iris's sobbing creates a counterpoint

to the gunshots and the dripping blood). Travis now puts a gun to his *Attempted*
throat and pulls the trigger, but it is empty. He sits down, and as the *suicide*
police enter (emissaries from the sane world who appear menacing as *fails*
they first peer through the door, but soon bring a calming order to the
scene), he puts a bloody finger to his head, works it like a gun, and,
smiling, lays his head back. The camera cuts to a high, overhead shot,
and, to a crescendo of music, tracks the carnage, down the blood-splat-
tered stairway and, through a series of lap dissolves, over the bloody *lap*
body of Sport and out the door, observing the police cars and the *dissolves*
crowds, in slow motion, gathering.

  I describe the sequence in detail partly to make a written record of
the climax of screen violence in the mid-seventies and to see if the horror of the sequence can be re-created in verbal description. It cannot, of
course, and the difficulty is to keep from exaggerating the description or
reflecting upon it verbally just enough to make it comic. And I wonder
if beneath its horror there is not something of the comic, or at least the
bizarre, ready to break forth, turning the sequence, with all its repetitions of shootings, fallings, and risings, its grotesque exaggerations, into
a parody of screen violence. Early in the film, Travis drives by a movie
house that is showing *The Texas Chain Saw Massacre*. The marquee is
prominently in view as the cab drifts through the streets. One may speculate whether the reference suggests the influence of violent films on
Travis (as, in the person of John Hinckley, Travis and his film would
someday influence someone "in real life"), reflects his violent propen-
sities, or alludes to cinematic violence that the climactic sequence will
parody. I would also suggest the shoot-out is another aberration of
Travis's mind. Not exactly a fantasy—it "happens" as part of the fictional events of the film—but happens the way everything else in the
fiction happens, as an exaggerated expression of the way a madman perceives and acts upon his world, an expression doubled by the viewer's
own perception of it as he or she watches the film. In other words, the
act of violence is another part of the inside/outside process of observation that Scorsese has followed throughout. So much so that Scorsese
plays a little game. After the event, there is a newspaper clipping on the
wall of Travis's room that shows an overhead diagram of the carnage—
a sketch, or story board of the high-angle shot that closed the sequence.
This is a reflexive gesture on Scorsese's part, as important as his own

*Reflexive elements*

appearance as the murderous husband in Travis's cab. The "outside world" in the film (in this case the press) imitates the interior world of Travis. The film reflects its parts against each other and against the spectator's observation of them, raising form to consciousness.

I noted that there is something predestined about the shoot-out. The violence grows out of Travis's mad self and the violent world he sees and absorbs until it becomes his reflection. Part of the *mise-en-scène* and the entire formal construction of the film, it is prepared for by gestures made, compositional strategies set up, words said throughout. The second time the viewer sees Betsy, she is bantering with a friend at campaign headquarters about a newsstand operator who has only one hand, and only two fingers on that hand. They speculate that the mob blew off his fingers. Travis does not hear this, and there is no suggestion that this ridiculous conversation suggests to him his treatment of the caretaker of Sport's brothel. It is simply a set-up and a contrast, the banal chatter of two people oblivious to the world in which Travis lives, words that will be ironically and grotesquely realized in the shoot-out and after. Reference to the Mafia turns up again when it is discovered that one of the men Travis kills was a mafioso. This is the event that, with the freeing of Iris, makes him a media hero.

In this sequence, Travis approaches Betsy and makes his pitch to her, telling her how he has observed all the people around her and all the work on her desk. When he says this, there is suddenly a cut to a point-of-view shot from Travis to the top of her desk, which the camera pans, following the sweep of Travis's hand. The shot is unmotivated; it adds nothing to the sequence and tells us little about either Travis or Betsy at this moment (though it is another signifier of the spatial and temporal distortions in Travis's perception). However, the high angle, the movement across the clutter of the desk, *formally* predict the high-angle shot of the carnage later on. In fact, Scorsese presents such a high-angle shot twice before: once at the cab company, where there is a similiar point-of-view shot from Travis to the cab owner's desk, and then again at the candy counter of the porn movie theater Travis visits. This may, I am afraid, sound more than a bit overingenious. But in a film as carefully structured as *Taxi Driver*, every shot is made to count, to be meaningful immediately or to prepare for meaning later in the work. This meaning need not be on a substantive level. Form can refer to, or in this case foreshadow, form. A high-angle pan of a cluttered desk is contextually different from a high-angle track of a room full of bloody bodies, but formally similar. Both are high-angle, and both move. A linkage is therefore set up that may not affect a spectator consciously on first viewing, but remains part of the structural system and the spectator's awareness of the film nevertheless.

Other foreshadowings are more apparent and direct. When Travis purchases guns from Andy, the gun fence, who sells his wares as if he were selling appliances, Travis holds one up and aims it through the window, the camera tracking along his arm to an anonymous couple on the street. Earlier, at the Belmore Cafeteria, when Travis takes Wizard aside in an attempt to tell him of the bad ideas in his head, a black cab driver looks up at him and points his finger at Travis as if it were a gun. There is a dolly back from this gesture—a shot from Travis's point of view—and then a reverse to Travis, who reacts with an odd look. Once outside the cafeteria, Travis attempts to unburden himself to Wizard, who cannot comprehend what he is saying. He calls him, with affection, "Killer." "Relax, Killer," he tells him, "you're gonna be all right"— words that will ironically ring true as Travis proceeds. Later, when Travis meets Sport for the first time, the pimp makes the same gun gesture with his hand at Travis. After the massacre, Travis repeats the gesture, at his own head.

Comprehension of these events, along with Travis's killing of the robber in the delicatessen and the manic preparatory rituals he undertakes, should make the main event less surprising and perhaps less gratuitous than it first appears. Unfortunately, no matter how much is revealed by such analysis, it remains an excrescence, a moment of grotesque excess in an otherwise controlled work. It damages the film, permitting it to be rejected as only one more entry in the list of violent exploitations rampant in the mid-seventies.[19] But even so damaged, the film is less cynical than many of its relatives, and no matter how much it may pander to the lowest expectations of an audience, it also holds back, tricks those expectations, and, save for those few minutes in which control is lost, remains a coherent, subtle work.

Through the structuring of point of view, the reconsideration of the *noir* milieu, the intense observation of the character's relationship to a carefully defined world that expresses his state of mind, and with its

reticence in analyzing or seeking motivations for that character and his
world, *Taxi Driver* sets up a closed narrative of loneliness and madness.
The film proves, finally, to be quite responsible, in the sense that it
offers, in a clearly defined form, the lack of clarity and the lack of definition that characterize solitude and madness, without falling into the
trap that romanticizes madness as a redemptive experience. In total, by
presenting its character and his semi-life as simply *there*, the film implicates the viewer and allows neither the character nor the viewer to be
removed from the consequences of events and of perception. It examines from the point of view of its character the clichés and the sentimentality that have come to be taken for granted in films and television,
conventions of masculine strength and feminine passivity, of heroism
and revenge that appear not merely banal but insane and destructive
when they are taken as meaningful.

I spoke earlier of the use Scorsese makes of cinematic allusion, the way
he follows the French New Wave filmmakers in drawing upon, paying
homage to, and in many instances changing the cinematic forms and
conventions that precede his work. In *Taxi Driver* that allusiveness is
carefully integrated into the film, making it rich and resonant. The Fordian lineage of Travis Bickle and his demonic re-creation of the John
Wayne persona in *The Searchers* has been mentioned. Even stronger
and more conclusive is the film's homage to Hitchcock, and to *Psycho*
in particular.*

What Hitchcock persistently examines in his best films are the ways
an audience can be manipulated in and out of morally ambiguous situations, and made to react not so much to what is happening on the
screen as to what is happening to their reactions to what is happening.
Hitchcock speaks to the power of images and sounds to manipulate an
audience into reaction and counter-reaction, and, within the narratives
constructed by these images and sounds, to the manipulative power of

---

*There are allusions as well to the master of cinematic allusiveness, Jean-Luc Godard.
Patterson and Farber point out the full-screen inserts of Travis's diary entries, a device
Godard employs, via Bresson, in *Pierrot le fou* and elsewhere. There is, as well, the camera
movement into a bubbling glass of Alka-Seltzer, an homage to the coffee-cup sequence in
*Two or Three Things I Know About Her.*[20]

*excellent Hitchcock Description*

sexuality and domination and fear that one character can wield over another. Throughout the forties and into the fifties, Hitchcock cloaked this inquiry, sometimes almost hermetically, in romantic melodrama (*Notorious*, posing as a love story, is as frightening an exploration of sexual and emotional abuse and political manipulation as one can find in American film). In the fifties he slowly began to drop the generic pretenses, first in *The Wrong Man* and then in *Vertigo*. By the time he made *Psycho*, he was able to create a world that was the dialectic to that of melodrama, a dark, loveless, brutal world in which the viewer is made emotional accomplice first to a petty thief and then to a homicidal maniac. The world of *Psycho* is a sub-division of *noir* territory, in which the isolation of a roadside motel takes the place of a barren urban landscape, and its parlor the reflection of a savage and savaged mind. *SAVAGE!*

Taxi Driver becomes at many points an analogue to *Psycho*. (Tangentially, *Taxi Driver* is related to *Vertigo* as well, the relationships of Travis to Betsy and Sport to Iris being curious echoes of Scottie's idealized and destructive relationship to Madeleine/Judy.) Both *Taxi Driver* and *Psycho* are studies of the impenetrability of madness, but where Hitchcock leads the audience by indirection, showing the effects of X madness, bluffing the cause and withholding the source, Scorsese concentrates on the central figure, never withholding a concentrated gaze on a disintegrating mind. But in both cases, though by different means, the viewer is permitted a degree of closeness to a character, reproved for that closeness, and made to feel horror and guilt because of it. Both Hitchcock and Scorsese play upon the desire to "identify," to sympathize with and understand a film's "hero." Both do this formally, through devices of framing and composition, through control of the *mise-en-scène*; so that as a viewer tends to move toward the character, the way he or she sees the character stimulates a move in the opposite direction, alienates the very desire to understand. Both films work through a sense of terrifying isolation. Norman Bates is completely removed from his world. Travis Bickle is removed *with* his world, half-seeing and half-creating it wherever he goes until it almost literally disappears into his own reflection. The sequence in which he looks at himself in the mirror—as if he were every antagonist he could ever fantasize—"You talkin' to me? . . . Who the fuck do you think you're talkin' to?"—signifies an almost total solipsism.

*MIRROR SEQUENCE, Almost Total solipsism*

*Psycho* and *Taxi Driver* attempt, finally, to delineate this solipsism, creating a world and a state of mind so enclosed and so unknowable that the viewer is fooled for attempting to understand it. Hitchcock fashions his enigma through a major device of manipulation. Norman's mother is discovered to be Norman himself, a killer with knife and wig shrieking in the darkness. The shock at this discovery is offered a palliative by means of a psychiatrist's rational explanation. In cold, deliberate tones, in the security of a police station, a doctor explains Norman's condition, placing it within the order of rationally understood experience. By all expectations, this explanation should end the film, close it neatly and with the promise of comfort. But it is not meant to be closed comfortably, or at all. After the psychiatrist's tidy and titillating words, the gaze is redirected at Norman himself. The camera tracks slowly to him, in a cell, draped in a white sheet, his "mother's" voice explaining how she wouldn't hurt a fly; the track continues to approach his manic face until, beneath it, Hitchcock slips in the image of mother's grinning skull, the two images punctured by the car in which Norman had buried his victims being pulled from the swamp. The face and the acts of madness, images of unexpected and uncontrollable violence, regain power over the psychiatrist's talk of complexes and psychoses. Rather than the security given by explanation, one is left with the enigma of the irrational.[21]

The closing sequences of *Taxi Driver* similarly play on a desire to understand and to assimilate the unknowable. After the carnage, the camera, as it has earlier in the film, pans along the walls of Travis's apartment. Travis is not present, only a version of him that has been created by his act, newspaper clippings announcing his heroism: "Taxi Driver Battles Gangsters," "Reputed New York Mafioso Killed in Bizarre Shooting," "Taxi Hero to Recover." Over this is the droning voice of Iris's father: "You are something of a hero around this household. . . ." The anti-social lunatic killer has become savior; a combination of Clint Eastwood, Charles Bronson, and now Sylvester Stallone— is born from the union of Norman Bates and John Wayne, with Kubrick's Alex acting as godfather. (What better offspring than Dirty Harry Callahan, the urban vigilante of *Death Wish*, and Rambo in the person of that working-class philosopher, the cab driver?) The desperate search for heroes in recent cinema has thrown up some odd characters, who seem to insist that only viciousness and excesses of anti-social behavior can lead to triumph in a society seemingly devoid of other means of self-expression. What prevents the viewer from accepting Travis as another manifestation of such salvation? Nothing, except that he clearly manifests the psychotic nature that is hidden in the film, heroes who are his antecedents and descendants. What is contained in the clippings on Travis's walls, and heard in the voice of the father whose daughter he has returned, gives the viewer permission momentarily to slip out of Travis's perception of the world. But if that opportunity is taken, the viewer is suddenly situated in an unsecured place and may find that he or she is as capable of seeing the world in as mad a light as Travis, discovering ludicrous heroes in unlikely places, indulging in fantasies as grotesque as Travis's own.

This hallucination continues in the following sequence. Travis is standing with his cronies in front of the St. Regis Hotel. This is the first time in the film he is seen in a setting not redolent of violence and perversity (although by this time his presence alone is sufficient to create the necessary aura). Betsy, the angel in white, gets into his cab, and Travis drives her to a leafy East Side street. The sequence continues the fantasy of the hero originated by the newspaper clippings and the letter from Iris's father. Travis is removed from Betsy, talking to her casually, not permitting her to pay the fare, playing the melodramatic role of the strong, rebuffed lover. Has he somehow been purified by his ritual act of destruction and its attendant glorification? Or does he think he has? Betsy is not seen for the duration of her ride, except as she is reflected through the rear-view mirror of the cab. When she finally emerges from the cab, it is in a far shot, and she remains a kind of ghostly projection of Travis's romantic fantasies. The momentary perceptual separation from Travis, the illusory reconsideration of his status, lingers. Is he, after all, a likable guy who just—as President Merkin Muffley says about Jack D. Ripper in *Dr. Strangelove*—went a little funny in the head? In truth, the sequence is a set up in a manner analogous to the penultimate sequence in *Psycho*, offering a false invitation to understand the character.

As Travis drives away from Betsy, she can be seen through his rear window. The camera pans across the cab's interior, past Travis to his eyes, strangely lit, reflected in the rear-view mirror. He glances toward

*[handwritten margin note: TRAVIS'S WIERDNESS NEAR END]*

the mirror and there is a cut to a shot from behind it, looking at him. Suddenly, as if catching sight of his eyes, he makes a lunge, twisting the mirror toward him. As he does this, a loud squeak is heard. There is a cut back to a shot from inside the cab, looking at the mirror and the street outside. Travis's hand pushes the mirror away and, as the credits come up, the lights of the streets are seen outside the cab window and reflected in its mirror. As the credits end, the percussive sound track rises, Travis's eyes briefly pass across the mirror, while outside is the grainy night-time street, the people moving, as they did at the beginning

*[handwritten margin note: PERCUSSIVE SOUND TRACK RISES]*

of the film, in slow motion. Like the end of *Psycho*, the end of *Taxi Driver* is a reminder of the abysmal impossibility of understanding madness or accounting for its violence. What it adds is the suggestion that the carrier of this madness has some awareness of his state. Travis's avoidance of his eyes in the cab mirror refers back to his conversation with Iris. When he told her that Sport is a killer, she responded, "Didn't you ever try looking in your own eyeballs in the mirror?" When he finally does, his reaction parallels that of the viewer who gazes into Norman's face at the end of *Psycho*: terror. New York's hero is still "God's lonely man," still a killer. He remains his own passenger, threatening to take others for a ride.

Scorsese was so fascinated by the madness and violence of Travis Bickle and the complex perceptual elements that constructed both the character and the viewer's reaction to him that he and De Niro re-created him in different guises three more times. Jimmy Doyle, in *New York, New York*, manifests a similarly unmotivated—though more contained—violence in a *mise-en-scène* that, as we shall see, extends the expressionist tendencies of *Taxi Driver* to the point of absolute artificiality. *Raging Bull* places its figure of violence within a setting more suited to his needs, the boxing ring. It tempers the expressionism of *Taxi Driver* by combining it with observation of the character's urban ethnic environment and more closely identifying point of view with the dissolution of the subject, the individual dissolved out into indeterminable drives and actions. But curiously *The King of Comedy*, a film whose wit and brightness link it more closely to *Alice Doesn't Live Here Anymore*, toys with some of the ideas of *Taxi Driver* more clearly (and dialectically) than its predecessors.

Visually and structurally, the two films are quite different. Because it is about television, *The King of Comedy* is shot analogous to the flat, neutral television style. The lighting is even and high key; the camera almost always at eye level and largely steady; the editing, except for some fantasy sequences, remains close to the standard shot/reverse shot pattern of television and ordinary filmmaking.[22] But despite its repression of visual exuberance and its use of comedy to reduce anxiety and threat, *The King of Comedy* plays out a central problem raised by *Taxi Driver*. The lone, disenfranchised individual is once again taken by the public to be important, heroic—or, in this instance, at least, entertaining—and is thereby absolved of his madness. De Niro creates a character named Rupert Pupkin, who, like Travis Bickle and Jake La Motta, has no superego, no controlling voice that permits him to live comfortably within the knowable bounds of middle-class convention. Unlike his predecessors, however, his subjectivity is strongly defined, so much so that it is unaffected by external realities. Rupert wants only one thing in his life, to become a talk show comedian. To that end, he will insert himself into any situation, any confrontation, without embarrassment. His madness is defined by his insistence on turning desire into act and refusing to flinch at situations that would be largely unthinkable to a normally inhibited person. He forces himself into the life of a popular talk show host, Jerry Langford (played with restraint and self awareness by Jerry Lewis), finally kidnapping him in order to assure himself a spot on his show. His success is enormous. Although jailed for his actions, he, like Travis, is taken as a hero by the media and becomes a popular star.

Like Jake La Motta and Travis Bickle, Rupert imposes his fantasies on the world—to such an extent that one critic suggests it is difficult to tell whether his final triumph is imaginary or not.[23] Unlike them, no one is physically hurt by the impositions. (At the beginning of the film, Rupert cuts his hand in the act of forcing his way through a crowd of admirers into Jerry Langford's car and Jerry gives him his handkerchief to stop the bleeding; when Rupert and his friend Masha kidnap Jerry, they bind him head to toe in adhesive tape. These moments of violence suggest the dangerous aberrations that occur within and between the characters, but are limited by the comic form of the film, existing as forebodings only.) Travis's and La Motta's fantasies take the form of perceptual dislocations that distort and transform the world outside of

The imagination of Rupert Pupkin. Robert De Niro and Jerry Lewis in *The King of Comedy*.

them. The world of celebrity and show business is already distorted, made up of the fantasies and aberrations of everyone who actively or passively takes part in it. Therefore, Rupert does not so much violently attack a world which is not "in reality" corresponding to his perceptions of it, but merely forcing room in that world for one more abberation—himself.

This provides another explanation for why Scorsese moderates his visual style, basing the film's structure on conventional patterns, and then modifying them just enough to indicate a perceptual disturbance. He will use some of his old devices to indicate the dubious perceptions of his central character, as in the pre-credits sequence when Jerry Langford, seen from Rupert's point of view, moves in slow motion. But he will also use the ordinary shot/reverse shot pattern in an unusual way to integrate "fantasy" and "reality" and indicate their proximity. At the end of their first meeting (aided by Masha, who gets locked in Jerry's car so Rupert can pull her out and take her place with his idol), Rupert tells Jerry they should have lunch. In the next sequence, Jerry and Rupert have lunch, and Jerry begs Rupert to take over the show. Scorsese cuts between the two in a standard fashion. But he also cuts away from the fantasy to one shots of Rupert, in his basement, talking, carrying on the dialogue with himself. By entering Rupert's imagination in this way Scorsese is, in effect, entering the solipsism that constitutes celebrity. Rupert's life as a star begins in his imagination, which he recreates in his basement, the space rigged out with life-sized posters of Marilyn Monroe and Humphrey Bogart, of Liza Minnelli and Jerry Lewis/Jerry Langford (after he becomes a star, Rupert himself will be a life-sized poster in a bookshop where his memoirs are being sold). Rupert sits between these two cut-outs, kissing them, laughing at their unheard jokes, pretending to be a talk show host, interrupted by his mother's offscreen voice (*Scorsese's* mother's voice, in fact), yelling at him to be quiet or to go to work. At one point, he records an audition tape for Jerry; he sits at a desk, talking into his tape recorder, his mother yelling at him. There is a cut to a photograph of a laughing and applauding audience. Rupert steps in front of it and begins to deliver his monologue (the words of which are mostly incomprehensible). The camera pulls back, the sounds of people laughing becomes distorted; when the camera finishes its movement, Rupert is observed at the end of a long, white corridor, standing before a poster of people frozen in hilarity. The space of the imaginary, of fantasy, becomes so powerful that it transforms reality, or more accurately, further subdues it. The onanist of entertainment will begin to impose himself on the outside world, which will finally be as pleased with him as he is with himself.

Travis Bickle's madness is read as bravery by the newspapers; Rupert Pupkin's obsessive activity, his invasion of privacy and commandeering of the airwaves by kidnapping, is turned into fame by magazines, television, and their audience. There is a wider and flatter plane of perception operating here, which may further account for the relative flatness of the *mise-en-scène*. Where Travis Bickle's terror was relatively localized, Rupert's literally subverts the country. He kidnaps a popular talk show host and as ransom demands that he be given a monologue on the show. His wish is granted, he delivers a grotesquely idiotic routine about his parents and throwing up, goes to prison, writes a book, and emerges a major figure in the popular imagination (these last two events are presented through a montage of magazines and book covers, reminiscent of the newspaper headlines near the end of *Taxi Driver* and a similar montage in *New York, New York*); the individual himself disappears beneath the signs of his fame.

. The question finally raised by both *The King of Comedy* and *Taxi Driver* is, who is crazy? If the viewer is implicated in the response to Travis Bickle's actions, the whole of television culture is implicated in Rupert's. His desire speaks to the desire for fame of everyone who sees him, and the film makes it difficult for the viewer to remain superior to the world the film addresses. Rupert is too bizarre to remain unattractive. He is the perfection of a crazed simplicity. Open and direct in his aspirations, his fantasies are relatively uncomplicated, and he cannot be embarrassed by them or by acting them out. Whether pursuing his girlfriend, Rita (played by the black actress, Diahnne Abbott, whose race is never an issue to Rupert), or Jerry Langford, or pursued by his overtly lunatic cohort, Masha (Sandra Bernhard, who dances around the bound Jerry Langford almost naked in a delirium of lost repression: "I wanna be black," she tells him, in an attempt to express her notion of sensual delight at having her hero near her), Rupert remains steadfast and smiling where others might run cringing. Travis Bickle deflects viewer comprehension, Rupert invites it. He is an avatar of the man on the make, simple enough to bring assent to his desire to enter the lucite and chromium offices of media stars, indeed to become one himself. His obvious madness is mitigated by the persistence we are always told is needed to get ahead. He succeeds through a criminal act and a television performance so bad that it stands as another embarrassment by which he—and apparently the television viewer—is unaffected. Travis's success is appalling; Rupert's almost welcome. In either case a cipher has been filled with celebrity, and the culture that seeks images to celebrate and gives fame to madmen is once again put in a situation as precarious as the subjects of its admiration.

Of the five films I have been discussing, *Mean Streets*, *Taxi Driver*, and *Raging Bull* are tightly linked through their formal presentation, each one experimenting further with aspects of perceptual play and point of view. *Taxi Driver* and *The King of Comedy* are thematically linked, and join with *Raging Bull* as studies in the enigmas of subjectivity and celebrity. They share as well an intensive concentration on the male figure. Two of Scorsese's films, *Alice Doesn't Live Here Anymore* and *New York, New York*, though very different stylistically, concentrate on a woman and on the couple, respectively, and therefore make an interesting comparison. *Alice Doesn't Live Here Anymore* directly precedes *Taxi Driver* and is so completely its opposite that it might be by another hand. Although it has great formal energy, it is as important for its subject as it is for its execution.

Rather than the dissolution of the subject, *Alice* is concerned with the discovery of subjectivity, the discovery of individual energy and the impression of that energy onto the world in a non-destructive way. It is one of the rare films of the contemporary period that offers a notion of optimism without resorting to avenging heros, extra-terrestrial forces, or an entirely debilitating sentimentality. In the context of Scorsese's work, *Alice* stands apart, almost as a dialectic to the dark violence of *Mean Streets* and *Taxi Driver*, seeming to offer the possibility that the violence can be contained and subdued. The one violent character in the film, Harvey Keitel's Ben, is seen partially as an intrusion, partially as a mode of behavior that exists and must be attended to. Ben is not allowed, as are similar characters in the other films, to encompass and diminish everything else. But he does exist, and besides his presence there is a sense of brooding and nervousness in the camera movements throughout the film that seems to portend something other than what these movements are covering. These stylistic events relate the film to the essential concerns of Scorsese's other works. Threat always exists; energies are always ready to be expended. Here, however, the threats are overcome and the energies directed joyfully.

*Alice* can be seen either as a comedy, a structure of outrageous and exaggerated incidents leading to a harmonious grouping of characters at the end, or as a feminist film that attempts to question and respond to the conventions of female behavior set by American film for decades. But neither of these approaches is consistent within the work. The feminist film has yet to be established in commercial American cinema, and probably will not be, considering the reaction to feminism in the culture at large and the dilution of its most easily assimilable ideas and modes of expression by advertising and television. In the years since *Alice*, feminist work and influence have flourished in serious film criticism and been expressed in non-theatrical film, but have been negated by cooptation in theatrical film at about the same rate as they have in the society as a whole. Its major critiques of patriarchy have been reduced to jokes or conventions. Though strong women directors may survive, like Susan Seidelman, more likely a woman may make one or two strongly feminist films and disappear, like Claudia Weill, or, like Amy Heckerling, director of *Fast Times at Ridgemont High* (1982), stay within commercial strictures in order to survive.

Comedy, while among the most established genres in film, is the most impure and unstable. There is no possibility of defining the generic bounds of comedy, as we can for the gangster film, or *film noir*, or even the broader form of melodrama. Generic definition is even more difficult since *Bonnie and Clyde*, which set the pattern for mixing conventions of comedy and melodrama within one film. A few things are clear, however. The incidents that make up a comic narrative are usually exaggerated and play against the norms of conventional (cinematic) behavior. And most importantly, comedy must permit its characters to survive without suffering or sacrifice, and ought to constitute or reconstitute images of ideal harmony as part of its closure.[24] The genre has the potential for being a subversive form. Melodrama, and its demand for sacrifice and transcendence, is the dominant form of most ideological structures. Comedy demands the opposite: the turmoil it presents is without consequence, no one of importance is hurt, and its central figures not only triumph (or at least survive) without being emotionally scarred by their adventures, but are often liberated from rather than subdued to an oppressive controlling power.

Like most of Scorsese's films, *Alice Doesn't Live Here Anymore* is about working-class characters, and in particular about a woman unfamiliar with freedom forced to try it out. In older film comedies about women—most especially the screwball comedy of the thirties—the freedom and equality of the central female character were a premise that allowed the even match between male and female characters to occur. In fact, the male character was sometimes put at an emotional disadvantage to a stronger woman—confronted by her energy, as in Howard Hawks's *Bringing Up Baby*, and forced to be an equal.[25] This was not a situation the culture was, or is yet, very used to. Neither was the compromise between individual energy and marriage that so many of the screwball comedies discovered. With the firm bourgeoisification and domestification of comedy in the late forties and fifties, the woman either gave up her strength to the male or used it to coax him into a domestic life. *Alice* begins in domesticity, the character seeks to escape it, and discovers a compromise with some minimal triumph.

Alice Hyatt (Ellen Burstyn) is not an independent figure. Her reach for liberation is the result of an accident and the memory of a fantasy. She moves out of the domestic order—the small, compacted, bleached world of a New Mexican suburb. Rather than seeking a man, she seeks escape from a world that has been dominated by one. Her husband dies and his death allows a return of her desire to be a singer and a very real need to support herself. What is important in this movement is that neither Robert Getchell's script nor Scorsese's direction allows any attempt at analysis of Alice herself. She neither agonizes over her decision to move (though she feels sad about leaving her friend) nor voices any distinct understanding of it. If anything, the opening sequences of the film indicate she is rather out of touch with the realities of her situation, and subject to conflicting fantasies. The film opens with an artificial studio landscape, a farmhouse and a country road, lit in red and reminiscent of thirties film, of Dorothy's Kansas in *The Wizard of Oz* or a John Ford homestead. Alice's past is a movie past, a surrogate for real experience in a three-by-four screen ratio, personalized somewhat by being embodied in a tough, foul-mouthed little girl, who insists she can sing better than Alice Faye. This fantasy of the past, the Monterey of her movie-made childhood, is what Alice wants to rediscover in her escape from her domestic life. At the end, this sign of the past becomes a sign, literally. Alice and her son Tommy walk down a Tucson street, still uncertain about their future, and over them, against the hills, in a compressed, telephoto shot, is a roadside advertising sign that says "Monterey." One place is as good as another, if all places are divested of fantasy and invested with a secure sense of one's self. This is a glib solution, perhaps, redolent of the seventies, but at least an initial step in the divestiture of illusion. For as fantasy, the "Monterey" of Alice's past entraps her as much as her domestic life, and one of the areas the film investigates is whether a way out of any of these traps is possible.

Alice's married life, which booms into the movie fantasy of her past with a loud noise and rapidly moving camera, is the obverse of her childhood myth. Her son has his head clapped between two loudspeakers blaring rock, and Alice can only sing along while she sews. Her husband is a prostrate figure on the bed, yelling at the noise. When finally seen, he appears a sulky, complaining, unresponsive man. In one rather touching and upsetting shot, the camera looks down at him and Alice in bed, she turned away, he hopelessly holding her from behind. Alice's "present" is sketched in with short but significant scenes, an offering of an immediate, unpleasant reality that wipes out past dreams and replaces them with small, suffocating oppressions. These scenes are somewhat stylized so that they not only present a great deal of information in a small time, but also play off of the fantasy sequence that precedes them. The childhood fantasy is presented in images that render the artificiality of an old movie set. Present "reality" is also artificial, even though it consists of images shot on location, in natural light, images that are comfortably "realistic" within the conventions of contemporary film. Yet it is artificial because this is film, of course, and artificial as well because of its almost stylized expression of domestic oppression. Finally, the childhood fantasies of the opening sequence and the "reality" of the domestic sequence are experiences from which Alice must free herself. They reflect and exaggerate two regrettable situations and set up a potential for escape. (If a time comes when the domestic order is liberated and women are not oppressed and made passive by it, then the scenes with Alice and her husband may be recalled or re-created as images of a lost nightmare, much as the childhood sequence is presented at the beginning of the film as the recollection of a lost dream.)

Another result of the sketchiness of Alice's domestic life is the ease with which the husband can be removed. He is a brutish jerk whose death in his Coca-Cola truck is presented with a cold, bright distance worthy of Godard. Scorsese cannot permit any emotional reaction to it, because it is not central to the narrative, only a catalyst. The husband's function is clearly to represent a hopeless situation, and with him gone, Alice and the film are free to inscribe other patterns. The first man she meets on her travels is a slightly more complicated figure than her husband. Ben appears warm and gentle, only to turn out to be a potential killer. (He makes the gesture that becomes so significant in *Taxi Driver*, of pointing his finger as if it were a gun—play violence preceding physical violence.) The sequences of their meeting and bedding down are created to indicate both Alice's strength and the potential danger awaiting an unattached woman. The dissolve from her in bed with Ben to her in bed with her son, listening to a fight in the room next to theirs, prepares for violence to come, as does the nervous hand-held camera work that precedes the visit of Ben's wife and his breaking into Alice's motel room, threatening murder. The entire episode is somewhat cautionary. The woman alone is vulnerable (as vulnerable as the woman married), and the long far shot of the interior of the smashed-up motel room as Alice and Tommy leave after Ben's attack serves to isolate them and to emphasize the tenuous nature of their life alone on the road.

These observations come to an end when Alice meets David (played by Kris Kristofferson, the singer Betsy asks Travis about in *Taxi Driver*), and the film begins to fall back on conventional elements. Alice takes a job as a waitress—a prime movie occupation for a single working girl—and she meets the rancher who attempts to accommodate her independence and also disburden her of her fantasies of becoming a singer in Monterey. Scorsese and Getchell choose to give this affair melodramatic overtones and to deny the possibilities of vitality that

Domestic life: *Alice Doesn't Live Here Anymore* (Billy Green Bush, Alfred Lutter, Ellen Burstyn).

marked Alice's character up to this point. They opt for a sentimentality that has so far been missing from the film and which the film has difficulty in accommodating. Ellen Burstyn's character has, until now, supplied too much energy suddenly to fall for the recessive machismo inevitably supplied by Kristofferson. Her admission to her co-worker, Flo— in a tender scene between the two women that takes place in a bathroom—that she is both afraid of not pleasing a husband and unable to live without a man, indicates that she remains burdened by old fantasies and cultural baggage, and points as well to the fact that the film will ultimately have to recuperate the old order. That she "falls" for David, even though she forces him to recognize her needs, betrays how close the film cleaves to the forties "woman's picture" in which the female character has strength only to manage until a man can usurp her personality. Few recent films that have pretended to focus upon women and consider them as individuals have succeeded in transcending the gravitational pull back into marriage and/ or a "fulfilling" relationship. The screwball comedies (to use my earlier contrasting example) did not depict marriage as "fulfilling" in the sense that it determined a woman's role. Marriage—or remarriage—was the end of most screwballs, but it was most often a celebration of battles continually to be fought and personalities continuing to be independent (it was often a placation of the Hays Office as well). *Alice* has disappointed many critics on this score, for it gives and takes away, depicts independence only to wind up back in dependence again. Though it ends with the termination of Alice's fantasies, there is no end in sight for larger fantasies, those that insist that a tall and handsome stranger will protect the weak and dependent woman. Patriarchy demands its saving heroes for the culture at large and certainly for any woman who believes she may not need one.

If the conclusions drawn by *Alice* are bright but less than radical, there are elements within it that do conceive responses to old conventions in new ways. The most important of these are the friendships between Alice and Flo (Diane Ladd), Alice and her son (Alfred Lutter), and her son and Audrey (née Doris, played by Jodie Foster). In each of these groupings there is an evenness and equality that belie the manipulation or sentimentality that usually marks friendships, indeed relationships of any kind, in American film. Flo and Alice make up an almost unconventional pairing. In past films women have sometimes been allowed understanding companions, but the companionship had to retain a certain distance and inequality. Flo and Alice parallel the friendship between Joan Crawford and Eve Arden in *Mildred Pierce*, except that here the two women are equal and Flo presents a grounding, stabilizing component to Alice's dreams. The sequence in which the two of them sit and talk in the midday sun, observed in profile, faces raised to the warmth, an image which dissolves to a long shot which places them in the midst of the blowing sands of an unpleasant desert landscape, presents in almost symbolic fashion an image of two strong women trapped in unaccommodating circumstances, yet attempting to find sources of comfort amidst the isolation.[26]

The humanizing quality exists more strongly in Alice's relationship with her son. A chapter in the history of American film could be written about its inability to come to terms with children, who exist either as small adults, as unconscionably cute, or as amazingly vicious. Beginning with some films of Michael Ritchie, such as *Smile* (1975) and *The Bad News Bears* (1976), an attempt was made to create children with fewer of the old stereotypes. More recently, the teenage films of John Hughes (*Sixteen Candles*, 1984, and *The Breakfast Club*, 1985, for example), and many of the films directed or produced by Steven Spielberg, have removed children from the adult world entirely, while at the same time creating a world accessible to adult fantasy and nostalgia. Instead of small adults, these children become adult surrogates, their world a place adults would like to inhabit. When Scorsese himself confronts a teenage character, with Tom Cruise's Vincent in *The Color of Money*, the result expresses some ambiguity. Paul Newman's Eddie attempts to take Vincent away from the sphere of teenage freedom and irresponsibility and father him into the adult world of pool hustling. The result is that the child learns well, turns upon the surrogate father and dupes him; the adult learns in turn to look after himself.

No such fantasies or moral pointers occur in *Alice*. Tommy and Audrey represent an attempt to deal with children without modeling them upon a predetermined notion of what their behavior should be or turning them into replacements for adult exprience. Once again, the characters are presented without any explanation of or motivation for their behavior (except for the brief appearance of Audrey's prostitute mother, no reason is sought for her toughness). They are created with-

out sentimentality. Tommy and Alice exist in a free and equal interchange that provides a measure of companionship and support Alice
does not get from strangers, as well as the major comic moments of the
film. Every opportunity to exploit Tommy's loneliness or Alice's potential guilt for leaving him in a motel room while she works is avoided.
Any profound concern that Tommy will start on a life of delinquency
because of such treatment and because of his friendship with the tough
Audrey is denied. Obviously this can be done because the film is a comedy; but it is not an evasion merely for the sake of the genre, rather part
of an attempt to avoid psychologizing or moralizing that is, with the
regrettable exception of the treatment of Alice and David, a mark of the
film's success (and, as we have seen, a major part of Scorsese's approach
to narrative).

Rarely does an American film, particularly when it takes the form of
a journey, a road movie, leave both its viewers and its characters in
peace, without indicating momentous events and major change. Except
for the event that sets Alice out (which is underplayed) and the violence
of Ben (which Scorsese cannot avoid), *Alice* is content to observe possibilities of change and freedom, however limited, without forcing its
characters to pay a price. No one dies (with the exception of Alice's
husband), no one gets emotionally or physically hurt or scarred. *Alice*
is perhaps one of the few films discussed in this book in which no character is seriously lonely, or mad, without recourse to community of
some kind. Coming, as it does, between *Mean Streets*, in which the
community is dark and volatile, finally destructive, and *Taxi Driver*,
where there is no community and the isolated man explodes into madness, *Alice* indicates that the dialectic is not dead and that American
film could, conceivably, survive with its characters intact, talking to
each other, listening, and responding. In its time, it stood, with all its
flaws, as an indication that American film could come to terms with
women characters in a way other than the conventional modes of melodrama or the condescension that has remained Hollywood's interpretation of "women's liberation." The film worked as a middle link
between Cassavetes's dark view of a husband and wife imprisoned in
their own inarticulateness in *A Woman Under the Influence* (1974) and
Paul Mazursky's sentimentalizing of a rich divorcée in *An Unmarried
Woman* (1978). Scorsese went no further with it, nor, with isolated

exceptions, such as Donna Deitch's *Desert Hearts* (a feminist film fairly well set in melodramatic conventions) or Susan Seidelman's *Desperately Seeking Susan* and *Making Mr. Right*, did any other commercial filmmaker. (Seidelman's *Susan* with its sequences set in lower Manhattan and its star, Rosanna Arquette, bears interesting similarities to Scorsese's *After Hours*, which was made at about the same time).

Scorsese himself went on to deal with the problem of the domestic couple in a film simultaneously old fashioned and innovative in both form and substance. In the three features before *New York, New York*, he showed an attraction to artificiality in setting or in the treatment of locations. The opening of *Alice*, where the camera booms around a mock-thirties studio set; the carefully controlled lighting, framing, and movement (indeed the generally expressionist approach) in *Taxi Driver*; the red-lit bar sequences in *Mean Streets*, photographed in slow motion are all part of Scorsese's desire to create a *mise-en-scène* that locates both his characters and the viewer's perceptions of them in a controlled space. Unlike Hitchcock, who used studio interiors and process shots long after they had gone out of fashion so that he could keep all aspects of the production under his control, Scorsese is not intent on making the artificial appear "real," but on drawing attention to the artificiality itself; he wants viewer perception of the unusual, the artificial, as such.*

*New York, New York* contains almost no location shots. With the help of production designer Boris Leven and cinematographer Laszlo Kovacs, Scorsese builds an artificial world. The result is odd, and I am not certain that what is perceived is the same as what was intended. The opening titles of the film, the painted city skyline, immediately refer the viewer to a pastel evocation of the forties and early-fifties studio musical. But as the film proceeds, this intended evocation begins to disap-

---

*The issue is a bit more complicated than this. Hitchcock's "realism" is a tenuous affair; he constantly seeks to elicit a perception of the strange and violent from the everyday. But it is true that he stuck to the studio long after studio sets and process shots, when compared with location shooting, began to look like the artifices they always were.

Scorsese has expressed his admiration for the films of Michael Powell and Emeric Pressburger, who made *The Red Shoes* and *Stairway to Heaven* (among many others). Many of their films demonstrate a marked attraction to the artificial and the fantastic, even for their time. Their influence on Scorsese is an interesting item for further research.[27]

pear and be replaced by a consciousness of the *methods* of evocation. The forties interiors and the strange, almost abstract suggestiveness of the exteriors develop their own attraction; the control of the *mise-en-scène* seems to become more important than why that control is being exercised, so that form threatens to refer only to itself. The viewer becomes aware not of *why* the studio sets are there (to evoke the atmosphere of the studio musical), only that they *are* there. Not that they are not fascinating in themselves. Jimmy Doyle's ascent up the steps of the El, as he gazes upon a sailor and a girl doing a Gene Kelly ballet in an empty and undefined street below; a high-angle shot of Jimmy playing his saxophone under a lamp in a deserted studio street; a meeting between Jimmy and Francine (Liza Minnelli) in the snow, with the silhouettes of cut-out trees behind them; a car driving off into a studio-red sunset, are all undeniably attractive. But they are only fascinating as aspects of design. And they are inconsistent. Most of the interiors, with the exception of an oddly lit motel room and a nightclub lit entirely in red neon, are conventionally "real." They look like interiors evocative of the forties, whereas the exteriors evoke not a time but the idea of studio sets.

Scorsese merges two levels of realism: illusory realism, in which the cinematic space and its articulations create the illusion of a "real world," and a realism of form, in which the cinematic space points to its own existence, prevents the viewer from passing through the form into an illusion of reality, and uses that obstacle to create other levels of awareness. This is what Kubrick attains in *Barry Lyndon*, but through a consistency of spatial articulations that point both to their own artificiality and to the way that artificiality is the very content of the film. If Scorsese was consciously attempting to correct the phenomenon of "evocation" films that followed upon *Bonnie and Clyde* in the late sixties and early seventies by demonstrating that the evocation of the past in film is only the evocation of the ways film evokes the past, the inconsistency of exterior artificiality and interior "realism" somewhat compromises his attempt. What remains uncompromised is the gesture toward the evocation of form, the insistence, through significant foregrounding of artificiality, that filmic reality is generated by its own image-making conventions. Along with *Barry Lyndon, New York, New*

*York* has influenced other films that seek to rediscover the possibilities of conscious artifice. Herbert Ross's *Pennies from Heaven* (1981) bases some of its design in American painting. Alan Rudolph's *Choose Me* (1984) and *Trouble in Mind* (1986) represent urban exteriors by means of studio sets. (Emphasizing the evocative power of the artifice in the last-named film, Rudolph turns an "actual" city into a fictional one and has his central character gaze at the model of an urban warehouse district, through which the camera moves as though it were an actual location.)

*New York, New York* experiments with other forms as well, exploring the artifices of genre as well as set design. The film is primarily a romantic musical in the post-*Cabaret* style, where musical numbers occur as part of the narrative, as an actual stage performance—or, in one sequence, a film performance—rather than expanding out of the narrative into another spatial plane, as was the convention from the Busby Berkeley Warner Brothers musicals through the Vincente Minnelli and

Studio trees: Robert De Niro and Liza Minnelli in *New York, New York.*

Gene Kelly-Stanley Donen films for MGM in the late forties and early fifties. Bob Fosse's *Cabaret* (1972, which also stars Liza Minnelli) attempted to turn the musical into a "realistic" genre, a melodrama with music. *New York, New York* continues that attempt, but at the same time undoes it by attempting to evoke older musicals that had no pretense to that kind of realism, while at the same time flaunting the unreality of its own appearance—representing its own representation. If that were not complicated enough, exteriors are so lit and photographed as to appear similar to the *mise-en-scène* of *Taxi Driver*, so that a claustrophobic, barren, and occasionally foreboding effect is achieved that saturates the film with the aura of *film noir*.

This element is not altogether novel. Some of the thirties Warner Brothers' musicals had a discomfiting darkness and despair about them. But it is not altogether clear what the darkness of *New York, New York* is reflecting, since the temporal overlays are so uncertain. The occasional despair about "putting on the show" or about personal and financial security that manifested itself in some thirties musicals grew out of the Depression, the time in which the films were made and the time they reflected. *New York, New York,* made in the seventies, is about the forties, and it is difficult to determine whether the *noir* elements of the film are merely part of the evocation of the forties *noir* style, part of the experiment in genre-mixing, or an attempt to create a setting for a romance that has its dark and anxiety-ridden moments. (Scorsese admits to the direct influence of two forties *noir* musicals, *My Dream Is Yours* and *The Man I Love*.)[28] With all of this, the film also has comedy and moments that recall the musical biography popular in the forties and fifties. Finally, these elements are placed at the service of the two major characters and their unromantic romance in a melodrama that attempts to squelch itself.

But here, too, an uncomfortable mixture of styles occurs. Liza Minnelli brings with her a persona full of vulnerability and almost masochistic passivity, in the tradition of her mother, Judy Garland (as well as her own past screen roles). De Niro, under Scorsese's direction, had, up to this film, developed a persona of barely restrained anger and violence. He has in general become a major figure of urban disenfranchisement, brooding, sado-masochistic, both restrained and unpredictable. The conflict between the energy and the control results in explosion and violence—except in *New York, New York,* where the anger is restrained, and Scorsese attempts to domesticate the character.*

Scorsese and screenwriter Earl Mac Rauch and Mardik Martin attempt a curious play upon the conflict of "star" personalities. The result is that, with all the other tensions of the film generated by its clashing genres and its artificial *mise-en-scène,* there are as well the tensions created by two individuals whose existence is strongly determined outside the narrative impersonating two fictitious characters within it, who themselves are full of tensions. The body of the narrative traces Francine's falling under Jimmy's domination and yielding to his enigmatic isolation (a trait he shares with Travis Bickle and which is hilariously alluded to when he is seen, in one shot, framed under a print of the *Mona Lisa,* a figure conventionally associated with the enigmatic). He insists at one point, after he has stayed away from her, that she cannot understand his need to be alone: "No, you don't understand that. Don't tell me you do, 'cause you don't really understand it. But I had to do it, baby." To which she responds, "Well, I understand that I don't understand." And he agrees, "Okay, that's being better about it." (The rhythmic repetition of phrases is a mark of Mardik Martin's style, evident throughout this film as well as *Mean Streets* and *Raging Bull.*)

Jimmy either talks about himself in romantic terms, or he bullies or withdraws. Although never quite as violent or obsessive as Jake La Motta is toward Vickie in *Raging Bull,* like him, he insists on a controlling distance from his wife. For her part, Francine can only with-

---

*An analogy can be drawn between De Niro and Marlon Brando. De Niro's screen persona becomes a repressed but articulate version of the fifties Brando and his mumbling energy (of course De Niro plays a young Brando—Vito Corleone—in *Godfather II*). In the fifties, the rebellious, eccentric character had to be restrained by confusion and uncertainty, a looking inward that tempered outward bravura and threat. In the seventies, the rebellious male needed to be more self-effacing, more in control, more wise to his discontent, or at least more accepting of it. In the eighties, rebelliousness was largely restricted to men without personalities who blow up society's designated enemies. Rupert Pupkin, the one character De Niro has played for Scorsese in the early eighties, is not the violent figure of the seventies films.

The Brando/De Niro pairing becomes most interesting when the two actors can be seen directed by the same individual: by Coppola, in the *Godfathers*; by Bertolucci, who directs Brando in *Last Tango in Paris* and De Niro in *1900*; and by Elia Kazan, who was Brando's best director in the fifties, and who unsuccessfully attempted to manipulate De Niro in a romantic melodrama, *The Last Tycoon,* in the seventies.

draw, slip behind him and make her way and her career by default. Jimmy's aloneness is by his choice and need; Francine's aloneness is a result of his need. At the end of many of their scenes, Scorsese has Jimmy leave the frame, or he will cut to a closeup of Francine, holding it to indicate her isolation, or permit a prolonged look at Jimmy, emphasizing his enigmatic character. In a sequence toward the end of the film, when Francine begins her own career and attempts a reconciliation with her husband at a nightclub, Jimmy goes off to speak on the phone. The camera observes him, standing silently after his phone call, with a very long, inarticulate gaze that reveals nothing but his silence and his inability to come to terms with himself, and the viewer's own inability to come to terms with him. This direct, long confrontation of viewer and character has a violent counterpart in *Raging Bull*. There, La Motta, jailed for prostitution of a minor, stands in his cell, banging head and fists against the cell wall. In both instances what is revealed about the characters is the viewer's inability to comprehend them, their inarticulateness, and their often violent behavior—things they cannot comprehend themselves.

Through the inarticulateness of the characters and the somberness of their situation and surroundings, Scorsese avoids some of the glibness (but also the brightness) of *Alice Doesn't Live Here Anymore* and replaces its nervous energy with a slow, sometimes ponderous rhythm of emotional liberation emerging with considerable pain and uncertainty. But like *Alice*, and indeed all of his films, *New York, New York* does its best to avoid the melodrama and sentiment inherent in its subject, denying the emotional glut that might easily have been built up. Those sequences in which Francine begins to act and move on her own and in which Jimmy's separation from her is made complete are among the best indicators of Scorsese's control over the narrative trajectory. In the nightclub sequence just referred to, Francine attempts her reconciliation with Jimmy by singing with him on stage. He forces her off by upping the tempo, using the self-contained power of his music to drive her away. She waits for him in their car, where an enormous battle ensues. Jimmy drives and beats on the dashboard, and then beats on her. He attempts to express his feelings, but in so doing creates a nice inversion of expectations. Physically they are equals in the battle (quite unlike Vickie and La Motta, where the woman receives all the verbal and physical abuse until she quietly leaves). Verbally, the emotions Jimmy expresses—his jealousy about their baby, his fears about being nothing on his own and nothing in relation to her—are feelings often reserved for the woman in a melodramatic situation, which dictates that it is the woman who must suffer in the face of an impassive man. Here we find that, once the man's impassiveness breaks down, he, too, suffers the fears and uncertainties that, in American film at least, are rarely allowed a man. But Scorsese is clever enough to have things both ways. If a reversal in the relationship of man and woman is permitted, melodrama is permitted as well. The sequence ends, after much yelling and slapping, with the pregnant Francine going into labor.

This might provide the moment of reconciliation melodrama would lead one to expect. But when she has her child, Jimmy walks out, because of his own frustration, his inability to conform to the passive paternal role, and because of her attempt to make him conform by naming the baby after him. He leaves the hospital, crying, refusing to look at his child. He walks behind a partition in the hospital corridor, and the camera remains on the partition for a long moment, providing a temporal and spatial transition to a recording studio, where Francine, her child now old enough to accompany her, is making the record that will bring her stardom. Again, the hospital sequence puts Jimmy in what is conventionally a feminine attitude. He feels used and hurt by Francine's control, over herself, over him—by naming his child after him without consulting him. The separation is complete. Francine stays, endures, and succeeds. Jimmy withdraws, moves away, but— again denying the narrative direction that seems indicated—also succeeds. *New York, New York* is not to prove another version of *A Star Is Born*, where the husband fails as the wife triumphs.

The recording session begins on Francine alone, isolating her in the studio as she sings a song about broken dreams and perseverance and fate ("The World Goes 'Round"); as she gets absorbed in her singing and the camera tracks in toward her there occurs a montage of fan magazines, scenes in a movie studio, indicating, in the grand old Hollywood style (repeated, with more irony, at the end of *The King of Comedy*), her rise to success. This ends with the appearance of her movie, *Happy Endings*, which Jimmy attends, watching her big production number on the screen. The movie is followed by a newsreel reporting Francine's triumphant return to New York, and the sequence ends with a shot of Jimmy in the audience, quiet, not applauding.* By employing the "career montage," Scorsese again refers to the movie origin of his movie; but he denies it as well. His film is not to be about the rise of one person at the expense of another. Jimmy will have his as well: his success, and his own montage signifying his success, a montage that follows directly upon his attendance at Francine's movie and which shows, via newspapers and record charts, the popularity of his song, "New York, New York," and his success as a nightclub owner.

One more potential for melodramatic reversal is offered as the narrative suggests the possibility of a reconciliation. Jimmy goes to see Francine perform her "big song" in a sequence where the complex of styles breaks apart. Suddenly it is not "Francine Evans," fictional character, but "Liza Minnelli" doing her nightclub routine, with a little more Garland than usual. The effect is not one of Brechtian distance, but rather of the collision of two fictions: the film fiction and the persona of Liza Minnelli in her act. After the show, Jimmy joins her at a backstage party, where they almost quarrel. He leaves, but then calls her from outside to ask if she will join him for Chinese food (a De Niro character is at his best when he can think of nothing more complicated for a reconciliation dinner than Chinese food; Rupert takes Rita to a Chinese restaurant in *The King of Comedy*). She agrees and the narrative provokes anticipations of a conventionally happy ending. Francine looks out at the street from inside the stage door, hesitates, and turns back. There is a shot of Jimmy outside, a shot of her inside pushing the elevator button. Scorsese cuts back to Jimmy, who quietly walks out of the frame. Inside, the elevator door closes on Francine. At this point, the film might have appropriately ended, but Scorsese needs more, and so he cuts back outside, to a high crane down on Jimmy on the street,

*The original sequence from Francine's movie, cut for *New York, New York*'s theatrical release, is deeply reflexive. Francine plays an usherette who dreams she meets a producer at the movie theater where she works. He brings her fame and romance, but, like Jimmy, leaves because he fears her fame will eclipse his. In the dream within the movie, he returns to her. Back in the theater—in the "reality" of the movie within the movie—she actually does meet the producer. The newsreel following the movie shows the "real" Francine being given a tumultuous welcome in New York.

down further to his shoes and umbrella, and then dissolves to a track of the empty, rain-slick, studio streets.

This final flourish is a further reminder of a cinema where the artificial expressed the "real," where a studio street called forth a response to an *idea* of "street-ness"—what an audience expected cinema streets to look like. But while the visual form evokes a reflection upon an older cinema, the narrative moves in another, perhaps newer, direction. The threatened reconciliation and its attendant melodrama do not take place. There is no violent provocation of viewer emotions, no happiness, no great unhappiness. The promise of domesticity has been broken and stays so, and the possibility of two people once together, now remaining apart is realized. In the tradition of the musical film, the ending is closer to those Warner Brothers musicals of the thirties, mentioned earlier, where a certain anxiety lurks about the success of the show.

But the closure of *New York, New York* is not anxiety-ridden, merely a bit sad, at least if one expects the couple in a romantic melodrama to get back together. It is a response to the conclusion of *Alice Doesn't Live Here Anymore* and a foreshadowing of *Raging Bull* and, in a way, *The Color of Money*. *Alice* emphasized the necessity and beneficiality of heterosexual bonding; *Raging Bull* indicates that the balance of power in the bond remains with the man and the most the woman can do is to withdraw passively. The adolescent couple—Vincent and Carmen—in *The Color of Money* share some of the attributes of Jimmy and Francine in *New York, New York*, but the focus of attention in *The Color of Money* is on the male couple, Vincent and Eddie. With them, Scorsese plays with the problem of male bonding, a basic theme in much contemporary American film (including his own, for it turns up in *Mean Streets* and, in curious ways, in *Raging Bull* and *The King of Comedy*). He goes no further than most filmmakers in examining the homosexual substrate of the male bond, though he does contemplate another perspective, that of the older man attempting to father the younger. Eddie's attempt to nurture and educate Vincent into the lucrative career of pool hustling is an enormous success and failure. Eddie learns too well, rebels against the father and humiliates him. But rather than destroying him, the experience brings Eddie to a new sense of independence. That the results of all of this are uninteresting is due to the flatness of the film's characters and *mise-en-scène*; yet *The Color of Money* is further indication of Scorsese's interest in the dynamics of the couple in circumstances beyond those of conventional melodrama, and a variation of the conclusion drawn in *New York, New York*, the notion that bonding of whatever kind is not always necessary or always beneficial.

But, *The Color of Money* notwithstanding, Scorsese himself will continue playing a necessary and beneficial role in contemporary American film. His inquiries into the potentials of cinematic form, the perceptual provocations present to some degree in all his films, serve among the few current reminders that cinema is an act of seeing rather than merely showing. His work is necessary to a cinema that might otherwise collapse into the banalities of convention. Yet there is a paranoia attendant to the experimentation. As each film continues to test the resistance of Hollywood to an intelligent and provocative cinema, that resistance becomes stronger and Scorsese's work becomes more isolated, and perhaps more ordinary as he continues making films. Within his work, the threats of isolation to his characters is enormous. Paranoia seems to enter into the pores of the films, saturating form and content. Scorsese's characters live under a threat of anomie, of collapse, of disappearing into the ordinary world. As a result, they try by all means to define and impress their subjectivity on that world. Because that subjectivity cannot be defined, their success is deeply compromised.

Jimmy and Francine Doyle's success as a couple is compromised by their celebrity as well as their own inarticulateness. Rupert Pupkin—the most innocent of Scorsese's characters—succeeds only because the rest of the world is more innocent than he, and certainly more passive. His celebrity is a mark of everyone else's failure. Jake La Motta, whose despair is articulated only by physical violence, can in the end articulate only a verbal reflection of his former power. Like Travis Bickle and Rupert Pupkin, like Jimmy and Francine, he depends upon public recognition to affirm himself. When he can no longer get that recognition by boxing, he seeks his celebrity through self-parody. Destroying himself physically, his obesity mocking his former strength, he becomes a kind of freak, reciting doggerel and movie dialogue in nightclubs. When last seen, he stands by a mirror in a dressing room, rehearsing Marlon

Brando's great speech from *On the Waterfront*, about being a contender and a bum. This film about a real boxer ends by referring to a boxer in another film, reflecting the necessary and painful intersections of fame and fiction. The possibilities of the self decline and diminish. Reflected in that same mirror is part of the figure of La Motta's director. Scorsese intrudes into the frame as the nightclub manager, asking his star if he needs anything before his act. La Motta then looks at himself in the mirror and says, "Go get 'em, champ." He shadow boxes and calls to his image, "I'm the boss. I'm the boss," and prepares to go on stage. One performance is as good as another, when either one offers an illusion of existence to a diminished personality and the illusion of participation to a diminished spectator. "Better to be king for a night than schmuck for a lifetime," Rupert Pupkin says. The paranoid attempts to avoid being undone by controlling as many people as possible, even if for a moment.

Without public affirmation, these characters would cease to exist. Their fictional being reflects their cinematic being: as figures of cinema they exist only when perceived. Their paranoia is based upon their fear of not being seen, not being recognized. When the characters are totally self-contained and desire for public perception is missing, as it is in *The Color of Money*, there is nothing for the characters to struggle against and no perspective against which to judge them. Eddie's and Vincent's world is, curiously, more hermetic than Travis's, La Motta's, or Rupert Pupkin's because it is open neither to public scrutiny nor subjective dissolution (Vincent's enjoyment of the pool fans' adulation is merely a sign of his egotism and arrogance, not of any paranoid need and terror, and serves further to define him against Eddie's controlled self-sufficiency). These characters need only satisfy their own well-defined desires. Rather than struggle against a diminishing subjectivity, they need only discover how to manage what they have within the world of pool hustling and their own sense of self. Without paranoia they are devitalized. Without the drive to be seen, they become uninteresting to look at.

Paranoia has its obverse side, a terror that results from being too much seen, too much recognized. The subject of *After Hours* is a character who, like Dorothy in *The Wizard of Oz* or like E.T., wishes only to go home, to withdraw a presence that has become too uncomfortable.

Paul Hackett (Griffin Dunne) works as a word processor and lives on
the East Side of Manhattan. All he seeks is a date. What he gets is a
night in lower Manhattan that plunges him into a complex of evil
events from which he barely escapes alive. He becomes so visible, so
much the object of everyone's ill intentions, that he is almost destroyed.
Joseph Minion's script provides the narrative with a seemingly infinite
series of coincidences that diminish the character while not allowing
him to withdraw. The more burdened with misfortune—on the way
downtown, Paul's money blows out of the cab window; his date, who
suggests she is the victim of hideous burn injuries, commits suicide
(when Paul examines her body, no burn marks are to be seen); the bar
owner who befriends him turns out to be his dead date's boyfriend; the
transit system raises its fares at midnight, leaving Paul with insufficient
funds to go back uptown; he almost has his hair shaved off in a punk
disco; he is mistaken for a local burglar and pursued through the streets;
a woman who lives in an apartment underneath a bar wraps him in
plaster, exactly like the hideous statue (which resembles the figure in
Edvard Munch's painting, *The Scream*) fashioned by his dead date's
roommate; in this state he is stolen and falls out of the thieves' truck in

Paul Hackett (Griffin Dunne) looking for a friend in the night of
downtown Manhattan. *After Hours.*

front of his office at dawn—the less able he is to discover the logic of his situation and to extricate himself.

Scorsese builds the narrative into a paranoid's comic dream and discovers allusive structures in the script which offer great room for play. With the exception of Alice, Paul Hackett is the least odd of Scorsese's characters and certainly the least possessed of any discomforting drives or troubled sense of self. He is also Scorsese's first markedly middleclass figure, without violence or mystery, which makes him perfectly liable to a Hitchcockian reign of terror. Like a parody of a Hitchcock figure (at one point, Paul sits on a bed, talking on the phone; Scorsese composes him slightly off center in a shot that recalls Roger Thornhill in a similar situation in *North by Northwest*), Paul gets caught up in a chaotic, threatening environment that evades his control. But script and direction have even higher aspirations than Hitchcock. In his subjugation to the illogical, Paul becomes lesser kin to Franz Kafka's Joseph K., and Scorsese sees the relationship not only through Kafka's novel *The Trial*, but through Orson Welles's film of the novel.

At the opening of the film, Scorsese's camera booms in, arcs around, and pulls back from Paul Hackett at his desk, movements which, as always in Scorsese's films, signify impending threat and violence. As a co-worker talks to Paul, a melody by Bach is heard, which is carried over into the following sequences in which Paul makes his fateful date. The melody is reminiscent of another baroque theme, this one by Albinoni, that plays throughout Orson Welles's film. The gates that close behind Paul as he leaves his office and open again the following morning when, after his terrible night, he is dumped out of the truck, wrapped up like a George Segal sculpture, echo the gates of the Law in Kafka's parable "Before the Law," which appears in the novel and is recited by Welles at the beginning of his film (accompanied by animated images of the gates, the gatekeeper, and the supplicant). When Paul attempts to enter a punk disco, called the Club Berlin, the doorman accepts a bribe. He tells Paul a bribe is not necessary, he is taking it only so that Paul will not feel he has left anything untried. The words repeat those of the guard, standing before the Law in the same Kafka parable. The labyrinthine streets of Manhattan's SoHo, the hidden and underground apartments that let out to unexpected places, the women who try to seduce or abduct or hurt Paul, the entire narrational apparatus of a man trapped for reasons unseen and unknown reverberate back to Kafka and Welles.

Unfortunately, *After Hours* alludes to but does not approach Hitchcock, Welles, or Kafka. It hasn't the social-political-psychological resonance of Kafka, the visual power of Welles, or the moral dynamics of Hitchcock. Nor does it contain the ironic perceptual play of Scorsese's previous work. The structure of allusion serves merely to anchor in literary and cinematic history a basic Scorsesian narrative of New York as trap for the subject who cannot overcome it. Scorsese's previous New Yorkers, despite the precarious state of their identities and psyches, dwelt comfortably in Manhattan. Travis Bickle created his own horror-filled New York to match his perceptual needs. Paul Hackett—not of the working class or of the streets, without an obsessive need to have his selfhood validated—has no protection against it. The gates of his office protect rather than imprison him. Once outside and cut off from the security of the middle-class world, he is helpless and at risk, surrounded by threats of mutilation, castration, and death. In fact *After Hours* is a comic film about castration, about the removal of potency, the ability to impress the self onto the world. Paul Hackett ends up where most Scorsese characters begin, powerless and in despair; yet he almost achieves what all these characters want—celebrity, in his case as an art object.[29] Celebrity offered life to Rupert Pupkin, survival to Jake La Motta. Here it all but embalms the poor word processor who only wants to go home.

*After Hours* is not, finally, a major item in Scorsese's output. Though full of energy, unnerving, and cinematically more interesting than most of the work coming out of Hollywood in the years surrounding its release, it does not have the drive and the significant structure of *Taxi Driver* or even *Raging Bull* or the irony of *The King of Comedy*. Much of the film is shot in rather straightforward, eye-level, over-the-shoulder patterns. Some of the tracking camera movements, such as the booms into the statue that holds its hands to its head in despair, the figure that Paul will become by the end of the film, are repetitive of movements Scorsese has done with more power in earlier films. The streets of lower Manhatten are not explored with quite the same sense of dread and threat as they were in *Taxi Driver*. The brilliant visual filigrees during the final credit sequence, as the camera weaves. and dances around

Paul's office, is as much a showing off of the talents of cinematographer Michael Ballhaus, who did similarly complicated work for Rainer Werner Fassbinder, as it is significant of the ironic security Paul receives in his safe quarters. The film is about paranoia and also exhaustion ("Is that all there is, my friend," sings Peggy Lee in a bizarre fifties song played during the final sequences) and betrays a certain exhaustion of imagination in its images.

Or a willing surrender of imagination. While preparing for *The Color of Money*, Scorsese was quoted as saying that "certain films" do not require slow and deliberate work. He says he no longer wants to be overwhelmed with the drive to make "every shot" the "greatest."[30] *The Color of Money* indeed bears out his wish. Without the obsessive drive to make form expressive and without a form that expresses characters caught in obsessiveness or in the paranoia that accompanies a dislocated self, this is the only film he has made so far that is visually and contextually uninteresting. As always, the filmmaker cannot be second guessed or denied. Perhaps a need to fit more comfortably into the economic, budgetary, and scheduling imperatives of the film business has forced Scorsese to review his methods and reconsider his forms of expression. Perhaps his bad luck in getting financing for a favorite project, a film of Nicos Kazantzakis's *The Last Temptation of Christ*, has forced him to lower his sights. Unable to find funds for high seriousness he may simply be playing for the safety of good returns. But whatever his reasons, the unhappy reality is that in giving up the obsessive search for the right shot, for the precise means of expression, Scorsese risks giving up whatever made his work different from other American filmmakers. The long, dead stretches of conventional over-the-shoulder, shot/reverse shot dialogue sequences in *The Color of Money*, uncharged by the powerful, ethnic speech rhythms of *Mean Streets* or *Raging Bull*, could have been made by anyone. With the exception of the pool-playing montages and a few other moments of visual inquiry, the film is another representative of the Hollywood anonymous style.

I suggested earlier that *The Color of Money* might be a Scorsesian allusion to the ordinary Hollywood "star vehicle" and to his own ability to make a film just like anyone else's. The other possibility is that it is only an embrace of necessity with the attendant loss of individual expression that occurs with such an embrace. If so, Scorsese may successfully have put to rest the romantic illusion of subjective expression in a form that, in reality, demands an impersonal voice—or a voice that homogenizes as many personalities as possible in its attempt to express ideological and stylistic unity. Dissolving the subject into anonymity takes care of the anxiety of subjectivity, along with the anxieties of fitting into the Hollywood system. Unhappily, it also puts an end to the subject's inflections of difference upon the anonymous style. The sleep of imagination becomes more profound.

## CHAPTER FOUR

## IN THE PATRIARCH'S BOSOM

# Steven Spielberg and the Politics of Recuperation

> Parents redeemed erase the sins
> of the past and become Paradise
> regained. . . . At the final
> eucharistic table of the free
> lunch, Ronald Reagan is the
> rehabilitated parent par
> excellence, the faded idol as
> reachable ideal.[1]

The desire to think and write seriously about Steven Spielberg's films produces a surge of conflicting reactions and activates the critic's discomfort about analysing recent, very popular works. The immediate response is to assume a classical, elitist position. Anything so popular is no doubt questionable and fleeting; in a few years the films will disappear into the back shelves of the video store never to be referred to again. Their glibness and polish, their ability to excite the most accessible emotions seem to force them into a position that defies serious analysis. But that very defiance produces a critical defiance in response. Spielberg is so proficient—so efficient—at structuring his narratives, controlling his *mise-en-scène*, and positioning the spectator within these structures, that the films all but guarantee that the viewer will surrender his or her self to them at some point during the narrative. Power like this needs to be understood; when film so easily manipulates emotion, there is every reason to find out how and why.

Less subjective reasons also emerge. Spielberg's work is obviously well crafted, technologically overdetermined, dependent upon cinematic effects, and at the same time determinedly realistic and manipulative. It brings to the fore the central problem of the illusionary form, the power of American cinema to create an unquestioning location of belief and assent. I have already discussed the ideological ramifications of this phenomenon, and must note a more immediate problem. The plain fact is that discussion of modernist form is far easier than discussion of the classical style. The way in which Scorsese's films, for example, so happily and energetically foreground their narrative and cinematic devices makes them readily accessible to formal analysis. The dominant classical style—the repetition of formal devices whose aim is to render themselves invisible—is much more difficult to analyze, precisely because the form is repetitive and hidden behind the narrative it creates. Spielberg's work is firmly in this tradition. Although he inflects its structure with a patina not of modernism, but of modernity, and includes frequent allusions to other films, he disallows distance and objectivity. He tightens his films like a trap, so that the viewer is unable to see beyond the image content and remains immediately unaware as to why there is no escape. From the outside, their camouflage is difficult to penetrate. But by defying analysis, Spielberg's films create a critical, perhaps even a political imperative to pierce their invisible cover and reveal the mechanisms at work.

An important part of the mechanism is the ideological structure of the films. The content of Spielberg's work is very attractive, but only to the degree that its formal structure gives it shape and meaning and manipulates viewer assent to it. The form and structure of the films produce images and narratives that respond or give shape to the current ideological needs of an audience, offering a safe and secure ideological haven. Their images and narratives speak of a place and a way of being in the world (indeed the universe) that viewers find more than just comfortable, but desirable and—within the films—*available*. Just here is where we see form and substance become inextricable. These films create for their viewers comfortable surrogates for an uncomfortable world, satisfying desire, clarifying, indeed forging relationships between the individual and the world *within the films' imaginative structures.* Unlike Arthur Penn's work, Spielberg's films are not simply ideological bellwethers, pointing to major cultural currents, summing up the state of things every five to eight years. They transcend the function of responding or giving shape to ideology, and instead become ideology, the very shape and form of the relationships we desire with our world. Louis Althusser writes, *"all ideology hails or interpellates concrete individuals as concrete subjects. . . ."* Individuals give their subjectivity willingly to the ideological discourse, because something obviously recognizable and desirable is there. "It is indeed a peculiarity of ideology," he says, "that it imposes (without appearing to do so, since these are 'obviousnesses') obviousnesses as obviousnesses, which we cannot *fail to recognize* and before which we have the inevitable and natural reaction of crying out (aloud or in the 'still, small voice of conscience'): 'That's obvious! That's right! That's true.'"[2] The ideological structures of Spielberg's films "hail" the spectator into a world of the obvious that affirms the viewer's presence (even while dissolving it), affirms that what the viewer has always believed or hoped is (obviously) right and accessible, and assures the viewer excitement and comfort in the process. The films offer nothing new beyond their spectacle, nothing the viewer does not already want, does not immediately accept. That is their conservative power, and it has spread throughout the cinema of the eighties.

Spielberg's films constitute a factory of ideological production, the great imaginary of the eighties, full of images the culture wanted to see, images and narratives that expressed the culture. The frequency, success, and influence of his films during a relatively short period of time have made them a kind of encyclopedia of desire, a locus of representations to which audiences wished to be called.* He is at the center of eighties American filmmaking, and I want to get to that center through

---

*Spielberg's immediate influence extends to the group of films produced under his aegis, including Robert Zemeckis's *I Wanna Hold Your Hand* (1978), Tobe Hooper's *Poltergeist* (1983, apparently largely directed by Spielberg); Joe Dante's *Gremlins* (1984) and *Innerspace* (1987), Robert Zemeckis's *Back to the Future* (1985); Richard Donner's *The Goonies* (1985); Barry Levine's *Young Sherlock Holmes* (1985); Richard Benjamin's *The Money Pit* (1986, an "adult" comedy, and therefore somewhat to one side of the other works); Don Bluth's animated film, *An American Tail* (1986).

some adjacent doors, examining other images and narratives of the period, before confronting the main texts. My selection is somewhat limited, for I am most interested in particular kinds of ideological representations; but they are typical of the way film has placed itself in the service of the dominant cultural discourse, and indeed document that discourse for future reference.

**1**

Discussing Penn's *Night Moves*, I noted the shudder that went through the dominant ideology during the sixties and seventies, beginning with the assassination of Kennedy and ending with the liberation of Vietnam in the late seventies. For a society unused to internal failures and external losses, unable and unwilling to analyze events historically, politically, economically, rationally, the result was a mixture of anger, guilt, and frustrated aggressiveness. In film, images and narratives of despair and impotence alternated or were combined with violent outbursts against the self and others. *Taxi Driver, Death Wish* and its vigilante offspring; Coppola's *The Conversation*; *Night Moves*; Alan J. Pakula's *The Parallax View*; Sidney Pollack's *Three Days of the Condor* are some examples, among many, of films which spoke defeat and powerlessness, with the occasional, isolated surge of violence as surrogate for social action.

Watergate, the revolution in Iran, the capture of American hostages, the accepted notion that Jimmy Carter was weak because he did not or could not make war threatened to cut away any of the remaining ideological props of liberalism. A turn came in the late seventies. The weakened structure began to be strengthened and the dominant voice retuned by the discourse of neo-conservatism. Within the relative ideological hegemony of American politics, liberalism and conservatism are not very disparate, and in fact coexist with only some tension. Both ideologies are centered upon the image of the male individual and his unfettered advancement in a "free enterprise" economy. Both are anti-collective, anti-female, anti-left, hierarchical, and aggressive. Liberalism embeds its aggressiveness within images of conciliation and myths of equal opportunity and reason ("Let us reason together" was Lyndon Johnson's call, while he waged war) and gathers to itself, almost like satellites, opposing ideological fragments, discourses that offer possibilities of help to those outside the central sphere of power, while that sphere remains essentially untouched. Conservatism repels any mitigating or modifying forces, demanding individual and groups be not merely unimpeded by, but denied of assistance or protection, while demanding that all dwell within a rigid, economically determined hierarchy. Contradictions develop instantly within both structures. Liberalism cannot comfortably contain images of social responsibility within its capitalist imperative. Conservatism gets tongue-tied as it insists upon unfettered individual initiative while promoting a protected, elite, patriarchal structure of ownership and administration. Infiltrating this central contradiction is a discourse of extraordinary belligerence in which the banalities of free enterprise are re-created into harsh statements of moral and political righteousness, protectionism (of all entrenched, non-communist political, economic, and social structures), and intolerance.

Liberalism generates, as part of its ideological contradictions, a loneliness born of its impossible promise of communal assistance. Conservatism fosters loneliness outright by insisting that each man must count on no help and each woman must be dependent upon the same unaided individual. At the same time, conservatism pretends to offer a voice to the lower middle-class, those to whom its goals of wealth and power appear to be vaguely in sight but are perpetually unreachable. This is the group that attends to its discourse, hears it repeat its litany that the most fulfilled life is one in which money is earned and a family raised and protected without government assistance—tasks that require single-minded effort, self-denying labor, and a refusal of all political action except assent. The right wing discourse also announces that the middle-class can win back national and international esteem and pride presumably lost when foreign governments assert themselves. Typically, the announcement is based on yet another contradiction: this esteem is rightfully ours, it says, but we are too weak to establish our right to it. As a result, aggressiveness and belligerence increase until military operations become all but unavoidable. In the end, conservatism must wage war or (more likely) recognize its impotence as a fact and then fantasize images that pretend to overcome that impotence.

This contradiction has been a most potent source for cinematic images in the eighties. In fact, film has created the images and produced the narratives that give ideological structure to what has often been a confused discourse punctuated by occasional desperate action. I noted earlier that, during the seventies, in response to feelings of social impotence, the subject as effective agent in cinematic fiction was diminished physically, emotionally, and politically. Francis Ford Coppola's *The Conversation* (1974) offers a better than typical example. The film's central character, Gene Hackman's Harry Caul, is a gray and recessive surveillance expert, who, in the course of the film, suffers a kind of moral destruction. Used to spying on others with delicately operated sound equipment, he becomes—or so he believes—witness to the murder of a corporate director. As a result, he suffers a kind of moral paralysis, subdued by his guilt and then by the very act that created that guilt. The man who attempted to subordinate his personality in order to become the secret watcher of other people's lives becomes the object of surveillance himself, by someone not troubled by anxieties. At the end of the film, he is a completely reduced figure, sitting in the corner of his room, which he has torn to pieces looking for a hidden microphone, playing a saxophone as if he were a child sucking a pacifier.

The character's fall is accompanied by a questioning of the viewer's own position of safety outside the narrative, in the world. Coppola structures events through Harry's sensibility, so that a complex of fear, guilt, and fantasy are created that sometimes defy straightforward comprehension of what happens. But he also articulates his camera so that it often creates images of passive, almost impersonal observation. In that last shot, the camera observes Harry from a high angle, mechanically swinging right and left, as if it were an instrument of surveillance. Therefore, the viewer must respond not only to Harry's sensibility, but to the absence of sensibility signified by the coldly observing camera. The result is a reduction of both subjects, the participant in the fiction and the viewer of the fiction, neither of which is given any moral ground. The film raises questions not only about the morality of spying and the effects of being spied upon, but about the efficacy, potency, and ethics of action itself.

*The Conversation*, as I said, was one of a number of films of paranoia and loss, fictions of impotence and despair which disallowed the effective heroic action American films had so often promised its audience.

There were, as well, responses to these statements offered by country and urban vigilante films, particularly the *Walking Tall, Dirty Harry*, and *Death Wish* cycles. These films drew directly upon the convention of the individual hero, resituating him in somewhat more clearly defined political contexts than in the past. While Buford Pusser was battling mob elements in a small town in *Walking Tall* (1973, directed by Phil Karlson, "based on a true story," yet essentially the same film as Karlson's 1955 *Phenix City Story*), Dirty Harry Callahan and Charles Bronson's architect hero of *Death Wish* were acting in political opposition to local government powers. The police adhered to liberal laws that permitted killers to walk the streets. The vigilantes, more closely in touch with the needs of the community, transcended these laws, bringing evil to violent justice.

These films articulated, quite simply and directly, one aspect of the growing conservatism of the seventies, generating images that articulated the Nixonian calls for law and order against anti-war activists (the mad killer in *Dirty Harry* wears a peace symbol) and other anarchic forces in the society that seemed resistant to control. As the Nixon regime turned paranoid and Vietnam caused a rupture in the ideological layer where cultural images of invincibility lay embedded, filmic expressions of violence became more inwardly directed and masochistic. There were symptoms that the society held itself collectively to blame for Vietnam (of course it was to blame, though the political aspects of this truth were not the ones examined), and many films focused upon the crazed Vietnam veteran. As always, cinema evaded political realities and, in this instance, focused upon Vietnam as a psychological aberration which processed innocent young men into psychopaths (*Taxi Driver* has some relationship to this group of films). On another, equally apolitical level, the war was seen as a challenge to conventional notions of civilized conduct (including traditional notions of the "proper" conduct of war), a destruction of individual comportment and control, and a demonstration of just how fragile were the conventions of western civilized behavior. Michael Cimino explored this somewhat aberrant version of right-wing humanism in *The Deer Hunter*, as did John Milius and Francis Coppola in *Apocalypse Now*, and Oliver Stone in *Platoon*. The Vietnam of all these films savaged hearts, minds, and bodies, making American boys crazy. *Apocalypse*

*Now* and (to a somewhat lesser extent, pretending to offer the perspective of the average field soldier) *Platoon* portrayed Vietnam as a hallucinatory, schizophrenic realm in which hierarchy, responsibility, and order were in decay. (Of the mid-eighties Vietnam films, only Kubrick's *Full Metal Jacket* concentrated on the destructive elements inherent in the training and disposition of the soldiers themselves.) The cause of moral decay and madness, particularly in *The Deer Hunter* and *Apocalypse Now*, was an enemy as anarchic as "the criminal elements" who needed extermination in the law and order films. Worse, they were Oriental and communist, able therefore to be represented as the alien other, who might infiltrate the Western soul and destroy its moral structure. The analogy to fifties anti-communist science fiction films is not at all strained.[3]

The regime of Jimmy Carter was a result, in part, of a search for calm after this latest assault, along with a desire to live out a fantasy of a nongovernmental government (Carter had his origins in the populist, indeed Capra-esque notion of the "man of the people," who might separate the nation from an established power that now appeared not only corrupt, but, after Watergate, self-absorbed and uninterested in people's needs). During Carter's tenure, various national interests outside the United States continued to assert themselves, and the internal economy faltered badly; the hoped-for calm turned into another cycle of frustration and desire for revenge. Arabs took the place of Orientals as the alien other, although their representation in film was limited to the comic or the devious. Middle Easterners are depicted either as rich and stupid men in robes or savage, irrational terrorists.

Clearly, the culture still required a period of calm, recuperation, and affirmation, even in the face of events that would appear to render such a period impossible. Ronald Reagan was able to enact an extraordinary phenomenon. With the actor's talent for assuming a persona requisite to the situation at hand, and a national audience ready to become subject to a discourse of security, power, and self-righteousness, he was able to focus various ideological elements. More, he became an ideology. For a moment it seemed possible that no further ideological displacement would be necessary. Reagan did not merely articulate the language of extreme conservatism; he was his own discursive center, displacing the reality of politics with the illusion of a personality who spoke deliberately, assertively, and with complete conviction. "The great communicator" was not merely a journalistic cliché. Ronald Reagan became what many people wanted to see and hear. More than what Reagan spoke, the way he spoke it, his aggressive, anti-communist discourse, his promise of a free-enterprise utopia where every one (of the appropriate gender, politics, and color) might do what he wished and thrive, with no interference; his implicit offering of himself as paternal guide into this utopia, made him an ideological magnet and a hegemonic force, equaled (in a rather different political context) only by Roosevelt in the thirties and forties.

But words are not enough. Ideology is structurally unsteady. Currents keep surging and contradictions keep occurring, causing shifts, forcing elements continually to realign in order to maintain validity as representations. Reagan's aggressive discourse, which presented most of the non-white, non-monied, or non-capitalist world as enemy, could only exist *as* discourse, as a way of addressing reality that finally ignored reality altogether. Except for a few invasions and the military and economic support given to reactionary guerrilla groups throughout the world, there was little Reagan and his government could do about the international and domestic complexities it attempted to simplify in its language. One result was a great deal of ideological energy that remained unconnected to tangible images. Fragments of discontent and desire continued to be generated and frustrated, breaking loose, seeking articulations. Reagan, or the Reagan discourse, kept articulating problems with solutions that could not be safely acted out in reality, notions of international hegemony and internal domesticity, economic self-sufficiency that could not be lived out by most people.

American film, as always, became an important generator of images through which that ideological energy was channeled. And since film had always created an imaginary realm of individual passions inflamed and satisfied, not much accommodation had to be made. Some generic adjustments, some variations on heroic stereotypes and a confusion of historical realities allowed filmmakers to supply the coherence that the general discourse lacked. Two areas—strength against communism and the virtues of the family—were much attended to, and often intermingled in odd ways. The cold war, an ideological knot tied in the fifties and continuing its hold in the eighties, provided basic material for two groups of films. One was directly anti-Russian and is best represented by Sylvester Stallone's *Rocky IV* and Taylor Hackford's *White Nights* (both 1985).

*Rocky IV* creates a rather peculiar set of oppositions. The cold-war films are based upon one ideological premise, the weakness of America. "Look at them," says Rostov, the agent who begins the Russian take-over of the United States in *Invasion USA* (1985), ". . .soft, spineless, decadent. They don't even understand the nature of their own freedom or how we can use it against them. They are their own worst enemy." Rocky Balboa decides he will be one man who can overcome this weakness, not through military force, but through a single act of willed hero-ism. Throughout the series of films bearing his name, Rocky has been an unconscious parody of the working-class hero, a character of inartic-ulate stupidity, good-hearted strength, and indomitable spirit. Here these qualities are manifested in a peculiar way. He becomes not merely a representative (and savior) of his society and culture, but—as in the first of the Rambo films—a very force of nature itself. His Russian opponent, Drago, is man-made, artificially created, his strength built by high-technology exercise equipment and steroids. Rocky trains not in a gymnasium or lab, but in the Siberian wastes, running through the snow, chopping wood, chinning on rafters, lifting a sleigh full of peo-ple—a comparison presented in a lengthy montage sequence in which the two fighters and their different preparations are intercut. Stallone—or his editor—is apparently not ignorant of cinema history, he merely stands Eisenstein on his head.

This montage of oppositions, the pitting of nature against technology, comes out of some interesting cultural and cinematic realities. The "back to nature" movement was a largely middle-class phenomenon of the seventies, part of the general withdrawal from direct participation in the political realm. By the early eighties, nature was once again upstaged by technology, as the computer became an obsessive cultural reference. Despite the ubiquitous images of and by computers, the promise that the machine would be useful in every home faded. They were not needed in every home, they were the threat to jobs and privacy everyone had feared, and the "information systems" they created remained the property of others, inaccessible to most people. Stallone was able to work upon these negative, somewhat threatening images and combine them with the dangers already foreshadowed in science fiction films. He begins by parodying the idea of domestic technology: Rocky owns a robot, who speaks like a woman and acts as a servant for his son and for his friend Paulie. He then goes on to consider the greater threat as represented by his technologically trained Russian opponent, who emerges as that stock figure of science fiction, the robot monster. Russia becomes a version of the future society often depicted in science fiction films in which individuals are reduced to automata. The country has especially forgotten that sports involves direct human activity, the struggle of strong individuals, and uses scientific intervention to create an unbeatable superman. International sports, as always, become a surrogate for war, and Stallone combines all the elements to create a film in which the power of nature overcomes politics and technology to work toward the victory of the American individual over the superior, inhuman forces of the enemy.

In the midst of all this, further ideological problems are settled. Conservative discourse holds that technology and the hard, external world of business are the male's domain. Women are part of nature and the internal world of reproduction and sustenance. Like nature, they are to be used for the good of men. Because of his success as a boxer, Rocky has become domesticated, with a wife, child, money, and a fancy house. Too domesticated, in fact. The indication is that he may be getting old and soft, which in the film's crazed political logic makes him representative of America itself, imperative that he fight the Russian boxer to prove himself and his country, and avenge the death of his friend and onetime opponent Apollo Creed. (In *Rocky IV*, Apollo is killed by Drago in a match tainted by Las Vegas glamor and show business posturings, unnatural, a further indication of the distance America has come from its natural strengths.) Rocky's return to nature helps him not only redress the imbalance of cultural superiority but of masculine and feminine roles as well. He leaves the comforts of his home, uses nature, bends it to his needs, makes it work for him during his training. He regains his strength—and, by extension, his country's—and manages to reassert proper domestic hierarchy. Rocky's wife, Adrian, is passive and compliant, but when he decides to go to Russia and fight Drago, she is fearful and refuses to accompany him. However, in the midst of his Siberian training, she appears, proclaiming her love and attachment.

She helps him in his extraordinary efforts to build his strength, becoming part of the natural order at his service. Drago's wife, on the other hand, is aggressive and prominent. Ludmilla speaks abrasively for her husband at news conferences and intrudes her presence whenever possible. She is, in the polarities created by the film, not "natural," not a true woman, just as her mechanically trained husband is not a true man.

These oppositions need a common ground in which to meet, or else they would remain contentions without the synthesis needed to create a point of ideological stability. In *Rocky IV* that ground is provided by a representation beloved of conservative populism, "the people." Like Rocky, "the people" are part of nature, their intuition is dependable; they prove able to tell good from evil. Throughout much of the film, the Russian people are shown as suspicious or the objects of suspicion. The police, the KGB, soldiers stare, everyone else is stared at, appearing almost soulless, out of touch with their individuality. As the match between Rocky and Drago goes on, as Rocky proves that he can take it, the Russian audience discovers where the real strength and honesty lie and begin to cheer him on. The combination of the natural force, the expression of pure will—Rocky—and the growing enthusiasm of the audience that recognizes how wonderful he is, brings the attending Politburo, led by actors who resemble Gorbachev and Gromyko, to their feet to cheer the American underdog. Drago falls victim to the clean, untainted, unsupported strength of America-in-Rocky; his people naturally understand the irresistibility of that strength; their new hero wraps himself (literally) in the American flag and makes a speech about global understanding.

Rocky far surpasses the generic limitations of the boxing hero. No despairing, uncentered sufferer like Jake La Motta, Rocky transcends his profession and influences governments. But at the same time, he does not. The film—typically—cannot articulate politics as something separate from issues of personality and the individual. Obviously, *Rocky IV* is as much or more about the discovery of inner strength and self-reliance as it is about cold war issues. And, curiously, political victory and self-discovery are measured by the individual's conquering of himself. There is here an odd, almost fascistic, and certainly melodramatic pattern of destroying the self so that a new self may emerge, an act of cleansing by pain and sacrifice that will allow the new, natural man to emerge. Rocky tells his wife, "No, maybe I can't win. Maybe the only thing I can do is just take everything he's got. But to beat me, he's going to have to kill me. And to kill me, he's going to have to have the heart to stand in front of me. And to do that, he's gotta be willing to die himself. I don't know if he's ready to do that." The sacrifice to death will prove the value of men and nations—an old cry from the depths of conservative ideologies. Rocky has to kill his old self, corrupted by the comforts America makes available and which in turn make it soft. The Russians have no selves to kill, for they have already given themselves up to the state (again the fifties science fiction images of the cold war prove ideologically accurate). They have to kill the collective, the communal spirit. Selves that already exist, like Rocky's, do not have to go through the trauma of being reborn, only rediscovered. During the match, as Rocky gains the upper hand, a member of the Politburo rushes to ring side and scolds the the Russian champ for losing. To the cheers of the crowd, Drago lifts the man up by his neck and shouts: "I fight to win . . . for me!" The communist automaton—pulverized by the new, natural American man—learns the value of self against the government. Politics and history disappear as strong individuals emerge.

The individual who affects the conduct of government or, preferably, works for an alleged good in spite of the conduct of government, has become a major narrative component of the conservative film. We will see the figure in its full glory in the eighties revenge films. *White Nights* attempts a more complex narrative for such a figure, while offering its audience a number of attractions: ballet dancing, tap dancing, cold war rantings, problems of race relations, miscegenation, and a prison escape melodrama. The film attempts to integrate these mutually exclusive elements through the conventions of psychological realism, in which two antagonistic characters must learn to care for each other. Once more, politics provides only a background to character struggle, resulting in some narrative operations that almost make one approve of Stallone's comic book directness.

Mikhail Baryshnikov's ballet dancer-defector, Nikolai, finds himself trapped again in Russia (a Russia similar to *Rocky IV*, cold and hard, a land of universal suspicion) and must overcome his arrogance and elitism. He must befriend, and eventually help, the black American defector, Raymond (Gregory Hines), who finds that racial oppression in the U.S.S.R. is worse than in the U.S.A., which he left to escape the terrors of Vietnam. Whereas *Rocky IV* creates a clear, direct, and fantastic narrative line, *White Nights* goes through a number of melodramatic diversions during which it seems to pose and answer seemingly important questions, maneuvering around its central tedious problem concerning the ability of the Russian bourgeois ballet dancer/defector reaching an emotional accord with the angry black American tap dancer/defector. The latter has fallen deeply in love with, married, and impregnated a Russian woman and has become a tool of Chaiko, the smirking KGB man. Obviously the resolutions to the problems are predetermined by every other melodrama that has preceded it. Political realities and complexities have no effect on the predeterminations; or, rather, the conventions of cold war conflict are themselves so much grounded in melodrama, the latter easily absorbs the former. *White Nights*, finally, is not a film about international relations or about class and color, which are only used something like the flippers on a pinball machine, to direct the narrative toward the inevitable escape of the characters from their captors.

The escape itself is not so much a manifestation of political urgency as it is of a more vague and therefore more easily fulfillable desire. Nikolai wants his freedom—although he seems to be offered as much freedom as possible in the U.S.S.R. Raymond wants only to take control of his life and "to go home." "I'm going home," he says, as he is exchanged at the border (he initially sacrificed his freedom so that his wife and Nikolai could make their escape). "For better or worse, I'm going home." He suddenly recognizes his need for that central image of conservative ideology, the mythical place of family and security that dissolves all other problems. Racism in the United States and in Russia goes unexamined (the demonstration that Russian KGB officers are racist seems sufficient to the point). The question of how Raymond may survive his return to the country he fled is unanswered by anything but the comment that "things have changed." To succeed in its ideological project, the film must only impress upon its most complex character— and its audience—the necessity of accepting an undefined place that promises security.

Home, it turns out, is a major focus of the new cold war films. This image and narrative goal, which received major encoding in *The Wizard of Oz* ("home sweet home" was pumped into the script throughout successive rewrites at MGM)[4] have become the sign of safety, promise, and rest. As I suggested, the vagueness of the image, its by now automatically generated connotations of security, make it irresistible to filmmaker and viewer, full of psychological, economic, and social potency. Inside this home is where the family is—that signifier of sexual, economic, and political order that resides as the obsessive center of conservative language.

E.T. phones home; a black dancer in Russia wants to come home no matter what the consequences (particularly when the KGB threaten wife and family); Vietnam veterans are brought home. Aggression against home and family in the *Death Wish* films provoked vigilante action. The inability to reunite families and complete the home initiates aggression against old enemies in the eighties round of vigilante films. I noted earlier that the seventies vigilantes worked locally, within their city or town. The eighties avengers work internationally, specifically in Vietnam (a province of Russia in most of the films involved); their purpose is to find those men—a son in the instance of Ted Kotcheff's *Uncommon Valor* (1983, co-produced by John Milius and Buzz Feitshans, the latter the producer of a number of right-wing Vietnam avenger films, including the two *Rambo*s), friends or simply abandoned American soldiers, as in Joseph Zito's *Missing in Action* (1984) or Stallone's and George Cosmatos's *Rambo: First Blood Part Two* (1985)—who were presumably left behind and forgotten. They must find them and bring them home. In John Milius's *Red Dawn* (1984) and Joseph Zito's *Invasion U.S.A.*, the Russians invade the United States, destroying homes and families. In the first film, primitive bands of heroic teenagers form to fight the Russians; in the latter, Chuck Norris and the army wipe them out.

To understand the politics and ideological structure of these films, it might be helpful first to look at one that extracts its avenger from the peculiarly right-wing, anti-Russian base that supports all of those just cited. J. Lee Thompson's Charles Bronson vehicle, *The Evil That Men Do* (1984), goes against the grain. The Bronson character—a retired avenger (little information is offered about him; simply being an avenger is now sufficient background for most of these characters)—takes on, for no pay, the job of destroying a hired torturer, who works for the United States and its client states in Central America, teaching counter insurgency by giving instruction in the destruction of the human body. The Bronson character tracks the man down and hastens his death at the hands of a group of his former victims, who work in a mine. The final act is not that of the lone hero, but of a collective, and is almost a revolutionary gesture.

This film is an all but unaccountable aberration, for few others of the period express such anti-American, pro-Third World sentiments (there are some vaguely liberal precedents in the seventies *Walking Tall* and *Billy Jack* films, and perhaps two eighties films that critically question American hegemony, racism, or anti-Russian feeling, each—Peter Hyams's *2010*, and the German director, Wolfgang Petersen's *Enemy Mine*—a work of science fiction). One must assume that the liberal establishment in Hollywood and the film's producer, Pancho Kohner, felt it necessary to make a statement somewhat to the left of center and hoped that the film's star, the violent action that informs his work and is present to an extraordinary degree in this film, would counter its politics. Or render them invisible. Fredric Jameson writes that melodrama is "a narrative instrument for managing social tensions and conflicts."[5] Perhaps *The Evil That Men Do* demonstrates that the avenger melodrama manages these tensions and conflicts simply by resolving them through the repeated figure of the lone man who performs the symbolic action of destroying a well-defined evil (the torturer's acts are much more clearly defined in the film than his politics). By so doing, the audience is absolved of political responsibility, performing its own symbolic act of social-political evasion by allowing the action to create catharsis while ignoring the causes and effects of the action. As long as it fits within certain narrative parameters that permit the hero to operate, and as long as it helps explain "the existence of social disorder,"[6] the evil of the avenger films *may* be of the right or the left.

The theory is partly born out in *Rambo: First Blood Part Two*. Although the villains are identified as Vietnamese and Russian, they appear as something quite different. They are determined one way politically, another cinematically. The Vietnamese are not Vietnamese, but a re-creation of World War II movie Japanese. Their Russian adviser is not Russian, but a representation of a World War II movie Nazi. (In the videotapes of *Rambo* prepared for countries sensitive to anti-Russian propaganda, the dialogue was easily re-dubbed so that contemporary references were effaced and the film set in World War II.) Simplemindedness is not the sole contributing factor to this confusion. On some level, the makers of *Rambo* realized that a popular narrative is facilitated both in its creation and reception if the codes are immediately apparent and easily recognized. An old signifying system is more easily re-created than a new one invented. Orientals and Germans have been typed and coded since the earliest years of cinema, their representation easily explains and defines "the existence of social disorder" and provides for its correction. Reverting to such representations is more convenient than attempting to describe who the Vietnamese soldiers were and what a Russian adviser might be like, and what, if anything, the two might have in common. By solving the problem without dealing with it, the film invites an easy participation and ready reception by the viewer. *Rambo* speaks the discourse of frustration satisfied and fantasies affirmed; it confirms what film has been saying throughout its existence, that Orientals are indeed all alike, without history or national differentiation; that nazism signifies any white, foreign evil, easily detectable by a character's uniform, insidious accent, and cruel gaze.

But the fact remains that, despite its transmission of current ideology through older film images, *Rambo* and the majority of avenger melodramas have an affinity for contemporary conservative discourse (or vice versa), which seems to indicate that their generic violence and dependence upon individual as opposed to collective action is, finally, more amenable to the ideological representations of the right. This rightward inclination is particularly strong in the eighties Vietnam revenge cycle because of the presence around them and, in a curious way, within them of Ronald Reagan. The ideological process works like this: the missing-in-action films contain two enemies, the U.S. government and the Vietnamese (as noted, in order to maintain a comforting familiarity, and not to strain political stereotyping, the Vietnamese are often depicted as mere tools of the Russians). The major fault of the United States is that it did not permit the soldiers to win the Vietnam war in the first place ("Do we get to win this time?" is John Rambo's most lucid, if not most historically useful, utterance when he is sent on his mission). To compound matters, the government now covers up the existence of survivors to save itself embarrassment (although, in reality, the government seems to ply rumors of the existence of prisoners of war to promote active antagonism against the Vietnamese). At the same time, Ronald Reagan, the head of government, based his career on separating himself from the government on all matters, including Vietnam policy. As a result, the government could be attacked for continuing to allow prisoners to suffer (the objects of this attack in the films are sometimes the CIA, but more often officials of some unnamed bureaucracy); the head of the government could stand apart as the mentor of brave, individual action, as the patron of the missing and—in the films—the mentor of the avengers. Even outside of the films, Ronald Reagan is not so much an individual as an ideological representation of the tough movie hero; through him and into the films passes the spirit of John Wayne, particularly the John Wayne of *The Searchers*—the lone figure, something of an outlaw, who can work against the system for the good that everyone knows the system is trying to ignore. Like Reagan himself, the avenger heroes become unique embodiments of that part of the dominant ideology the dominant ideology itself does not wish to recognize, the desire to discover and act upon foreign injustices to Americans, safely, through the intervention of an individual who will act for everyone.

The avenger films, finally, offer an ideological contract, promising to represent that which is *only* available in representation in return for the committed gaze of the viewer. If representing a representation seems to be a redundancy, recall that the ideology of the right presents a barely coherent discourse full of possibilities that cannot be acted upon without enormous military and social cost. The films articulate these possibilities, representing the assenting viewer's own fantasy, uniting his subjectivity (I am assuming that the intended subject of these films is male) with characters who enact the ideology's great wish fulfillment: destruction of the "enemy," ending opposition by annihilating it, placing the entire burden on a single individual. The only cost is the price of admission, which includes a most terrible and hopeless admission, that the world spoken by the ideology and the images given it by these films have validity.

The validation of the imaginary has some peculiar consequences, affirming patriarchal structures and absorbing the individual into them. Here a detour from the avenger films is necessary in order to return to them with some greater clarity. The classical description of psychological processes, as revised by the French psychiatrist, Jacques Lacan, represents the father as a castrating force, cutting the child from union with the mother and the imaginary world of comfort and sustenance, forcing the child into the symbolic realm of language and culture, the phallocentric, patriarchal world of power. Here, in the "adult" realm, the subject is in flux, continually repositioned, alternately (or simultaneously) at the mercy of the other, *being* the other as the object of someone else's gaze. But the hailing of the subject into the imaginary realm of these films (indeed *all* films to some extent) reverses the oedipal process.[7] The subject is not cut off from comfort and sustenance, he is offered them. He is given an illusion of power. Rather than being positioned against or at the mercy of the patriachy, the subject is put under and made witness to its protection. The patriarchy assumes a maternal position, of care rather than authority. In the process, an extraordinary event happens as the ideological material from the larger discourse of the government is given shape by its image-making arm, eighties film. Ronald Reagan (re)enters cinema as the guiding patriarch offering maternal care.

Earlier I mentioned that Reagan created a persona who stands apart from the government he attacks, acting as the brave mentor to great deeds that cannot be done. I am suggesting here that, more than external guiding force, he becomes a disguised narrative figure in these films, a paternal figure who guides the hero. The image of older mentor—the wise fatherly surrogate—keeps appearing in contemporary American film in a variety of guises. I must emphasize that, as an ideological and psychological presence, this figure is hardly new; the maternal patriarch is present throughout literature and film, usually coded as a protector and the well of great wisdom. In the late thirties and early forties, Roosevelt would appear often in films—in *Yankee Doodle Dandy* (1942), for example, when George M. Cohan visits the White House and "Roosevelt," who is viewed from behind, represented by his shoulder and back, a metonymic figure of the great man who may not be fully represented, yet whose presence accompanies everything. When the Joads enter the government-run migrant camp in *The Grapes of Wrath*, they are greeted by the man in charge, who looks like Roosevelt and offers them the security and help that was an extension of Roosevelt's ideological aura.[8]

The entry of the Reagan persona into film is different, taking the form of an older man who teaches and legitimizes the hero and, perhaps even more important, protects the audience. While the hero goes beyond the mentor in his deeds, the mentor is still present as a control, as a safety limit. He looks out for the hero and looks out for the audience as well. With him present, the viewer is assured that the hero will neither get hurt nor go too far beyond established bonds (mentors in pre-Reagan contemporary film might be unreliable: in *Taxi Driver*, Travis goes for advice to the older cab driver, Wizard, who says he doesn't know what Travis is talking about; the mentor fails and Travis goes beyond all socially acceptable bounds of behavior). This is particularly true where the older figure mentors an adolescent. The young man is still learning, still vulnerable and capable of wrong action if uncontrolled. Here the mentor fully emerges as father surrogate, a wiser and more protective influence than the hero's actual father (who is either dead, separated from the family, or completely ineffectual), who manages to create a sounder patriarchal situation than any actual father could. Replacing the biological father, giving the hero direction and control, the new mentor-maternal-patriarch supplies the ideological demand for family, without the need to bring forth the insoluble problems regarding the family's viability.

This is nowhere better observed than in Robert Zemeckis's *Back to the Future*. Here, under the guidance of a somewhat looney scientist, Doc Brown, Michael J. Fox's Marty McFly goes back in time before his birth and helps to arrange his parents' marriage. His own father is mild-mannered and cowardly, and therefore Marty must be sure the match occurs, lest he and his family become uncreated. Unfortunately, his mother-to-be falls in love with him, thus creating a most interesting variation on the oedipal triangle. Marty is under the obligation not only to get his mother matched to the correct person, but also to save his scientist friend. Just as Marty left, Doc Brown appeared to be assassinated by Libyans who sold him the plutonium for his time machine (a Delorean car) in return for his promise to build them a nuclear bomb. As a result of these efforts, the son manages to go through oedipalization before he is born, create his family to his own liking (when he returns from his trip, his father is no longer a hopeless coward, but a suave writer, thanks to Marty's interventions), and save Doc Brown. Through it all, the scientist acts as a kind of *idiot savant*, both an equal and elder guide, who does not make paternal demands, is vulnerable, and who offers not only support but adventure. (*Back to the Future* creates an interesting counterpoint to another Spielberg produced film, Joe Dante's *Gremlins*. Here, too, the young man's father is mild and somewhat passive, an inventor of useless objects. The mentor figure plays only a small role in this film, an Oriental elder who entrusts the boy with a small beast which multiplies into a horde of mean little demons. The boy becomes father to the anarchic creatures over whom he must regain control.)

The Japanese gardener, who becomes karate master to the fatherless adolescent in *The Karate Kid* (1984, directed by John Avildsen, who made the first *Rocky*), is a much stronger figure. He offers discipline and paternal support, Oriental magic (he can heal with the touch of his hand), and he provides a mystical inner strength that links him to the figures of Ben Obi-Wan Kenobi in *Star Wars*, Yoda in *The Empire Strikes Back*, and Spielberg's E. T. These figures—the first two offering patriarchal wisdom to an adolescent (whose natural father has become evil), the last giving fatherly and motherly security to a child—inhabit the fantastic. *The Karate Kid* offers a more accessible location: the present, in Southern California, with characters who appear to represent existing possibilities. This film links the desire for protection with the desire for revenge, and is therefore connected to the military revenge films I have been discussing.

The bullies who torment and hurt young Daniel Russo are trained in their karate by a somewhat fascistic, military minded fellow whose motto is "Strike first. Strike hard. No mercy." In contrast, the Japanese gardener, Miyagi, controller of hidden powers, is a figure of enormous self-control and self-effacing wisdom, irresistibly kind and willing to give himself over to his young student. More than physical prowess, Miyagi teaches self-control (a powerful and desirable ideological trait that promises deadly force kept hidden under a calm exterior). He allows Daniel to put up with an extraordinary amount of physical abuse before he may put his knowledge to use, and before that knowledge is even imparted, he forces Daniel to go through training by doing things a father might ask: cleaning cars, painting his house. In the process the paternal guide has a softening effect on his young charge and is in turn softened, given some finer details of personality most often lacking in movie Orientals. But despite all the softening, and like the more aggressive revenge films, the narrative context is so arranged that physical retaliation is the only option left for its hero. In fact, the film is so strongly directed toward this end that the revenge Daniel finally visits on the bullies seems not quite commensurate with the punishment they have given him. As I said, the film attempts to advocate a considerable self-control over the expression of violence it nevertheless finds necessary. This control, created through a figure of exotic kindliness and strength, places the viewer at a somewhat frustrating intersection of desire: for revenge, for restraint, for desire itself—that one could have a man of such wisdom as guide.

As a result, a set of contradictions operates in *The Karate Kid* which confuses its ideological structure. The film offers revenge as the most appropriate action while withholding it at the same time. Part of this emerges from the character of the father-teacher and his placement in a historical context unusual for its liberal interpretation of the past. Miyagi was trained in bonzai cultivation and karate by *his* father (who dies in the sequel, permitting the teacher and his student to travel to Japan, where the boy receives further lessons in control and the necessary unleashing of violence). He became a soldier in the American army. His wife was sent to a Nisei detainment camp and died in childbirth. Rather than becoming bitter, Miyagi's sense of restraint was only strengthened. He transcends his own history and that of the country that caused him pain. History is finally forgotten (when, in the sequel, there is reference to Japan's past militarism and World War II, Miyagi only asks, "Why we all so stupid?") and replaced by a call to inner strength. Miyagi tells Daniel, as the latter learns the proper meditation for battle, "If it comes from inside you, always right. . . ." This insight is another variation of the *Star Wars* motto, "May the Force be with you," that call for movement away from community and history to an unformed reliance on an ill-defined interiority, driven by some external mystical power. Like its science fiction predecessors, *The Karate Kid* denies its own pretensions. Rather than encourage self reliance, it confounds understanding by offering a magical father who will guide the child not to wisdom and analytic power, but to physical action against his enemies.*

This brings us back full circle to the avenger films, in which unrestrained physical action is offered as the only solution to political complexity, and all power comes not from a mystical force, but from the barrel of a sub-machine gun. The restraint and gentleness proffered by *The Karate Kid* as a prelude to a somewhat limited violence is abjured completely. The avenger has no restraints; he and his audience are left with no unfulfilled desires in the face of the enemy. The patriarchal figure, as exemplified in the second *Rambo* film, offers his charge unlimited license to destroy. Having trained him, his only job is to support him and protect others whose destruction might end the destroyer's career.

In Ted Kotcheff's *First Blood* (1982), the film that introduces Rambo and Col. Trautman (Richard Crenna), the relationship is slightly different, because the film aims at a modicum of complexity. Called in when Rambo runs amok, Trautman is revealed to be Rambo's military leader and the one who formed his personality. He says that he "created" Rambo by training him to be a counter-insurgency fighter, a trained killer of Vietnamese guerillas (the notion of Rambo as "killing machine," which recurs in the second and better known of the two films, makes an interesting comparison to the shark in *Jaws*). Unfortunately, with the war over and the political object of his destruction gone, he is now a displaced subject, wandering, lonely, his fighting mechanism primed to go off with the right catalyst. When the redneck officials of a small town provoke him, he declares war and nearly destroys them all. Trautman, the father-mentor, begins as something of a Frankenstein with his son-monster barely under his control.

In this first incarnation, Rambo is presented as a version of the crazed Vietnam veteran stereotype, here modified as the misunderstood tool/

---

*Magical figures of the patriarch appear in the most extraordinary circumstances during the eighties. Ron Howard's *Cocoon* (1985) is, on one level, a moving and somewhat valid narrative about old age. Validity, however, is canceled as fears of physical decline and death are answered by visitors from space, who take the old people off to a distant planet where they will do useful work and no longer age!

victim of the society of the seventies. Rather than an avenger, he is lost
and needing a protector. Trautman must reclaim his responsibility—
which is the responsibility of the society—and offer some haven to his
wandering child. At the end of the film, after Trautman has stopped
Rambo's destruction just short of the murder of the sheriff, Rambo tells
him of his Vietnam experience. His description of a friend who was
blown up in his arms by a Vietnamese saboteur reverberates with other
stories or depictions of atrocities in earlier films about the war: Kurtz's
tale in *Apocalypse Now* of the Vietnamese who cut off the arms of peas-
ants vaccinated by Americans; the Russian roulette fantasy in *The Deer
Hunter*. These tales and scenes are meant to evoke the image of an
enemy so vicious and uncivilized that he is capable of driving ordinary
men insane by his barely speakable acts. They are meant to prove that
it was not the war itself that damaged American soldiers, but the terrifying, unscrupulous enemy who, we would believe, caused the war in
the first place. It is as if the dehumanization created by American intervention in Vietnam could be mitigated by stories of even greater dehumanization on the part of the enemy. The effect of such atrocities has
damaged Rambo and uprooted him; he has nowhere to go and no outlet
for the killing instincts implanted by Trautman. Without the war, he is
a violent, abused child with no guidance.

Within the narrative, Trautman must regain the trust of and responsibility for his offspring and act as the mediator between the narrative
and the audience. As he provides explanations for Rambo's actions, sets
limits, knows how far Rambo can go, how far he can permit the sheriff
to make a fool of himself, his control becomes apparent. Trautman, in
effect, directs the narrative and the viewer's response as well. As Rambo's creator and the audience's guardian, he permits enjoyment of the
violence because his wise hand is in control. In *Rambo: First Blood Part
Two*, that control is somewhat more restrained and less restraining. A
guide is no longer needed, only a representative of the patriarchal right
to destroy enemies. *First Blood* was part of the opening movement in
the recuperation of Vietnam; *Rambo* is the full fantasy of winning the
war—"this time."

Rambo himself changes from a confused figure damaged by the war,
needing help, to an angry adolescent, denouncing the political father for
refusing to let him fight. There are many contradictions here, the fathers

are split many ways; yet they form an interlocking patriarchal web. "The supreme achievement of patriarchal ideology," writes Mary Ann Doane, "is that it has no outside."[9] Rambo battles society and supports society; fights one representative of government and is supported by another. He never has to move outside, because finally the patriarch is always with him and he within the patriarchy. His major political battle is against that image of all governmental action—or inaction—that we disapprove of, the bureaucracy. Like the external enemy, communism, the bureaucracy is intractable and cannot be done away with; it serves as constant irritant and a catalyst to action. This time, however, Rambo is aided in his struggle not only by Trautman (a soldier, and therefore part of the bureaucracy—although the indication is that he is somehow working on his own, outside normal military channels because the bureaucrat who opposes him has soldiers working for *him*), but by the figure who guides Trautman and, through him, gives Rambo support: the great enemy of communism and bureaucracy, Ronald Reagan.

Trautman has Rambo released from prison to carry out a photo-reconnaissance mission on a prison camp in Vietnam where American prisoners are believed to be held. Marshall Murdoch, the recalcitrant and double-dealing bureaucrat, tries to prevent Rambo from finishing his mission, in order to keep the existence of prisoners secret. Rambo is stranded alone amidst Vietnamese and Russians, while, at the base, Trautman curses the bureaucrat for his actions. A number of significant objects are seen, at various times, surrounding Murdoch. On his desk is a copy of G. Gordon Liddy's *Will*. On the wall behind him is a pho-tograph of Reagan. The book by the former Watergate thief (and admirer of Hitler) focuses the actions of all the participants, each of whom demands adherence to the righteousness of their cause. The book reflects positively on Rambo, whose will allows him to overcome tor-ture and the force of three armies—the Vietnamese, the Russian, and the American—to free the prisoners single-handedly. It reflects nega-tively on Murdoch, whose will is not free, who is at the mercy of selfish political desires, and whose intransigence and paranoia are associated with an older politics that Reagan has transcended. Early in the film Murdoch asks for "something cold," and one of the soldiers goes to an unlocked Coke machine to get a can for him. Observing this, Rambo registers interest and displeasure in a man who orders soldiers around and abuses the privileges of private property by getting free Cokes. A Coca-Cola machine is played for a joke in *Dr. Strangelove* (Lt. Mandrake has it shot open in order to get change to call the White House, much to the chagrin of Col. Bat Guano, who warns that he will have to answer to the Coca-Cola company for destroying private property). Here it is a serious sign of the abuse of privilege, of Murdoch's assumption of power and authority.

The significance of Reagan's photograph on the wall is a bit more complex; it offers the role of a silent character in the various confrontations. Reagan, of course, as head of the government, is Murdoch's superior, and therefore somehow responsible for his unforgivable action. But the masterstroke of Reagan's ideological maneuverings was his ability to remove himself from the discomforting realities of *Realpolitik*. Like the father of a large family of unruly children, Reagan disapproved, cautioned, even punished, and remained aloof and untouched at the same time. He is Murdoch's superior; he may, in his role of President, have to disapprove of an illegal action; but ideologically he is on Rambo's side. Rambo, in fact, fulfills the Reagan discourse of retribution against enemies. During two sequences, when Trautman confronts Murdoch, the photograph is composed close to Trautman. During the sequence in which Trautman curses Murdoch for betraying the mission and abandoning Rambo, the photograph is first directly behind and to one side of Trautman; then, when Murdoch presents his cynical justifications for abandoning the mission, Murdoch's face eclipses the photograph, just as his actions attempt to deny Reagan's will to correct the "errors" of the war. Trautman's proximity to the photograph validates both his and Rambo's position and places Reagan on their side. More than on their side: Trautman becomes a surrogate for Reagan in the film, a figure who sums up all the patriarchal representations in the films we have been discussing. He guides, directs, controls. He is almost helpless against bureaucratic opposition, but his offspring is powerful enough to overcome all odds—even his momentary despair when he believes Trautman himself has betrayed him—and kill the enemy. In the process, Rambo himself is transformed. He is no longer merely Trautman's "son," but through Trautman Reagan's son as well, the ideal issue of an ideal patriarch, who does his father's business without assistance and without question. Finally, as he achieves an apotheosis, Rambo becomes the offspring of the culture itself, the child of his society's desire for revenge against the loss of their sons. An enormous rush of ideological concentration occurs in these representations. Desire for revenge that had been ignited by the language of aggression is offered images that neatly organize the desire into a narrative that appears to fulfill desire on an imaginary level.

And a physical one. Rambo's body itself becomes a transcendent point of attention, a place on which desire and action may be inscribed. So grotesquely muscled, it looks like a child's warrior doll, which is perhaps its function. Rambo is everyone's toy soldier, placed in fantasies of war, beyond harm even when captured and tortured, the apotheosis of the virile posing that Susan Sontag pointed to as a mark of fascist aesthestics. He is the perfect human machine, making new ideological history in which, because of his efforts, "we get to win this time." As transcendental son, he also rewrites the family's history. He goes off to war not only to protect the dignity of those back home, but to restore dignity to those in prison. He gives everyone new faith in military prowess and at the same time, by doing everything himself, puts no one but himself in danger. He falls in love with a woman he meets on the mission, but she is killed in the course of his operation, and his aloneness remains inviolate, as do the emotions of the viewer, safe in his own isolation. (The woman is Vietnamese, and though not one of the enemy, safely outside the racial pale and the viewer's sympathies.) When Rambo is through with his job, he does what every family hopes its child will do: he makes no further claims. He does not even kill Murdoch, but merely frightens him so that the bureaucrat will now know his place. His reclamation of honor and his job of saving those without hope completed, he wanders off alone, no one's responsibility.

The act of reclamation is most important for the avenging hero and a major facet of an aggressive ideology. Something is presumed lost or undone and must be gotten back or finished. This process lies at the core of all melodramatic structures (and ideology is, finally, melodramatic). While melodramas and ideologies may contain contradictions, they cannot be maintained without guarantees of closure—not merely closure in the usual sense of a satisfactory ending, but the creation of an ending that will bring events back to a better place than where they started or were originally left unfinished. The Vietnamese war did not

Rambo's body. Sylvester Stallone in *Rambo: First Blood Part II*.

"work" ideologically because while it was going on there was no clear notion of its closure, and when it was over it was not closed. Loss was interpreted as incomplete action. Not only was victory denied, but peace for the culture that suffered the loss seemed impossible. There were conflicting ideas about what wrongs had been committed during and because of the war, but no notion as to how those wrongs could be undone. Because of the domestic and international upheavals after the war, there was no immediate hope that things would be better. The desire for reclamation and recuperation was enormous. The films that created narratives for a conservative ideology attempted, through aggressive (but safe) fantasies of individuals reconquering Southeast Asia, or fantasies of domestic concord gained by overcoming difficult obstacles, or fantasies of visitors from other worlds comforting small children, to assure the culture that an imaginary world—a world of images—in which security and power were regained was indeed possible. These films give visual structure to ideological discourse. In return, that discourse was nourished by the films. "After seeing *Rambo* last night," the President of the United States is reported to have said after a Middle East hostage crisis in 1985, "I'll know what to do next time." And, in fact, he actually thought he did. By the mid-eighties, history and ideology, film and fact got terribly mixed, and in the persons of Oliver L. North and Robert C. McFarlane, Reagan found his own "real life" incarnations of Rambo and Trautman.

## 2

Steven Spielberg is the great fantasist of recuperation, every loving son, calling home to find out how things are and assuring the family that everything will be fine. He is the great modern narrator of simple desires fulfilled, of reality diverted into the imaginary spaces of aspirations realized, where fears of abandonment and impotence are turned into fantasy spectacles of security and joyful action. This description may not seem applicable to the maker of fascist film I spoke about in a previous chapter, until one realizes that the security and joy is neither offered by his films nor earned from them, but rather forced upon the viewer, willing or not, by structures that demand complete assent in order to survive. His films are not so much texts to be read and understood, but machines to stimulate desire and fulfill it, to manipulate the viewer without the viewer's awareness of what is happening.[10] While he is hardly the first American filmmaker to manipulate or assure his audience, he is the first to do so with such insistence and consistency. He is the contemporary master of the mode and plies his trade with a subtlety (as much subtlety as the form allows) not to be found in those films outside his immediate school.

His work is closely related to the ideologically bloated films we have been discussing, in fact he is very much father to them, although most of the progeny—with the exception of those films to which he is related as producer—are unrecognizable. Beside the relative subtlety, a major difference between his work and its relatives lies in the fact that there are few explicit political images or references in Spielberg's work. When one does appear, it is blatant and played for full ideological effect. *Raiders of the Lost Ark* (1981) takes place in the thirties and uses Nazis as figures of evil. The historical-political allusion is subdued; there is no discussion or exposition of nazism *per se*. The Germans are useful in the wider narrative context of adventurer-archaeologist Indiana Jones's quest for a Jewish religious object, the Ark of the Covenant. Both religion and politics are reduced to elements easily amenable to plot, to cliché, and to special effects. Religion becomes an aspect of the supernatural, the supernatural an overarching protector of the good, the Nazis an anti-Semitic force of destruction and perversion of this protective aura. (The cruelty of the Nazis is complemented by obstructionism of the U.S. bureaucracy, who, when Indiana Jones brings the Ark to America, hide it in a government warehouse, where the camera seeks it through thousands of crates in a sequence mimicking the end of *Citizen Kane*). The most resonant political representations in the film are the Arabs, and one must recall that the film appeared at a high point of anti-Middle East feeling in the United States, just after the Iranian hostage situation and at the beginning of the Reagan regime. Even though Indiana has an Egyptian friend and protector in the character of Sallah (a version of the patriarchal substitute we have been discussing), the Arabs are seen mostly as cunning, swarming, somewhat dim-witted tools of the Nazis and victims of the hero's physical prowess.

One sequence in particular stands out. At the end of a long search through Arab-thronged streets for his beloved, Marion, who has been spirited off by the Nazis, Indy suddenly finds himself confronting an enormous Arabian figure. Bearded, turbaned, dressed in black robes with a red sash, this giant stands alone twirling a large sabre. He is the fantasy of every hated Arab enlarged into one figure. He grins malevolently at his helpless prey. A cut to Indy shows him with a somewhat quizzical and contemptuous expression. The narrative pattern of *Raiders of the Lost Ark* presents its hero with a series of insurmountable obstacles, which he then surmounts by cleverness or physical skill. He gathers up the subjectivity of the audience, removes from it the reality of danger, and then repositions that subjectivity within a kinetics of victory over physical obstacles and escape. Neither the viewer nor the viewer's adventuresome surrogate ever loses, and the meeting with the Arabian giant is no exception.

The quizzical, contemptuous gaze offered by Indy is not a manifestation of uncertainty about what action he will take. Quite the contrary. He simply pulls a gun and shoots the Arab dead. The significance of his look turns out to be amazement that the Arab would assume such useless posturing; should even for a moment think himself a threat. The ideological positioning of the viewer is made quite certain. Subjected to imagined humiliations at the hands of Middle Easterners—figures so outside known cultural limits that they have only just barely achieved the rank of stereotype—the audience, having given itself over to the hero, finds it can now subject the villain to instant, guiltless retribution. The response to this sequence in a movie theater was overwhelming. The hero's bravura, his ability to dispatch enemies without himself getting seriously hurt, assured the viewer an instant and untroubling gratification. Reaganism had its first explicit filmic representation.

But, as I said, this is a rare moment of direct political-ideological address for Spielberg, though the general methodology of positioning the viewer is typical. He is, if not more subtle, usually more indirect and often more insidious. His narrative discourse speaks to yearnings for security, help, reclamation, and amelioration; the formal articulation of this discourse so situates the viewer as to make both the yearning and Spielberg's assuring response to it irresistible. The methods Spielberg employs to compose his images and build them into narratives offer interesting examples of how film represses individuality and creates an ideal and responsive subject. A universal subject. When a Spielberg film works, the response of one viewer ought to be the same as every other. This is, as I've noted before, not an original phenomenon. The existence of classical Hollywood cinema depends upon an audience's assent to its formal and substantive conventions, and an acceptance—indeed belief—in the illusory fullness and presence of the fictive world these conventions create. Spielberg is particularly precise in the calculation and execution of the conventions, almost Hitchcockian. But Hitchcock's manipulation of imagery and narrative has always a second level of articulation, so that the primary response is inflected by an awareness of the response and even, somehow, by an awareness of the methods used to achieve that response. The viewer is permitted a space to reflect upon his or her own reaction, to reread almost immediately and see through the illusion.* For all the reflexive gestures in his own films—most notably through quotations, which are often taken from his own films—Spielberg never permits the viewer reflective space. Should they occur, they might bring down the entire structure of belief each film works so hard at erecting.

Though Spielberg does not permit even the degree of reflection that Hitchcock built into his narrative structure, he is himself acutely conscious of what needs to be done to make that structure work, even when it is not working. *1941* (1979) is Spielberg's only film that failed commercially and textually, and, given its expense, might have marked a major hiatus in his career had he not quickly joined producer George Lucas to make *Raiders of the Lost Ark*. There is a sequence in the film that takes place in a movie house. Outside, hysteria is mounting over a feared post-Pearl Harbor invasion of California by the Japanese. The hysteria is expressed through the lunatic behavior of soldiers, sailors, and civilians, arming, fighting, attempting various sexual encounters, in an incoherent series of gags, all of which are overstated and intercut

---

*Hitchcock's best films explicitly promote this reflexive process: *Rear Window* is about the act of cinematic seeing and voyeurism; *Vertigo* investigates the creation of narrative illusion; and *Psycho* tells its tale from two directions simultaneously, revealing itself as it creates its mystery. Spielberg is quite conscious of his debt to Hitchcock. In *Close Encounters* he imitates a shot from *North by Northwest*. In that film, Roger Thornhill gives his hand to pull Eve Kendall up the rocky side of Mount Rushmore. Here, Jillian offers her hand to help Roy Neary up the side of Devil's Tower. In the first film, that helping hand leads to the marriage bed; here to the witness of the alien landing.

with one another to create a tottering narrative of pubescent anarchy. Inside the movie house, General Stilwell (Robert Stack), a character who attempts to represent mature, paternal control, is watching *Dumbo*. The juxtaposition is meant to be amusing—the military man in charge ignores the chaos surrounding him and watches a children's cartoon. But outside the plot, something else is going on. General Stilwell, in effect, represents Spielberg himself, the head of this chaotic production, escaping by watching the kind of images he most likes and which express emotions he most likes to express. (Roy Neary, the Richard Dreyfuss character in *Close Encounters of the Third Kind*, wants to take his recalcitrant children to see *Pinocchio*: it is full of "a lot of furry animals and magic," he tells them. They want to play miniature golf. At the end of the film, the music of "When You Wish Upon a Star" accompanies the spacecraft's take off. During the sequence in which *Pinocchio* is discussed, the parting of the Red Sea sequence from De Mille's *The Ten Commandments* is on the family's television set—more movie magic that foretells the magical effects in Spielberg's own film.) The first sequence from Disney's film that the General sees shows Dumbo's approach to his caged mother and her reaching through the bars, rocking her baby in her trunk. The music swells, elephant tears fall from the cartoon creatures' eyes, and the viewers—General Stilwell inside the film and the audience watching *1941* and its film within the film—react with emotion. The sequence from *Dumbo* is a moment of absolute Disney sentimentality—the desire for parental love, reconciliation, yearning, and comfort within the artifice of a totally enclosed animal world. Spielberg, whether speaking of killer sharks, visitors from space, or poor blacks, seeks the same absolutes, the same promise of enclosure, indeed the same enclosure and safety offered to General Stilwell by the movie house and the film being shown there.

No safe haven is offered by *1941*. There is a maximum of spectacle, but so beyond what the narrative calls for that it does not even impress with its virtuosity. Nothing the fictive humans do in this film *represents* any significant and comprehensible behavior on the cultural, ideological, or even symbolic level. The characters are in a profound sense unborn, insufficiently made for the world Spielberg has exploding around them. In spite of the quasi-historical setting (or because of it), the adolescent gags refuse to connect. However, Dumbo and his mother, non-human, outside the narrative proper, supply those basic signifiers of need and satisfaction that make up the nursery of the Spielberg world, which the other inhabitants of this film refuse to enter.[11] Except for General Stilwell at the movies. His is the dedicated gaze at the sentimental object that Spielberg is most often successful at constructing.

The construction methods are surprisingly simple, and I would like to move through them, in order to gain some understanding of how this filmmaker articulates the classical style, and then out into a more general discussion of what exactly is being constructed. What follows, therefore, is a kind of catalogue of devices and techniques, a taxonomy of Spielbergian form with some discussion of the form's significance, itself followed by a discussion of the ideological structures set up by that form.

Perhaps the most immediately recognizable formal element in a Spielberg film, almost a stylistic signature, is light—blinding light shone directly into the camera lens. During the sixties, breaking with long cinematographic tradition, filmmakers began allowing light to flood the camera, showing its refractions through the elements of the lens. Shooting into the sun rapidly became a convention, as did the glare of headlights on a nighttime street. Stanley Kubrick uses severe backlighting, allowing light to come in through windows behind characters or from fluorescent lights above them. Spielberg goes beyond this, making bright, sometimes overwhelming light, a major element of his *mise-en-scène*. *Close Encounters* begins with a dark screen that suddenly bursts into the light of headlights piercing through a desert sand storm. Roy Neary's first encounter with a spaceship is shown by a blinding light that floods his truck in the night—a night made darker by the fact that all man-made lights have gone out. Light creeps through the door jamb as the aliens come to remove young Barry from his mother's house. The spaceships are seen mostly as lights, and the spectacle that ends the film is told with light on light, a play of brightness and color whose intensity is threatening when it begins, but which ends as an invitation to its finally unthreatening mystery. The presence of the extraterrestrial in *E.T.* (1982) is noted by light streaming from the shed of a suburban house. Threatening at first, this light becomes a signifier of a friendly creature, itself threatened by other lights—the flashlights of the government men slashing the darkness in search of the visitor. Elliott, E.T.'s earthly friend, is almost always backlit and surrounded by light, significant of his protective and protecting aura. When Shug Avery and Celie go upstairs to read Nettie's letters in *The Color Purple*, light streams in through the window behind them. "Look for me in the sunset," Nettie writes.

Threat and protection, fear and security are the opposing poles of Spielberg's thematic. The light piercing through his films plays on both, violating the viewer's safe distance from the narratives by demanding attention, forcing the gaze, hiding objects and then revealing those objects, surrounding them with its protective glow. The light offers enlightenment but blinds the viewer to it at the same time. Light is the most visible means of Spielberg's game with his viewer, his act of temptation and promise; his demand for attention. And it reveals as well his love of his medium. Film only works because of light; light initiates the filmic image. Spielberg takes this physical fact and turns it into a stimulus of narrative perception.

His other means are somewhat less explicit and occasionally more subtle, though they all have the same ends. In his fitting together of narrative parts, Spielberg follows the convention of strict continuity cutting, linking sequence to sequence chronologically, or intercutting two sequences which are meant to be happening simultaneously, though in different places. In all cases, he sutures the viewer's perceptions into the linkages so that the linkages themselves are invisible. He employs some very traditional methods of linking shots, covering a cut with a passage from John Williams's symphonic score (or Quincy Jones's in *The Color Purple*); by moving from one shape to another (the bright round light of a helicopter to a white, round radar dish in *Close Encounters*); or from one physical movement to a similar one in the next shot. Sometimes he will use cutting for a whimsical or virtuoso effect. *E.T.* contains a sequence linking together Elliott, his friend from space, and a John Ford film. Elliott is in school and E.T. is at home, drinking beer. As the creature gets drunk and falls down, so does Elliott. E.T. then watches *The Quiet Man* on television. John Wayne pulls Maureen O'Hara to him and kisses her. The action is matched and cut to Elliott at school who echoes John Wayne's movements with a classmate. The cutting in this sequence not only serves to indicate the bond

of human and alien across domestic and psychic space, but to intercon-
nect fictional spaces as well, linking all movie images together. If ever
any reflexive openings occur in the sentimental glaze of *E.T.*, they are
at points such as these, when the film admits its relationship to other
film romance, other film fictions. (The process is continued without cutting in a later sequence when the children and their alien playmate, cos-
tumed for Halloween, walk down the street. E.T is drawn to a child
dressed as Yoda—two movie fictions recognizing one another.) Such
self-conscious gestures are, as I noted earlier, never distancing; they
continue to propel the viewer into the fiction. The spaces of recognition
(of filmic allusions, of editing style) heighten the viewer's affection for
the images and their affective pull.

As dictated by the classical style, Spielberg's cutting—rarely as self-
conscious as this, but often consciously manipulative—moves the narrative from one temporal or spatial point to another. It almost always
drives or is driven by the expectations set up for the viewer by or within
the sequences themselves. But, like Hitchcock, Spielberg occasionally
makes the viewer a participant in the cutting process. By offering partial
information and withholding the rest, Spielberg manages a continuity
of suspense, expectation, desire, and fulfillment which molds both the
cutting pattern and the viewer's gaze into one interlocking web. Here is
an example from *Jaws*, not one of security or comfort—except for the
comfort of being safely manipulated into fear and anticipation, which
is what this particular film is about. After the first shark attack, Chief
Brody (Roy Scheider) decides to shut down the Amity beaches. There
is much confusion and some panic on Brody's part as he gives orders.
A marching band goes down the street, interrupting Brody's assistant as
he tries to tell Mayor Vaughn about the attack. Brody goes to the ferry,
where he is joined by the Mayor, the coroner, and another town official.
In a long take, Brody attempts to explain his actions, while the mayor—
dressed in an absurd blazer printed with little white anchors—insists
that the beaches cannot be closed because summer tourism will suffer.
The coroner changes his original story, suggesting that a boat rather
than a shark may have caused the victim's death. (The references to the
corruption of public officials during the Watergate scandal would have
been immediately noted by an audience in the mid-seventies).[12]

During all this, the audience, primed by the scene of the first attack, its fear hightened by the expression on the policeman's face when he discovers the remains of the body, waits in anticipation of further grisly events. The viewer, of course, knows that the mayor is planning a cover-up, knows that a shark is lurking. This is a major clause in Spielberg's contract with the audience. Hitchcock often pointed out that if, in the course of the narrative, a bomb is planted under a table, the characters must remain ignorant of it, but the audience must be keenly aware of the situation, so that they may fear and wonder over the outcome. In the same vein, Spielberg often provides the viewer with just slightly more information than the major character has, thereby giving the viewer superiority over that character, fear of what may happen, and promise that the hero will succeed and join the viewer in a fantasy of triumph. But Hitchcock said the bomb must never go off; Spielberg always creates an explosion of one kind or another. As the scene on the ferry ends, the mayor warns against panic. "It's all psychological," he says, taking Brody's arm and moving forward into the frame. "You yell 'barracuda,' everybody says 'huh, what?' You yell 'shark,' we've got a panic on our hands on the Fourth of July." Appetites are further whetted. Fear is supplemented by expectation of chaos. There is a cut to a shot of the ferry returning to the dock, and then a cut to the beach, as a large lady moves across the frame from right to left. Expectation and fear in *Jaws* are based upon the body and the injury that might be done to it. The corpulent lady walking into the water emphasizes both the body and the fear.

As she moves into the water, a young boy in red trunks walks out in the opposite direction. The camera reverses its movement, tracking the child to his mother, who gives him permission to get his raft and go back swimming (unknown to the viewer, this is the child who will be the shark's next victim; here special knowledge is offered but not recognized). The child continues walking to the right, past Brody, who sits, in profile, on the right side of the screen, gazing out at the ocean, while his wife and others carry on small talk behind and to the left of him. A cut to his point of view of the beach reveals the large lady floating in the water, a young man running past with his dog (he had been observed earlier when the lady walked by). He throws a stick for his pet, who will also become the shark's victim. The child in red trunks returns to the water, a rapid cut taking him from the beach into the ocean. A number of shots of bathers—the large lady, the boy in red trunks, the boy with his dog playing on the beach—follow, ending with a frontal shot of Brody staring intently. One after the other, two figures walk in front of him, the motion of each hiding a cut which, when the figure passes, presents an even closer shot of the Chief. The intensity of the gaze at him and of what he sees makes him a surrogate for the viewer, looking intently, waiting. Whatever reactions he shows will be a signal to the viewer that something terrible (and wonderful) is happening.

Point of view shots are complex events, organizing the visual space from three different perspectives: that of the director and his or her camera, who creates and orchestrates the film's matrix of perspectives and glances; the character in the film for whom the camera is seeing; and the viewer, who is meant to be seeing what the character sees, via the camera. The illusion of the camera gaze—its eye that stands for the eye of character and viewer, which in turn becomes the I of those two subjects it creates or represents—gives the viewer particular ownership of the space and the character, a privileged place of seeing and knowing. Jean-Louis Baudry writes, "if the eye which moves is no longer fettered by a body, by the laws of matter and time, if there are no more assignable limits to its displacement—conditions fulfilled by the possibilities of shooting and of film—the world will not only be constituted by this eye but for it."[13] When the camera assumes a first person perspective, the viewer is doubly constituted by the world of the fiction (the diegesis) and the particular eye viewing this world at a particular moment in its fictional existence. To complicate matters, a point of view shot can, indeed often does, contain the figure whose view we are meant to be sharing. The stare *at* that figure locks the viewer more firmly to the character. When the two subjects merge, the fictional world is then constituted for both.

The play of gazes continues on the beach. Another cut to Brody's point of view shows the large lady bathing. A figure crosses the line of sight and once more hides a cut which returns the gaze to Brody himself. These figures crossing his field of vision are interruptions, obstacles that make him and the viewer nervous. Another such interruption occurs and the gaze returns to the ocean, this time closer to the floating lady, and then back to Brody just as something black is seen moving toward her in the water. Brody starts, but the reverse shot reveals it only

as the head of a man swimming. Expectations have been raised further
and then released. Brody relaxes for a moment and is interrupted by a
man with a trivial problem. The man bends down to speak to Brody,
blocking his and—since the two have been drawn so close—the audience's view. Brody lifts his head above the man's shoulder and Spielberg cuts to a point of view shot that looks over the man's shoulder to
the ocean. A woman is seen in the water, screaming, and on that scream
Spielberg cuts to Brody getting up, looking. The reverse shot reveals it
to be a girl and boy playing in the surf. Another momentary rise and
fall in tension is created. Brody's wife—composed behind and below
him in the frame—speaks to him about their children, who have been
swimming. The old man whose bobbing head Brody—and the viewer—
thought was a shark, comes up to talk. Brody looks at his children, who
are seen running. His wife rubs his shoulders and he relaxes some.
There are further shots of children swimming and screaming; Brody's
small son on the beach; the boy calling after his dog; the stick he threw
for him, floating on the water. Finally the underwater shot of dangling
legs and the accelerating sounds of bass fiddles indicate the shark is
approaching. The interlock of points of view is momentarily broken,
shifting to that of the monster, a device that repels the viewer rather
than makes him or her complicit with the attack. It is difficult to "identify" with the point of view of a shark, and by forcing the viewer to do
so, Spielberg raises anticipation, expectation, and a desire to see the
unseeable—a monster destroy a human.* There follow a number of
shots of the attack, thrashing bodies, the boy with red trunks going
under, blood boiling in the water, intercut with people rising up on the
beach, all of which are climaxed with a combination zoom and track to
Brody and his wife, who is behind him, rubbing his neck (a shot remi
niscent of the point of view device Hitchcock uses to represent Scottie's
reaction to heights in *Vertigo*). The effect is to bring Brody rapidly for-

---

*Many critics have pointed out that in those horror films in which a knife wielder stalks a
woman, the point of view from the killer is both titillating and debasing, offering the viewer
the misogynist's gaze. Indeed, the first shark attack, in which a young woman is devoured
while a drunk and sexually aroused young man watches, is related to those degrading
images. Here, however, the point of view of the shark is neither sympathetic nor degrading,
but rather a warning sign, a preparation for disaster. For more on this point of view shot
in the horror film, see my earlier discussion of *The Shining*.

ward in the frame while making the background seem to slip away from him. The movement is expressive both of his response and the viewer's own reaction to the long delayed event, an interesting visual representation of panic.

With such an effect, Spielberg charges the spaces of the shot itself with fear and desire. During one sequence early in *Close Encounters*, air traffic controllers huddle around a radar screen on which they observe the blip of an airplane having an encounter with a spaceship. The camera observes their faces reflected in the screen, or gazes intently at them, lit and photographed from below; focus is shifted from one face to the other. As the UFO makes its pass the anxious voices of the airline pilots are heard on the loudspeaker, and the camera tracks in toward the controllers' anxious gaze. Again figures within the narrative become surrogates for the viewer's own anxious look, this time for something which exists only as an enigma, something as yet unseen.

The intensity of the gaze: air traffic controllers in *Close Encounters of the Third Kind.*

This conventional camera movement, a slow dolly forward to a figure, becomes charged with emotion. Such a movement has been coded—since the early thirties at least—as a gesture of approach or as a visual exclamation within an otherwise static scene (in this latter guise it becomes an almost clichéd gesture in postwar, pre-New Wave French film). Spielberg inflects the movement just enough to change its conventional effect. He makes it slightly faster than usual (though not enough to make it suggest a frightened lunge at the object to which the camera is moving), and usually places the camera at a slightly low angle. This upward angle, combined with the movement, communicates the threat or danger to the character being approached and, at the same time, encourages the viewer to react to the threat uneasily. In effect, it becomes a point of view shot for the audience, inviting the viewer into the narrative space, indicating the danger or enigma of that space at the same time.

The angle and movement are persistent throughout *Close Encounters of the Third Kind*, a film in which Spielberg plays against the generic expectations of science fiction, frightening his audience with alien invasion, which such films usually present as dangerous, but which here turns out to be friendly. At the beginning of the film, as the army and scientists meet the Mexicans who have discovered the lost air squadron of 1945, the camera persistently moves toward the various figures. The confusion, the blowing sand, the low angle movements, the scientist's almost hysterical questions about the discovery, "Where's the crew. . . . How the hell did it get here?" serve as a provocation to the viewer. Fear, hysteria, enigma lead to a *desire* to discover what has happened, to penetrate the mystery and overcome the resistance of the screen space and its figures to which the camera moves without, yet, revealing anything. Movement and cutting throughout the early part of *Close Encounters* offer both an obstacle and an invitation, fear and longing for explanation which is not so much offered as climaxed by the spectacle of awe, joy, and regeneration which ends the film. At this point, the sheer size of the spaceship and the attendant apparatus dwarf the human figures. By this time, the low angle tracks—in combination with the gargantuan images—completely subject the viewer. They reduce him or her in relation to the images and, by their very dynamic, organize the movement and direction of viewer perception into a predetermined state of bliss and wonder. The shot becomes a controlling force, a tool of the director as dictator. So much so, that, when he is ready, Spielberg can reverse the movement of the shot and thereby use it as a release from the narrative. After a final dolly in to the wondering face of Lacombe (François Truffaut), who proceeds to communicate with an alien from the ship, there are a series of low angle tracks moving *away* from the wondering humans, releasing tension, preparing the viewer not only for the departure of the spacecraft, but for his or her own separation from the narrative—though the final separation is not complete until the viewer is further subdued and excited by the massive forms of the ship and the overwhelming soundtrack.

An interesting variation of the low angle track occurs in *The Color Purple*, Spielberg's ethnic domestic melodrama, whose genre demands that he eschew the more dramatic visual effects of the fantasy and adventure films. Yet his own style—the complex of forms he has developed as particular variations upon existing conventions—tends to overlay more traditional requirements, or extend them into somewhat different configurations. When Celie (Whoopi Goldberg) first approaches her new husband's house, which will be a place of pain and humiliation, there is a low angle shot from her point of view. The camera booms forward, at a low angle, directly at the house and the children lined up in front of it. On first viewing of the film, the audience is unlikely to know of the brutal events that await Celie, and this almost violent movement is an important preparatory device. In fact the violence begins in the course of the tracking shot, as one of the children hurls a rock toward the camera eye/I of Celie. After that event, the bloody imprint of Celie's hand—the result of her head wound—is seen on a rock.

The movement is, as always, dramatic and foreboding, but finally too much for this particular film. A stylistic element imported from another genre, it signifies the film's director more than it does a major narrative event. While it imparts important information, the form outstrips its signifying potential and indicates that Spielberg's stylistics may be limited and therefore open to repetition. Of course repetition is necessary for the creation of a style. Kubrick's tracking shots, Scorsese's methods of shooting New York streets, Robert Altman's use of the zoom lens or of off-screen dialogue mark the way these individuals inflect and individuate formal material, and they occur in film after film. But when such inflections overdetermine narrative material and do not create a formal significance within the narrative context, then the *auteur*, designing and shaping his film, gets caught within his own devices and desires. In this case, the point of view shot represents Spielberg more than it does the narrative it is supposed to form.

Another spatial construct favored by Spielberg is a bit more interesting. With the exception of *E.T.*, *The Color Purple*, and the short piece for *Twilight Zone: The Movie*, all of his theatrical films are made in an anamorphic ratio. He often takes great advantage of the horizontal breadth of the composition by placing figures off center, on the left or right of the screen, and then situating other, equally important figures in the other parts of the frame, in the background and in soft focus (turning to advantage the difficulty in creating deep focus with an anamorphic lens). He will then often change focus so that the figure originally seen clearly in the foreground goes out of focus and attention is shifted to the figures in the rear. The effects of such compositions are less insistent than the dolly-in and depend more upon the viewer's willingness to explore composition. Rather than manipulate by dynamic movement, such shots require active observation of the frame (and anything in Spielberg's work that offers the viewer an opportunity to exercise his or her own will is to be noted with appreciation).

An example of the method is found in *Raiders of the Lost Ark*. Indiana Jones has just survived an enormous chase across the desert. He has been shot, run over by a truck he has been clinging to, dragged by the same truck down the road, and generally abused beyond the endurance of any normal human body. He and his lover, Marion, arrive at a dock, where Sallah, his friend and protector, has prepared passage for him on the boat of an African, Katanga. The camera tracks Indy and Marion walking to the dock from right to left. Sallah greats them, and the camera continues its track, bringing Katanga into the frame on the left. There is a shift of focus to Katanga as the three original figures are now in soft focus in the center background. Katanga lights a cigarette (the sequence takes place at night, and the lighting effects are subtle and effective). Indy asks Sallah if these people are to be trusted, and Sallah calls to Katanga, who walks over to them, the focus changing as he approaches the original group in the center of the frame. Katanga offers them his cabin and then walks out of the frame. Indy moves to Sallah and embraces him, moves to the rear and makes way for Marion to say her goodbyes. Sallah sings a song as Marion and Indy walk to the rear and to the boat. The camera follows Sallah off to the right as he passes a group of sailors and waves goodbye to his friends who are now standing on the gang plank.

*Raiders*, to an even greater extent than Spielberg's other work, depends almost entirely on cutting to maintain its rhythm and create the illusion of rapid and dangerous action. This long, complicated shot in which figures and camera are almost choreographed together offers a moment of rest and collection (which is, in fact, what the characters enjoy at this point in the narrative). But if it seems to change the register of activity, it is in fact only a modification of that register that permits it to encompass another ideological effect. Spielberg's films are always concerned with melodramatic conventions of friendship and assistance, with the attractive myth of individuals coming to the aid of other individuals to ward off danger and loneliness. Only Dennis Weaver's David Mann in *Duel* is without external support; he is the only Spielberg character who must depend entirely on his own resources. Otherwise, each of Spielberg's characters has a special friend who helps: in *E.T.*, Elliott has his alien; Brody has Hooper in *Jaws*; Celie is brought to maturity by Shug in *The Color Purple*; Lou Jean and Clovis are befriended by the very policemen whose laws they break in *The Sugarland Express*; Jillian and Roy help each other get to the alien landing in *Close Encounters*, where the aliens themselves prove to be universal friends. In the films Spielberg produces, children are often supported by their friends and family, as is Marty McFly by his scientist friend in *Back to the Future*, or the group of children who look after one another in Richard Donner's *The Goonies*.

These friendships and groups, whether human or cosmic, are always of a fantastical kind, providing intensive support under overwhelming conditions. They are exclusive groupings and never pose wider questions of community. On the contrary, the larger community is often seen as indifferent or antagonistic, and the friendships are so isolated as to form a cell within it. Spielberg's major discourse is precisely about the security of exclusive, protective, and non-threatening companions.

There are no communal spaces in his films (the beach in *Jaws* is a place of threat; the town in *The Color Purple* either anonymous or, again, a place of danger; the landing field for the spacecraft in *Close Encounters* is the closest Spielberg can come to a large area of people working together; but their work, of course, is for a purpose that will finally diminish the group, and in the course of the film, the community contacted by the aliens is whittled down to a single couple, Roy and Jillian). In *Raiders*, a good part of the globe becomes a field for an individual of almost supernatural powers to prove his cleverness and endurance. When Spielberg decides to encapsulate him within the tentative confines of rest and protection, he does it with a remarkable cinematic grace that affirms the need for isolation, with friends, from a dangerous world.

This encapsulation process includes the film viewer. For he or she is invited—often forced—to partake of the groupings and become a privileged participant in the illusory world of adventure and salvation. Earlier, I mentioned the contract that Spielberg draws up, promising to offer the viewer slightly more information than that held by the characters. The contractual obligations are fairly one sided, the films parcel out information, entice the viewer by means of manipulation of point of view, but in fact never get beyond the manipulation, for someone outside the fiction can never actually become part of it. The terms and methods of that manipulation, however, can seem quite agreeable, and their visual articulation interesting. The first part of *Close Encounters*, for example, is built upon alternating sequences of strange and ordinary events—the discovery of the lost fighter squadron in Mexico, the UFO sightings by airliners and controllers, the appearance of the flying saucers to the little boy, Barry, in Muncie, the domestic discord in Roy Neary's house, and his encounter with a spaceship out on the highway.

Spielberg balances the global events with the domestic, and is most interested in the effects of the space visitors on the little child and on Roy, the man with the heart of a child. Full-scale domestic melodrama threatens in the case of the latter. Roy becomes obsessed with the vision of the mountain—the sight of the spacecraft's landing that the aliens have implanted in his mind. He falls apart, loses his job and his family. The latter is an event any Spielberg film construes as intolerable; Spielberg cannot permit a rupture in domesticity to last very long. Roy soon joins forces with Jillian, Barry's mother, who shares with Roy the imprint of the mountain shape. Once they discover their shared vision, they continue their quest together.

In order to hasten the healing of the domestic break and the concurrent separation between viewer and character, Spielberg uses a widescreen compositional effect we have been discussing to give the viewer privileged information and finally assure us that Roy's isolation will not be a permanent state. When Roy's wife and children leave him, he is alone in their midwest, suburban house (such a house is the location of much Spielbergian melodrama, where passion is turned into a commodity to be consumed by the viewer who inhabits similar quarters). In the shot that climaxes the first part of the sequence, Roy stands on the left of the composition, staring out at the suburban landscape, rendered all the more banal by the momentous, cosmic events he is attempting to understand and the psychological upset he is suffering. (In the first version of the film, Roy had gone almost mad and built his model of Devil's Tower out of garbage and garden dirt he hauled in from the front of his house. Spielberg removed this scene in order to incorporate more gigantic special effects as Roy enters the spaceship in the "special edition" made for the film's re-release.) As the sequence continues, there is a leap in time. The television set, placed to the right of the model, plays the end of a soap opera and then a beer commercial. Roy crosses in front of it just as the news comes on. Howard K. Smith, the former news broadcaster (who hires out his image to filmmakers so that they may make reference in their fiction to another form of mass entertainment, the network news), is delivering a story. He reports the army's closing of Devil's Tower in Wyoming and he shows an image of the mountain Roy has been trying to model. Roy is now on the phone to his wife, walking across the room, then sitting in front of the television screen, on which the image of the Tower and the model he has been building match up. For the moment, however, he is oblivious to it, for his despair over ruined domesticity interferes with his search for higher truths. But when the images match up for a second time, he finally notices what is going on.

The viewer, however, is permitted primary access to the space, registers the information, but of course cannot pass that information to the fictional character. A gap is opened by the very fullness of the shot, partially closed when Roy finally sees what the viewer already knows, and then sealed shut with a cut to Jillian, who is also seeking a correspondence to the image in her head (as well as seeking her son who has been taken by the aliens). She sees the same news program on her television set. The recognition and the joining of the two characters is now immediate, and in the next sequence Roy is driving to Wyoming, where he will meet Jillian. Both will finally reach the site which the government has closed off (another gap in knowledge: the viewer knows the army has created a false story of a toxic spill to evacuate the area; Roy and Jillian must overcome further obstacles in order to discover this themselves and must then endure considerable hardship to reach the landing site). The ability to see the mound Roy builds and its analogous television image within a single shot and before the central character does creates both knowledge and frustration. It directs the viewer's entry into the space left empty by the departure of Roy's family and encircles the viewer within the formation of the character and the narrative process itself. The cut then relays the knowledge about Devil's Tower, held mutely by the viewer, across narrative space, connecting the characters to the viewer's already held information, relieving frustration, allowing the narrative to proceed and a new domestic unit to form.

There are other instances in Spielberg's films where composition generates a tension between desired security and narrative uncertainty, especially on the domestic level. In *Jaws*, a few brief sequences quickly establish a domesticity that is set at odds with the horror of the shark attacks and the resistance of the town leaders to closing the beaches. Immediately after the first attack, and before the beach sequence described earlier, there is a domestic sequence with Brody and his wife and child. The couple get out of bed; their son comes to them with a cut hand. Brody goes to the phone to receive the call about the shark attack. He is framed on the right of the screen, in sharp focus, his wife and son in soft focus in the left rear of the composition, standing in the kitchen—the domestic space—where she tends the son's injury. The family unit is present, but visually fading in importance in face of the task that lies ahead, while the cut hand assumes a significant relationship to the large bodily assaults inflicted by the shark. Later, in a moment of domestic calm, father and son watch television, the son playfully mimicking Brody's gestures. This sequence begins with the camera focused on the mother; but she quickly moves again to the kitchen, remaining in soft focus behind them until Hooper enters and the three sit around the table discussing the shark.

As a peace loving, middle-class man, wife and child are the comfort and quiet Brody wants. But they must be positioned correctly. The wife may not dominate, only remain the soft-focus anchor of the domestic group. And that group is threatened, as always in American film, and especially at times of cultural stress. A major thematic of films during the fifties and from the mid-seventies on is that middle-class comfort and security is a frail thing. Not only must it be fought for, but continually tested. Two things have to happen: the family unit needs to be secured against external threat and the male member of that unit needs not only to protect (or in some instances avenge) the family, but in the process must prove himself. During the late forties and fifties, gangsters often intruded upon the family and had to be defied by the husband; or the husband got involved with gangsters—an act which threatened the stability of his family—and had to extricate himself. The classic variations on the theme occur in Michael Curtiz's *The Breaking Point* (1950), Fritz Lang's *The Big Heat* (1953), and William Wyler's *The Desperate Hours* (1955). Recent variations place other obstacles in the domestic path and permit a certain amount of role reversal. To save her family, Lou Jean initiates the journey to reclaim her son and forces her actions on a somewhat passive husband in *Sugarland Express*. Similarly in Richard Pearce's *Country* (1984), the wife must struggle to keep her farm against the insensitivity of both a hostile government bureaucracy and a beaten and unreactive husband. In Robert Benton's *Kramer vs. Kramer* (1979), however, the husband proves to be the strong parental figure, caring for his son after divorce, and in Robert Redford's *Ordinary People* (1980), the wife proves to be a major force in promoting domestic discord. The wife in Hooper and Spielberg's *Poltergeist* undergoes a considerable ordeal at the hands of the living dead in order to preserve the family unit.

The intrusion upon domesticity in Spielberg's films most often takes takes the form of insuperable or superhuman forces: the malevolent truck in *Duel*, the more malevolent shark in *Jaws*, the law in *Sugarland Express*, extra-terrestrials in *Close Encounters*. The Indiana Jones films stand outside the pattern by focusing upon a male figure who refuses the comforts of family entirely. However, in *Raiders of the Lost Ark*, he finds comfort with a strong woman, nearly his equal in bravery, and an older friend and guide. *Indiana Jones and the Temple of Doom* (1984) presents the hero with a conventionally dumb and hysterical woman companion, but also with a young Oriental boy who bravely accompanies him on his adventures, offering wisecracks in place of strength. *The Color Purple* inverts some of the codes by creating the husband himself as the seemingly insuperable and disruptive force and placing in the narrative a woman who reorganizes the domestic structure, giving the central female character strength and support to break away. (However, as I shall discuss further on, the inversion does not turn out to be subversion.)

*Jaws* uses the family group as a point of reference and departure, and the ramifications of its narrative take us beyond stylistic devices and the problems of pictorial composition into larger areas of ideological

Men—bonding. Brody (Roy Scheider), Quint (Robert Shaw), and Hooper (Richard Dreyfuss) in *Jaws*.

formation. The film rapidly integrates itself with the seventies sub-genre of the buddy film—men joining with other men and casting the woman out. The soft-focused mother and children eventually disappear from view entirely as the screen is filled with the presence of Brody, the young scientist Hooper, and the obsessed old shark fighter, Quint, who form a new family grouping. Within that family, Brody must prove himself the brave son, although he, in effect, fathers himself. Hooper is too young, too much the intellectual, too unattached, and too rich to emerge as the film's hero. He may only aid Brody, ending up hiding under the water for the climax of the battle with the shark, joining Brody on a piece of the wrecked boat as they paddle to the shore after the victory. Quint is too old-fashioned, too single-minded, and too much the individual to emerge the unadorned hero. He is too old and, simultaneously, too paternal and too mean to survive. His death—in the film's most grisly scene—is the death of the old father. Brody, however, is the perfect middle-class man, who must be initiated into heroism (although police chief of the seaside resort, he is a New Yorker who is afraid of the water), and may return to shore and family only after undergoing his rite of passage. As Stephen Heath points out, this battle at sea occurs "in the summer of America's final year in Vietnam," during which the three men enact a ritual of "destruction and conscience and manliness and menace and just-doing-the-job. . . ."[14] Of the three, the unassuming, middle-class man does the job best and emerges from struggle renewed. Likewise, Roy Neary, in *Close Encounters*, is offered a severe, cosmic test, which he endures because of his childlike faith and his ability to join with Jillian in the quest for the new utopia of the aliens. Both Brody and Neary, though serious about their tasks, do not take themselves too seriously, which is a prime requisite of the modern hero. Commitment and seriousness of purpose isolate an individual, make him threatening, and therefore unacceptable (Rambo is the curious exception to this). The man who proves himself best is nothing special, an ordinary man who fights for domesticity (or, in the case of Indiana Jones, for the hell of it). With his victory, Spielberg proves that the traumas of the seventies and eighties may be overcome by an ordinary heroism supported by domestic desires.

All of Spielberg's films operate to prove the validity of, and to recuperate any possible losses to, the domestic space. Their specific formal devices work toward the success of this project, which becomes finally the universal *mise-en-scène*. In *Close Encounters*, the visitors from space send their children out to greet the earthlings, thereby promoting an intergalactic family, already initiated by their calling first on Jillian's small child and then Roy to join them (Jillian remains on earth, in soft focus, as it were, waiting first for the return of her son and then of Roy). E.T. descends to perform the role of father, secret friend, and baby for young Elliott. Even the Indiana Jones films (infected by George Lucas's fantasies of adolescent adventure and an invulnerable hero who seems to want none of the normal ties to home and family) betray Spielberg's central concern. Indy has two lives: one as mild-mannered bespectacled archaeology professor, the other as adventurer, something of a sublunar Superman. Were he *only* an adventurer, the viewer would be unable to find the securing point. The narrative space would be open ended; its activity would find rest in the conclusion of the adventure, but not in the satisfactory return of the subject to a place of comfort. So, the first film has Indy return home; the second has him save hundreds of Indian children captured by an evil sect, returning them to their desolated village. The hero takes on the role of paternal savior, that major figure in eighties cinema who forms the narrative core of Speilberg's work. The father must prevail.[15]

The Spielbergian world is absorptive and distributive, forcing the spectator into it, obsessively replacing discontent with satisfaction, insisting that the child's desire for comfort and companionship is a persistent state that cannot be fulfilled in a mature, earth-bound, communal environment. This world refuses the possibilities of an individuality that is responsive to social needs. In fact, it refuses individuality, certainly in the sense of a meditative subjectivity, secure within its own knowledge and activity. All individual acts are done in the service of returning or bringing the self and the world to a state of calm protected by a strong, patriarchal force. Spielberg absorbs uncertainty and fear and redistributes them into narratives in which they are replaced either by a self-effacing hero who actively engages a threatening world or by an unheroic man or child whose passivity is filled by an external, unearthly presence.

In either instance, a hierarchical order is created (as it must be in melodrama) in which the subject viewing the film and the subject within the film are placed in a relationship of child to succoring adult, a relationship impossible to sustain outside the film itself. I noted that *Jaws* is very much a film of the Vietnam-Watergate period when the culture felt itself at the mercy of all manner of sharks. Spielberg's representation of political and social threats by a monster spawned in nature is itself an act that removes any responsibility for the threat, reducing the world to helpless victims in need of a salvation. The shark has no rational motivation, but merely destroys, without reason or premeditation, the least suspecting and deserving individuals. The enemy is a natural and instinctive force; no one is responsible for it. When it is destroyed the world can be restored to a knowable and safe order—a more trustworthy order because a protecting figure is now at hand. The petty politicians of Amity (or the corrupt land developer in *Poltergeist*) have a hand in prolonging or, in the latter instance, provoking the threat. But the threat, finally, is greater than they are—a situation, paradoxically, more manageable than if it were caused by mere human agency. Heroic action may right nature and create succor. It is less than successful in dealing with the subtle machinations of corrupt adults.

If *Jaws* is a response to the cultural shocks of Vietnam and Watergate, *Close Encounters* responds to the period of transition after these events, and *E.T.* to the long night of complacency and withdrawal begun in the late seventies and continuing into the eighties. The films emerge not so much from order disrupted, as they do from a desire for a more dependable, exciting, and sustaining order than that which exists. *Close Encounters* is about patriarchy lost, about the domestic unit in decay, about the authority of the father in confusion. The job of the film is to reorder that patriarchy on a cosmic level. Therefore, as Roy Neary and his family fall apart, the aliens begin constituting a new one for him, through Jillian and her son. Mediating these actions is the paternal figure of Lacombe, who travels the world in order to integrate various UFO sightings and help the army prepare for the arrival of the aliens. (Lacombe's paternal role is doubled: in the film he is the quiet, assured investigator and guide to the new world; but he is also François Truffaut, director of films about children and innocence, the father of Spielberg's own imagination. He appears again, by allusion, in *The Color*

*Purple*. When Nettie teaches Celie to read by attaching pieces of paper with words on them to the objects the words name, she is doing what Truffaut's character, Itard, did to teach language to the wolf boy in *Wild Child*).

Lacombe's voyages, interspersed throughout the early part of the narrative, confirm a cultural hierarchy that assures the reigning place of white, middle-class patriarchs in the new order to be brought by the spacemen. Lacombe is wise and knowing in his quest. The people he discovers who have encountered the aliens are capable only of barely articulated awe. In India, for example, masses of people chant the music communicated to them by the aliens and point their fingers heavenward to indicate the origin of the sounds. In the United States, the army intervenes with technology and subterfuge, while "ordinary" people wait passively or, in the case of Roy and Jillian, finally resort to heroic resourcefulness to reach Lacombe at the landing site in order to convince him that Roy has been especially chosen. Jillian remains behind; her boy has gone aboard the spacecraft and now her lover will make the voyage. Only two women are among the army personnel that go aboard the ship. The aliens in that ship seem to be only males ("He's a boy," Elliott tells his sister—and reassures the viewer—about his own alien in *E.T.*). Male authority is unthreatened by the new forces that bring comfort to the earth, which comes in the form of new fathers to man. The groups that formerly represented order—the army, science, the family—dissolve in the face of the blinding light of new protection. I said that the space visitors seem to be male children; in fact the first alien figure seen is a huge, white figure hovering protectively over many small white figures. Another double paternity is formed: the aliens who will be mankind's guide and protector are in turn protected by a fathering figure. The terrifying is turned into the benign. Enormous power, demanding and receiving enormous obeisance, is so represented as to offer masculine protection to a needful child.

This affirmation of protection is repeated with greater intimacy in *E.T.* The upsets of the seventies seemed to call for large interventions. At the beginning of the Reagan era, the culture was ready for simple, uncomplicated, direct communication with an unthreatening leader. The film represents this ideological shift to a childlike dependence upon a kindly patriarchal force, a solution to anxiety and insecurity repeated by many other filmmakers. To achieve its effect, *E.T.* inverts the narrative structure of *Close Encounters* while keeping its direction and purpose largely intact. The scale is smaller; the low tracking shots and oblique lights shining in the dark are less overwhelming. Yet they still signify a threat and mystery, though the threat quickly becomes detached from the aliens and attached to adult earthlings who search for the visitor. The essential mystery of the film concerns only how E.T. and Elliott will get along and survive. The child is faced with a barely understanding mother—who manages to remain ignorant of the visitor in her house for much of the early part of the film—a troublesome brother and sister (Elliott is significantly without a father) whom he must win over to his side, and scientists and government officials who want to study the creature. Spielberg creates, in effect, two aliens, Elliott and the space creature, finding their way in the troublesome adult world.

They manage through a process of total identity. I have mentioned that the initial goal of a Spielberg film is to position the spectator so securely within the narrative movement that his or her subjectivity is given up to that movement. More than "identifying with the characters," the viewer is made part of the imaginary complex of the fictive world, subject to its events and rhythms, his or her individuality suppressed into the narrative weave. *E.T.* doubles this process. Elliott and his alien become so close that they share experiences, to the point where, when E.T. sickens, Elliott does too, and almost dies. While the viewer cannot achieve as close a physical proximity to the fictions on the screen, she or he can be situated in so intense a state of longing for that proximity that, for the duration of the film at least, those fictions become the illusory fulfillment of the viewer's desire.

Earlier, I spoke about the ways in which certain films hail the spectator to them in a way that seems to counter the oedipal threat, offering a kind of dual matriarchal/patriarchal protection—sustenance, security, and power. I want to elaborate that argument here, because the narrative processes of *E.T.*, its effect of identifying the two characters in the film and the viewer with those characters, exemplify it better than any other film. The French psychiatrist Jacques Lacan hypothesized a moment in the development of the child that he called "the mirror phase." At this point, the child, as if seeing itself and its mother in the mirror, receives its initial notion of the self as separate being, another self who is, at the same time, not another. Because it is the reflection of the child still in the state of maternal protection, it exists in the fullness of being and security. This is the imaginary realm, a place of images whose reality are only those of images. For Lacan, this moment is also the beginning of sexual identity—or mis-identity. The child discovers that it either has a penis or not, that it is like its mother or its father, and with that discovery begins the desire to own the symbol of potency, a desire which allows the child to enter and become subject to the sym- bolic stage of language, culture, and power in degrees depending upon its gender.[16]

*E.T.* is a curious working out of the Lacanian theory. The alien crea- ture both is and is not Elliott, and it is everything Elliott wants it to be. Because Elliott's father has left him, E.T. becomes not only another self and an imaginary friend (in multiple senses of the word imaginary), but a paternal *and* maternal surrogate, even more powerful than those other matriarchal patriarchs I discussed earlier. Even more, they become mother and father to each other. E.T. has wisdom, the power of flight, and can cure a cut finger with a touch. Elliott teaches the alien human language; the alien teaches Elliott feeling and care. Each is the other's baby, each takes on the other's self, and Elliott is offered the possibility of bypassing the adult world and escaping Oedipus altogether. Their relationship offers Elliott power without the concomitant castration, the subjugation of self to other selves—to the patriarchal order—that is part of normal movement into adulthood. "I have absolute power," Elliott tells his brother before introducing him to E.T. And he maintains this power, with E.T.'s consent, until his other self—unable to return home—sickens and dies. At this point, the scientists who have been searching for the alien invade Elliott's house and threaten to return him and the viewer back to the world of male authority. These men are rep- resented thoughout the film by their flashlights piercing the dark, threat- ening Elliott's secret, or in the case of the one scientist who will most sympathize with Elliott, by the keys clinking on his belt, a synecdoche marked by its phallic suggestiveness. This figure emerges as the absent male patriarch. However, he proves to be not a threat, but a positive paternal figure, who has—like the viewer—concern and envy for the relationship between Elliott and E.T.[17]

The fortunate child of fantasy has complete control over his own oedipal process, can enter into the world of power and differentiation with his subjectivity and control intact (it is such an inviting fantasy that Spielberg repeats it via Robert Zemeckis's *Back to the Future*). The viewer is not in such a fortunate position. I said that *E.T.* doubles the process of identification. Elliot and E.T. merge as father/mother/son, boy/best friend, self/other self. The viewer merges with the film, gives up his or her subjectivity to it. If Elliott proclaims complete power over his relationship with the alien, so Spielberg proclaims his power over the viewer. The film becomes the viewer's mirror. But whereas in the Lacanian mirror phase (to quote Christian Metz), "the child is both in [the mirror] and in front of it," the mirror of the cinema "returns us everything but ourselves, because we are wholly outside it. . . . The spectator is absent from the screen *as perceived*, but also (the two things inevitably go together) present there and even 'all-present' as *perceiver*. At every moment I am in the film by my look's caress."[18] The perceiver's gaze caresses the cinematic mirror and, in the case of a Spielberg film, is caressed in turn. *E.T.* does everything to make the viewer forget that he or she is absent from the screen by sealing the viewer's gaze within the anti-oedipal fantasy of the film's two main figures. With the mutual caress, the viewer is returned to a childlike state, and enters the imaginary world.

". . . I don't know how to feel," Elliott says as E.T. dies. Within the fiction, Elliott becomes dependent upon the creature; outside the fiction, the viewer is dependent for his or her feelings on the filmmaker's manipulation of the fictional characters and the viewer's response to them. Spielberg makes us feel what he wants. He is the ultimate, arbitrating patriarch and knows, much better than his characters do, that the relationship to the imaginary cannot go on indefinitely. Elliott himself is forced to enter into the next and final stage of development, Lacan's symbolic order, the realm of language, of difference, of the need to position the self among other selves within shifting strings of power. After all, that self was threatened by E.T., and while Spielberg seeks to assure the protection of the self, he does not wish its total dissolution. The narcissistic identification of child and space creature is finally broken by the latter's need to go home or die and by the former's need to come home to the paternal voice, provided by the friendly scientist.

E.T. is resurrected by the promise of home and Elliott confronts the adult world once more, helping the creature engineer his escape. "This is reality," Elliott tells his friends who ask if E.T. couldn't just beam up to his ship.

The escape itself is a scene that at once recalls the Freudian imagery of infantile dreams of flying and the last sequence of Vittorio De Sica's *Miracle in Milan*, where the poor take off for heaven. The police and the government in pursuit, E.T. leads the children in flight into the forest where his spaceship and comrades will come to take him home. With mother and friendly scientist present (suggesting the reformation of the earthly domestic unit), E.T. makes his separation from Elliott. The imaginary disappears and Elliott is left in the world of men. The viewer has considerably more trouble leaving the imaginary of the screen. The shower of tears that clouds the gaze at the end of the film also clouds the ability to move away from the fiction, which lingers in the imagination, in the form of memory, of consumer goods, in journalistic references that may be consumed over and over. The narrative may have permitted E.T. to go home; its ideological effect keeps the viewer in a state of rootless want and yearning. The fiction had to provide separation in order to close itself; but in its closure it opens the gap of dissatisfaction with the mundane and creates desire for even more images that pretend to close that gap.

Spielberg manipulates the space between his texts and reality itself, creating melodrama within his films and between them. The desires he satisfies within the films return again when they are over and may be satisfied by re-seeing the film, or waiting until the next one. An enviable circuit of exchange is created in which the viewer is ready always to purchase more assurance, more satisfaction, while the product is manufactured both to satisfy and create greater need. Conventional melodrama closes down its narrative by insisting that desire must be sublimated and redirected. "Don't let's ask for the moon. We have the stars," Bette Davis tells Paul Henried in *Now Voyager*, when they realize their love must remain platonic. But Spielberg is off in another direction. He affirms what the culture has always suspected, that gratification can only be achieved within the imaginary realm of film—his films, which promise moon, stars, and gods who will save us. Jean-François Lyotard states that the old narratives are no longer of use in the postmodern world.[19] Spielberg finds that the problem can be overcome by absorbing the world into his narratives, creating a melodramatic oedipal machine, delivering protection, yet denying what it seems to offer, keeping the viewer attached to it at all times, threatening/promising loss whenever the attachment is broken. The machine generates surplus value for its manufacturer and delirium, satisfaction of desire, and a need for more from its spectators. Promising fulfillment of the dreams of childhood, the machine places everyone who comes in contact with it in the position of a child under the control of the father who gives, takes away, promises to give again if the child reacts correctly.[20]

The patriarch exercises his full power in *The Color Purple*, a film which seems to offer liberation from old repressions, only to restate them with such force that the initial subversive act is itself subverted and the old order reclaimed. Alice Walker's novel, the film's source, is a strong statement of female strength and bonding, an affirmation that women can place themselves in the center of knowing and acting. The film offers moments as strong as the novel; indeed, Celie's denouncing of her husband and proclamation of her freedom is a powerful feminist statement. But the statement is ultimately retracted, rephrased, and finally refuted in a film that cannot break from older cinematic tradition or the tradition Spielberg himself has developed during his own career.

*The Color Purple* was publicized as Spielberg's departure from childhood fantasy and cinematic spectacle. In fact it merely tones down its spectacle and resituates its fantasy, transferring longings for protection and security from the realms of space visitors into a world of rural houses, fields, and poor towns reminiscent of older Hollywood films about blacks in the South: *Cabin in the Sky, The Green Pastures, Pinky*. The influence of John Ford on the film is consuming, a force that helps pull it inward toward convention and the conservative reclamation of its liberal project. Of course, Ford's presence hovers over most of Spielberg's work. Both filmmakers are preoccupied with families and security, with threats to domestic (and in Ford's case, communal) order and its reestablishment. In *The Color Purple*, Ford's influence is profound enough to affect the very compositional structure of the film. When Spielberg closes his narrative with Nettie's return from Africa, Celie, Shug Avery, and others of the household are composed on and around the porch of Celie's house, gazing at the approaching group, exactly as

Domination of the patriarch. Mr. (Danny Glover) and (in soft focus) Celie (Whoopi Goldberg) in *The Color Purple*.

Ford composed similar family groupings around housefronts in, for example, *Fort Apache* and *The Searchers*.

But Ford was always concerned with issues of community, as well as the individual and the family. Spielberg is not. I mentioned earlier that community always lingers around the peripheries of his films, and that issues of order are either on a personal or universal level, never involved with the body politic. Ford looked to adjust his individual figures into the movement of American history, seen from a conservative perspective—but at least seen. In his film about a black community in the first half of the century, Spielberg shows almost no interest in the political, economic, or ideological forces at work at the time, only the personal and the domestic ideologies of the eighties transferred back into the fictional realm. His narrative, despite the brutality and emotional deprivation that occurs within it, is a melodrama set in a pastoral realm—with a few brief visits to the city—strangely cut off from the rest of the world. When the brutality is ended and emotional deprivation curtailed with Celie's liberation and the return of her sister, the pastoral realm enfolds everything, and the film becomes an idyll of regenerated souls. Walker's novel offers Spielberg and his screenwriter, Menno Meyjes, an opportunity to evade larger problems, for it creates an almost mythical southern, rural landscape in which economic and community problems do not seem to exist. But this is countered by the fact that, in Walker's fiction, black poverty is a given, understood by its pervasive presence. Within that poverty, the central female characters are clearly defined and clearly aware of their difference, of their being black and not white, female and not male. Spielberg's fiction is strangely lacking in awareness of difference. To be sure, his characters are black, but their rural accents, as well as their appearance and surroundings, are more authentically movie Negro than southern black. Walker's characters break out of stereotypes; Spielberg's attempt to do so, only to be reclaimed. Spielberg dissolves Walker's fiction into the conventional patterns of the only thing he knows, movies, and the only ideological patterns with which he feels comfortable, patterns of return to domestic order controlled by men.* On its most profound level, *The Color Purple* is an effective, authoritative narrative that confirms the necessity of male-dominated structures of power.

The confirmation begins with ambivalence manifested in the character of Sofia (Oprah Winfrey), the first figure to show signs of revolt. Full of spirit and rebellion—she denies Celie's pathetic advice to her husband, Harpo, to beat her in order to keep her in line—she is used as a signifier of black oppression. The only character who suffers directly from contact with white people, her humiliation seems to be played out for more than sympathy alone. Standing up to a condescending white woman (who is depicted as slightly mad, and therefore safely not representative of a more general, abiding racism), she is attacked by the woman's husband and finally knocked down by a policeman, crippled and jailed for many years. When the policeman pistol whips her, Spielberg cuts to a high angle, the camera distanced as Sofia falls, her skirts

---

*I do not wish to engage in a detailed comparison of novel and film except when necessary to make a particular point. Most of the events in the film that I will concentrate on are peculiar to the film, with only some small analogy in the novel or none at all.

coming up over her head. She is, in effect, laid bare for the audience, whose enjoyment of her high spirits is broken at the same time as those spirits are broken themselves. Yet the shot seems also to objectify Sofia, making her body and what is done to it a source of derision. Sofia is not conventionally attractive in the first place, but rather stereotyped as a fat, raucous black woman. The shot of her sprawling on the ground seems to express not merely her vulnerability to an oppressive white world, but her ridiculousness (and it curiously echoes another shot, meant to be explicitly comic, of two women sent sprawling in a hole, skirts above their heads, in *1941*).

Her suffering not only suggests the terrible price blacks and women pay for rebellion, but the terrible uncertainty Spielberg suffers in portraying it. Sofia is punished by whites and diminished in spirit and capacity. Shug Avery is everything Sofia is not. She is good looking, talented, and a completely free spirit, Mr.'s lover and Celie's. She is the the catalyst for Celie's freedom, a sexual guide and maternal spirit. But Shug has a father, a preacher, from whom she is painfully estranged and wishes recognition. When Shug sings in Harpo's juke joint, the scene is intercut with her father preaching against her in church, pointing up their separation. After Shug first makes love to Celie—the initial moment of the latter's liberation—she goes to her father's church to attempt a reconciliation. He refuses her, and the sequence is played out mostly in one shots of each character, separated from each other, Shug unable to obtain the absolution of her father's love.

Later, after Celie's break with her brutal husband, and after she and Shug return from the city, an extraordinary series of events occurs that moves the narrative onto its recuperative path. Celie finds that the man she thought was her father was not, a discovery that removes the threat of incest and safely prepares for the return of Celie's children and sister, Nettie. Once again Shug sings in the juke joint. Once again Spielberg intercuts this with her father preaching. His sermon is about the need "for the Lord to drive you home to truth." The choir sings and their music infiltrates the juke joint and interferes with the music being played there. Shug has the band join in with the church music and an antiphony begins which is not only musical, but visual as well: the sequence alternates between the church and the little rural nightclub. Within the montage of these two opposing places and antagonistic characters, Shug and her father, Spielberg inserts a shot of Mr. He is now a man reduced in power by the refusal of his wife to submit to his brutality. He sits in his rocking chair, smiling at the antiphony of church and juke joint, as if with some secret knowledge of the outcome. Shug proceeds to lead her friends out of the club to the church. The cutting progressively narrows the distance until father and daughter confront each other in the church. Finally, they embrace. The film's two other major female characters, Celie and Sofia, are also present in the church and the reconciliation prepares for the final apotheosis of the father.

Shug and Sofia begin as independent and strong-willed women who are forced back into positions of subservience to men. Sofia winds up tending bar at her husband's juke joint; Shug's freedom is unfulfilling without her father's recognition. She must enter his house to find it. Celie, on the other hand, begins with no independence. From the beginning of the film she is physically and emotionally abused by men who take things from her—children, sister, identity. She is made chattel to Mr., who throws Celie's beloved Nettie out of the house because she won't sleep with him and keeps her letters from Celie out of pure meanness. He is something of a human equivalent of the shark in *Jaws*, a domestic evil in this case, a figure drawn with certain racist stereotypes of the evil black buck. (One of the most questionable images in the film occurs when Celie and Shug discover Mr.'s secret chest in which he has hidden Nettie's letters. Amidst his private cache are pictures of naked white women—as if the white creators of the film could think of nothing more secret, more illicit or shocking for a black man to covet. Walker merely refers to "nasty picture postcards.")[21] Celie's victory over Mr. becomes a major melodramatic triumph of good, a gaining of selfhood over the language of brutality. Her movement to slit his throat—articulated by Spielberg in a complicated montage that intercuts Celie's movements shaving Mr., her son in Africa having his face cut in a tribal ritual, and Shug running to prevent Celie from acting on her anger—releases the desire for revenge created in the audience. That desire is then more effectively channeled in the dinner table sequence that follows, where anger and self-recognition are articulated in language. Words give Celie a measure of freedom and the result is one of the great liberating moments in contemporary film.

But this measure of freedom must be contained. After her break with her husband, Celie leaves with Shug and becomes successful in a business of her own devising (she manufactures trousers that fit both men and women). But she must be brought home—quite literally, as she discovers she has inherited her father's house. Mr., his life ruined by Celie's new-found energy, must also be brought back, in fact reinserted within the film's central grouping. The film's ideological project could not be successfully closed were he left out of the general reclamation that ends it. Mr. must be recuperated not only into the narrative, but into that greater narrative fantasy of mid-eighties America in which families are returned to their proper order. Alice Walker offers a quiet return of Mr. into the fold of decent human behavior. He learns to look after himself; he and Celie talk gently with each other. Spielberg eschews quiet reconciliation for melodramatic reversal. As the events with Shug Avery and her father proved, the patriarchy must be somehow reestablished. But Mr. cannot be the figure who offers the reconciliation; he has been too brutal and Celie's break with him too complete. Were they to come back together, the narrative movement would be not merely reversed but broken. Rather he must be reconciled into a more general scheme, and the narrative allows this to occur by making him an agent for the recuperative process and then allowing him a share in the spaces of reunion.

The process begins with that shot of him smiling, rocking on his front porch, which is inserted into the movement of Shug to her father. Placed by the editing into the middle of this specific return of the father, he is joined into the general act of reclamation, which he facilitates by arranging with the U.S. Immigration Service for the return of Nettie and Celie's children. When that reunion occurs, when the entire family, which was broken up first by Celie's stepfather and then by Mr., come to each other and embrace, Mr. is again edited into the process so that he is sutured into the harmonious space. Celie and Nettie run to each other in the fields and embrace; Celie meets her children. Intercut with these events are shots of Sofia, Harpo, and Shug, smiling happily, observing the proceedings from the front of Celie's house. At one point, Shug turns, and as if she were looking at Mr., Spielberg cuts to a shot in which the camera dollies in on him in the fields. He is looking downward with contentment (the dolly in, that favored camera movement I described earlier, does not represent uncertainty or threat here, but a dynamic move to proximity with the character, a reduction of space between him and the viewer). There is another shot of Shug followed with yet another of Mr., this time seen from a distance in the fields, walking off. Finally, as Celie and Nettie clap their hands together against the sun, Mr. can be seen walking by behind them.

Though unable narratively to re-enter Celie's new-found happiness, he is composed within it visually, and in turn helps to compose it. His presence that was so violent and destructive before is now the necessary part of closure. The matter is not simply one of a happy ending, of a fairy tale in which all figures, evil and good, are reconciled in the end, but of an inability to cast out the male figure. *The Color Purple* cannot allow its female figures a space of their own and insists that the male figure—Shug's father and Celie's husband—be present and part of a transcendent reordering of freedom back into the domestic unit. Many uncertainties are solved inside and outside the narrative. Any fears that black women—any women—may proclaim their independence from patriarchal structures are soothed; any notion that independence may exist apart from the confines of a happy, loving family with a controlling male figure is annulled.

The conservative concept of the family annuls individuality and the various images of family are used to purchase emotion at the expense of analyzing alternatives. Spielberg turns desire into a commodity, utopia into the mundane, and the politics of relationships into a spectacle that confirms power and hierarchy. The only realities in demand here are those that involve the attention and response of the viewer. "Spectacle demands our attention," writes Dana Polan. It is "a command to 'look here' that needs no cognitive assent other than the initial fact of looking. The specific content of a spectacle is only a very small part of its attraction. . . . Spectacle offers an imagistic surface of the world as a strategy of containment against any depth of involvement with that world."[22] But something, of course, must be contained. In the case of *The Color Purple*, as with all of Spielberg's films, the promise of regeneration, of social, personal, political change is contained within the spectacular pleasure of ideological assent. The viewer buys the commodity of spectacle and is repaid by exciting images which offer the dangers of subversion rendered harmless by the affirmation of secure convention. Since the spectacle's command to look is by definition a patriarchal one (the American cinema is part of the general discourse of male power, and commands are part of that discourse), the viewer is assured that what is looked at will affirm the secure, known discourse of the culture at large. Narrative images of home and safety, of protecting fathers and securing families are a part of that discourse, which has turned them from social, psychological realities into consumer goods, packaged as exciting narratives and sold with the promise that their purchase will assure contentment and an appropriate place in the cultural imaginary.

Terry Eagleton nicely describes the shift of "family" from its reality as a refuge from the public sphere into a commodity whose purchase offers validation of one's place within that sphere. "Mass culture," he writes, ". . . to some degree displaces the family as the arena in which needs and desires are negotiated, and indeed progressively penetrates the family itself."

> In the classical public sphere, private experience provided the very basis of public association: participants encountered each other precisely as private citizens, and the subjective autonomy of each was the very structure of their social discourse. The "intimate" realm of the family and household was at once a refuge from this world, and one matrix of its modes of subjecthood. In late capitalism, privatization becomes the dissolution, not the enabling condition, of public association; it is at once the effect of a real separation between family and society—of the absence of a public sphere which might mediate between them—and, paradoxically, of that deprivatization of the family brought about by the absorption of some of its traditional functions into the state, which maroons the family with little beyond its affective and consumptional experience. The family remains in part a refuge from civil society, nurturing vital impulses unfulfilled by it; but since it is also ceaselessly penetrated by commodity culture, this potentially positive arena of the personal is continually caught up with forms of privatization which atomize, serialize and disconnect. At the same time, the forms of public *association* of the traditional bourgeois sphere are replaced with an ideologically powerful *homogenization*, an *ersatz* sociality which is little more than the levelling effect of the commodity.[23]

"Privatization" is the process of removing all community and its protection, for permitting all spheres of activity to be turned into commodities and entered into the balance sheets of exchange. "The family" has become one of these commodities, fetishized, sentimentalized, and gutted of substance in political discourse, sold on television and in film as something viewers must desire, that they might in fact be able to own if they purchased its images and cultivated them with their own financial and moral capital. The family is no longer a refuge, but a command and a judgment—a law of the patriarch. Spielberg's spectacles demand that we look at the kindly statement of these laws, that we permit ourselves to be dissociated from reality by the promise of a private realm where reality will never impinge. Like all consumer products they promise to soothe fears and satisfy desires. They complete a circuit of demand with a ready supply of promise. The terrors of the world remain untouched by them; our understanding of these terrors are short circuited by the ease with which the films overcome them. The subject is itself privatized and reconstituted by spectacle that can push the world aside and replace it with an imaginary realm willingly consumed. In this way, ideology reproduces itself.

## CHAPTER FIVE

# RADICAL SURFACES

---

# Robert Altman

At the end of Robert Altman's film *Secret Honor*, Richard Nixon screams a mad, defiant "Fuck 'em" at all his presumed and imagined enemies, all the voters who elected him, condemned him, and elected him again. "Fuck 'em," he screams—his image echoed on the television monitors in his office that multiply and re create him. "Fuck 'em," he yells, fist upraised, his television image responding, throwing out more images. "Fuck 'em."

Robert Altman tells a story about negotiating a project with Warner Brothers some years ago. After much talk and some compromise on the director's part, a Warner's executive became uncomfortable and hesitated. He still was not sure about the proposed film and he told Altman "We don't want this to seem too much like a Robert Altman movie."[1]

In 1976, Altman made *Buffalo Bill and the Indians, or Sitting Bull's History Lesson* for Dino De Laurentis. A big film with big stars—Paul Newman and Burt Lancaster—it turned out to be a dry and angry denunciation of the myths of show business and the distortions of people and history that those myths engender. Few people went to see it, and it could only have been taken as an insult by its producer, who cut it for European distribution. The affair resulted in the breakdown of a project Altman was planning, a film of E. L. Doctorow's best-selling novel *Ragtime* (later made into an indifferent film by Milos Forman). However, Altman was able to return within a year with *Three Women*, a difficult, enigmatic, and not very commercial film. In the late seventies, Altman had a multi-film deal with Twentieth-Century Fox. *A Wedding* did well critically and commercially. *Quintet* and *A Perfect Couple* did very poorly. Fox refused to distribute the last of the films, *Health*, and Altman had to take it to colleges and festivals himself. (In 1984, Altman made a film for MGM called *O.C. and Stiggs*, based on some *National Lampoon* characters. It was not seen until 1987, and then only in limited release.) In 1981, his last large-scale production, *Popeye*—made for Paramount and Disney—behind him, other projects getting canceled, Altman sold his studio, Lion's Gate Films, and started what is essentially a new career of low-budget, independently distributed films made from plays and, occasionally, for television.[2]

I would not suggest that Altman (of all people) identifies with Richard Nixon, but rather that the final outcry of that paranoid figure created by Altman, writers Donald Freed and Arnold M. Stone, and actor Philip Baker Hall, carries enfolded within its hysteria some of the very calm, unparanoid defiance expressed in Altman's own work and career. For ten years, he had been able to use the economic and emotional system of Hollywood filmmaking to the advantage of his work and to the benefit of exceptional filmmaking. His one "blockbuster," *M.A.S.H.* (1970)—something of an accident, since the project was offered to Altman, who was far from its producer's first choice as director—provided the security for his future work. Producers were willing to back his films on the promise that he would make another enormous commercial success. He never did, but the promise allowed him to direct one or two films a year, made relatively inexpensively and returning relatively small profits. More important, he was able to make them under his own auspices and to elaborate within them and from film to film a consistent approach and point of view. Altman's seventies films are formally and contextually of a piece, so much so that, once his style is understood, it can be recognized in almost any one part of any film he makes. Few American filmmakers have so confirmed the fragile legitimacy of the *auteur* theory with such a visible expression of subjectivity in their work. Few have, with this expression and insistence on control, so annoyed producers and distributors.[3]

Part of the consistency came from Altman's ability to create around him a dependable community of production people and players, a ministudio in which the logistics and complexities of his films were worked out among individuals who were familiar and comfortable with his methods and approach. His associate producers, Scott Bushnell and Robert Eggenweiler, and assistant director, Tommy Thompson, formed the nucleus of this group. Editor Lou Lombardo and production designer Leon Ericksen worked on some of his best films, as have cinematographers Vilmos Zsigmond and Paul Lohmann. Alan Rudolph was an assistant director on *Nashville* and co-author of *Buffalo Bill and the Indians*. Altman, in turn, produced Rudolph's first films, *Welcome to L.A.* (1977) and *Remember My Name* (1978), and Rudolph's later work still bears traces of Altman's influence. (Altman also produced Robert Benton's *The Late Show* (1978), and Robert Young's *Rich Kids* (1979).) Until they began branching out into their own careers, he had a stock company of players, including Shelley Duvall, Michael Murphy, Keith Carradine, René Auberjonois, John Shuck, and Bert Remsen. This group helped provide security within an insecure environment and made it possible for Altman to explore and expand upon his ideas from film to film, without having to start from zero each time.

Scott Bushnell and other associates remain with Altman's new company, Sandcastle 5 Productions, and cinematographer Pierre Mignot has filmed all of the theatrical adaptations to date. Secure environment is so important to Altman, that he has—at the time of this writing— removed himself from the West Coast and set up production facilities in Paris. One of the delights of *Beyond Therapy* is the way Altman disguises Paris to look like New York, until the very last shot, when the true location is revealed.

I am aware that such a narrative runs the risk of turning Robert Altman into a hero, making him the *auteur* not only of a body of films, but of a romantic personality, fighting the mean-minded, commercially crass system, succumbing, regrouping. He is not a hero, only a good filmmaker, and he has merely pulled back from the fray to do other kinds of films, organizing a new production company with similarly dependable people. But perhaps for the purposes of remaining optimistic about the future of American film, Robert Altman must be seen as a fighter against the system. For the purposes of critical inquiry, however, that persona is less important than the films Altman makes, and it is those films that manifest the subject which is important for the inquiry. I spoke of their consistency, but must point out that a break occurs in 1981, when Altman began making films of plays. These recent works are quite different in form from the preceding films, more contained, held fast by their verbal source and their budgetary constraints. They continue to explore many of the same problems as the work of the first period, and some may be seen standing in a dialectic relationship: *Streamers* to *M.A.S.H.*, for example; *Come Back to the Five and Dime, Jimmy Dean, Jimmy Dean* and—at least in terms of location—*Fool for Love* to *Three Women*; *Secret Honor* to *Buffalo Bill and the Indians*; *Beyond Therapy* to *A Perfect Couple*. In the discussion that follows, I want to incorporate that dialectic and do some comparison of the recent to the earlier work.

Given the extent of Altman's output and the relative consistency of his formal approach within each of the two periods of his career, I want, in the discussion that follows, to create something of an arbitrary division between form and content. I will first look at the ways Altman alters conventions of cinematic space and narrative structure and will then examine the major films. However, since there are twenty-five of these, from 1957 to this writing, it will be impossible to discuss all of them or give equal attention to each. The method will necessitate some doubling back and some fragmentation of exposition. But this seems the best way to encompass the scope of Altman's work, which itself encompasses nothing less than an inquiry into the images of contemporary America and the way those images have been set by our films and our politics (among other forms of entertainment, representation, and misrepresentation). The films, themselves engaging entertainments, continually reflect their origins and their status as films as they reflect from us and back to us the images we hold of ourselves and our culture.

In creating these inquiries and reflections, Altman dissociates himself from the closed forms of classical Hollywood story-telling, turning the screen into a wide, shallow space (he used the 2.35 to 1 anamorphic ratio almost exclusively until 1981, and again in *Fool For Love* (1985), filled with objects and people, with movement, with talk and sounds and music woven into casual and loose narratives that create the appearance of spontaneity and improvisation. But it is only an appearance, for the apparent casualness is carefully intended, and the sense of arbitrary observation calculated to situate the viewer in the narrative in specific ways. In the theatrical adaptations, he reverses his approach almost completely. Filmed in standard ratio (sometimes in 16mm or videotape), the post-1981 films draw attention directly to their dramatic center. Confined to a very few sets, and carefully locating and exploring the figures within their milieu, the films seem to deny the openness and apparent randomness of the earlier work. After having broken up the narrative and dispersed the viewing subject into its various parts in the earlier films, Altman now attempts to reconstitute that subject, urging the viewer to concentrate on carefully developed dramatic dynamics. However, in his rapid move from modernism to post modernism, Altman only rediscovers the difficulties in locating a secure subject. Once his films moved from center to periphery, now they go in the opposite direction, but still do not often find a secure point of rest.

Altman made two features in the fifties. One of them, a "documentary" on James Dean, employing stills and interviews, is an artifact of the kind of sentimental myth-making he was to attack in the seventies. He did television in the early sixties and in 1968 a feature for Warner Brothers called *Countdown*. This potentially interesting study of astronauts, concentrating on their jealousies and tensions, is filmed and cut in a frontal, static, eye-level mode which allows for little but a straightforward exposition of the story. Made in what could be called the Hollywood anonymous style, its form is unobtrusive, linear, with no detail to detract from the headlong perpetration of plot. *Countdown* is a studio film and gives no idea of what Altman was to do, though it does offer an example of the early work of two major seventies actors, James Caan and Robert Duvall. The film would hardly be worth mentioning were it not an example of the kind of formal structure that Altman and most of the other filmmakers discussed here are working against. It is a prepared text that the director has only to transfer to film; there is no space for the inflection of style, which, for Altman, makes its initial appearance in *That Cold Day in the Park* (1969).

The subject of a repressed spinster driven to murder by her activated but unrealized sexual desires seems at best a cliché (at worst a bit of rampant sexism) and offering at most the opportunity for some conventional psychology and brooding, foreboding compositions, perhaps some shock cuts in the manner of an AIP horror film. Indeed, *That Cold Day* offers all of these, and, were it an isolated work, could easily be dismissed by the reviewer's phrase "atmospheric." The film is not isolated, however, but rather an initiation, and Altman's attempts to render the subjective states of a female consciousness, though crude here, will be refined in *Images* (1972) and fully realized in *Three Women* (1977), *Come Back to the Five and Dime, Jimmy Dean, Jimmy Dean* (1982), and, with less emphasis on expressionist components, in a made-for-cable piece, *The Laundromat* (1985). Most important is that Altman begins to develop in this film the opening of the aural-visual space of his narrative, diffusing its center by taking notice of the peripheries. The camera continually drifts away from the main action, zooming past a face into a window to pick up the out-of-focus light reflected on the glass, defining the central character and her state of mind by bringing to the viewer's attention the otherwise unnoticeable objects and minutiae that surround her. Dialogue shifts, too, away from the central speakers. In a bar, a diner, a doctor's office, Altman picks up conversation to the side, almost off screen. When Frances Austen (Sandy Dennis) visits her gynecologist, she sits in the waiting room apart from the other women. Attention is on her, but at the same time diverted from her, diffused by the fact that she is observed, through the length of the sequence, from outside a window, and further diffused by the fragments of tantalizing gossip that drift around her as the other women talk about sexual problems.

On the face of it, there is nothing unusual about one character set off against a group of strangers, those strangers speaking of matters that somehow reflect the main character's state of mind. Certainly a key development in American film of the sixties involved greater attention paid to peripheral action, a sense of life existing around the main focus of action (Penn's *Mickey One* is a good example). In conventional film narrative, attention is concentrated on the central characters and their relationship. Sequences carefully moved from an establishing shot to a mid-shot and then to closeups of individuals or couples who spoke in turn, the dialogue and the cutting directing attention to the central concern of the sequence. In a sequence that took place, say, in a nightclub or other public area, the "extras" were precisely that, extra to the sequence, filling the space rather than participating in the sequence. An exterior, such as a street scene, would be peopled by anonymous bodies, and, were any commentary on the main action needed from them, a closeup from the crowd would be cut in and quickly removed.

D. W. Griffith is the forerunner of this tradition of centralized, exclusionary screen space. He used the closeup to narrow the narrative field and concentrate attention inward, removing unwanted surroundings by inserting what he considered the center of those surroundings, the emotionally charged human face. Certainly an ideological force is operative in this: the focus in traditional American cinema on limited, concentrated areas, dominated by a few central characters, reflects long-standing myths of individual potency as well as the pre-cinematic tradition in middle-class art that the only serious and engaging dramatic interests are those of the individual in conflict with him or herself or another person, the individual spectator being the privileged observer of that conflict. Responses to this narrative tradition in film did not begin with Altman or the other contributors to recent film but can be seen in the work of filmmakers as diverse as Eisenstein and Renoir.

Eisenstein's montage in his silent films creates a sense of constant movement from periphery to center and back again, from masses of people in action to the faces within those masses and the small events that make up the action. Cause and effect, action and reaction play against each other, the "center" of events occurring ultimately off screen, in the spectator's consciousness, which the montage guides but keeps somewhat distant. Eisenstein, of course, is working out his filmic structures from an ideology more clear and immediate than Griffith's—an ideology of revolutionary action and dramatic change in social and aesthetic structures—and Griffith's films became a model for Eisenstein to work against. Jean Renoir's responses to the American narrative tradition in the thirties are less radical. His redefinitions of the visual field and the focus of individual sequences within a film are closer to what

Altman would be doing in the seventies (and, to a lesser extent, to what Spielberg does in those shots that allow the viewer to examine the space surrounding the central figure). *Grand Illusion* and *Rules of the Game* are structured with an acknowledgment that narrative blocks do not have to be built out of single, concentrated areas of activity. Renoir recognizes that the screen is capable of indicating an extension of space beyond the frame rather than denying the existence of that space. Through deep-field composition and the use of the pan he extends the spatial limits of the shot, indicating, by continually expanding it, that there is more to the space than is immediately depicted. In a sequence in *Grand Illusion* where a soldier puts on a woman's costume while the others stare at him, the pan of the men's faces not only indicates surprise, longing, and sadness, but also quantity. There are many men, in a large area, and they all share, at this moment, the same feelings. As the camera moves from face to face, the effect is incremental and expansive; the viewer is permitted visually to embrace the physical presence and the emotions of the men. In *Rules of the Game*, Renoir orchestrates his characters and camera so that there is an expanding and contracting flow of spatial movement in response to the emotional and intellectual movement of the narrative, encompassing that movement and opening it out, permitting observation of many activities and not allowing the viewer comfortably to focus on any one character or point of view.[4]

As I said, American cinema since the sixties has taken more cognizance of peripheral activity. But with few exceptions this has not been in the manner of Renoir nor, certainly, of Eisenstein. The periphery recognized usually encompasses onlookers, and the sense is that of giving the extras a bit more work to do. With the rise of location shooting and the setting of action sequences within those locations, the possibility arose of counterpointing the central action against those observing the action but irrelevant to it. A source for this is Carol Reed's *The Third Man* (1949), whose post-war Vienna exteriors are punctuated by workers in the dark, barren streets, old faces observing speeding cars. Reed's onlookers constituted a kind of historical conscience, silently commenting upon the action. In recent film the faces that are inserted into a sequence of a shooting or a car wreck are only observers, commentators on the action who have nothing to do with the "plot," the central characters and their activities, and they signify only a passing, outside

world. Therefore, the suggestions of activity beyond the central character in *That Cold Day*—the women at the gynecologist's, for example—are a bit special. Altman is imposing peripheral action onto the
central focus of the sequence, not merely indicating its presence but
playing that presence over and against the main figure and her concerns,
forcing the viewer to take equal notice of both while at the same time
removing the viewer from both by shooting the sequence from the other
side of a glass window (a device Altman uses again, for comic effect, in
the therapy sessions in *Beyond Therapy*). So, too, with the camera drifting off, away from the main character, and zooming to objects and
blurred lights. Here Altman uses the zoom to suggest a subjective sense
of vagueness and disorientation; elsewhere he will use it to capture the
particulars of a defined area, reorganizing the space of a given sequence
by developing it as a place of inquiry rather than accepting it as a pre-
existent whole (a method he will continue, on a much more restricted
scale, in the theatrical adaptations). More than Renoir, Altman
launches an investigation of the ways one observes filmic constructions
and the ways one reads the narratives to which these constructions give
form.

The investigation moves forward rapidly in *M.A.S.H.*, the film Altman did not originate or choose, but which he was able to use both as
a means to develop new formal approaches and, coincidentally, as a
financial base upon which to build his future work. In *That Cold Day
in the Park*, the shooting style is an extension of the basic horror-gothic
approach. Most of the action takes place in the dark, heavy apartment
of the main character, Frances Austen. Browns and blacks predominate;
there is little red, so that the act of violence that concludes the film is
all the more shocking because of the sudden appearance of the color of
blood. A standard focal length lens (which approximates the spatial
relationships of the eye) seems to be used throughout, allowing Altman
and cinematographer Laszlo Kovacs to explore the rooms and their
shadows and the characters trapped within them.

*M.A.S.H.* is shot largely out of doors, but the area is an isolated one,
cut off. The men live in flimsy tents; they are pressed in by their situation, not only as a hospital unit stuck inside the war zone (this aspect
is underplayed, for the war is never seen or heard, only its casualties),
but by the fact that their spirits are imprisoned by military order. (In

*Streamers*, the action is confined completely to the interior of a barracks, parts of the outside glimpsed only through windows. But the imprisonment here is actually psychological, the pressures of confinement and the possibility that the men will have to go to Vietnam generate racial and sexual tensions and violence rather than a struggle against their oppression.) To create the appropriate *mise-en-scène* of confinement in *M.A.S.H.*, Altman employs two devices which effectively contradict each other, resulting in a curious spatial illusion that grows out of the contradiction. *M.A.S.H.* is photographed (by Harold E. Stine) in Panavision, whose great width is often used to suggest large horizons or actions. But Altman wishes to constrict the space of *M.A.S.H*, and to this end he employs a telephoto lens for most of the sequences, which compresses space, making it flat—a device that had sometimes been used to great effect by Akira Kurosawa. Unlike shallow-focus cinematography, which foregrounds the figures in focus, creating an undefined background, and deep focus, which articulates the objects from foreground to back, telephoto cinematography tends to background everything, or at least to put foreground and background on the same plane. Within the extreme width of the Panavision screen and the compressed depth created by the telephoto lens, Altman fills the screen space with people and objects, all of which are drained of any bright colors, save for the spurting blood in the operating room, and observes them from a distance.

The result is visual conflict rendering an experience of claustrophobia, a sense, on the viewer's part, of being locked into an observation of a *mise-en-scène* which refuses to open up or to give way, to yield immediately to the viewer's investigation of it. The visual denseness is supported and perhaps exacerbated by the sound track. There is not a silent moment in *M.A.S.H*: dialogue, music, announcements on a loudspeaker are continuous, sometimes at odds with, or in ironic counterpoint to, what is happening on screen, sometimes all things at once. Altman takes from Welles (and Howard Hawks) the notion of overlapping dialogue, people talking at the same time without waiting for a response. The effect is an aural space that parallels the decentralization of the visual space. By refusing to allow the comfort of pauses in the dialogue any more than he allows the comfort of simple visual orientation, Altman creates a demanding and busy visual and aural field.

But the terms of his demands are not those that André Bazin spoke about in his discussions of the long take and deep-focus cinematography, with their capability of opening the image to active participation on the part of the viewer. In *M.A.S.H.* and the films that follow, Altman rarely uses deep focus, and he cuts a great deal. The visual structure of his films requires not that the viewer pick and choose among various visual and aural options but that he or she observe and understand the whole and integrate into the larger unit those parts of the whole that the director wishes to emphasize. What Altman creates is not the conventional structure of a whole that is analyzed into its parts, but a simultaneity of the whole *and* its parts, a simultaneity the viewer must always attend to.

*M.A.S.H.* creates and sustains its busy, constricted, claustrophobic structure for about half its length, then dissipates itself as the action leaves the army camp for antics in Tokyo and on the football field. The spatial experimentation occurs only sporadically in the film that follows, *Brewster McCloud* (1970). Two sequences within this film—one in a police laboratory, the other a police investigation of a murder on the street—are constructed with large numbers of people talking all at once and at cross purposes, bad jokes weaving in and out of the conversations, no one element taking precedence over the others. These sequences tend to be isolated, for Altman is working out other problems of narrative structure. *Brewster McCloud* jokes around with itself, falls in love with its bird-shit jokes and the looney characters that fly and squawk around its demented assemblage. With *McCabe and Mrs. Miller* (1971) he thoroughly grasps the possibilities of his spatial experiments and sees them through.

*McCabe and Mrs. Miller* is among the richest works of seventies cinema; form and content are so well integrated that a split is difficult to make, even for purposes of analysis. It will bear talking about once in the context of its visual and narrative structure, and once again in relation to its genre and the way it responds to other westerns. In each case, analysis is enlightened by placing the film in the context of the work of John Ford.

In *The Man Who Shot Liberty Valance* (1962), Ford worked out the possibilities of an indoor western, eschewing wide-open spaces for the dark interiors of saloons and homes, a newspaper office and a meeting hall. Ford, near the end of his career, wanted to examine the transition of the frontier wilderness to the closed, law-bound community. He was saddened by this transition, though he realized its historic reality and inevitability. More important, he knew that the myth of the West had to be tempered by the reality of capitalist expansion. His film is an elegy for the past and an almost begrudging celebration of the change to the bourgeois security of a structured civilization. Altman has no stake in either part of the western mythos. A man with a late-sixties, early-seventies consciousness, with a certain left-liberal perspective, he sees the western, and most other film genres, along with the attitudes and ideology they embody, not as healing and bonding lies—which is the way Ford saw the western—but merely as lies. Like Ford, Altman responds to the elegiac element always latent in any myth of the past. But, unlike Ford, he does not mourn the passing of the frontier and investigate the coming of law and order: he mourns rather the lost possibility of community and the enforced isolation of its members.

Out of this paradox of community and the isolation it creates Altman builds the *découpage* (the compositional and editing structure) of his film, working from the reorientation of space and sound he began experimenting with in *M.A.S.H.*[5] Over the Warner Brothers logo at the beginning of the film are sounds of a harsh wind blowing. As the credits begin we see a man on horseback, heavily wrapped in furs, riding through the pine trees of a northern winter landscape. A sad lyric by Leonard Cohen accompanies the movement, a song about a gambling stranger. The space, as in *M.A.S.H.*, is enclosed, narrow, and flat, and the color is almost bichromatic: the greens of the trees standing out, barely, from a general blue haze. The man on horseback—as in so many westerns—enters a town. He pauses by a church, removes his furs, dismounts, mumbles something angry and incoherent. Visual attention shifts to some of the men in the town, standing about in the rain, looking, observing the stranger from a distance. McCabe (Warren Beatty) is seen again in a telephoto shot, from a vantage point inside a saloon; he is crossing a footbridge, moving toward the camera until his face is framed in the saloon window, looking in.

There is a cut to the interior of the saloon, dark, filled with low voices. The color, what little there is, appears warmer than the exterior blue. Various faces are picked out. Through a barred partition we see the owner, Sheehan (René Auberjonois), lighting a candle under a statue of the Virgin and saying a prayer. More faces are picked up; McCabe asks for the back door. Various comments from the men in the saloon regarding his gun can just be heard: "Is he wearing a gun?. . . Do you know what kind of gun that was . . . that was a Swedish . . . from Sweden . . . What the hell is he wearing a gun for? . . ." These comments appear freely on the sound track, not assigned to any speakers directly seen. McCabe returns with a tablecloth and spreads it out. Some people comment on the weather. A small fight breaks out over a chair. Again various faces are observed. McCabe asks for a bottle. As they are about to  begin playing cards, McCabe asks to go fifty-fifty with Sheehan, and as they talk of a business arrangement Sheehan lights a lamp, infusing the space with a warm golden light. There is talk of the game, of betting, a shot of hands dealing cards. McCabe's hand points to the table and his voice, off screen, says, "Jack off." With the accompanying laughter, the camera cuts to the whole group and then to a zoom to McCabe's face, smiling, revealing a gold tooth, cigar clenched happily.

For this verbal description of the film's opening sequence to work properly, I would somehow have to break the sentences up, slip some parts of them under others; still others would have to be bent sideways or placed at a diagonal. For in a more radical fashion than *M.A.S.H.*, Altman has created in *McCabe* a tight and enclosed space, peopled with figures who, though contained in that space, seem unconnected to it and, even more, unconnected to each other. There is little eye contact between the various characters in this opening sequence. When McCabe looks, he doesn't get a direct look back. The camera rarely observes the characters squarely, at eye level, centered in the frame. They are rather picked out, seemingly at random, glanced at and overheard. The Panavision screen and telephoto lens serve, more than they did in *M.A.S.H.*, to inhibit observation by compressing the screen space. The cutting and the sound mixing create a barely localized environment and a sequence of events that are just suggested.

Through it all, Altman produces a fine dialectical effect. The more random fragments of faces, figures, and conversation that are given, the more coherent the space becomes. The viewer is often unaware, momentarily, of just what location he or she is observing, or even why it is being observed. But the confusion itself becomes a coherent expression of this loose, unfocused community, existing in disorder, with its members operating not out of friendship but in a sort of mutual antagonism. And the less definition Altman offers, the less securely is the viewer fixed in the narrative and instead is offered the opportunity to help construct the proceedings from the interlocking fragments. To repeat what I noted earlier, this is quite a different phenomenon from what Bazin had in mind when he spoke of the filmmaker allowing the viewer to retrieve a range of information and experience from the image. Bazin's concept suggests an activating of the otherwise passive filmgoer; but this is only sometimes the case. The long deep-focus take may do little more than concentrate attention and permit the viewer to observe the details of the *mise-en-scène*. It may intensify reactions by allowing them to build slowly rather than by commanding them through editorial direction. But Altman does direct the attention and the gaze. However, unlike the conventional *découpage* of American film, he does not order that gaze into, and then within, a determined and delimited space (as, for example, Kubrick does). He creates—or, more appropriately, allows the viewer to create—an idea of place out of visual and aural fragments and suggestions. This fragmentation is, of course, never as severe as that of the European cinemodernists, like Jean-Marie Straub and Danièle Huillet, for instance, and the town in *McCabe and Mrs. Miller* is, ultimately, well defined. However, his dependence upon viewer cooperation in constructing the *mise-en-scène*, his refusal to situate the viewer comfortably in an easily observable space, break sharply with the codes of conventional film.

The effect achieved is, again, reminiscent of Renoir: an extension of the screen space, the suggestion of rich and random activity of which the focus of narrative attention is only one part. Like Renoir, Altman attempts to indicate a wholeness, a continuum of space. Unlike Renoir he does it by cutting and by sound, rather than by panning and tracking. When movement occurs, it is most often executed by a zoom, which by its nature does not encompass space but narrows or extends it, depending on the zoom's direction. Like his cutting, Altman's use of the zoom offers more by showing less. But it defines the relationship of a character and his or her surroundings, or the relationship between two characters, by directing attention more coherently than would a direct cut. More gently too. Altman's zooms, at least in *McCabe*, invite regard of faces and objects, they reveal a private moment or an intimate reaction on the part of a character. They reveal even a violent action without sensation and offer proximity without embarrassing either viewer or character. They inquire and connect within and even between the films, for the zoom is the major technique Altman brings from the seventies films to the adaptations of theatrical works in the eighties. Within the limited space of the latter films, the zoom inquires even more carefully, directing viewer perception within the scene, acting more as a centripetal force, preventing stasis through the persistent probing of the characters in their setting, countering the artifice of the theatrical space that might be created by a steady camera and conventional cutting.

Let me pick up the description of the early sequences in *McCabe and Mrs. Miller*. The busy, rambling, off-centered gambling scene is brought to a small climax as the camera zooms into McCabe's smiling face, isolating and accenting it, presenting an image of a man momentarily in control of his situation. But this zoom closeup is broken by a cut to a telephoto shot of the footbridge outside and the feet of a figure walking away from the camera, which pulls up and zooms back. The warm and embracing movement to McCabe is broken by the cold blue exterior  from which the camera withdraws as soon as it is seen. The figure on the footbridge turns out to be the minister of the town (which is named Presbyterian Church), the one person who cannot engage himself in the activities of the town and who, later, shares in McCabe's destruction by refusing him sanctuary in the church. In this instance the zoom serves to link the viewer closely with McCabe, then to link McCabe with one of the individuals who will prove to be his nemesis, and to define sharply the two areas: the warm gold interior of the saloon and the cold  blue exterior of the town. The act of linkage is most important, for if Altman had merely cut from the card game to the approach of the minister outside, only separation and opposition would have been implied. By first offering proximity to McCabe by the means of the zoom to his face and then cutting to the footbridge and zooming back from that, Altman associates the places and the individuals and introduces important narrative tensions.

In a later sequence, McCabe brings three ragged whores to town. The event is a major turn in his entrepreneurial efforts. He shows them off to the men; a fight breaks out between the whores and the men; McCabe takes the women to their temporary, ramshackle quarters. He is deeply confused over what he has gotten himself into. "I've got to go to the pot," one of the whores tells McCabe, "and I don't think I can hold it." The camera zooms into her face and, in a reverse shot, zooms to McCabe, who looks distressed and uncertain. Out of a kaleidoscope of faces and events, the zoom isolates a moment, a relationship, a set of reactions. It does not necessarily bring the characters close to each other; in fact, the zooms to the whore and to McCabe indicate the extent of incomprehension between them. But the zooms indicate as well their forced proximity and the necessity of the viewer's dealing with that proximity.

The zoom for Altman is a narrative probe, an attempt to understand characters and *mise-en-scène*, the signifier of a cautious but assured approach, a means to discover detail and emphasis. It does not have the positive sense of space transgressed as does the tracking shot.[6] Rather—in Altman's hands, at least—it inscribes the parts and details of the visual field. With the zoom, and in conjunction with his editing, Altman can create a field of action and event that is detailed and particularized. The point of view given the viewer is that of discoverer and connector. The zoom functions as an offering of perspective and detail, of coaxing, leading but never totally or comfortably situating the viewer, or closing off the space that is being examined.

The visual and aural field created in *McCabe and Mrs. Miller* sets the pattern that Altman will build upon in the films that follow. As much as he alters the pattern to fit the needs of each film, the basic preoccupations remain: the urge (prior to the theatrical adaptations) to decentralize the incidents and the area in which those incidents are acted out; the use of the zoom to probe details and emotions. There is, too, a reticence, a desire not to overwhelm the viewer (another quality Altman shares with Renoir), to show him or her some respect and to allow a comfortable distance. Even the violence in his films, often random, sometimes gratuitous, is not brutalizing, but a part of the abrupt changes and alterations that make up his narratives.

Only rarely does he alter the distance and demand that the audience be implicated in the *mise-en-scène*. There is an attempt to communicate the claustrophobia and the developing violence throughout *Streamers*, but with only limited success. *Fool for Love* employs flashbacks that present material contrary or simply different from what the characters are saying in their voice-over commentary about those flashbacks, thereby demanding the viewer account for the perceptual discrepancies and, in effect, work out an alternate *mise-en-scène*. In *The Long Goodbye* (1973), Altman so radically and subtly manipulates the perception of cinematic space that the viewer becomes aware of this manipulation through a sense of discomfort and uneasiness. The film is an attempt to re-examine the figure of Philip Marlowe, Raymond Chandler's private eye, traditionally embodied in the figure of Humphrey Bogart in Howard Hawks's *The Big Sleep*. Altman's Marlowe (played by Elliott Gould) is a puzzled, passive, deeply abused man, caught in an environment and a moral structure he refuses to comprehend. To allow the audience a comprehension of Marlowe's dilemma, Altman and his cinematographer, Vilmos Zsigmond, uproot perceptual stability, preventing a secure, centered observation of the characters in their surroundings. Almost every shot in *The Long Goodbye* is either a very slow, never completed zoom into or out from the characters observed, or a slow, almost imperceptible, arc around or track across them.

In one sequence, Marlowe and Roger Wade (Sterling Hayden), the broken, drunken writer, sit by the ocean, talking, drinking aquavit from enormous cups. The dialogue is broken down into one shots of each of the participants, isolating them from each other visually as they are isolated from each other emotionally and by the misinformation each has about the other. The one shots are punctuated by shots of both together, but these only serve to emphasize their separation by showing their physical distance. This would be a fairly standard *découpage* of a dialogue between two mutually wary antagonists, except for the fact that they are never observed with a still camera. A slow zoom back from Wade is cut to a slow arc around Marlowe, to a slow zoom back of both, to a leftward arc of Wade, to a right arc of Marlowe, and so on until, at the end of the sequence, the camera zooms in and past both to the ocean behind them. More than what is said by the characters in the sequence, the viewer may be affected by what the sequence says about the characters. Here and throughout the film the movement comments, insists that there is more to be known, catches us up in an instability and an incompleteness.

In a later sequence, Marlowe is in Mexico investigating the assumed death of his presumed friend Terry Lennox. He speaks to an official and his aide while the camera observes them through the open window of a building. The dialogue, in which Marlowe is thoroughly lied to by both men, is created by a series of slow lateral tracks across the bars in front of this window. When Altman cuts to a closer shot of the group, the camera is still outside the bars and still tracking, yet near enough so that the bars are out of focus and barely visible. The combination of the telephoto lens, the proximity of the bars, and the slowness of the track gives an immediate appearance of a static shot, yet the sense of movement is inescapable, and the effect insidious. Like Marlowe, the viewer is made uncertain of the seen and unseen, insecure about perception itself.[7] Unlike *Raging Bull*, for example, where slow-motion point of view shots communicate Jake La Motta's failing grasp of his own situation within his world, the movements in *The Long Goodbye* implicate the viewer with the central character's tenuous perceptions of the world.

*The Long Goodbye* is Altman's most extensive experiment in altering the spatial coordinates of the film narrative. I referred to it as being manipulative, but in fact that is not the appropriate term (particularly when compared with Spielberg's work). Like the *mise-en-scène* of *McCabe and Mrs. Miller* it asks a different perceptual response than a more conventional film would; it is more insistent in its demands and more unsettling than is *McCabe*, or indeed any other of Altman's films. But as in the others, suggestion takes precedence over direction, and the peripheries of action take on equal importance with the centers. In an important sense, Altman is a director of peripheries. The dislocation of space that makes up the visual world of his films is part of a wider dislocation that concerns him. That is, the well-made American film, with its steady and precise development of story and character, appears to Altman to be itself a dislocation and a distortion. By attending to different spaces, both visual and narrative, he can reorient the ways an audience looks at films and understands them, and the ways they reflect cultural fantasies back to that audience.

The narrative structure of Altman's films—from *M.A.S.H.* through *Health*—develops out of, or as part of, their spatial structure. The movement from center to periphery demands an abandonment of straightforward narrative development. Events on the edges gain equal importance with events in the middle. More is seen and heard than one is accustomed to. Throughout the offhand conversations that make up the first sequence of *McCabe*, Altman cuts away to the bar, where a running and finally anticlimactic conversation about a beard is taking place. McCabe wanders in and out of the saloon to look around, to urinate ("That man out there takin' a pee . . . ," says Sheehan the barkeeper, inventing a legend for McCabe that will help undo him, "is the man who shot Bill Roundtree"), and as he wanders, so does the conversation, in and out of what should be the main concern: McCabe's buying into the town and his reputation as a gunfighter. But nothing definitive is ever said and no direction given to the narrative. The sequence ends as it begins, gently, humorously, and indirectly. McCabe returns to the gambling table, he tells one of his endearing filthy jokes, and the camera quietly zooms past everyone to a fiddle being plucked in the background.

When, in *The Long Goodbye*, Marlowe gets off the bus in Mexico and wanders, incongruous in his jacket and tie, through the squalid town square, the camera quietly moves from him to zoom in on a pair of fornicating dogs, who wind up snarling at each other (surely the finest example of the often-mentioned improvisational methods of Altman's direction). As fortuitous, offhanded, and incongruous as this particular zoom is, it enhances a narrative of offhanded and incongruous movements and of casual, Southern California couplings that lead to snarling and to death. Snarlings, fistfights, acts of violence continually break out in Altman's films, not so much as they do in Scorsese's as a portent of even greater violence to come, but at unexpected moments, always to punctuate the tenuous calm of any given scene and to indicate the disruption that underlies any situation.

People and events are always disrupted in an Altman film, as are viewer expectations and assumptions. The spectator no more expects to have attention drawn to a pair of fornicating dogs than to a Philip Marlowe who cannot tell lies from truth—and does not seem to care—or to a frontiersman who is only interested in being an entrepreneur, or to a Buffalo Bill who is nothing but a preening, fatuous racist, or to a boy who lives in the Houston Astrodome while he builds a pair of mechanical wings so that he can fly off to nowhere, or to the political infightings of candidates for the presidency of a health food convention. These films do not merely contain unexpected turns; they are unexpected turns. They are quiet attempts at a deconstruction of the narrative and generic truths that are taken for granted in American film, which Altman unfastens from their position as absolutes and relocates within the formal, cultural, ideological structures that created them.[8] In dislocating their visual and narrative centers, the films dislocate their generic centers as well, and begin to reveal some of the ways in which the smooth, undistracted, and unquestioning forms of cinematic story-telling have lied. Altman will no more construct alternative truths to the lies he perceives than will any other American filmmaker; but the deconstruction is insightful, funny, sometimes angry, sometimes off the mark, and always respectful of uncertainty and plurality.

*Brewster McCloud*, though a less than perfect film, is a good place to start an examination of the deconstruction process and to extend the investigation of Altman's use of space to the wider areas of narrative and generic inquiry. The very opening of the film indicates what Altman will be up to. The MGM logo appears, but instead of the expected lion's roar, there is a voice saying, "I forgot the opening line." The film cannot quite get itself started. No smooth entry into a story is promised. A rather strange man appears, a lecturer (René Auberjonois), who talks to us about birds, men, the dream of flight, and environmental enclosures. As he is about to speak of the last, there is a shot of the Houston Astrodome and in it Margaret Hamilton, the wicked witch of *The Wizard of Oz*, attempting to lead a marching band of black musicians in the national anthem. The credits begin; Hamilton stops the band and attempts to get them to sing on key. The credits begin again, and the band breaks into gospel, completely out of control. This film, which will concern itself with the conflict of freedom and constraint, announces this conflict from its beginning, not only in its images, but in the difficulty it has in getting its images started. *Brewster McCloud* parodies itself, its existence as a controlled formal structure, from the very start.

It parodies other films as well—*The Birds, Bullitt*, and *The Wizard of Oz*—while intricately shuffling its elements—a boy training for flight in the bowels of the Astrodome, under the care of a mothering bird-woman; the deaths by bird droppings and strangulation of various bigoted and brutal characters; the posturings of an artificially blue-eyed "super-cop" named Frank Shaft (played by Michael Murphy, drawing on the absurd elements of an earlier character created by Steve

McQueen but in name looking forward to the black cop John Shaft, who appeared a year later in a film by Gordon Parks, also made for MGM). All the while the film playfully comments on its own silliness while refusing to face its serious intent. The film's individual parts—the complicated sound track of radio announcements; the voice-over of the lecturer, who comments on the bird-like endeavors of the various participants and slowly turns into a bird as the film progresses; the intricate intercutting of foolish police investigations with Brewster's dream-like isolation; the car chases; the touching connotations of dreams of flight, of Icarus, and of Oedipus—are successful, but only as parts. They refuse to yield up a coherent statement about the anger that informs them. *Brewster McCloud* is a film about sexuality, power, and freedom, and about how these fundamental personal and ideological components were being changed, questioned, repressed, and corrupted under the Nixon regime at the turn of the seventies ("Agnew: Society Should Discard Some People, A Certain Number Who Won't Fit In," reads a newspaper seen early in the film and rapidly covered with bird droppings). Altman attempts to realize the transformations and distortions of these three forces within a doomed adolescent fantasy of freedom and flight. This fantasy is in turn enclosed by another fantasy, that of the super-hero policeman, that aberration of the heroic which our culture allowed to be foisted upon itself, in film and on television, in the late sixties and early seventies, and which reappeared as the international avenger in the eighties. But although Altman feels the tensions inherent in repression and the need to escape it, and although he understands the absurdity of the heroic images that the culture chooses to embody its various desires to escape untenable situations, he cannot bring the playful openness of the narrative to do more than suggest them. The crushed corpse of Brewster—whose flight to freedom, doomed from the start, ends in an agonizing fall—lying amid the characters who are prancing about in circus garb (the mock-Fellini ending of the film is about the most unfortunate thing Altman has ever done) further rends the fabric of the narrative, rather than mending it with an intended irony.

   *Brewster McCloud* is a significant and successful failure. More clearly than *M.A.S.H.*, it lays out Altman's formal and thematic concerns (though sexuality, power, and freedom are themes so general that almost any film can be said to deal with them, they are specific to Altman in that they do inform most of his work and he consistently deals with their manifestations in the culture). *Brewster McCloud* is important also in that it shakes him free of the potential trap of *M.A.S.H.*, for *Brewster* examines some of the contradictions in the "youth rebellion" of the late sixties—its inherent aimlessness and dependence on the existing social-political order—whereas *M.A.S.H.* is merely a gratification, indeed a pacification, of that rebellion. *M.A.S.H.* feeds a given audience what it wants and shocks others in a perfectly acceptable and unthreatening way. While the compression of space, the crowded *mise-en-scène*, and sound track are important for what will come out of them in Altman's films, *M.A.S.H* presents very little for an audience to deal with contextually. Its narrative is constructed from a series of episodic gags, each representative of the anarchic individual fighting against a restrictive order, with no analysis offered as to the nature of that order and why it should be fought against. Military order is held up as "bad," the heroes of the film as "good." *M.A.S.H* may indicate a difficulty inherent in any film about the military. The genre is too weighted by larger ideological fears and aspirations. Attitudes toward discipline and suffering and enemies, patriotism and death are too fraught with contradictions to be worked out clearly. (Only Stanley Kubrick in *Paths of Glory* came close to dealing with the complexities.) Altman has no luck with it even when he reverses perspective. *Streamers*, which attempts to concentrate upon the psychological tensions of a group of men waiting for service in Vietnam, substituting melodramatic confrontation for comic hijinks, ends with a clear and violent manifestation of racial and sexual instability, but comes to no more certain understanding of how individuals react to the reality of war and the military state than *M.A.S.H.*

*M.A.S.H.* is not a good place to find the beginnings of Altman's investigations of genre. It is finally no more of an antiwar film than is *Paths of Glory* or, for that matter, Lewis Milestone's celebration of selfless bravery in a Korean battle, *Pork Chop Hill* (1959). *M.A.S.H.* is anti-authority only. With a happy band of committed surgeons substituting for the committed band of fighting men omnipresent in earlier war films, and the substitution of operating room for battlefield, it merely teases its audience with an attitude of liberated non-conformity. The war is not really present in *M.A.S.H* (the bleeding bodies have no faces and merely provide more foils for the antics of the heroes) and therefore need not be confronted. There is a smugness not merely in the characters but in the way the narrative allows them to prevail without forcing them to confront anything—such as a notion of why they are where they are.[9] *M.A.S.H.*, like *The Graduate*, that other hymn to the paradoxically passive rebellion of the sixties, is a gentle massage. While the happy surgeons prevail over military order, it remains unchanged and enduring. *Brewster McCloud*, though it also goes some way in depicting the stupidity of the prevailing order, indicates too how difficult it is to overcome with infantile fantasies of evasion and escape. *Brewster* is therefore a much less happy film than its predecessor. Only in its refusal to take itself seriously does it manage to avoid being rather grim.

*M.A.S.H.*, despite its sense of self-parody, takes itself too seriously and perhaps the only way it can be saved is by regarding it not as an army comedy but as part of the sub-genre of POW films.[10] If the war were regarded as a prison and the surgeons of the M.A.S.H. unit as its captives, their hopeless rebellion might be seen as a kind of protection against the destruction of the spirit. This reading gives the film an aura of hopelessness that provides an otherwise absent dialectic. Without it the narrative is all flashy episodes, running jokes, and unexamined assumptions, a balm to the viewer who wants to believe that the structure of authority can be destroyed (or humiliated) by either laughing at it or ignoring it (and being good at your work). Altman's later films try to avoid or at least to confront such false assumptions. That too few such assumptions are confronted in *M.A.S.H.* and too many in *Brewster McCloud* indicates that Altman needed a way to stabilize his perspective, to integrate and control the visual and narrative experimentation that goes on in these early works. He finds that way in *McCabe and Mrs. Miller*, through organizing his film both within and in opposition to one of the most established of American film genres. Where *M.A.S.H.* parallels the war film, *McCabe* sets up an active analysis of the western. Where *M.A.S.H.* celebrates the community that exists in opposition to military authority, *McCabe* is an elegy to the loss of community and the isolation of the individual on the frontier. I said earlier that Altman, unlike Ford, does not see the transition of wilderness to civilization as somehow natural and pre-ordained, incorporating the struggles of individual heroes into secure bourgeois enclaves of law and order. Rather, he sees the conquering of the West as part of the inevitable movement of capitalism, with its attendant brutality, betrayals, and selfishness. The town of Presbyterian Church is no frontier bastion, no Fort Apache or Dodge City. Its inhabitants are not upright citizens or gunfighters. They are merely rather dull and passive people trying to keep warm. The bumbling entrepreneur, John McCabe, has only to walk in to bring a semblance of order, via a gambling saloon and whorehouse. His enemies are not savage Indians or anarchic outlaws but the very passivity of the people, his own misplaced sense of heroism, and the agents of a mining company (who include a savage Indian and anarchic outlaw). He is undone by refusing a business deal and by believing he is a gunfighter.

Altman offers no one in the film, or watching the film, the comforts of convention, the easy assumptions that there are ideals worth dying for or communities worth preserving, at least as those ideals and communities are constituted in our movie myths. In *My Darling Clementine* (1946), Ford creates a sequence in which the townspeople hold a square dance within the unfinished frame of a church, with American flags flying and the wilderness of Monument Valley safely in the distance and effectively sealed off by the structures of the community. He creates it with no irony and no subtext, but as a pure symbol of human order controlling and impressing itself upon the wilderness.[11] In *McCabe*, the comforts of civilization are on a cash basis only and the church a place of denial. Its interior alone of all the buildings in town remains unfinished; its inhabitant is an antisocial, mean little man. But it does serve ironically as a place of congregation. When the church catches fire, the townspeople flock to save what they have heretofore ignored, leaving McCabe alone in the snow, pursued by the mining company's gunmen. He acts the hero despite himself and dies—unlike most heroes embedded in the ideology by cinema—for absolutely nothing. In an alternating montage sequence worthy of Griffith, McCabe is placed alone with the stalking gunmen while the townspeople gather to save a worthless building. Unlike Griffith's, however, the two parts of the montage never join. The community is left to its own devices; McCabe to his death.

The church fire and the gunfight in the snow continue and conclude a set of visual ironies set up early in the film. When Sheehan, on McCabe's arrival, lights the lamp in his saloon, it infuses the area with a warm and golden light that continues to bathe the interiors of the gambling house and whorehouse throughout the film. Conventional association offers this as the light of warmth and security, contrasted with the cold blue of the exteriors. But this is a film in which warmth and security are shown to be delusions and snares and community a fraud. Altman and cinematographer Zsigmond manipulate the warm-gold-interior and cold-blue-exterior light to warn against false comfort.  When the mining company gunmen ride into town, they are bathed in gold light; when McCabe first confronts their leader, the enormous Englishman Butler (few would expect a western gunman to speak with an English accent) in Sheehan's saloon, the gold light is replaced with  the cold blue of the exteriors. The simple glow of protection, security, and community is easily transferred and broken down. The church, conventionally associated with refuge and security (a convention Alt-man acknowledges early in the film when he photographs it against the sunset as its cross is placed on the spire—one of the most photograph-  ically beautiful shots in all his work), burns up. Golden warmth is replaced by destructive fire, destructive not merely to the church (which everyone has ignored previously), but to McCabe and the sense of com-munity obligation. The gold light proves to be false, fooling the viewer as it has the characters of the fiction. When seen for the last time, in contrast to the blue cold in which McCabe dies, it is suffusing the opium den where Mrs. Miller (Julie Christie) has withdrawn. All connotations  of security and community are stripped from it. Still expressing warmth, it is here the warmth of withdrawal, avoidance, and isolation. Mrs. Miller is looking within herself, able to see no further than the marble egg she turns in her hands. (That image returns as self-parody in *Popeye*, where a visit to a gambling and whorehouse reveals a Mrs. Miller look-alike reclining, staring at a vase she holds in her hands—an apt event in this somewhat imagination-starved film where Altman looks back and seems to find only elements for parody in his own work.)

The shots that end the film—Mrs. Miller's eyes and the marbled pat-terns those eyes see—seem to be in perfect opposition to the opening shots of McCabe's entry into the town. But if we recall those opening shots, the enclosed space they embrace, McCabe mumbling to himself

McCabe (Warren Beatty) after his first meeting with Mrs. Miller.

as he dismounts from his horse, the vacant and directionless stares of
the men hanging about in the cold, it is clear that Mrs. Miller's state of
isolation and self-absorption is only an intensification of the state
of things at the beginning. If we realize, in retrospect, how the cutting
of the film and its crowded, fragmented spaces and sounds create a
sense of pervasive isolation in the midst of community, the end comes
as little surprise.

Isolation and self-absorption are qualities Altman discovers in many
of his characters and most of the places they inhabit. He finds the idea
of a successful community difficult to imagine and the smaller units
within communities—conventional romantic couplings and domestic
unions of the kind usually celebrated by American film—impossible.
Only once, in *A Perfect Couple* does he create an unassuming, middle-

class man and woman who manage to find successful love with a minimum of pain and within a context almost devoid of irony. (Successful
love consummates *Beyond Therapy*, but only after long, ironic sexual
battle.) The relationship of Mrs. Miller and McCabe is indicative of difficulties Altman usually sees in romantic conventions. Their initial isolation from one another is a result of the business arrangement that
determines their actions. McCabe wishes to be an independent businessman. "Partners is what I come up here to get away from," he tells
Sheehan, asserting his independence in a scene that is punctuated by
the brutal stabbing of a customer by one of the whores McCabe clearly
cannot control by himself. As he attempts to break up the fight, the
scene is once more broken by violence, this time the scream and smoke
of a steam engine bringing Mrs. Miller into town.

Her intrusion into McCabe's life is not physically violent, but it is
disrupting and complicating. She proves to him his lack of entrepreneurial knowledge, particularly when it comes to running a whorehouse;
but, more, she shows him how dumb he is trying to do business alone.
This is a difficult thing for the hero of a western to hear, and from a
woman especially. The shot that occurs after the initial dialogue
between McCabe and Mrs. Miller at a table in the saloon, she eating an
enormous meal, McCabe manfully downing his scotch and raw egg, is
a slow reverse zoom of McCabe alone, in slight disarray, belching and
farting. This is a rare little shot, not merely because one is not used to
hearing a character break wind in a film, but because of its effect as an
immediate response to the dialogue preceding it. McCabe is a lone man,
and his aloneness has just been assaulted; the brief insert permits the
viewer a sort of offhanded observation of his confusion and his attempt
to reassert himself, if only to himself. The fact that the camera zooms
away from him rather than toward him implicates the viewer in his
solitude, his desire to be alone, and his feeling of having been violated.
The shot affirms the vulnerability of the would-be hero and indicates
his end.

Mrs. Miller is rarely observed alone, except for the very last sequence.
She is occasionally set off from her girls, once glimpsed just in the background at a birthday party for one of the whores. The few times that a
sequence begins with just her, McCabe appears shortly, and their conversation inevitably involves business, and inevitably puts McCabe in

a bad light. She is not alone because, unlike her generic forebears, she is a woman of business and not the center of a family. She is not the frontier wife or the schoolteacher from the East who domesticates the hero. She is a whore and the administrator of a whorehouse, jobs she knows and does well. She demonstrates no desire to be other than what she is. (There is little domesticity in the film as a whole: only two "families" exist: a black barber and his wife, who are rarely seen, and Coyle (Bert Remsen) and his mail-order bride, Ida (Shelley Duvall). Coyle is killed in one of those flash brawls that punctuate the film, and Ida becomes one of Mrs. Miller's girls.)

Constance Miller does not provide the expected romantic, domesticating role. Curiously enough, McCabe does; he is, despite himself, a character with romantic pretensions. Unfortunately, like his pretensions as a businessman, he cannot handle them. He remains at the mercy of convention and platitude. Neither Mrs. Miller nor anyone else will accept them. In a touching sequence that denies the fulfilment of romantic expectations usually set up by film, McCabe comes to make love to Mrs. Miller, full of bravura and tenderness: "You're a funny little thing. Sometime you're just so sweet. . . ." Well, in this instance she is not sweet, but stoned. Her reaction to McCabe is to hide coyly under the sheets and point to her money box. He dutifully counts out his payment, and the camera zooms into Mrs. Miller's—very literal—heart of gold.

The only time McCabe is allowed to express his feelings is when he is alone. At one point, so tied up in his own inarticulateness and inwardness, he paces a room and faces the wall, drinking, mumbling to an absent Mrs. Miller, "If just one time you could be sweet without no money around. . . . If you just one time let me run the show. . . ." "I got poetry in me," he says; "you're freezin' my soul." McCabe sounds like a pubescent rock balladeer and is expressing himself from the same source of conventional, sentimental clichés that has fed movie lovers and songwriters for years. In his hopeless innocence and aloneness he can only confront himself, and with language that expresses only that innocence and aloneness without responding to anyone else's needs. He is at this point one with almost every melodramatic character ever created in cinema who cannot call upon any other mode of discourse but that which expresses his own barely articulate, self-satisfying emotions.

Since there is no one who cares to share these emotions, he winds up talking about himself to himself.

The threat to McCabe is not merely that Mrs. Miller will not return what he thinks is his love for her (she does, in fact, demonstrate—to herself—some concern and even some affection for him), but that she and everyone else in the film speak a language different from his. And he cannot understand the language of others anymore than they can understand his sentimental gibberish or his mock-tough gibberish. He will pretend comprehension of other clichés, if they seem to fit in with his own understanding of things. The lawyer, Clement Samuels, feeds McCabe a most atrocious line of half-liberal, half-conservative nonsense when McCabe consults him about the threat of the mining company. Samuels talks of protecting big enterprise and small, of busting up the trusts and monopolies. "I just didn't wanna get killed," says McCabe. "Until people start dying for freedom," says the lawyer, in a line redolent of patriotic illogic, "they ain't gonna be free." Samuels convinces McCabe he can be a hero, that he can "stare 'em down and make 'em quake in their boots." In other words, that he must be Gary Cooper or Henry Fonda, or even John Wayne. Poor McCabe buys it.

Altman's fiction continually turns in on itself and its predecessors, placing itself in a critical perspective to history and to the myths of history propounded by other westerns. Certainly McCabe would like to fancy himself a hero, if not actually be a hero. When he parrots the lawyer's words to Mrs. Miller, her expression of concern for him and his stupidity is more than a bit tempered by her concern for her investment should he be killed. Altman unfailingly responds to any outpouring of romantic individualism on McCabe's part with one or another expression of economic self-interest. The West, Altman tells us, contrary to what we have been told in film after film, was not so much the testing ground of our culture's initiative as it was an outgrowth, or the outward growth, of the wielding of economic power. The initiative was taken by those with the power to initiate. Mrs. Miller seems to understand this, so that at every moment she denies whatever emotion she might have—she might even wish to have—in order to protect herself.

McCabe kills the three mining-company killers, and he does it alone, like a good gunslinger should (and unlike that weaker cowboy, the sheriff of *High Noon*, who had to depend on his wife to help him). Like their relatives in *High Noon*, the townspeople ignore his plight, not out of cowardice particularly, but rather out of passivity and distraction; the church is burning down. Mrs. Miller deserts him; what could she do to help him? McCabe finally lives up to the "big rep" the townspeople have created for him (and, could the fiction be extended, probably creates a bigger rep in his wake). He is shot and dies in the snow, buried in it, no more than a mound of white, his heroism unseen, unapplauded, and unwanted.

*McCabe and Mrs. Miller*. like Coppola's film, *The Conversation* and Arthur Penn's *Night Moves*, denies absolutely the possibility of the individual triumphing, in fact or in spirit; and it could be criticized for reinforcing the ideology of defeat and powerlessness that we noted was common in the seventies. The film is saved, however, by its own lyricism and gentleness, its sense of process and suggestion of other modes of behavior. For while there is an immediate expression of hopeless activity and inevitable loss, there is the possibility of the opposite. The film is without despair and with the suggestion that, perhaps between the adolescent romanticism of McCabe and the hardness of Mrs. Miller, love might possibly exist on terms other than the raucous sentimentality American film insists upon. There is a suggestion too that a community might cohere on terms other than self-interest and a brutality that arises out of greed. The film suggests these alternatives, but only by their absence.[12]

Altman will not admit them openly; but he at least tempers his film with a softness that somewhat denies the hopelessness of what is seen. This is not to suggest that the film is in any simple way "optimistic." Altman cannot easily slide into any one extremity of point of view and stay there long. The very pluralism of his visual and narrative form forbids it: there is too much happening, too much diversity for any one mood to dominate any other. In his other films the alterations of mood are usually more extreme than they are in *McCabe*, where a sadness of lost opportunity is most persuasive. The predisposition on the part of the viewer to respond to configurations of lost love and blighted romance provides a tension with the film's political and ideological nuances. The hazy quality of the images and Leonard Cohen's songs (poor by themselves, yet very effective in combination with the images) also provoke an emotional response. The continual and ironic contrasts

McCabe, alone as the townspeople fight the fire, flees the gunmen.

of cold exterior and warm interior work out an idea of needed protection and desired community which garners a response despite the fact that the film continually denies them—a denial that assures a regret over their loss. An effective balance and tension are achieved between desire stimulated by conventional expectations and the response to what is actually happening in the narrative. Tenderness is achieved out of its opposite as the film evokes a longing for the very attitudes it attempts to deny.

Later, in *Quintet*, Altman will do his best to suppress any lyrical response. *Quintet* is the pessimistic, indeed nihilistic extension of *McCabe and Mrs. Miller*. The frozen frontier community becomes the frozen, desolate city at the other end of history, at the end of the world. In creating this world, Altman does not play off the horizontal expanse of the Panavision screen against the compressed space of the telephoto lens. The film is shot in standard ratio and the peripheral circumference of the camera lens is smeared, so that the gaze is moved inward toward the center, which is itself in frozen decay. If the possibility of vital expansion is just slightly suggested at the peripheries of *McCabe*, it is denied altogether by the absence of peripheries in *Quintet*. Here gambling is no longer an enterprise and a pastime, but an obsessive way to death, the ritual of an aristocracy that seems able to warm itself only on each other's blood. As in *McCabe*, "friendship" is replaced by "alliance," but even that is only a pretext for murder. Essex (Paul Newman) enters the dying city from the frozen wastes, loses his wife and her unborn child to one of the murderous players of the game of Quintet, almost loses his own life to other players, and ends by walking out of the city to the wastes alone. No warmth, not even the illusory security of an opium den is offered to any character. There is no sad, lyrical soundtrack, only dissonant music and the sounds of shearing ice.

*Quintet* is an unsatisfying film because of its singleminded desolation. Its pessimism is part of a later and tentative expression in Altman's work, an experiment in despair and the reduction of the spatial openness of the earlier films, and can be observed in the grimness and disillusion that infiltrates *Buffalo Bill and the Indians, Three Women*, and *A Wedding*, and which comes to an end with the unusual romanticism of *A Perfect Couple*, the political hysteria of *Health*, and the silly doodlings of *Popeye*. The mood returns in the theatrical adaptations where restricted space again becomes charged with a melodrama which often gives voice to deadness of spirit and environment, and is broken once again in *Beyond Therapy*, where the expanses of the Paris skyline offer liberation from neurotic confusion. In the mid-seventies, however, his inquisitiveness kept the perspective of his films shifting and refracting rapidly through and across many genres and many moods.

If *McCabe and Mrs. Miller* portrayed the community as a place of isolation, and romantic love as individual fantasy determined, externally, by economic necessity, *Thieves Like Us* (1974) reverses the point of view, attempting to locate a possibility of love within a larger social and economic context, a love that attempts to counter that context but inevitably fails in the face of it. The film also establishes a different notion of community. There are three communities in *Thieves*: the American heartland in the thirties, Depression-ridden, listless, barely cohesive; the three thieves, Bowie (Keith Carradine), Chicamaw (John

Shuck), and T-Dub (Bert Remsen), who attempt to form a bond of friendship in necessity, rob banks because it is the only thing they know how to do, and protect each other because they are the only ones who can; and the lovers, Bowie and Keechie (Shelley Duvall), who remove themselves from the male group, attempt a community of two, sealed off from the larger world, isolated and finally destroyed when Bowie is killed by the police.

The film contains little of the ironic lyricism and spatial dislocation of *McCabe* or the psychological intensity of *Images*, and certainly none of the restrained hysteria of *The Long Goodbye*, the film that immediately preceded it. Filmed in standard ratio, it does not play off a horizontal width against a compressed interior space (but neither does it suggest a sense of collapse and claustrophobia like the later *Quintet*). Its framing is loose and casual, and Altman indulges in a deep-focus sequence for only the second time in his major work. The first such sequence appears in *Images*, where Cathryn's living room, with its smoking fireplace, is composed in the left foreground of a particular shot, while to the right and in the rear, she can be seen working in the kitchen. In *Thieves*, Bowie, Chicamaw, and T-Dub sit together in a living room, while to the right and in the rear, Keechie goes about her work in the kitchen. In both shots we find a woman in her "proper place," oblivious to some larger event occurring outside her observation. Unlike such shots in Spielberg's films, Altman charges these compositions with irony and portent. The women in his films rarely remain in conventional situations, rarely allow themselves to be "placed."

Despite the departures in the film's spatial construction and its casual, even kindly, treatment of its characters, *Thieves Like Us* follows through some of Altman's major concerns. Like most of his seventies work, it is a film of generic protest, and the genre it protests is of recent origin. Altman looks directly at *Bonnie and Clyde*, and with that look denies the heroic, even mythic status that Penn gives his characters. They attempt to control their world by asserting their energy and spirit upon it. The characters of *Thieves Like Us* are always controlled by their world, enjoying a tenuous freedom from it only when the three men are alone in a joking camaraderie, or the two lovers withdraw within themselves. But even in these instances the world is present, either in the newspaper accounts of the gang's exploits or in the radio programs that create a background to all of their activities. If the Barrow gang create their own community and briefly dominate their world, the thieves and lovers of Altman's film are always dominated by a community that oppresses them in the form of the soap operas, gangster stories, cheap poetry, and political and religious speeches that dominate the film's sound track. This very domination emphasizes the distance of the characters from their environment, while simultaneously Altman is at pains to distance the viewer from the characters' activities. When the three robbers take a bank, the camera remains outside, gazing at mundane activities on the street as if refusing the viewer privilege to the gang's activities, which are replaced on the soundtrack by a broadcast of "Gangbusters" that ironically mocks their exploits. When a robbery is observed directly, it is a disaster: the gang is forced to kill, and it marks the end of their success. In this instance, in ironic counterpoint to the activities, the soundtrack plays a speech by FDR about security, peace, happiness, and the power of a democratic government to protect its citizens. When Bowie and Keechie make love, their closeness is punctuated by a radio soap-opera version of *Romeo and Juliet*. Over and over the radio voice drones, "Thus did Romeo and Juliet consummate their first interview by falling madly in love with each other." The radio commentary mocks the couple but makes their adolescent passion the more endearing at the same time. Even more, it refuses to let them alone. None of the characters are free from the authority of their world and the images that diminish them. Like McCabe and Mrs. Miller—though without their entrepreneurial opportunities—Bowie and Keechie are held down (within their fiction) by economic oppression and (outside their fiction) by the myths of their cinematic predecessors. They are oppressed by the demands of their culture whose banality drains from them any possibility of heroic action. McCabe and Mrs. Miller inhabit a moment in American history when that banality was just coming to be (its birth is witnessed in the characters of Eugene Sears and Ernie Hollander, emissaries from the mining company, who represent violence by wearing a bland face, and by the lawyer Clement Samuels, who mouths the clichés of free enterprise as if they were new truths). Bowie and Keechie are alive at its maturity. Bonnie and Clyde transcend for a moment the emptiness and banality of their culture; Bowie and Keechie merely sink beneath it.

If Altman refuses to indulge in the heroic nonsense of *Bonnie and Clyde* he also refuses to indulge in the total grimness of oppression and loss that Penn's myth-making leads to. He refuses as well the grimness that accompanies an earlier version of *Thieves Like Us*, which is also an influence on Penn's film, Nicholas Ray's *They Live by Night* (1949), based on the same novel that is Altman's source. The two films offer a revealing comparison of style and temperament. *They Live by Night* is a *film noir*, although it makes some important shifts in the *noir* structure by dealing with rural thieves rather than urban gangsters and private detectives. Ray's characters are trapped within their world, enclosed in a darkness that seals up their innocence like a coffin. His lovers are betrayed and humiliated; Altman's make at least an attempt to confront their situation, to work out the allegiances that Bowie has both to his friends and to his lover. In Ray's film, Bowie has to be physically coerced to stay with the gang; in Altman's, he chooses to help Chicamaw escape from prison, though his friend proves so bitter and murderous that Bowie is forced to abandon him. At the end of both films, Bowie is killed and Keechie is left alone. But the different forms of the endings indicate an important change in points of view. In Ray's film, Keechie is left by Bowie's body, the viewer's gaze concentrated on her, while her own eyes are averted and her face full of hardness and despair. She then fades into the darkness. Altman's Keechie watches her lover's death from a distance, restrained by Mattie, the woman who betrays Bowie to the police—explicitly in Ray's film, implicitly in Altman's. Keechie is seen behind a screen door, the bright red of a Coca-Cola icebox punctuating the blue haze, a romantic poem punctuating the sound track. As the police shoot to pieces the shack Bowie is in, Keechie smashes her omnipresent Coke bottle, violently screaming in slow motion (a welcome removal from the brutality forced upon the viewer at the end of *Bonnie and Clyde*).[13] But Altman does not leave her there. After Bowie's body is carried out of the shack, there is a cut to the waiting room of a railroad station. On the sound track Father Coughlin, the right-wing thirties radio evangelist, speaks to the need of bearing our burden in silence, like men. Keechie talks for a while to a woman (Joan Tewkesbury, co-author of the screenplay), telling her the child she carries will not be named after his father. She then joins the crowd going up the stairs to the platform. There is one more shot of her

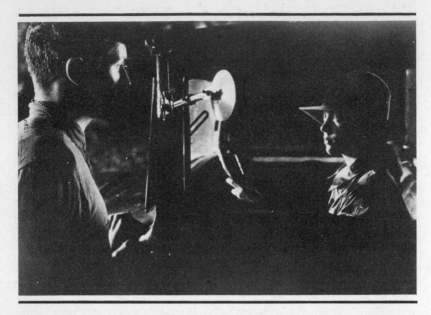

Two versions of Bowie and Keechie: *(above)* Farley Granger and
Cathy O'Donnell in the *noir* world of Nicholas Ray's *They Live by Night;*
*(opposite)* Keith Carradine and Shelley Duvall in the brighter world of
Altman's *Thieves Like Us.*

impassive face and then a cut to a far, slow-motion shot of the crowd
disappearing up the stairs.

   Where Ray ends in despair, Altman ends on a notion at least of a
world in which some sad flow of life continues. He lifts the *noir* fatality
that trapped Ray's characters, diffusing it into a wider context, the larger
trap of the world they inhabit. His Keechie endures, trapped as she is
and strong as she is. She does not withdraw like Mrs. Miller, and she
does not quite give in. She will exist ensnared in the promises of bourgeois comforts and security, ever-present in the radio shows she hears,
promises negated by the narrow, disenfranchised life she must lead.[14]
But at least some community, even the faceless, slow-motion crawl of
a crowd in transit, exists, and no *film noir* offered even that much.

   Out of *film noir*, Altman has made something that approaches *film
lumière*, and which, like his western, indicates a potential of community

as well as its inevitable dissolution. He indicates that neither male camaraderie nor heterosexual love is able to survive in a culture that denies the very security it promises to those unable to abide, for intellectual or emotional or economic reasons, by its rules. But he indicates as well that a kind of endurance is possible, albeit a passive, lonely one. Keechie's survival is in fact similar to Mrs. Miller's, similar as well to the survival of the crowd at the end of *Nashville*: isolated, with false comfort or none at all, unable or unwilling to change their situation. But Keechie at least moves on, and although it is a movement in sadness and resignation, it is more movement than Mrs. Miller's, and more certainly than any *noir* character ordinarily makes.

Another kind of movement, more extreme, but no more hopeful, occurs in the film that precedes *Thieves Like Us*, a version of *film noir*, this time by way of the forties detective film *The Long Goodbye*. The film is at once a direct descendant and a powerful denial of its ancestry. The detective has fascinated Western culture since he was invented in the nineteenth century. An urban and urbane quester, he could descend into worlds the middle-class reader—and, later, viewer—could never approach. Even more, he could do what the reader and viewer could only dream of doing, gain control of complex and dangerous situations through reason and perception and with a moral superiority that allowed him to be engaged in, but untouched by, the moral squalor around him. The classic detective was also the surrogate of the reader in the act of detection, an act that permitted an interplay, in the traditional "whodunit," of many voices: the author, the criminal, the detective, and the reader, creating a complex discourse which always promised that one voice would prevail, a voice that enunciated the pristine and integral solving of the problem.[15]

When, via Dashiell Hammett and Raymond Chandler, the detective entered the *film noir* world of the forties, changes occurred. He became less morally pure, less certain, less sure of his perceptions. The dark, oppressive *mise-en-scène* he worked in did not permit clear understandings and pristine solutions. The rich, devious perpetrators of criminal acts, their low and vicious henchmen, and the dark, treacherous women of the *noir* universe allowed for no easy comprehension and apprehension. The *film noir* detective was a sullied individual and almost always harmed morally and physically by his business. Yet he prevailed. Bogart's Sam Spade, in *The Maltese Falcon* (1941), had a sense of moral obligation and self-protection, as well as a sense of bluff and bravura, that allowed him some success. The various Philip Marlowes, especially Dick Powell's in *Murder My Sweet* (1944) and Bogart's in *The Big Sleep* (1946), had a strength of self-protective wit and cynicism that distanced them somewhat from the complexities and compromises of their work.[16] They also had, for the audience, at least, a recognizable *milieu* in which to operate. This would appear to be an immediate contradiction: the *film noir* world is dark and oppressive; yet the forties detective operates in a recognizable *milieu*. The contradiction arises from some curious results of convention. Forties *film noir* rapidly became set in its visual forms so that its threat was somewhat lessened through the almost comforting repetition of its images. The shadows and rain-soaked streets, dark nightclubs and narrow alleys, the half-lit faces and claustrophobic rooms with shadows of venetian blinds became instant icons of a quickly recognizable fictive world. This easy recognition, transmitted by an often stable, neutral camera, contradicted the amoral, indeed dreadful, vaguenesses of the world being created.

If, as has been suggested many times, *noir* worked as a subversive element in the classical Hollywood style, that subversion was rapidly neutralized by a repetition that created the familiarity of met expectations.* One need only look at Aldrich's *Kiss Me Deadly* and Welles's *Touch of Evil*, two late *noir* films deeply conscious of the way they are put together, to discover how disturbing the genre still can be when its forms go beyond the conventions that were established by the late forties. The fact that the *noir* model is so often copied or investigated by recent filmmakers indicates both its potency and the readiness with which its elements can be used for effect. *The Long Goodbye* continues this self-conscious re-examination of original *noir* forms, rediscovering their potential for subverting old codes. Its form, analyzed earlier, creates an unstable and unsettling perspective, a sense of disorder and lack of comprehension so extreme that it expresses as much or more in camera and lens movement than its forties predecessors did through chiaroscuro and the claustrophobic framing of their characters. If *Touch of Evil* is the last *film noir* in black and white, *The Long Goodbye* may be the first in color, eschewing the expressionism of the forties and of Welles (reintroduced by Scorsese in *Taxi Driver*), replacing it with a drifting, unlocalized, uncertain perspective. Rather than being witness to a dark and doomed world, as in classic *film noir* (and that other seventies revision of the *noir* detective film, *Night Moves*), the viewer shares the point of view of a Marlowe so completely out of control of his world that there is no possibility of detection, but only, perhaps, of accidental discovery. The voices woven into the text of detective fiction become here a confused mumble.

Many critics, some with outrage, have discussed how weak, fooled, and finally violent Altman's Marlowe is—particularly compared with his Bogart forebear in *The Big Sleep*. But a closer look reveals some

---

*Some early *films noirs*, like Wilder's *Double Indemnity* (1944) and Lang's *Scarlet Street* (1945), still have a desolation about them that belies the subsequent familiarity of their form and content.

interesting similarities, or at least extensions of Hawks's 1946 film. Hawks portrays a closed, dark, and curiously stable world over which Marlowe seems to exercise almost complete control. But Altman and his screenwriter, Leigh Brackett (who co-scripted *The Big Sleep)*, perceive that control to be tenuous at best, fraudulent at worst. The Hawks/Bogart Marlowe becomes, despite himself, deeply entangled in the world he enters, caught in the very morass he attempts to clear. His control over things is apparent only in his wit and his ability to find momentary attachments based upon the least amount of mistrust. In fact, the Hawks/Bogart Marlowe is played for a fool by everyone and is reduced to committing murder as vicious as any committed by the various thugs, grifters, blackmailers, and rich young women who drift in and out of the film's complex narrative. *The Big Sleep* ends in a litter of corpses (dead of Marlowe's doing), with police sirens punctuating the night and sharply undercutting the apparent romantic calm Marlowe shares with Vivian Sternwood (Lauren Bacall).

In *The Long Goodbye*, Altman and Brackett merely strip away the security of the Bogart persona: his wit and his ability to stand back from a given situation in a posture of self-preservation. Their Marlowe is a man out of time. "I'm from a long time ago," he tells his police interrogators. He is a character without physical or emotional anchorage in the world. "Remember, you're not in here; it's just your body," he tells David Carradine, who happens, in one of those small, offhanded, tangential sequences of Altman's, to be sharing Marlowe's jail cell. He is a man whose every connection with the world is faulty and non-comprehending. The discourse he carries on with the world is barely coherent and neglectful of the basic logic even of conversation. As he passes on the ramp that separates his apartment from that of a group of girls who practice yoga in the nude (and go mostly unnoticed by Marlowe), the following interchange ensues. He asks them if they've seen his cat (who ran off the night before when Marlowe couldn't provide it with the proper brand of food). One girl answers, "I didn't even know you had a cat, Mr. Marlowe. . . ." Another girl emerges, saying, "Say you wanted a hat?" Marlowe replies, "No, no, you don't look fat." And as the verbal language drifts and glances in incoherent directions, so the camera— our gaze onto Marlowe's world—drifts and pans, zooms slowly in and out (never completing its motion), arcs and dollies until the viewer's own perceptions are inscribed into an orderless, almost random series of interchanges and events.

The self-defensive Marlowe wit has turned into incomprehension. Mumbling passivity—Marlowe's key and favorite response is "It's o.k. with me" (a phrase that will turn up again in somewhat different form and a more disastrous context in *Nashville*)—is what has become of the Marlowe persistence and drive for moral order. And in his insular state Marlowe merely allows himself to be had. For no particular reason, he decides to refute the accusation that his friend Terry Lennox murdered his own wife. It is as if this notion of trust and friendship that Marlowe irrationally holds somehow provides a center to his drifting world. In fact, it furthers the drift and results in terrible betrayals, that of Marlowe himself certainly being the worst. Friendship is always a difficult subject for Altman, and his films constantly probe the proximity of friendship to betrayal. Bowie, out of emotional necessity, betrays his friends when he goes off with Keechie in *Thieves Like Us*. McCabe is betrayed by Sheehan and eventually by the whole town. *Nashville* can be seen as a complex of betrayals, of people refusing to admit to each other's emotional validity and individuality, looking rather upon one another as objects to be used. In *Quintet* a character explicitly states that "alliance" has been substituted for "friendship" in their freezing, dying world. The father of *Fool for Love* has shockingly betrayed his children by having kept two wives: the children are each the result of the separate unions, and they fall in love with each other. Only in *California Split*, *A Perfect Couple*, *Popeye*, and somewhat tenuously in *Beyond Therapy* does Altman see the possibility of two people sharing a modicum of trust. However, in the first, the two are men and their relationship is tentative. The cartoon frivolities of *Popeye* allow no serious consideration of the relationship. The sexual meanderings that occur in *Beyond Therapy* are no guarantee of permanent union. *A Perfect Couple* remains the one major film in which betrayal does not destroy a relationship. (In the made-for-cable film, *The Laundromat*, the two female characters reach some understanding after a brief, tortuous, and painful encounter.)

Marlowe's unquestioning and irrational belief in his friend cuts him off from even the limited comprehension of things he may have had. And just here we can see how clearly Altman is changing the conventions of the detective film. His Marlowe does not detect anything, actively or passively. He attempts to prove wrong the charges against his friend, but in so doing accepts any lie that is thrown his way. The Bogart/Hawks Marlowe persists in an attempt at discovery, no matter how dark and futile the attempt may be (so too, for that matter, does Penn's Harry Moseby). Altman takes the inevitability of failure as a fact, and starts from there. He sees the *film noir* detective as a patsy and chooses not to have him struggle manfully to prove otherwise. (Interestingly, the core of Altman's revision may lie in a sequence in *The Big Sleep* where Marlowe, trapped in the shadows of a warehouse office, looks on helplessly and hopelessly as Lash Canino murders Harry Jones; Marlowe afterward reveals an unexpectedly sentimental attachment to "little Jonesy," for whose death he bears responsibility.) Finally, Altman creates, out of the dialectical extension of the Philip

Two versions of Philip Marlowe: *(below)* Humphrey Bogart in the *noir* warehouse office in Hawks's *The Big Sleep;* *(opposite)* Elliott Gould brought to bay by Mrs. Wade's dog in Altman's *The Long Goodbye.*

Marlowe of the forties, a perfect fictive surrogate of a major cultural phenomenon: the modern passive individual, who accepts everything, questions nothing, and is had continually by anyone less gullible than he. But this very passivity creates its own irrational activity and deeply implicates Marlowe in the destruction of others.

One character who loses because Marlowe cannot and will not act is Roger Wade. He is one of the more melodramatically powerful men that Altman has created, a precise and conventional rendering of the burned-out, alcoholic writer who has been part of romantic mythology since the nineteenth century. His appearance in a film that otherwise denies conventional figures and acting styles (the kindly, vicious Jewish gangster, Marty Augustine—played by film director Mark Rydell—is an example, along with Marlowe, of this unconventionality) makes him stand out as an immediately attractive, because familiar, figure. He stands out so clearly that Marlowe, a figure made up of anti-conventional unromantic elements, cannot even see him. "Looney Tunes" is Marlowe's response to Roger Wade. The romantic, boisterous loser, full of anger and sorrow, only looks mad to the modern, recessive, passive loser. With a just irony, Wade calls Marlowe "Marlboro Man," and both remain vulnerable and outside each other's spheres.

In one of the film's great set pieces, Marlowe goes out to the beach, while Roger and Mrs. Wade argue, the writer expressing his passion to his cold wife (a *noir* woman, she is part of Terry Lennox's crime and uses Marlowe to push her husband to ruin and to further her escape to her murderous boy friend Terry). Their conversation is observed and listened to from outside the glass door of their beach house, the camera slowly zooming in on each and on both together. Marlowe, playing on the beach, is reflected in the window in front of the couple (technically the sequence is more complicated than this, for it appears that one shot of Marlowe on the beach is superimposed on the window; therefore, when the camera zooms back from the window, there is a coordinated zoom back in the superimposed shot, doubling the spatial slipperiness and uncertainty). This complex spatial and perceptual interaction serves as a metaphor for the film as a whole. The viewer is suspended between two points of view, seemingly unconnected with either. Because the Wades are observed through the glass for much of the sequence, the viewer is distanced from their conflict. The constant movement of the camera emphasizes this removal, this inability to confront the action as the viewer expects he or she has a right to. Marlowe, who is blind and deaf to what the Wades are doing and insensible to information that would go against his obsessive allegiance to his friend, is outside, dancing in the waves like a child. He is reflected on the same glass through which the camera observes, and because he is reflected, only his back is seen, and from a considerable distance. Every participant in the sequence is cut off from every other, emotionally, physically, and in their mutual misunderstanding. I said the viewer is suspended between points of view. In fact, the authorizing point of view still belongs to Marlowe, even though his back is to the scene. The recording apparatus—microphone and camera—may be trained on the Wades, but the instability created by image and sound projects the uncertainty, the lack of clarity that mark Marlowe's perception.[17] He cannot master any scene, any situation.

Later, after Wade is humiliated at a party by the slimy psychiatrist Dr. Verringer, he commits suicide by walking into the sea (like Norman Maine in *A Star Is Born*). Marlowe and Mrs. Wade are talking by the window, she misleading Marlowe by discussing Roger's affair with Mrs. Lennox, hiding her own connection with Marty Augustine, who has been pursuing Marlowe. Through the window that stands between them, Roger can be made out in the darkness, walking to the ocean. The camera zooms past Marlowe, past Mrs. Wade, to the figure approaching the waves. The movement is not an urgent one, merely another series of slow spatial drifts, not hurrying the viewer's gaze or the characters' to this pathetic event, but merely alluding to their obliviousness to it. They do not react until a reverse shot is given, a slow zoom up to the window from outside. Again, as so often in Altman's films, a window is used as a barrier to direct emotional contact. (The device reaches a climax in *Fool for Love*, where the characters, at strong emotional odds with each other, are observed almost continuously through windows.)

What follows is a scene of enormous energy for Altman. Marlowe attempts to save Wade from the ocean. This is his most active moment, and the noise of the surf, the darkness and confusion, Wade's dog running in the ocean with his master's cane, provide an engagement of viewer and action, and the participants in the action, unlike any other scene in the film. The problem is that this action and engagement are to no avail, for Wade is dead. The emotional peak the action creates and carries over to the investigation that follows reaches a level of hysteria that makes it impossible for either viewer or Marlowe to hear a policeman tell him that Wade could not have been responsible for Sylvia Lennox's death (as Mrs. Wade had said he was), information that further implicates Terry himself and further implicates Marlowe in the consequences of his own stupidity and neglect.

Altman is appropriately wary of highly emotional situations, of melodramatic crises and confrontations. These are the stock-in-trade of American film and represent a method of easily engaging the audience and, occasionally, obviating narrative difficulties. In television, even more than in classical Hollywood film, a sequence of overwrought feelings, of melodramatic hysteria, will be used to suture up narrative weakness, depending upon the audience's emotions to take the place of perception. Altman refuses such orchestrated climaxes and prefers to dissipate emotional intensity by observing peripheral action. When he does create an emotional scene, like Wade's suicide and its aftermath, he uses it to indicate its deceptive qualities. Later, in the theatrical adaptations, where such emotional climaxes are built into the drama out of which Altman must construct his film, he attempts, with varying success, to create them as dynamic ruptures in his *mise-en-scène*. The revelations of lies and repressed lives in *Come Back to the Five and Dime, Jimmy Dean, Jimmy Dean*, the brutal murders at the end of *Streamers*, the memories of bigamy and incest in *Fool for Love*, are pushed up by the tensions built throughout the film; they break out and are then reabsorbed—with the exception of the last work, in which resolution results in a kind of apocalypse, as the motel inhabited by the main characters goes up in flames. The dynamics are not as controlled as they are in the seventies films, not as ironic or as powerfully significant of false perceptions. They no longer question melodramatic structures and the ways such structures hide more important realities, but rather accept them as the necessary consequences of theatrical form.

At the end of the suicide sequence in *The Long Goodbye* Marlowe gets hysterical when he believes that Wade killed Sylvia Lennox; it is the highest emotional peak he reaches in the film, and it is based on lies. But neither he nor the viewer (unless the latter listens very carefully, for the camera is on Marlowe when it is said) hears the police inspector tell him that Wade could not have done it. Marlowe cannot hear or see; he is the detective as somnambulist. He is the bandaged mummy whom he meets in a hospital room in the penultimate sequence—his own double, as Jonathan Rosenbaum points out, who hands him a tiny harmonica that Marlowe will play as he skips off from his last encounter with Terry Lennox, the only encounter in the film in which Marlowe, his head somewhat cleared of misapprehensions (though not of misperceptions), takes definitive and immediate action.[18] This action was found so distasteful that, when the film was recut for television, it was altered and rendered ambiguous. In the film Marlowe kills Terry, shoots him without hesitation. They confront each other in a series of slowly accelerating zooms. "So you used me," says Marlowe. "Hell," answers Terry, "that's what friends are for. . . . Nobody cares." The camera is on Marlowe's face as Terry offers this response, and it zooms in closer as Marlowe answers, "Yeah, nobody cares but me." For the first time in the film, spatial proximity with the character is achieved. Still an isolating proximity, for nothing is offered that could make one believe that Marlowe is in touch with anything but a brief awakening of anger. There is another shot of Terry and zoom in closer, faster on his face: "Well, that's you, Marlowe. You'll never learn, you're a born loser." The shot returns to Marlowe, zooms back—"Yeah, I even lost my cat"—and he pulls his gun and fires. Terry falls into a pool, rolling in the water like the cowboy shot by the punk gunman in *McCabe*, or the gunman himself when he is later shot by McCabe. The camera zooms in again on Marlowe's face as he watches Terry, spits, and leaves. He walks down the road, oblivious to Mrs. Wade, who passes him in a jeep, heading for her now dead lover. On the sound track, the musical theme of the film, which in parody of forties films has been repeated throughout, coming from every conceivable source—doorbell to Mexican marching band— is distorted and moaning. Marlowe begins blowing the harmonica given him by the mummy. As he diminishes in size down the road, he begins dancing; on the soundtrack is the music of "Hooray for Hollywood" that opened the film. The mummy comes to life, having activated himself by murder.

I detail the ending of *The Long Goodbye* because it is an unusually definitive one for Altman, though still highly diffuse and multivalent. The fact that neither Chandler's Marlowe, nor any of his forties film incarnations, could kill a friend coldly and unflinchingly is a convention of Hollywood morality that Altman cannot abide, and he detects the weakness and falseness of it. At the end of Hawks's *The Big Sleep*, Marlowe pushes Eddie Mars (toward whom he once felt friendship) out the door to meet the certain machine-gun fire of his henchmen. Within the context of the film, the act seems appropriate, for certainly Mars would have killed Marlowe, and besides he is being forced into a death equal to his own viciousness. But Marlowe is responsible for the death nonetheless, as he was for the murder of Harry Jones by Lash Canino, a murder he passively observes. He is responsible for the death of Canino himself, whom he shoots out of revenge for Jonesy and out of a need to escape (at this point in the narrative Marlowe has no choice but to shoot his captor). The Bogart Marlowe is a killer whose killing is always morally accounted for. In Chandler's novel *The Long Goodbye*, Marlowe does not kill; he accepts Terry's having used him with sadness and understanding. The important thing for him is to remain true to an idea of friendship.

Altman cannot accept either the morally justified murders or the passive acceptance of abuse under the guise of loyalty. The act of his Marlowe is therefore a response to both, a murder as gratuitous as any shown on the screen and an action of a sleepwalker momentarily awake. There is undeniable satisfaction in Marlowe's act, the pleasure felt when a narrative includes revenge is immediate—a response proved by the endless series of films for which revenge is the central narrative dynamic. There is particular satisfaction here because Marlowe finally does something, acts rather than being acted upon. Yet the act is repulsive, as repulsive as Marty Augustine smashing a Coke bottle in his girl friend's face to scare Marlowe ("Now that's someone I love, and you I don't even like"). Peckinpah may have insisted that violence is a purgative; Penn may insist that it is the necessary result of defiant action; Kubrick and Scorsese may see it only appearing and disappearing, neither explained nor explicable, or, if explained, always something more than the explanation; the makers of revenge films use violence as the exploitation of impotence. Uninterested in examining the act, they use it to activate the unsatisfied desires of the viewer. For Altman, the causes of violence are almost as vague as Camus's *acte gratuit* and inevitable as well as erratic and unpredictable. And the violence hurts everyone concerned. Altman is one of the few American filmmakers who examines the results of the violent act, which more often than not only reaffirms the state that existed previous to it. The act of violence alters nothing. After the killing, Marlowe is still a jerk, still unconnected to his world. McCabe is dead along with the three gunmen. After the assassination in *Nashville*, everyone remains gullible and manipulable, singing their great anthem of passivity, "You may say that I ain't free / But it don't worry me." The murders in *Quintet* are the ritual acts of a dead society. The violence that ends *Streamers* grows out of and then sinks back into the groaning depression that marks the narrative as a whole. The conflagration that closes *Fool for Love* takes the life of the father who kept two wives, disperses the other characters, symbolizes the explosion of misdirected passion, but finally closes the narrative with no questions answered. Perhaps only the death of Edgar in *Three Women*—unseen, only referred to—has some positive value; it changes a situation, though the change itself is a grotesque one. Usually no one is helped, ennobled, or purged by the violence that occurs in Altman's films, least of all the audience. If a viewer applauds Marlowe's shooting of Terry, that same viewer must answer for its ramifications: is a person who has been played for a fool only able to rectify his or her passivity by murder? If, on the other hand, the act is appalling, then why are we not appalled by other acts just like it in our cinema? Why is the futility of Bogart's Marlowe "heroic" and the futility of Gould's Marlowe repulsive?

Altman is well aware that the ambiguities are generated by movies, and that is why "Hooray for Hollywood" opens and closes the film. Whatever its other qualities and faults, American film, with other forms of popular entertainment, has helped make the larger culture as gullible and passive as poor Marlowe, unable to discriminate between actions represented, reactions to them, and the social-political contradictions that play amongst everything, fudging the lines between valid individual activity and destructive heroic fantasies. If Altman is not attempting to clarify the confusions, he is at least attempting to reveal them, to demonstrate how perceptions have become befuddled by false heroics and irrational acts that present themselves as being true to life, as believable, when all they are actually true to are conventions of behavior that exist only in a film fiction. But *The Long Goodbye* is not a goodbye to Hollywood. Altman's affection for it is too strong. He needs its conventions as material to dismantle and reconsider. After the angry correctives and discomfiting ambivalences offered by *The Long Goodbye*, he softens his approach in *Thieves Like Us*, still diminishing the heroic myth, but with more restraint and certainly a more kindly disposition to his characters.

*Thieves Like Us* is the closest Altman comes to a conventional film narrative. But it is only a momentary pause, for he follows it with one of his more ambitious reorganizations of narrative structure. *California Split* (1974) can be taken on one level as another entry into the subgenre of buddy films, prevalent since the late sixties, which includes *M.A.S.H.* as well as *Easy Rider, Midnight Cowboy, Scarecrow, Deliverance, Butch Cassidy and the Sundance Kid, The Sting*, almost any film by Peckinpah, *Jaws, E.T.*, the Indiana Jones films—in which the position of the "buddy" is taken by the viewer—the *Star Wars* trilogy, *Running Scared*, and *Stakeout*. These films banish women from any major role and substitute a repressed or unstated homosexual or father and son relationship between two or more men engaged in extreme adventure.[19] *California Split* manages to escape some of the more uncomfortable sexual evasions and misogynistic attitudes of these films by keeping its emotional level low, by allowing, as few American films do, emotions and emotional relationships to be chancy, fleeting, nondestructive, unscarring. Unlike other buddy films, it gives its women characters equal status and equal strength. Though the Gwen Welles and Ann Prentiss characters are whores, they do not suffer and are not condescended to, nor are they any more oppressed by their situation than their male counterparts are by gambling. George Segal's Bill is sad a good deal of the time, but mostly because he does not experience either the thrills or the agonies in gambling that so many other films on the subject have insisted one must feel. (Compare *California Split* with Karel Reisz's essay in metaphysical angst, *The Gambler* (1974): Altman eschews completely the heavy masochism that Reisz sees as the motivating force of the compulsive gambler. However, in *Quintet*, metaphysics does threaten as Altman presents gambling as the surviving ritual of a decaying world.)

In *California Split*, Altman substitutes for melodrama a sort of emotional *laisser-faire*, and does so mainly by organizing not only the subject but also the narrative form of the film around gambling. The structure of *California Split* is that of a game of chance, a playful, random, offhanded series of events full of accident, coincidence, and peripheral action brought to the center in a more extreme way than in the previous films. But the adjective is misleading, for the film is not "extreme" in any way. If anything, it is extremely gentle and undemanding, requiring only a pleasure in its playfulness.

For example, there is a sequence in which a despondent, debt-ridden Bill enters a massage parlor, walks through it to a bedroom where some children are watching a cartoon of "Basketball Jones" on television, and passes by them to a poker game in a back room. Here Altman purposefully sidetracks, improvising not so much upon the acting or the elements of plot as on viewer expectations and responses. Each element of the sequence could be developed to major melodramatic proportions. An unhappy character in need of money to pay off gambling debts is reduced to the squalid comforts of a seedy brothel. But that is not what he does. He seems to be visiting some wretched family forced to live on the very premises—and expectations rise that the narrative will focus on this unhappy situation. But the family is ignored; the focus of the sequence must be on the card game in the back room. Convention suggests that these will be a group of unpleasant gangsters, playing in a place like this. But it turns out to be only a card game, and Bill loses, and leaves, and the place is never seen or referred to again, just as Sue and Barbara, Charlie's roommates, are never seen or referred to after a certain point. And a coincidence occurs: on the television set in the apartment in the massage parlor is a cartoon about basketball, a betting sport, a game that Charlie (Elliott Gould) will later hustle to get money for the big trip to Reno. A coincidence, too, that at a certain point in the film songs by Phyllis Shotwell, who will later appear as an entertainer in a Reno casino, suddenly begin to be heard on the sound track, commenting on the action. At one point, when Charlie is crossing a street in Reno, humming to himself, something he sings suddenly merges with a song on the sound track. The off-hand and out-of-hand keep occurring in sequence after sequence, with no climaxes, no directions. The film is carefully crafted to be open not to various interpretations but to various reactions to its juxtapositions and anomalies; it is made to be analogous to the wheel of fortune that closes the film, spinning and stopping where it will.[20]

This is, of course, not improvisation in the usual sense. Though much of the dialogue may have been made up in rehearsal and in preparation for shooting, the structure of chance and coincidence, the joking interplay of events in the film and the expectations of the viewer, would have to have been carefully planned. *California Split* holds an important place in Altman's work: experiment, joke, a game about gaming, it also moves him a bit beyond the generic revisionism of *McCabe* and *The Long Goodbye* into a greater revision of narrative structure in general, of the ways movies tell their stories and can be made to tell them differently.

With *Nashville*, Altman attempts to refine and enlarge upon the open structure of *California Split*, adding many more characters, each with his or her own small narrative to be worked out. Much more than its predecessors, Altman wanted *Nashville* to be a grand cultural statement, a "metaphor for America" (as he himself called it). Unlike its predecessors, however, *Nashville* falls short of the notion of the open narrative, in which the viewer is asked to participate in, question, and respond to new forms of expression. The film tends to lose its way, become ambiguous rather than responsible and temper its anger with sad contemplation. Pretending, perhaps disingenuously, to encompass many attitudes and points of view, its own perspective is somewhat restrictive. "All you need to do is add yourself as the twenty-fifth character," writes Joan Tewkesbury, in her introduction to her screenplay, "and know that whatever you think about the film is right, even if you think the film is wrong."[21]

Film, however, does not allow the spectator to become a participant on the same level as the fictions who inhabit its narrative. Even Altman and his screenwriter cannot change the immutable status of an imaginative work as an object made separate from the viewing subject and inviolable. As open and malleable as its structure of meaning might be, the elements that make up that structure—the immediate forms of what the viewer sees and hears—are permanent and removed. All a screenwriter and director can do is attempt to position the viewing subject as a more active and responsive element, less manipulated and con-

structed by narrative and character conventions. The fact that a narrative is made a certain way and that its characters say and do specific
things (the same things, each time one sees the film) makes it impossible
to believe that *whatever* we think about them is right. We may change
our attitudes on subsequent viewings (as, indeed, my own response to
*Nashville* keeps changing each time I see it), or even our reflections
upon a single viewing, but a certain structure and perspective remain.
Altman, more than any other American filmmaker, has insisted upon
positioning the viewer within the *process* of narrative, requesting that
she or he observe and comprehend the interacting details that cohere in
sometimes non-directed ways. But cohere they must on some formal
and contextual level, or narrative is impossible. If narrative is possible,
then *some* basic meaning system is created.

I am trying to provide some limits to modernism and the notion of
the open narrative. If Tewkesbury and Altman insist that any reading
of their film is the right one, then no meaning exists, and the film's status as narrative disappears into an arbitrary arrangement of incoherent
parts, mutually exclusive characters, and anomalous events (of course,
if that were true, a very definite meaning system would emerge). *Nashville* is none of these. Rather it is precisely located in time and place
with many characters, and Altman takes great care to relate them, even
if by apparent accident, and to define them. Even though it has no conventional story line, the various "stories" of the various characters
move easily and neatly. The frame narrative—the organizing of a rally
for candidate Hal Phillip Walker—easily holds the parts together, and
the controlling thematic of celebrity, power, their illusions and abuses,
is addressed in each sub-narrative and through each character. Finally,
the structure of *California Split* and *The Long Goodbye* is more complex, for *Nashville* actually only extends the parallel or alternate montage structure basic to American film. *Nashville* merely has more parallels and alternations.

As an experiment in smoothly integrating a number of alternating
narrative units into a whole, *Nashville* does succeed with much energy
and a sense of delight in its scope. As an integration of the fragments
that made up American culture in the mid-seventies, it remains close
to *Brewster McCloud* though without that film's manic silliness, and
*McCabe*, without its lyricism. Altman continues to be struck by the self-

serving, passive nature of the culture, but adds here something more, a notion of hypocrisy and meanness that can be glimpsed in *McCabe* and begins to surface more in *The Long Goodbye* (it is present in *Thieves Like Us* but only as an envelope, as the false ideas and mean hopes foisted by the culture upon Bowie and Keechie, which they cannot possibly achieve). In *Nashville*, all the characters are fools, manipulated or manipulating, hurt or hurtful, each using what little power they have to affect someone with less power. Barbara Jean, perpetually in a state of nervous breakdown, is booed by her audience and shot down at a concert, but not before she is treated like a child by her husband manager, Barnett, who is in turn insulted by Connie White and her manager. Tom, the pop singer, insults a poor soldier whose life is spent following Barbara Jean around and treats his women as sexual objects to be conquered and discarded. Opal from the BBC uses everyone as a sequence in her non-existent documentary and insults Haven Hamilton's son Buddy and the chauffeur, Norman. Del Reese, Linnea's husband, makes little attempt to comprehend his deaf children, helps Triplette, the political operative, organize his rally, and makes a pass at Sueleen after she has been first fooled into doing a striptease at Triplette's smoker and then humiliated during the performance. Linnea cheats on Del with Tom. Haven Hamilton condescends to everyone, but falls for Triplette's promise of political power. L. A. Joan refuses to visit her uncle's wife in the hospital, thereby causing him great pain. Triplette manipulates everyone into performing at his rally for the invisible Hal Phillip Walker, whose campaign is based on the clichés of a meaningless populism. Kenny, the assassin, has the last word by shooting Barbara Jean and, with this gratuitous act of political violence, throwing everyone into chaos and revealing their inherent passivity.

A major difference between the humiliations visited by one character upon another here and similar acts in *M.A.S.H.* is that the audience cannot share the victory over those who are hurt or identify with them. Altman keeps the viewer decidedly on the outside. In the very few instances where an emotional attachment threatens to break out, it is immediately squelched. Mr. Green learns of his wife's death in the hospital as the soldier, Kelley, is telling him how he watches over Barbara Jean for his mother's sake. The camera zooms in on Green as Kelley walks off saying, "You give my best to your wife." Green begins to grimace, to laugh in pain, but, before the viewer indulges in this rare expression of emotion, Altman cuts to Opal and Triplette laughing, she giving him her theory of assassination. On that there is a significant cut to Kenny, the actual assassin, on the phone to his grasping, protective mother. Other moments of emotional expression in the film are similarly compromised. Lady Pearl's feelings about the Kennedys are decidedly neurotic; Sueleen's shame at having to do a striptease is a result of her own self-delusion.

The distance at which the audience is kept is an important part of Altman's narrative control, for it positions the viewer as discriminating observer. The problem, however, lies in the uncertainty of what is to be observed and how. The ugliness of the behavior of most of the characters is not much dwelt on or commented upon, and is easily dismissible as part of the "flow" of events. If it can be argued that Altman is indeed somehow attempting an enormous "metaphor" of democracy, with all its flaws and all its attractions, then it can then be argued in return that what is shown is the very opposite of democracy: the great passive sink where those with some power manipulate those with less power and everyone sings a chorus of "You may say that I ain't free / But it don't worry me." And this in the end may be Altman's point. Passivity and the alienation from power are a major subject of the film, from the opening speech of the unseen presidential candidate, Hal Phillip Walker, who denies the right to be apolitical, through the insistence of most of the characters throughout the film that they are apolitical, to the revelation that politics is the function of everyone's manipulation of power over others. Altman accurately perceives that the ideology of the apolitical is a trap that conveniently allows those with politics and power the ability to control and manipulate. He confirms his perception by observing the manipulations of power conducted by the various characters on one another and on their audience, by presenting his "candidate" as just another political idiot, and the political rally, toward which all the events and characters of the film lead, to be the arena of yet another unexplained assassination whose resulting trauma permits all the errant couples of the film to be rejoined and another talentless country and western singer to achieve stardom. The fools remain fooled; the viewer, made distant and superior to the activity, is permitted only a sad resignation toward the events.

The pluralism of the film undoes itself—by condemning passivity while seeming to condone it, exposing the banal hypocrisy of country and western music while applauding its vitality, observing the vicious vacuity of "stars" while indicating that they're just folks, and giving everyone his or her due—and ends in ambiguity and evasion. A catastrophic event brings everyone together, but in a devitalized state, ready to be herded and manipulated once again. No answers are offered; indeed, the many vital questions raised by the film disappear in the general drift. Literally so, for it ends in a most uncharacteristic camera movement for Altman, a movement away from the field of action up to the sky. This seems to be the final evasion, and it needs a response. If *Nashville* suggests that America is divided into those who are in show business and those who passively watch the performance, it stops short of encouraging an analysis of this massive act of cultural manipulation. If everyone is at the mercy of everyone's lies, including their own, is there any meaning to individuality, is there any trust or any possibility of community?

The questions have become even more potent in the years since *Nashville*, and the film seems even more pertinent than it did in 1975. Altman has himself often returned to the problems posed by it, the cultural facts of celebrity and passivity becoming as important a thematic in his work as in Scorsese's. Unlike Scorsese, however, Altman is not interested in exploring the neurotic drive for recognition (even in his "meditation" on that great neurotic of the modern age, Richard Milhouse Nixon) or the responding, somewhat psychotic drive on the part of the culture to accept the image of celebrity. Rather, he is concerned with the visual and verbal language of spectacle and its reception, with the exchange value inherent in the illusory security offered by the owners of the spectacle to those who puchase and subject themselves to it.

*Nashville* is a multivalent observation of this phenomenon. *Buffalo Bill and the Indians, or, Sitting Bull's History Lesson* is narrower, an attempt to find the origins of certain kinds of cultural domination and its representations in history and language. As opposed to *Nashville*'s openness, it is an immediate, didactic, unambiguous, and closed essay on the substitution of personality for reality and the turning of history into lies—filmed with a jaundice-yellow wash over its images. *Buffalo Bill* is a narrative about narrative, about making stories and assuming that those stories adequately account for an individual's perceptions of the world. In short, the film is about the generation of ideology itself. Ned Buntline, writer of dime novels, creates Buffalo Bill out of William F. Cody, and Buffalo Bill creates the Wild West in which the white man always and effortlessly triumphs over the savage Indian. America and its history is an enclosed compound of actors and producers who keep sucking the past into their arena and re-creating it into a banal and simple present. "Everything historical is yours, Bill," says one of the boss's toadies. "I'm going to Codyfy the world," promises Nate Salsbury, producer-director of the Wild West. In the process the world is reduced to false assumptions of racial superiority, manifest destiny, and the complete gullibility of anyone not a party to the show.

Partly satire, partly farce, partly, as its sub-title states, history lesson, *Buffalo Bill* creates a set of exaggerated characters whose lives are devoted to exaggeration and to turning the false into the real. "Halsey doesn't mean a word he says," comments Buffalo Bill on Sitting Bull's interpreter. "That's why he sounds so real." Their words (in some of the best dialogue in Altman's work, co-written by Altman and Alan Rudolph) constantly expose their own absurdity without their ever showing an awareness of what they are saying. Except for the somber and dignified Sitting Bull, Halsey, and Burt Lancaster's Ned Buntline, who act as chorus, commenting sadly and ironically on the events, the characters stay enclosed within their world and their lies, feeding on each other and off of Bill, who feeds off the image of himself created by Buntline and compounded in his show (Bill is played by Paul Newman, and the result of this casting is to have one star of mythic dimensions play another who is playing the myth of himself that was created by someone else).[22]

The structure of the film is analogous to that of Kubrick's *Dr. Strangelove*. There is a similar use of language that signifies one thing to those inside the fiction and another thing to those on the outside; a similar blindness of the characters to the implications of their actions; and, like Kubrick's characters, the inhabitants of the Wild West are trapped in the logic of their lies, perpetuating an insulated and self-serving perception of the world that is destructive in its simplifications and assumptions. The film invites comparison as well with Penn's *Little Big Man*. But where Penn's picaresque narrative of a white man caught between his own corrupt world and the Indians' innocent and gentle culture suffers from special pleading, from an attempt to perpetuate another myth, that of the noble and gentle savage, Altman chooses another route. He is not concerned with the Indians *per se*; he realizes that their diminution and ruin have been accomplished and are irreversible (when the small and unprepossessing Sitting Bull first arrives at the Wild West, everyone mistakes Halsey for him—"That Injun's seven feet tall," someone says. "He's getting smaller every year," replies Buntline, aware that the myth cannot sustain itself). Rather, Altman speaks of the perpetuation of that ruin and of the self-deception that permits the perpetuation. Bill is in love with the image of himself (he looks in mirrors, gazes at his portrait), and that image is turned into an ideology of supremacy, of victory and hegemony. When Bill dreams of the dead Sitting Bull, who appears, as always, silent, self-contained, private, and assured, he can only insist that this hegemony *must* be real, for, if it is not, he is alone and without value.* "God meant me to be white," he says. "And it ain't easy. I got people with no lives livin' through me!. . . You see, in one hundred years I'm still going to be Buffalo Bill. Star! And you're still going to be the Injun." Gazing, yet again, at his portrait, Bill asks a question whose connotations pervade the film: "My God, ain't he ridin' that horse right? But if he ain't, then how come all of you took him for a king?"

Buffalo Bill and his Wild West must be right. Everyone assents to him and his myths. No one has ever questioned him. The mystical dreams and humane demands of Sitting Bull result only in his humiliation and defeat (the last thing seen of him is a charred bone). Buffalo Bill lives on in power and victory. These must be real. In the last sequence of the film, Bill "fights" Sitting Bull in the arena of the Wild West as hundreds cheer. The Sitting Bull he fights is actually Halsey, the tall Indian who everyone figured must have been Sitting Bull when they first rode into the Wild West together. Everyone was right after all. "When the legend becomes fact, print the legend," says the newspaper man at the end of Ford's *The Man Who Shot Liberty Valance*. Ford was quite serious. His conservatism demanded assent to cultural myths. Altman is both

---

*Bill's dream is filmed in a rather theatrical manner, almost as if it were on a stage. *Buffalo Bill* is, in fact, based on a play by Arthur Kopit and, no doubt unconsciously, foreshadows the theatrical adaptations that would preoccupy Altman in the eighties.

amused and appalled by the ease with which the myths prevail. Buffalo Bill has his own way. He fights the Indian everyone expected him to fight, and he beats him by merely pushing him to the ground. He stands in phony triumph over his phony captive, and the fraud is climaxed by the camera pulling far away to a high shot of the Wild West arena surrounded by the wilderness. The shot seems to signify entrapment. Bill and his company are alone and isolated by their lies. But it is a troubling point of view, for it is not very clear to whom it belongs. Is it meant to indicate new-found superiority to the lies of "the Show Business" on the part of the viewer? Having seen this film, does the viewer now see clearly how he or she is abused by cultural myths? Has this analysis of the semiology of cultural production freed us from subjugation to the signs the owners of the culture create to manufacture a predetermined response? Actually, all Altman has done is describe the present in terms of the past. The dynamics of cultural response, of politics, of film continue to prove his point that the society remains gullible to the fraudulence of celebrity, movie heroism, and white male supremacy. "The show business" and its spectacles continue to command attention and assent, and the culture seems contented by its passivity in the face of those dominant images. In the seventies there was the passivity of disenchantment and disengagement. If the heroes are dead, the culture seemed to say, if heroism is itself a fraud and no other alternatives seem possible, then all that remains is simply to bemoan the fraud and mourn the death. In the early eighties the hero was revived. On screen, muscular men destroyed foreigners, and visitors from outer space protected children. An aging movie star regenerated the fantasy of white, male, middle-class, Christian dominance that can secure the world under the protection of heroes made in its image. "Everything historical is yours. . . ."

Altman revived Bill Cody once again just at the point of transition from the seventies into the eighties in a film that marked an end to the first phase of his career and summarized all that he had done before. *Health* is a great carnival of a film, a hilarious documentation of politics and culture at the end of the Carter era when passivity began to disguise itself as self-satisfaction and marginal interests requested majority attention. The focus of the film is narrow and precise, even though the form of the film, like the best of Altman's work, is loose and open, full of peripheral action, off-screen dialogue, and, occasionally, a number of sight gags going on in one shot, after the manner of the French director Jacques Tati. But here, instead of linking together many narratives to make a larger commentary on the politics of manipulation as he does in *Nashville*, Altman creates a very precise event. A Florida convention of health food enthusiasts becomes a small mirror of larger political follies, of silly, self-serving people so convinced of their importance that they take for granted the fact that major significance attends their ridiculous activities.

The event is the perfect parody of political spectacle in which self-importance is raised to a historical (and perfectly hysterical) imperative, and gestures are made for the sole purpose of calling attention to themselves in front of the television cameras that observe them. There are flacks, advance persons, people dressed up as a variety of fruits and vegetables, a television talk show host, and candidates. One candidate is Esther Brill (Lauren Bacall), an eighty-three-year-old virgin who believes that each orgasm a woman has shortens her life by twenty-eight days. Her motto is "Feel Yourself" and she tends, in the middle of a sentence, to raise her hand and fall promptly to sleep. Her rival is Isabella Garnell (Glenda Jackson) who orders the furniture removed from her hotel room—"our worship should not be of material achievement," she pontificates, "but of human values and ideals"—drinks hot water with nothing in it, idolizes and quotes Adlai Stevenson, and records all of her thoughts onto a tape cassette. A third candidate, Dr. Gill Gainey (Paul Dooley, who co-wrote the film), has an ostentatious patch of white hair on his head, proclaims himself a member of the extreme middle, a mediator between the people and nutrition, and sells a product that has "all the sea water without the salt." When his candidacy gains no attention, he lies at the bottom of a swimming pool as if dead. Carol Burnett plays Gloria Burbank, a White House representative on nutrition who, after pleading neutrality, declares herself for Isabella Garnell and becomes romantically involved with her former husband, Harry Wolff (James Garner), Esther Brill's campaign manager. (The least clever item in the film is Gloria's propensity to become sexually aroused whenever she is frightened.) A political trickster (Henry Gibson) dresses up as a woman and advocates breast feeding in an attempt to gain Isabella's confidence in order to discredit her by proving that she is really a man.

The general chaos is given some order by two figures, one of whom is the only woman of sanity in the film. She is the black public relations

Entertainment, political spectacle, carnival. *Health* (Lauren Bacall, Dick Cavett, Carol Burnett, Glenda Jackson).

director for the convention hotel, who observes the events with a distanced amazement and bemusement that places her as a surrogate for the viewer within the film. The other figure has a more complex role. Dick Cavett appears as himself, a talk show host who is covering the convention. Earlier, in *Nashville*, Elliott Gould and Julie Christie appeared as "actual" Hollywood celebrities among the country and western celebrities impersonated by the actors in the film. As the characters in the fiction fawn over the personalities who enter their fiction from the outside, a hierarchical structure of illusion is created among actors playing celebrities and actors who are celebrities already and play themselves. Cavett's role in *Health* turns this around somewhat. He is, of course, the "actual" celebrity and the point to which all the characters tend to gravitate. The television program he is doing from the health food convention draws everyone to him, including the viewer—the electronic titles marking the start of taping are superimposed on the screen as the show within the show begins. (As in *Brewster McCloud*, the film begins by pointing to its existence as documentation of a spectacle. Someone yells "Hit it!" and, under the studio's logo, the Twentieth Century-Fox drum roll is replaced by the convention band.) Cavett remains calm and aloof from the lunatic activities of the other characters. Twice in the course of the film, as the other characters go through their machinations, Altman cuts away to Cavett, zooms gently into him lying in bed, watching Johnny Carson. The actual celebrity, entering a fiction filled with would-be celebrities, removes himself from the frenzy to commune with a colleague on television.

As in *Nashville*, a collision of fictions and illusions push the already eccentric structure of the film further off center. Altman creates a world that is a parody of a political phenomenon that is itself already a parody of show business, for political conventions always mediate the realities of power with the signifiers of spectacle. *Health* is, finally, a representation of a representation. And Dick Cavett, the talk show host, a celebrity who acts as mediator and midwife to other celebrities and moderator of the spectacle, is in the perfect position to be ringmaster of this carnival, remaining aloof to the very situation he has a responsibility for creating.

Into this crazed parody of political buffoonery comes a strange, frightening figure with a familiar name. Col. Cody (played with a violent Southern accent by Donald Moffat) appears, not as Buffalo Bill, but as a right-wing ogre who claims to own the health food convention and, by implication, the government itself. During two sequences played out in a threatening darkness, one with candidate Isabella Garnell, the other with Gloria Burbank, he speaks of a corporate power that diminishes everything in its wake. "You're into government programs," he tells Isabella, "we're into foreign governments." He claims responsibility for the death of the group's President, the event that has lead to the current campaign battle. "You work for me, woman...," he tells the White House representative, "you are finished making moral stands. Your work is meaningless. You ain't gonna change a thing." And to Isabella he delivers a most chilling judgment that affirms completely the power of manipulation and lies over reality. "Lady," he tells her, "you have told me what I wanted to hear. You are for real. That means you are no threat to anyone." The words echo what Altman's original Col. Cody said about Sitting Bull's Indian interpreter: "Halsey doesn't mean a word he says. That's why he sounds so real."

Lying, as Franz Kafka's Joseph K. feared, is raised to a universal principle. The appearance of truth is given more power than any possible realities might have—including the reality of Col. Cody himself. The great liar and owner of all things historical proves, in his reincarnation in *Health*, to be still a fraud. He is not the right-wing lunatic he sounds like, but rather Esther Brill's crazy brother pretending to be a right-wing lunatic. Everything, finally, is what it seems, a perfect illusion, a manipulation of words, images, and individuals in a great, silly game. Everyone willingly enters into a trance. The convention of health food enthusiasts is to be followed by a convention of hypnotists. Dinah Shore, who will cover that group, greets Dick Cavett as he leaves.

Altman is so fascinated by that particular manipulator and corrupter of images, Buffalo Bill Cody, that he re-creates him yet again—much changed in form—in another film. *Secret Honor*, the one-person play about Richard Nixon filmed by Altman in 1984, stands as a coda to the meditations on politics, celebrity, and spectacle carried forward in *Nashville, Buffalo Bill and the Indians*, and *Health*. Altman's Nixon is Buffalo Bill turned schizophrenic. Part of him is the great fraud who would mould history into a reflection of his televised image and an echo of his tape recorded voice. Another part is a passive hysteric, hiding behind a self-induced nightmare of conspiracy in which he becomes the willing political tool of the rich and powerful. The result is a Nixon made up of cringing bravura: an obscene, racist, anti-Semitic, all-American paranoid, who denies his power and corruption, replacing it with delusions of conspiratorial forces to which he has no choice but submit. During the course of the film, which takes place in the confines of an office, he drinks, yells, exclaims, whines, talks into his tape recorder (an extension of his personality), addresses his image on four television monitors (the confirmation of his personality), or an imaginary judge, or his dead mother. He strangles on language, sometimes finds it impossible to get words out of his throat. He stands dwarfed by portraits of Lincoln, Woodrow Wilson, and the alter ego he despises, Henry Kissinger, alternately defying the world and contemplating suicide. He blames his career on the "Committee of One Hundred," a shadowy group of businessmen who, he insists, used him to keep control of the world and allowed him the illusion of power. "There I am," he says, "down in the sewer, waiting for my turn just like every-fucking-body else." This Nixon is a vile and profane Rupert Pupkin, who became President instead of a television star. Rupert at least blamed his notoriety on no one else.

The All-American paranoid. ''Nixon'' (Philip Baker Hall) in *Secret Honor*. (© Courtesy Cinecom International Films)

Like so many of Altman's characters, Nixon uses passivity as a means of action. The contradiction is a bold one. By refusing to act, or only reacting to situations caused by inaction, or blaming actions on the power of others, or by being a willing subject to someone else's spectacle, these characters remove themselves from responsibility. Or are removed from it. Altman is especially drawn to the passivity that is the result of gender, a passivity that is not wanted, but enforced. In four films (and a short work made for cable television), he attempts an examination of women who react in strange and sometimes destructive ways to their subordinate situations. The films raise the inevitable problem of whether a male can explore female consciousness from anything but a male perspective (whether the reverse is true is difficult to determine, for in commercial narrative film, at least, there has been little serious work about men by women). Therefore, those films whose subjects are women—*That Cold Day in the Park, Images, Three Women, Come Back to the Five and Dime, Jimmy Dean, Jimmy Dean*—must be understood as films about women from the point of view of a particular male. And it is not an entirely dependable point of view. The films in which women are active though not necessarily central figures—*Nashville, A Wedding, Health, Beyond Therapy*—do not offer terribly flattering representations. The women there are often foolish, and when they act, it is sometimes stupidly. A question of consistency is raised, and of authenticity. Secondly, Altman finds it difficult, in the films whose subjects are women, to escape from some old Hollywood or theatrical conventions of rendering psychological states: strained camera angles and odd point-of-view shots, dreams, hallucinations, memories, mirrors that serve as windows to the past, eerie music. He is not entirely successful with these devices, as is Scorsese in *Taxi Driver*. And unlike Scorsese, who managed an almost creditable film about a woman in *Alice Doesn't Live Here Anymore* by avoiding psychology, Altman gets caught in a dilemma. His attempts to define states of mind in novel ways run the risk of being compromised by his use of expressionist interventions. With the exception of *Three Women*, the narrative inquisitiveness and formal playfulness with which Altman explores character and event from the outside, avoiding psychological analysis and defining character by what the character does and what is done to him or her, is largely missing in these films.

*That Cold Day in the Park*, as I noted earlier, is important as an indication of Altman's early experimentation in reorganizing the spatial centers of his narrative. Thematically, its attempt to present the cliché of the sexually repressed spinster who can only release her repressions in deviant behavior would hardly be worthy of comment, were it not for the respect that Altman shows for the character of Frances Austen and his skepticism toward the boy she brings in from the cold. She mothers, attempts to seduce, imprisons, and procures for him, and then kills the whore she has procured. Both Frances and the boy are presented as being equally repressed: she traps herself in the accouterments of old age, surrounds herself with old people; he is a passive onlooker to the sexuality of others. Both of them can be seen as the first of Altman's passive characters, acted upon, in this case, by their repressions and their environments—the gloom of Frances's apartment and the shallow brightness of the streets the boy wanders. Their environments help to define them, but they are at the same time set off from the worlds they inhabit. A sense of isolation and inwardness is achieved by the shots that zoom away from Frances in her apartment to a wall of glass bricks or the lights of the street seen out of focus through the window.

This movement is Altman's central attempt at rendering an internal state, a lack of emotional anchorage, a sense of surroundings precariously or incompletely grasped. He uses similar techniques in *Images* and *Three Women*, and in all three cases his use of the zoom is unlike that in the other films where it accents a face, picks out a detail, indicates the extension of space. In *The Long Goodbye*, the zoom, along with the arc and the tracking shot, is used to create an unstable space, but that space is not merely reflective of the internal state of the central character; rather it indicates an almost universal instability of perception. In *That Cold Day*, movement is to blurred or reflected objects; in *Images* to a wind chime, which becomes a kind of fetish, an instrument that is insistently played upon, but is itself passive, an apt reflection of the central character. Reflective surfaces become apertures of memory in *Come Back to the Five and Dime*, where images of the past appear through a mirror, and the zoom and pan are directed across time from one barren moment to an earlier one.

Like *That Cold Day* (indeed, like *The Long Goodbye* and *Nashville*),

*Images* is about a passivity that turns to the destruction of someone else. Rendered in the most extreme subjective terms—the viewer, a good part of the time, sees only what the character sees—this passivity results in the breakdown of the character's perception of the "real" world and a withdrawal into an interior, surrogate one, which then redefines "reality." Altman does something very clever here. *Images* contains his most sharply defined images (made by Vilmos Zsigmond). There is little apparent tinkering with the color (the "flashing" technique, a method of pre-exposing the film that renders the gold and blue in *McCabe*, the blue-green haze of *The Long Goodbye*, and the jaundice-yellow of *Buffalo Bill*) and a greater use than in the other films of deep-focus cinematography. By unlocalizing the place of the film (it was shot in Ireland, but the locations are never named) and then rendering that unnamed location in bright, hard, deep images, Altman makes the hallucinatory world of the central figure, Cathryn (Susannah York), very immediate and very vague simultaneously. There is little narrative byplay in the film; the events are precisely focused among only five characters who become interchangeable in Cathryn's mind.* *Images*, in appearance and in narrative construction, is one of Altman's clearest films, and he takes great delight in playing that clarity and immediacy against the deranged and incoherent sensibility of his main character.

In retrospect (the film was not well received or understood in 1972), *Images* is also very clear and immediate in its statement about a particular kind of withdrawal and passivity. Cathryn is trapped by a dilemma basic to many women: how to reconcile the demands of the self with the demands of domesticity, of being a dutiful wife to—in this case—a meticulously bourgeois husband. Both in rebellion against and withdrawal from this conflict Cathryn retreats and then exteriorizes her other, a sexual being with lovers and with strong demands. She fears this other and the sexuality she represents. Her conflict undoes her, and in her imagination kills her former lover, René, with a shotgun and stabs her husband's lecherous friend, Marcel (René is actually already dead when he appears to Cathryn's imagination, and Marcel reappears

---

*The name of each actor is given to another actor's character: Susannah York is Cathryn, Cathryn Harrison is Susannah, Hugh Millais—who plays the killer, Butler, in *McCabe*— is Marcel, Marcel Bozzuffi is René, and René Auberjonois is Hugh.

quite well and happy after she stabs him). In a final hallucinatory attempt to confront and destroy her other self, she kills her husband "for real." The events and conclusion of the film propose an excess of imaginative zeal in the representation of madness.

Yet Altman's desire to show madness as a manifestation of a particular social-political phenomenon, in this case the cultural oppression of women, is sound. He is perhaps more successful when he comes to the problem from the outside, as observer, than as analyst. Mrs. Miller is a better creation of a woman attempting to be free, and Keechie of a woman oppressed by her helplessness, than Cathryn is of either. *Images* may suffer from being too clear, too simple, and too much centered on the abnormal psychology of its main character, problems with which Altman continually struggles when exploring feminine consciousness. *Come Back to the Five and Dime* splits its subject five ways. Five women gather in the Woolworth's of a desiccated Texas town to celebrate the reunion of their James Dean fan club. Images of their past and discussion of their present reveal a complex of lies and delusions each has visited on herself. The dramatic—indeed theatrical—sequence of unveilings, in the course of which more and more neurosis, repression, and pathos is discovered as each character exposes more and more of her life, yields finally to a notion of patriarchy as mutilation.[23]

Each of them has undergone a diminishment of self, physically and psychologically. Sissy (Cher), who, in order to please men, fetishizes her breasts as her most sexually attractive feature, reveals that she has in fact lost them to cancer. Joanne (Karen Black) is literally castrated. Humiliated as a boy because of effeminate characteristics and denied by Mona, whose child he fathered, he has had himself surgically rendered female. Mona (Sandy Dennis) lives in the belief that she bore a retarded child fathered by James Dean during the filming of *Giant*. She has surrounded herself with pictures and masks of Dean, turned herself into the Virgin Mary of a celebrity cult figure. In an illusory world, bordered on one side by the mirror of their past, on another by relics of a fifties movie star, and all around by the lifeless heat of the desert, these characters represent women not merely as victims of patriarchal demand, but crippled by it. Unable to sustain themselves in the patriachal structure, they have neurotically withdrawn from it, or denied it or themselves. The only member of the group who insists she is happy is a

Mona (Sandy Dennis), Sissy (Cher), Joanne (Karen Black) in *Come Back to the Five and Dime, Jimmy Dean, Jimmy Dean.* (© Courtesy Cinecom International Films)

woman who is perpetually pregnant, who finds comfort in the secure anonymity of domesticity.

Like *That Cold Day in the Park* and *Images* and the short film, *The Laundromat, Come Back to the Five and Dime, Jimmy Dean, Jimmy Dean* deals with the crisis of women confronting the oppressions of patriarchy by dissolving them into neuroses. Unable to struggle, these figures first collapse within themselves and then extrapolate their delusions as protection against the world that surrounds them. *Fool for Love*, though not specifically about women, is also concerned with the oppressions of patriarchy—quite literally, as it describes the effects on his children of a man who kept two wives. Here the delusions of repression and emotional pain are drawn through two visual/narrative devices. More than in his other films, Altman shoots characters and their actions—sometimes whole sequences—through windows, separating figures from one another and from the viewer, suggesting a constant desire to see things which cannot be seen directly or clearly. When

the characters—the Old Man (Harry Dean Stanton), Eddie (Sam Shepard, author of the play upon which the film is based), and May (Kim
Bassinger)—attempt to recall their past and relate its emotional terrors,
their words and the images that accompany them do not quite match.
The gestures and actions of the characters in the flashback may simply
deny what the character is saying in voice-over, or may be out of narrative sync, occurring at a different time, perhaps—or at all times.
(Early in the film, a family stays at the Royale Motel, a place in the
middle of the desert that contains most of the action, the place where
May and the Old Man live; they turn out to be the mother and father
of May, and May herself as a little girl. Past and present become coter-
minous.)[24] The mirror in *Come Back to the Five and Dime, Jimmy
Dean, Jimmy Dean* presents direct entry to the past, perhaps revealing
more than the characters wish to remember. The flashbacks in *Fool for
Love* indicate that the past is either unreachable, or too present, or that
it must be changed, romanticized, revised in the present in order for the
characters to deal with its unpleasantness.

   In no instance is the result entirely satisfactory. Narratives of victimization internalized and then emerging as destruction of self or others
remain stories of victimization. And melodramatic revelations, no matter how cleverly generated, tend to cancel profundity through their
excess. Altman is most successful when he generates his subjects out of
a rich and cluttered field of images and sounds from which he can
appear casually to pick and choose, defining his characters by indirection rather than melodrama. *Three Women* works the best among his
films on women because it attempts to avoid exclusive concentration
on neurosis and combines a number of narrative approaches. The film
works simultaneously from the inside out—from the characters' minds
to the world beyond them—and from the outside in—from the contemporary, nightmare landscape of Southern California to the people that
landscape defines. To this is added another element. Mediating the interior and exterior worlds is the continual presence of a group of grotesque murals painted by one of the characters. These murals depict
three reptilian women: one shows them at each other's throats; another
shows two under the domination of the third; and both show all of them
diminished by an enormous male figure. The result of the interplay of
interior states, exterior landscape, and the bizarre murals that punctuate

the film at strategic moments is an expressionism of sorts. Not the almost classical expressionism of *Taxi Driver*, in which the appearance of the external world is moulded through the perceptions of an agonized mind, but rather an expressionism created through the counterpointing of the world in its physical and ideological presence with reflections of that world off of the emotional states of the characters. The world of *Taxi Driver* is terribly concrete and immediate. The world of *Three Women* seems an appendage to the world of ordinary experience, not quite real, not quite nightmare, not even a fully articulated world, but a realm of existence that combines parts of each and whose most distinguishing feature is aridity and banality. It is all but empty of anything but the bizarre and the commonplace.[25] (The geographical locations of *Come Back to the Five and Dime* and *Fool for Love* are similar to *Three Women*, but because he must restrict locations, Altman cannot visually play the counterpoint of exterior and interior as he does here. Aridity and barrenness, however, are qualities shared by the three films.)

At one point, Millie Lammoreaux (Shelley Duvall) is driving her roommate Pinky's parents to her apartment. The camera observes the mother through the windshield of the car as she says, "Sure doesn't look like Texas." The camera pans away to reveal a featureless desert landscape that could be Texas, Southern California, Arizona, New Mexico, anywhere that is dry and hot and without features or human habitation. Pinky's mother sees a difference where there is none, attempts to give meaning to that which is barren of meaning. She brings a present for her daughter, a plaque with a gruesomely oppressive rhyme: "In this kitchen, bright and cheery, daily chores I'll never shirk. So bless this kitchen, Lord, and bless me as I work." "It's for the kitchen," she says. In *Three Women* everyone is trapped by clichés, by an inability to speak beyond the ordinary and the commonplace, their minds rendered sterile by having nothing to think about, nothing to feel, nothing to say, nothing to see.

Throughout his films, Altman has shown a painful sensitivity to the banal and an awareness of its destructive capabilities. *Three Women* takes the banal as its subject. Its characters, Millie, Pinky Rose (Sissy Spacek), and Willie (Janice Rule), as well as everyone who surrounds them, are ciphers, empty vessels in an empty landscape. Most are filled by whatever floats by. Millie ("I'm known for my dinner parties"—

Millie and Pinky (Shelley Duvall and Sissy Spacek) in the arid landscape of *Three Women*.

which consist only of packaged, processed food) is filled with the language of women's magazines and so insulated by its dehumanizing jargon that she seems oblivious to the fact that she is ignored by everyone. Pinky is filled by Millie, for she has no self at all. She is first seen when the camera zooms to her face, wide-eyed and blank, staring through a window at the health spa for old people where she has come to work. Later, at the spa, when she talks incessantly about Millie and how she misses her, the camera slowly and deliberately zooms to and past her face—achieving an effect akin to having her face slide slowly off the side of the Panavision screen—to the bright windows behind her, which go out of focus. There is an immediate cut to a metered television set on the wall of Pinky's dark, close room. The set is on, but there is nothing on it, and the camera pulls back from the bright empty screen (which suddenly goes off) to Pinky lying asleep. This movement and cut accomplish what Altman was trying to do in *That Cold Day* and *Images*, to find a visual surrogate for a subjective state. Pinky is as blank as a curtained window or a television screen, a creature without a personality, without thought. The third woman, Willie, is less detailed. She is pregnant, and finally delivers a still-born baby, a barren birth into a barren world. An artist, she creates the murals of reptilian women (one of whom is pregnant) and the monstrous male who controls them. She is married to Edgar, a parody of a macho male, an ex-stuntman and gun-toting buffoon who sleeps with Millie (the only man who will) and is the analogue to the male figure in Willie's mural. Willie is mostly silent, seemingly removed from the banality around her, yet constantly commenting on the terror of that banality in her art. Having given up the language of patriarchy, she seeks to comment on its oppression in another language, in the monstrous, almost mythic images she paints.[26]

The great problem that Altman has with these figures and their world is integrating them within a coherent design. As I said, he attempts to create a modified expressionist point of view, indicating states of mind by the faces and the surroundings of those faces. The early sequences in the health spa, with the silent old people being walked about by Millie and her colleagues; the first sequence in Millie's yellow apartment and Edgar's dilapidated bar where she hangs out, with motorcyclists and target shooters in the back and Willie painting her murals in an empty swimming pool; Millie's early relationship with Pinky; the sequence in which Millie enters her bedroom to find Pinky's decrepit parents locked in a sexual embrace—all form a complex point of view that oscillates between a recognizable world and a frightening, disengaged, disorienting one where identities are uncertain because unformed and unformed because there is no sense of self or of location.

The point of entry into the film for the viewer, however, is also uncertain. There is no possibility for "identification" with the characters and little sense of understanding, on a rational level, this discourse of absent personalities. The film may be an attempt—more extreme than in the other works—to split perceptions, remove their foundations, as the characters are split and unfounded. In the sequence where Willie gives birth to her dead child, the camera is placed just outside the doorway of this gruesome scene of pain and loss, placing the viewer at a distance, but at the same time forcing on her or him the point of view of Millie inside, helping Willie, and Pinky outside, frozen in terror. Here and throughout the film, the viewer is caught in a forced perspective where the immediacy of the event and its detached and disorienting structure conflict. The result is a sense of being unanchored, with no firm or assured position, drifting, like the subjects within the narrative, through shifting images and significations. As a result, the viewer tends to gain no knowledge greater than the characters have, to see and understand no more than they do, which was not the case in the earlier film of unstable perception, *The Long Goodbye*.

Altman seems intent on overmystifying the narrative, or, perhaps more accurately, overdetermining it with expressions of mystery and a forced sense of the portentous. There is little of the playfulness present even in the most serious of his other films (a problem the film shares with *Quintet*, *Streamers*, and, to a certain extent, *Fool for Love*). The exchange of identities between Millie and Pinky, for example, is an excellent idea, but managed with a strained sense of profundity. Altman had toyed with it in *Images*, where Cathryn and her young friend Susannah are seen reflected together in mirrors, and finally with their faces superimposed in a window, suggesting that Susannah, as a woman, will follow Cathryn's path of madness. The more explicit exchange between Millie and Pinky (who says her name is really Millie) seems an inevitable result of the emptiness of their personalities. But Altman cannot disengage himself from the Bergmanesque pretentiousness of the situation. Fortunately he does not infuse the situation with the metaphysical vaguenesses of *Persona*; he is too much in touch with the immediate presence of our culture. The world is present in *Three Women*, and its influence marked on the characters. But that influence remains diffuse. The *idea* of interchanging identities is itself diffuse, too fanciful and too abstracted from the otherwise concrete and immediate indicators of barren souls in a barren world.

The tension between abstract and concrete is strongest in the final sequences of the film, as Altman attempts to re-anchor the psychological transformations of character back into the environment they came from. When Pinky absorbs Millie's personality, she expresses it in a spirit of meanness and coldness, without her host's cliché-ridden vocabulary and without the pathetic quality that vocabulary lent her. Millie buckles under Pinky's meanness, her passive nature submitting to Pinky's new-found and misdirected strength. But another change occurs

after Pinky's nightmare—perhaps the most portentous, if not pretentious, sequence in the film, in which all the faces appear doubled or in
violent and distorted form and the events of Willie's still-birth are foreshadowed. After the nightmare, Pinky is more docile; her fear brings
her to Millie for mothering, she wants to sleep with her, and Millie comforts her, placing her hand on her face. A new relational complex is
forming, which will be completed after the horrendous sequence of Willie bearing her dead boy.

During the still-birth, Millie acts with a strength she has never before
demonstrated. Pinky is frozen in fear, unable to call for a doctor. After
Millie emerges from the house, hands bloodied and shaking in front of
her, as she had appeared to Pinky in the dream, she slaps her, again
demonstrating an unexpected sense of power and control. The sequence
ends on Pinky's face, bloodied by Millie's hand, which has in effect
transferred to her the sign of Willie's agony. From Pinky's face a cut is
made to a long, far shot of a desert road, barren and hot, power lines
marking the background. A yellow Coca-Cola truck comes into view
(yellow is the bright, bland color that Millie chooses for everything: her
apartment, her dress, her car). The truck pulls into the "Dodge City"
bar that Edgar owned and that was Millie's hangout. Pinky is behind
the bar, chewing gum, reading a magazine. When the delivery man asks
to have his Coca-Cola signed for, Pinky says she'll call her "mom," who
turns out to be Millie. In the dialogue with the delivery man, there is
the revelation that Edgar has been shot, "a terrible accident, we're all
grieved by it." Millie orders Pinky to the house to fix dinner. At the
house Willie sits on the porch, telling of a dream she had and cannot
remember. The camera zooms back from the house; Millie is heard
ordering Pinky about, Willie asking why she has to be so mean to her.
The camera pans to a pile of old tires, the last image of the arid landscape. The shot dissolves to the mural of the three reptilian women bent
to the ground. The enormous male figure has one of the females by the
tail; he raises his other hand in a fist. One of the female figures points
up to an occult symbol, a cross in a circle, around which emerge four
snakes.

The film concludes with Altman's most bitter observation of domination and passivity, of assent to ritual and assumption of cultural
myths. The three women, ridding themselves of men (Willie's child was

male and is born dead; and the suggestion is clear that the women shot Edgar—"I'd rather face a thousand crazy savages than one woman who's learned to shoot," he had said earlier), proceed to re-enact a family structure with one dominant member, now maternal rather than paternal, and two passive members. The enclave they form in the garbage-strewn desert is a parody of the male-dominated society reflected in Willie's mural and whose patterns of domination and passivity Altman sees spread through all relationships. Millie and Pinky are dominated by the hard and thoughtless doctors who run the health spa, and they in turn manipulate the old people as if they were children. Millie is controlled by the prose of female exploitation in women's magazines. Pinky allows herself to be manipulated by Millie, briefly exchanges roles to become the dominating figure, and in turn becomes a compliant daughter to her. Willie, Millie, and Pinky are all controlled by Edgar, and with Edgar gone, they can only exist in an isolated re-enactment of power and passivity within the structure of the family, that central image of psychological and economic control, the place where the ideology is delivered, nurtured, and reproduced.

As opposed to Spielberg and the filmmakers discussed in the preceding chapter, Altman sees the family as a barren place, as barren as the ideology it reproduces and which reproduces it. The family is literally barren at the end of *Three Women*, where its grim imitation of life takes place in the dry desert, and is destructive of all emotional balance in *Fool for Love*, where a father's attempt to have two families, equally attended to, results in a oppressive sexual relationship between the son and daughter of his different wives. Only when characters escape the grip of family, as in *A Perfect Couple*, or transcend the limits of ordinary emotional demands, as in *Beyond Therapy*, does Altman offer any hope of victory.

His most vicious attack on domestic institutions occurs in *A Wedding*, a film which offers a climax to Altman's explorations and revelations of hypocrisy, duplicity, manipulation, and humiliation. The subject of attack here is the very ritual that constitutes the institutionalizing of love in the culture, and Altman uses that ritual to work through many of his concerns.[27] Formally, the film is another experiment in the interaction of large numbers of people within an open narrative form. Contextually, he continues to explore the breakdown of community, the difficulties—indeed the impossibilities—of romantic engagement. While often a clever and funny film, its anger and, too frequently, condescension tend to make it flippant and evasive. Almost every cut, every zoom, reveals another bit of banal or embarrassing behavior without seeking to reveal the root causes of the banalities or to explain why they are so ridiculous. A senile priest, a pubescent bride with braces, her sexually promiscuous sister (pregnant by the groom), a pompous lesbian wedding coordinator (played by Geraldine Chaplin, who merely expands a bit on her unpleasant character in *Nashville*), a mother addicted to heroin, a love-sick in-law who attempts to seduce the mother of the bride—these and other caricatures appear and reappear to be laughed at or degraded. Altman shows, with only some insight or concern, that the rich are foolish and the *nouveaux riches* superficial and uncaring. The emotional contours of *Nashville* and the intellectual engagement that informs *Buffalo Bill* and *Three Women* are not much in evidence.

*A Wedding*'s cleverness always threatens to become a smugness that, for the first time in Altman's work, comes at the expense of its characters, and finally the spectators. When the farce is turned upon the viewer, who is led, at one point, to believe that the newlyweds are killed in a car wreck, the manipulation becomes too extreme. When it is revealed that it was not the newlyweds who were killed, but another young couple, a rather attractive man and woman somewhat less odious than the others who populate the film, the manipulation of emotions becomes too facile. The viewer is asked suddenly to reflect on the situation, to be horrified by the fact that the parents of the newlyweds are oblivious to the death of the other couple when they discover that their own children are safe. This becomes the final shame visited upon them, and they remain unaware of their emotional poverty. The only noble act in the film is a passive one: Luigi Corelli (Vittorio Gassman), the patriarch who has been held down by his wife's money, leaves the whole group behind for freedom.

But the leaving behind is the problem. Like Mrs. Miller, who withdraws into an opium den, or Essex, who treks out into the ice wastes at the end of *Quintet*, or May, who walks out into the dark at the end of *Fool for Love*, or Prudence and Bruce who transport themselves from New York to Paris, away from the conflicting claims of lovers and therapists in *Beyond Therapy*; like the drift of the camera to the skies at the end of *Nashville*; or the high shot that ends *Buffalo Bill*, the suggestion remains that the best way out of an impossible situation is simply to leave it behind. In some of these films, the withdrawal is informed by the narrative, by insight into the sources of hypocrisy and self-delusion in *Buffalo Bill*; by a lament for missed chances in *McCabe and Mrs. Miller*; by an understanding of the powers of ritual over life in *Quintet* or the results of distorted domesticity in *Fool for Love*. But *A Wedding* has offered only a stony gaze at a pack of unattractive people, a gaze like that of the statue in the garden to which Altman's camera is occasionally drawn: blank and uncomprehending. The gaze permits a privileged position, a position of safety and superiority, unlike *Buffalo Bill*, which attempts at least to offer an active demythification, to explore some of the foundations of cultural lies. *A Wedding* leaves the viewer simply alone, a situation by now too familiar.

But Altman, finally, cannot be singled out for a failure to deal directly with the abhorrent situations he perceives or to seek more deeply for causes. No other American filmmaker does, and Altman is the only filmmaker who has sought as much and as consistently. Certainly no other has worked so thoroughly on redefining the forms of his cinematic inquiry and few have focused so persistently on the distortions of personality caused by patriarchy. While he may not have total success in discussing the structures and consequences of patriarchy (and few male filmmakers have), he has had extraordinary success in dismantling the patriarchal structures of cinematic narrative. While his films may take as their subject the cultural propensity toward passivity, a willingness to be oppressed by manufactured images that are accepted as historical realities, the images manufactured by Altman to inscribe these subjects refuse to dominate the viewer. The open narrative construction—the flow, the sense of process and accident that so many of his films achieve—attempts to take apart the very subject they create, deconstruct them by exposing their manufacture and affirming the fact that it is the viewer who must make sense of them. Two distinct voices seem to be speaking these filmic discourses. One announces the inevitability of defeat through the hopeless yielding to domination. The other enunciates a freedom of perception, and therefore a control over what is seen, understood, and interpreted. However, the dialectic can become mere contradiction. There is an open narrative structure offering the viewer the potential of engaged response; and there is, no matter how great the openness, the insistence that, for all that engagement, the only possibility is to consider the varieties of our lack of freedom. These conflicting voices, speaking against passivity and lack of control while simultaneously declaring their inevitability, risk simply canceling each other out.[28]

Roland Barthes, writing about the phenomenon of the *avant-garde*, said something that is quite applicable to Altman's situation.

> ... The bourgeoisie delegated some of its creators to tasks of
> formal subversion, though without actually disinheriting them: is
> it not the bourgeoisie, after all, which dispenses to *avant-garde* art
> the parsimonious support of its public, i.e., of its money? ... The
> *avant-garde* is threatened by only one force, which is not the
> bourgeoisie: political consciousness. ... It seems that no sooner is
> the *avant-garde* won over to the necessity of revolutionary tasks
> than it renounces itself, agrees to die. ... The *avant-garde* is
> always a way of celebrating the death of the bourgeoisie, for its
> own death still belongs to the bourgeoisie; but further than this
> the *avant-garde* cannot go; it cannot conceive the funerary term it
> expresses as a moment of germination, as the transition from a
> closed society to an open one; it is impotent by nature to infuse
> its protest with the hope of a new assent to the world: it wants to
> die, to say so, and it wants everything to die with it. The often
> fascinating liberation it imposes on language is actually a sentence
> without appeal: all sociability is abhorrent to it, and rightly so,
> since it refuses to perceive sociability on any but the bourgeois
> model.[29]

Robert Altman liberated filmic language from the old models but cannot (will not) liberate a social vision. He found a point of escape out of the dead hand of Hollywood filmmaking, but could not go beyond visions of the closed, oppressive society that his liberated language addressed. In Hollywood, however, any deviation, any pretense toward the *avant-garde*, to *difference* is cause for repression. For his pains, his failure, and his success, the owners of cinema removed their already parsimonious support. But Altman has played a good game. His films were and, though somewhat restrained by their economic poverty, still are energetically involved in the conflict. He will never "infuse [his] protest with the hope of a new assent to the world," or perceive sociability on any but bourgeois models, but neither will he assent to the world or to film as it is. He has successfully influenced a new filmmaker, Alan Rudolph, who is one of the few people in commercial American cinema to share Altman's delight in opening up narratives to the play of their peripheries and to images that deflect away from, rather than toward, the dead center of plot. And, in the face of all odds, Altman has himself begun a new career and a new place of operations in Paris with a body of films that still fly in the face of commercial expectations and which, in time, will redefine the relationship of film to theater.

Although he remains trapped in the ideology of losing, of gaining and then losing, of profit and loss, Altman has more generosity, more sense of possibilities than anyone making commercial film in America. The other directors I have discussed here, even in their experimentation, seem determined to match narrative form and content, to deploy images of loneliness and entrapment, isolation and fear, to reinforce that desperate perception we have of ourselves. If any of their characters prevail, it is for a while only, and they seem only to prevail in order to make their fall all the more hard. When they do succeed—as Spielberg's characters do—their success is so fantastic, so predicated on spectacular events far removed from the social realities of everyday life, that they cancel out the very affirmation they seek to make. They leave their viewers lonely with reality. Altman, when he offers the plurality of a cinematically mediated world in its fullness and variety, at least presents the opportunity of seeing more, of perhaps seeing beyond the prison that our contemporary cinema seems dead set on insisting we inhabit.

And there is in Altman's work always the hope, and sometimes the reality, that someone, even if it is a fictional surrogate for Richard M. Nixon, will raise his fist and call out loud and clear—"Fuck 'em!"

# NOTES

## PREFACE TO THE SECOND EDITION

1. If there was little agreement on a definition of modernism, there is even less on postmodernism. One excellent source is Fredric Jameson, "Postmodernism and Consumer Society," in *The Anti-Aesthetic: Essays on Postmodern Culture*, ed. Hal Foster (Port Townsend, Washington: Bay Press, 1983), 111–25. See also the essays in Jonathan Arc, ed., *Postmodernism and Politics* (Minneapolis: University of Minnesota Press), 1986.
2. For a good discussion and defense of *auteur*ism, see Robert Self, "Robert Altman and the Theory of Authorship," *Cinema Journal* 25 (Fall 1985), 3–11.
3. Alan Williams, "Is Sound Recording Like an Image?" *Yale French Studies*, No. 60 (1980), 59.
4. Edward Buscombe, "Film History and the Idea of a National Cinema," *Australian Journal of Screen Theory*, Nos. 9–10 (1981), 150.

## INTRODUCTION

1. Some of the ideas for the decline of Hollywood production values and shifts in studio personnel during the late forties were developed with David Parker and Douglas Gomery. An excellent summary of the changes in Hollywood from the late forties through the sixties—from which much of the information in this section is drawn—can be found in Robert Sklar, *Movie-Made América: A Cultural History of American Movies* (New York: Ran-

dom House, 1975), 249–304. See also Gordon Gow, *Hollywood in the Fifties* (New York: A. S. Barnes, 1971); John Baxter, *Hollywood in the Sixties* (New York: A. S. Barnes, 1972); Axel Madsen, *The New Hollywood: American Movies in the Seventies* (New York: Crowell, 1975); William Paul, "Hollywood Harakiri," *Film Comment* 13 (March-April 1977); Stephen M. Silverman, "Hollywood Cloning: Sequels, Prequels, Remakes, and Spinoffs," *American Film* 3 (July-August 1978), 24–30. For an excellent study of the financial character of the studios, see Douglas Gomery, "The American Film Industry of the 1970s: Stasis in the 'New Hollywood'," *Wide Angle* 5, No. 4 (1983), 52–59.

2. See Michael Rosenthal, "Ideology, Determinism, and Relative Autonomy," *Jump Cut*, No. 17 (April 1978), 19–22.

3. See James Monaco, *The New Wave* (New York: Oxford University Press, 1976), 3–12. Monaco's is the best study of the French movement and has served as something of a model for this book.

4. In the seventies and eighties, filmmaking in France has fallen on hard times. The initial cohesion is gone, and while critical commitment remained strong—at least until the early eighties—production has reverted to the classical, linear style. Many French films are now made with an American audience in mind. See David L. Overby, "France: The Newest Wave," *Sight and Sound* 47 (Spring 1978), 86–90; Annette Insdorf, "French Films American Style," *New York Times* (July 28, 1985), P. H16.

5. Many people have examined the phenomenon of film effacing its existence as film. Two out of many possible references are Colin MacCabe, "Realism and the Cinema: Notes on Some Brechtian Theses," *Tracking the Signifier* (Minneapolis: University of Minnesota Press, 1985), 33–57; Christian Metz, *The Imaginary Signifier*, trans. Celia Britton, Annwyl Williams, Ben Brewster, Alfred Guzzetti (Bloomington: Indiana University Press, 1982), 3–68. For the idea of fiction as lie and substitution, see Umberto Eco, *A Theory of Semiotics* (Bloomington and London: Indiana University Press, 1976), 6–7.

6. *Language and Materialism* (London: Routledge & Kegan Paul, 1977), 67. The second quotation from Althusser comes from *For Marx*, trans. Ben Brewster (New York: Random House, Vintage Books, 1970), 252. For a direct application of ideological theory to cinema studies, see: Jean-Louis Comolli and Jean Narboni, "Cinema/Ideology/Criticism," in Bill Nichols, ed., *Movies and Methods*, Vol. I (Berkeley and Los Angeles: University of California Press, 1976), 23–30; Editors of *Cahiers du Cinéma*, "John Ford's Young Mr. Lincoln," in *Movies and Methods* I, 493–529. The April 1978 issue of *Jump Cut* (No. 17) has an excellent series of essays summarizing the issue. See also Bill Nichols, *Ideology and the Image* (Bloomington: Indiana University Press, 1981).

7. *Literary Theory* (Minneapolis: University of Minneapolis Press, 1983), 172, 210.

8. Rosenthal, "Ideology, Determinism."
9. Some tentative work is beginning. See Richard Dyer, *Stars* (London: The British Film Institute, 1979); *Wide Angle* 6, No. 4 (1985), has a number of essays on film acting, though most of these are on history and economics.

# 1. ARTHUR PENN

1. Cf. Diane Jacobs, *Hollywood Renaissance* (South Brunswick, N.J., and New York: A. S. Barnes, 1977), 35–37.
2. Robin Wood, *Arthur Penn* (New York: Frederick A. Praeger, 1969), 44.
3. Alexandre Astruc, "The Birth of the New Avant-Garde: *La Caméra-Stylo,*" in *The New Wave*, ed. Peter Graham (New York: Doubleday, 1968), 17–23.
4. Paul Schrader, "Notes on Film Noir," *Film Comment* 8 (Spring 1972), 8.
5. A great deal has been written about *film noir*. Schrader's article remains the best. Other works include the November-December 1974 issue of *Film Comment*, devoted to *noir*; Larry Gross, "Film Après Noir", *Film Comment* 12 (July-August 1976), 44–49; Charles Higham and Joel Greenberg, *Hollywood in the Forties* (New York: Paperback Library, 1970), 19–55; J. A. Place and L. S. Peterson, "Some Visual Motifs of Film Noir," *Film Comment* 10 (January-February 1974), reprinted in *Movies and Methods*, I, 325–38; Robert G. Porfirio, "No Way Out: Existential Motifs in The Film Noir," *Sight and Sound* 45 (Autumn 1976), 212–17; John Tuska, *The Detective in Hollywood* (Garden City, N. Y.: Doubleday, 1978), 339–42. Alain Silver and Elizabeth Ward, *Film Noir: An Encyclopedic Reference to the American Style* (Woodstock, N.Y.: Overlook Press, 1979); E. Ann Kaplan, ed., *Women in Film Noir* (London: BFI Publishing, 1980). For a thorough, cross-indexed filmography, see John S. Whitney, "A Filmography of Film Noir," *Journal of Popular Film* 5 (1976), 321–71. For background on the technological changes that made *noir* possible, see Barry Salt, "Film Style and Technology in the Thirties," *Film Quarterly* 30 (Fall 1976), 19–32, and "Film Style and Technology in the Forties," *Film Quarterly* 31 (Fall 1977), 46–57.
6. The essays in *Women in Film Noir* cover many aspects of this central generic problem.
7. Wood, *Arthur Penn*, 44–45.
8. *Dreams and Dead Ends: The American Gangster/Crime Film* (Cambridge, Mass.: MIT Press, 1977), 288, 303–4. It is important to note that Shadoian does not approve of this self-consciousness.
9. John G. Cawelti, "The Artistic Power of *Bonnie and Clyde,*" in *Focus on Bonnie and Clyde*, ed. Cawelti (Englewood Cliffs, N. J.: Prentice-Hall, 1973), 57. Cawelti's is a major essay on the film and there are some parallels with what is discussed here, the most important of which are noted.

10. *Ibid.*, 59–60. For another view of sexuality in the film, particularly for the sympathy aroused by Clyde's impotence, see Wood, *Arthur Penn*, 84–86.

11. For a discussion of shot length see Barry Salt, "Statistical Analysis of Motion Pictures," *Film Quarterly* 28 (Fall 1974), 13–22. Daniel Dayan's essay, "The Tutor-Code of Classical Cinema," in *Movies and Methods*, I, 439–51, is the classic discussion of the structure and ideology of the shot/reverse shot. See also Nick Browne, "The Spectator-in-the-Text: The Rhetoric of *Stagecoach*," *Film Quarterly* 29 (Winter 1975–76), 26–38, reprinted in Nichols, ed. *Movies and Methods*, Vol. II (Berkeley, Los Angeles, London, University of California Press: 1985), 459–75.

12. Many writers have addressed themselves to the vitality of the characters set against the barrenness of the landscape they inhabit (see, for example, Stephen Farber, "The Outlaws," *Sight and Sound* 37 (Autumn 1968), 174–75). Some have found their situation revolutionary and praised it (Peter Harcourt, "In Defense of Film History," *Perspectives on the Study of Film*, ed. John Stuart Katz (Boston: Little Brown, 1971), 266–69) or condemned it (Charles Thomas Samuels, in *Focus on Bonnie and Clyde*, 85–92). As should become clear, I do not see the film as a call to revolution, but, to the contrary, as a warning against being too free.

13. Richard Burgess brought this to my attention.

14. Cawelti, "Artistic Power of *Bonnie and Clyde*," 79.

15. *Ibid.*, 82.

16. For the car as icon in gangster films, see Colin McArthur, *Underworld USA* (New York: Viking Press, 1972), 30–33.

17. Robert Warshow, "The Gangster as Tragic Hero," in *The Immediate Experience* (Garden City, N.Y.: Doubleday, 1962), 127–33. See also my article, "Night to Day," *Sight and Sound* 43 (Autumn 1974), 236–39.

18. Shadoian, *Dreams and Dead Ends*, 1–6.

19. Cawelti, "Artistic Power of *Bonnie and Clyde*," 79–84.

20. Michael Walker, "*Night Moves*," *Movie*, No. 22 (Spring 1976), 37–38.

21. *Ibid.*, 38.

## 2. STANLEY KUBRICK

1. John Russell Taylor, *Directors and Directions: Cinema for the Seventies* (New York: Hill and Wang, 1975), 132.

2. Robin Wood discusses the matter of the horror film and family madness in *Hollywood from Vietnam to Reagan* (New York: Columbia University Press, 1986), 84, 150ff. In this and other matters, Wood's insights and mine are often closely aligned.

3. I have not seen *Fear and Desire*. Description and some analysis of Kubrick's earlier work can be found in three book-length studies of his films: Norman

Kagan, *The Cinema of Stanley Kubrick* (New York: Holt, Rinehart and Winston, 1972); Gene D. Phillips, *Stanley Kubrick: A Film Odyssey* (New York: Popular Library, 1977); Alexander Walker, *Stanley Kubrick Directs* (New York: Harcourt Brace Jovanovich, 1971). Another fine full-length study, and a beautiful piece of production, is Michel Ciment, *Kubrick*, trans. Gilbert Adair (New York: Holt, Rinehart and Winston, 1984). Each of these books, and Walker's in particular, has been of use in the study that follows. Walker's discussion of Kubrick's use of space is a special influence. See also Thomas Allen Nelson, *Kubrick: Inside a Film Artist's Maze* (Bloomington: Indiana University Press, 1982).

4. Walker, *Stanley Kubrick Directs*, 55–66.

5. Welles himself refers to his work as labyrinthine. Although Kubrick has mentioned Max Ophuls as an influence on his moving camera (see Walker, *Stanley Kubrick Directs*, 16), the influence of Welles is much more evident (see Terry Comito, "Touch of Evil," *Film Comment* 7 (Summer 1971), 51–53).

6. Quoted by Dilys Powell in Peter Cowie, *A Ribbon of Dreams: The Cinema of Orson Welles* (South Brunswick, N. J., and New York: A. S. Barnes, 1973), 27–28.

7. So great is the communal need in Ford that in his later films the individual who is asocial by his nature and inclination—Ethan Edwards in *The Searchers*, Tom Doniphon in *The Man Who Shot Liberty Valance* (both characters played by John Wayne)—removes himself so the communal unit may survive. (See Joseph McBride and Michael Wilmington, "Prisoner of the Desert," *Sight and Sound* 40 (Autumn 1971), 210–14). The notion that Ford became less interested in deep focus cinematography when he began to work in color was suggested by Joe Miller.

8. Cf. Walker, *Stanley Kubrick Directs*, 84; Kagan, *The Cinema of Stanley Kubrick*, 65.

9. Walker, *Stanley Kubrick Directs*, 112, emphasizes the enclosed, geometric situating of the figures during the courts-martial.

10. For Kubrick and the fifties, cf. Kagan, *The Cinema of Stanley Kubrick*, 64–66. For an excellent discussion of the "end of ideology" syndrome, see Roland Barthes, "Neither-Nor Criticism," in *Mythologies*, trans. Annette Lavers (New York: Hill and Wang, 1972), 81–83. Ideas on the interpretation of history in the eighties were suggested by Angela Dalle Vacche, "History, the Real Thing in Postmodern Culture," a paper delivered at the Society for Cinema Studies, May 1987. The irony of the woman sniper in *Full Metal Jacket* was suggested by Rita Kempley, " 'Full Metal Jacket': Indirect Hit," *The Washington Post*, June 26, 1987, p. B1.

11. Cf. P. L. Titterington, "Kubrick and 'The Shining'," *Sight and Sound* 50 (Spring 1981), 119.

12. Walker, *Stanley Kubrick Directs*, 160–62. Margot Kernan pointed out to me the significance of the first line of dialogue cited later in the text.

13. *Sade, Fourier, Loyola*, trans. Richard Miller (New York: Hill and Wang, 1976), 33–34.

14. Gerald Mast, *The Comic Mind* (Indianapolis and New York: Bobbs-Merrill, 1973), 317, 319. See also F. A. Macklin, "Sex and *Dr. Strangelove*," *Film Comment* 3 (Summer 1965), 55–57.

15. "Kubrick's films have always dealt with characters who mechanized themselves. . . ." Don Daniels, "A Skeleton Key to *2001*," *Sight and Sound* 40 (Winter 1970–71), 32. The mechanization of human behavior has been long recognized as a major element in Kubrick's work.

16. *Anatomy of Criticism* (Princeton: Princeton University Press, 1957), 224–25. Most commentators on the film have seen it as satire. What follows is an attempt to clarify the details of the generic form.

17. *Signs and Meaning in the Cinema* (Bloomington: Indiana University Press, 1972), 164 and *passim*. See also Roland Barthes, *S/Z*, trans. Richard Miller (New York: Hill and Wang, 1974), 10–11.

18. Theories of the subject and its placement in and outside the fictional narrative have received much attention. Two general treatments can be found in Kaja Silverman, *The Subject of Semiotics* (New York: Oxford University Press, 1983), and Terry Eagleton, *Literary Theory*, 127–193.

19. Kagan, *The Cinema of Stanley Kubrick*, 161–62.

20. *Directors and Directions*, 129–32.

21. "This Typeface Is Changing Your Life," *Village Voice*, June 7, 1976, pp. 116–17. Fredric Jameson writes, "form is immanently and intrinsically an ideology in its own right" (*The Political Unconscious: Narrative as a Socially Symbolic Act* (Ithaca: Cornell University Press, 1981), 141).

22. *Expanded Cinema* (New York: Dutton, 1970), 140–46.

23. "Fascinating Fascism," in *Movies and Methods*, I, 40.

24. Cf. Jonathan Rosenbaum, "The Solitary Pleasures of *Star Wars*," *Sight and Sound* 46 (Autumn 1977), 209.

25. For the ending of *Star Wars*, see Rosenbaum, "Solitary Pleasures"; for a more detailed analysis of the politics of Spielberg's film, see Robert Entman and Francie Seymour, "*Close Encounters of the Third Kind*: Close Encounters with the Third Reich," *Jump Cut*, No. 18 (August 15, 1978), 3–5; and Tony Williams, "Close Encounters of the Authoritarian Kind," *Wide Angle* 5, No 4 (1983), 22–29. I will deal more thoroughly with the form and substance of Spielberg's work later in the book.

26. François Truffaut, *Hitchcock*, trans. Helen G. Scott, rev. ed. (New York: Simon and Schuster, 1983), 282.

27. Cf. Robert Hughes, "The Decor of Tomorrow's Hell," *Time* (December 27, 1971), p. 59.

28. Anthony Burgess, *A Clockwork Orange* (New York: Norton, 1963), 158. My thanks to Richard Simmons for helping me connect the names.

29. For another, more favorable reading of the film, which attempts to fit it into a pattern within Kubrick's work, see Hans Feldmann, "Kubrick and His

Discontents," *Film Quarterly* 30 (Fall 1976), 12–19. See also Nelson, *Kubrick*, 133–64.

30. Mark Crispin Miller, "*Barry Lyndon* Reconsidered," *Georgia Review* 30 (Winter 1976), 843.

31. Cf. Michael Dempsey, "*Barry Lyndon*," *Film Quarterly* 30 (Fall 1976), 50.

32. Alan Spiegel, "Kubrick's *Barry Lyndon*," *Salmagundi* (Summer-Fall, 1977), 204.

33. Cf. Miller, "*Barry Lyndon* Reconsidered," 834–35. Feldmann, "Kubrick and His Discontents," 14, discusses the ritual of eating in *2001*.

34. Spiegel, "Kubrick's *Barry Lyndon*," 199.

35. Feldmann, "Kubrick and His Discontents," 17.

36. Spiegel, "Kubrick's *Barry Lyndon*," 206.

37. Cf. Feldmann's analysis in "Kubrick and His Discontents," 18. Spiegel, "Kubrick's *Barry Lyndon*," 201, fully analyzes the symmetrical repetitions in the film.

38. Cf. Feldmann, "Kubrick and His Discontents," 17.

39. Cf. Andrew Sarris, "What Makes Barry Run," *Village Voice*, December 29, 1975, pp. 111–12.

40. Michel Foucault discusses the concept of the all-seeing gaze in *Discipline and Punish: The Birth of the Prison*, trans. Allen Sheridan (New York: Vintage Books, 1979), 195–228. The classic essay on the male gaze in cinema is Laura Mulvey, "Visual Pleasure and Narrative Cinema," in *Movies and Methods*, II, 305–15. For another discussion of patriarchal structures in the film, see Flo Liebowitz and Lynn Jeffries, "*The Shining*," *Film Quarterly* 34 (Spring 1981), 46, 48. See also Greg Keeler, "*The Shining*: Ted Kramer Has a Nightmare," *The Journal of Popular Film and Television* 8, No. 4 (Winter 1981), 2–8, cited in Vivian Sobchack, "Child/Alien/Father: Patriarchal Crisis and Generic Exchange," *Camera Obscura*, No. 15 (1986), 15.

41. The stereotyping of women in the horror film is discussed by Gérard Lenne, "Monster and Victim," in *Sexual Stratagems: The World of Women in Film*, ed. Patricia Erens (New York: Horizon Press, 1979), 31–40.

## 3. MARTIN SCORSESE

1. For a discussion of this generation of filmmakers, see Michael Pye and Lynda Myles, *The Movie Brats; How the Film Generation Took Over Hollywood* (New York: Holt, Rinehart & Winston, 1979).

2. *Point of View in the Cinema: A Theory of Narration and Subjectivity in Classical Film* (Berlin, New York, Amsterdam: Mouton Publishers, 1984), 57.

3. Cf. Leo Braudy, "The Sacraments of Genre: Coppola, DePalma, Scorsese," *Film Quarterly* 39 (Spring 1986), 17–28.

4. Jacobs, *Hollywood Renaissance*, 124.

5. Pye & Myles, *The Movie Brats*, 192.

6. *Godard on Godard*, trans. Tom Milne (New York: Viking Press, 1972), 21, 28.

7. David Denby, "Mean Streets: The Sweetness of Hell," *Sight and Sound* 43 (Winter 1973/74), 50.

8. *Ibid.*, 48–49.

9. Braudy points out Scorsese's response to Stallone in "Sacraments of Genre," 26.

10. Braudy discusses the commentary on celebrity in Scorsese's recent work and uses the term "sacrament," *ibid.*, 26–27.

11. Lotte Eisner, *The Haunted Screen*, trans. Roger Greaves (Berkeley and Los Angeles: University of California Press, 1973), 23–24.

12. See Michael Dempsey, "Taxi Driver," *Film Quarterly* 29 (Summer 1976), 37–41; Jacobs, *Hollywood Renaissance*, 143–44. See also Robert B. Ray, *A Certain Tendency of the Hollywood Cinema, 1930–1980* (Princeton: Princeton University Press, 1985), 349–60. I have not examined the original, but the description of Travis Bickle that appears in a script extract published in *Film Comment* 12 (March-April 1976), 12, does present him in extravagantly romantic terms, very different from the character created by Scorsese and De Niro in the film. See also Schrader's comments on his script in the same issue of *Film Comment*.

13. *Transcendental Style in Film: Ozu, Bresson, Dreyer* (Berkeley and Los Angeles: University of California Press, 1972), 72.

14. "Notes on *Film Noir*," 12, 13. Colin Westerbeck notes the *noir* influence via Schrader in "Beauties and the Beast," *Sight and Sound* 45 (Summer 1976), 138.

15. See Fredric Jameson, *The Prison-House of Language* (Princeton: Princeton University Press, 1972), 50–53.

16. Jacobs, *Hollywood Renaissance*, 146. Jacobs does speak of the camera reflecting Travis's state of mind.

17. Patricia Patterson and Manny Farber, "The Power and the Gory," *Film Comment* 12 (May-June 1976), 29.

18. See Peter Birge and Janet Maslin, "Getting Snuffed in Boston," *Film Comment* 13 (May-June 1976), 35, 63.

19. The view of Patterson and Farber, "Power and the Gory," 30.

20. See *ibid.*, 27.

21. Cf. Robin Wood, *Hitchcock's Films* (New York: Paperback Library, 1970), 132–33; Raymond Durgnat, *Films and Feelings* (Cambridge, Mass.: MIT Press, 1971), 217–18.

22. Steve Mamber discusses the imitation of the television style in *The King of Comedy* in "Parody, Intertextuality, and Signatured: Kubrick, DePalma, and Scorsese," a paper delivered at the Society for Cinema Studies, April 1986.

23. Richard Combs, "Where Angels Fear to Tread: *After Hours*," *Sight and Sound* 55 (Summer 1986), 208.

24. For a discussion of the form of comedy, see Northrop Frye, *Anatomy of Criticism*, 43–48.

25. See Molly Haskell, *From Reverence to Rape* (New York: Holt, Rinehart and Winston, 1974), 126–30. For an opposite view of the screwball comedy, see Tom Powers, "His Girl Friday: Screwball Liberation," *Jump Cut* (April 1978), 25–27.

26. Jacobs, *Hollywood Renaissance*, 141–42, covers some of the points discussed here.

27. See Kevin Brownlow, "Telluride," *Sight and Sound* 47 (Winter 1977–78), 27.

28. *Film Comment* 14 (September-October 1978), 64.

29. Braudy refers to the mutilations and to Hackett becoming his own art object, "Sacraments of Genre," 26–27.

30. In Terrence Rafferty, "High Stakes," *Sight and Sound* 55 (Autumn 1986), 265.

# 4. SPIELBERG

1. Garry Wills, *Reagan's America: Innocents At Home* (New York: Doubleday, 1987), 388.

2. "Ideology and Ideological State Apparatuses," *Lenin and Philosophy*, trans. Ben Brewster (New York, London: Monthly Review Press, 1971), 173, 172. Italics in original. This concept of ideological address or "hailing" is discussed by Silverman, *The Subject of Semiotics*, 48–50. For discussion of the formal structures of ideology, see Fredric Jameson, *The Political Unconscious*, 140–45.

3. *Wide Angle* 7, No. 4 (1985), contains a number of essays on cinematic treatments of the Vietnamese war.

4. See Aljean Harmetz, *The Making of The Wizard of Oz* (New York: Limelight Editions, 1984), 51.

5. *The Political Unconscious*, 171.

6. *Ibid.*

7. See Althusser, "Freud and Lacan," *Lenin and Philosophy*, 189–219; Metz, *The Imaginary Signifier*, and, for a fascinating meditation on film, narrative, and Oedipus, Teresa De Lauretis, *Alice Doesn't: Feminism, Semiotics, Cinema* (Bloomington: Indiana University Press, 1984). Robin Wood, in *Hollywood from Vietnam to Reagan*, and his article on recent American film, "80s Hollywood: Dominant Tendencies," in *CineAction!* 1 (Spring 1985), 2–5, discusses Oedipus, the patriarchy, and the spectator as child in an analysis that runs parallel to my own. See also Sobchack, "Child/Alien/Father: Patriarchal Crisis and Generic Exchange."

8. David Parker reminded me of this. For the representation of Roosevelt in film, see Dana Polan, *Power and Paranoia: History, Narrative, and the*

*American Cinema, 1940–1950* (New York: Columbia University Press, 1986), 66–67.

9. "The Voice in the Cinema: The Articulation of Body and Space," *Yale French Studies*, No. 60, p. 50.

10. The idea of Spielberg's films as machine is in Stephen Heath, "*Jaws*, Ideology, and Film Theory," in *Movies and Methods*, II, 512, and James Monaco, *American Film Now* (New York: Oxford University Press, 1979), 176–77. Monaco also briefly discusses the beach sequence and Hitchcock zoom in *Jaws* that I will treat in detail further on.

11. See Dana Polan, " 'Above All Else to Make You See': Cinema and the Ideology of the Spectacle," *Postmodernism and Politics*, 59.

12. See Heath, "*Jaws*, Ideology, and Film Theory," 510–11.

13. "Ideological Effects of the Basic Cinematographic Apparatus," trans. Allan Williams, in *Movies and Methods*, II, 537. See also Branigan, *Point of View in the Cinema*, 73–100.

14. Heath in "*Jaws*, Ideology, and Film Theory," 511. For a discussion of the three male figures, see Wood, *Hollywood from Vietnam to Reagan*, 177. Fredric Jameson offers a fascinating reading of Quint's death as "the twofold symbolic destruction of an older America—the America of small business and individual private enterprise of a now outmoded kind, but also the America of the New Deal and the crusade against Nazism, the older America of the depression and the war and of the heyday of classical liberalism" ("Reification and Utopia," *Social Text* 1 (1979), 143–44).

15. Frank P. Tomasulo provides an interesting mythic/political reading of *Raiders* in "Mr. Jones Goes to Washington: Myth and Religion in *Raiders of the Lost Ark*," *Quarterly Review of Film Studies* 7 (Fall 1982), 331–38. He points out that in a 1952 anti-Communist film entitled *Hong Kong*, the actor, Ronald Reagan, is seen wearing "leather jacket, brimmed felt hat, three days' growth"—an earlier image of Indiana Jones.

16. For a lucid account of this complicated theory, see Nichols, *Ideology and the Image*, 30–33, and Christine Gledhill, "Recent Developments in Feminist Film Theory," *Quarterly Review of Film Studies* 3 (Fall 1978), 476–80.

17. See Wood, *Hollywood from Reagan to Vietnam*, 176.

18. Metz, *The Imaginary Signifier*, 49, 54.

19. *The Post-Modern Condition: A Report on Knowledge*, trans. Geoff Bennington and Brian Massumi (Minneapolis: University of Minnesota Press, 1983).

20. A fascinating and strange political reading of the oedipal process is offered by Gilles Deleuze and Félix Guattari in *Anti-Oedipus: Capitalism and Schizophrenia*, trans. Robert Hurley, Mark Seem, Helen R. Lane (Minneapolis: University of Minnesota Press, 1983). They use the image of the body as machine.

21. Alice Walker, *The Color Purple* (New York: Simon & Schuster, 1985), 129.

22. "Above All Else to Make You See," 63.

23. *The Function of Criticism: From The Spectator to Post-Structuralism* (London: Verso, 1984), 121–22.

## 5. ROBERT ALTMAN

1. Gary Arnold, "Filmmaker Robert Altman—Back in the Swim," *Washington Post* (May 8, 1977), p. E4.
2. Some information on Altman's career comes from Gerard Plecki, *Robert Altman* (Boston: Twayne Publishers, 1985), 103–26.
3. See Robert Self, "Robert Altman and the Theory of Authorship."
4. The ideological differences between Eisenstein and Griffith were most clearly articulated by Eisenstein himself. See his essay "Dickens, Griffith, and the Film Today," in *Film Form*, trans. Jay Leyda (New York: Harcourt Brace Jovanovich, 1969), 195–225. See also Noël Burch, *Theory of Film Practice*, trans. Helen R. Lane (New York: Praeger, 1973), 17–30; André Bazin, *Jean Renoir*, trans. W. W. Halsey II and William H. Simon (New York: Simon and Schuster, 1973), 87–91. Bazin's seminal writings on the long take and deep focus cinematography are contained in *What Is Cinema?*, Vol. I, trans. Hugh Gray (Berkeley and Los Angeles: University of California Press, 1967). For a wide-ranging, speculative essay on the problems of screen space, see Stephen Heath, "Narrative Space," *Questions of Cinema* (Bloomington: Indiana University Press, 1981), 19–75. A number of critics have indicated the Renoir influences on Altman.
5. For a fuller analysis of *The Man Who Shot Liberty Valance*, see William Luhr and Peter Lehman, *Authorship and Narrative in the Cinema* (New York: G. P. Putnam's Sons, 1977), 45–84. The notion of *découpage* comes from Burch, *Theory of Film Practice*, 4.
6. See Paul Joannides, "The Aesthetics of the Zoom Lens," *Sight and Sound* 40 (Winter 1970–71), 40–42.
7. For a detailed description of the camera work in *The Long Goodbye* see Michael Tarantino, "Movement as Metaphor: *The Long Goodbye*," *Sight and Sound* 44 (Spring 1975), 98–102. In the same issue, Jonathan Rosenbaum's essay "Improvisations and Interactions in Altmanville" (91–95) considers the narrative dislocations in the film.
8. I borrow the notion of "deconstruction" very loosely from Jacques Derrida; cf. *Of Grammatology*, trans. Gayatri Chakravorty Spivak (Baltimore and London: Johns Hopkins University Press, 1976). See also Jonathan Culler, *On Deconstruction* (Ithaca: Cornell University Press, 1982).
9. Cf. Jacobs, *Hollywood Renaissance*, 71.
10. As a student of mine, anxious to love the film, once suggested.
11. See Stefan Fleischer, "A Study Through Stills of *My Darling Clementine*," *Journal of Modern Literature* 3 (April 1973), 243–52.

12. Michael Dempsey sees the hope for community more positively stated than I do. See his essay "Altman: The Empty Staircase and the Chinese Princess," *Film Comment* 10 (September-October 1974), 14–17. For an excellent survey of Altman's treatment of romantic love and the couple, see Robert Self, "The Perfect Couple: 'Two Are Halves of One' in the Films of Robert Altman," *Wide Angle* 5, No. 4 (1983), 30–37. Self refers to the unusual romanticism in the film *A Perfect Couple*, 36.

13. Jacobs, *Hollywood Renaissance*, 66.

14. I owe this insight to John Pacy.

15. See the analysis of detective fiction by Tzvetan Todorov, in *The Poetics of Prose*, trans. Richard Howard (Ithaca, N. Y: Cornell University Press, 1977), 42–52.

16. Two excellent essays review the history of Marlowe on the screen: James Monaco, "Notes on *The Big Sleep*, Thirty Years After," *Sight and Sound* 44 (Winter 1974–75), 34–38; Charles Gregory, "Knight Without Meaning?" *Sight and Sound* 42 (Summer 1973), 155–59. The following analysis is indebted to them.

17. Edward Branigan talks about the notion of point of view projected into the *mise-en-scène*. See *Point of View in the Cinema*, 137–38.

18. "Improvisations and Interactions," 95.

19. The best discussion of this phenomenon is in Joan Mellon, *Big Bad Wolves: Masculinity in the American Film* (New York: Pantheon, 1977), 311–25.

20. Cf. Rosenbaum, "Improvisations and Interactions," 91.

21. *Nashville* (New York: Bantam, 1976), 3. Altman made the "metaphor of America" comment in *Newsweek*; cf. John Yates, "Smart Man's Burden: *Nashville*, *A Face in the Crowd*, and Popular Culture," *Journal of Popular Film*, 5 (1976), 23.

22. Karen Stabiner, "*Buffalo Bill and the Indians*," *Film Quarterly* 30 (Fall 1976), 55. Joan Mellon has a good discussion of the myths of male supremacy that are attacked in the film; *Big Bad Wolves*, 339–41.

23. Cf. Self, "Robert Altman and the Theory of Authorship," 8–9.

24. See Richard Combs, "*Fool for Love*," *Monthly Film Bulletin* 53 (July 1986), 196.

25. For a discussion of the film as dream, see Marsha Kinder, "The Art of Dreaming in *Three Women* and *Providence*: Structures of the Self," *Film Quarterly* 31 (Fall 1977), 10–18.

26. See Alice Ostriker, "The Thieves of Language," in *The New Feminist Criticism*, ed. Elaine Showalter (New York: Pantheon Books, 1985), 314–38.

27. Margot Kernan helped develop this argument.

28. For a parallel argument, see Leonard Quart, "On Altman: Image as Essence," *Marxist Perspectives* 1 (Spring 1978), 118–25.

29. "Whose Theater? Whose *Avant-Garde*?" *Critical Essays*, trans. Richard Howard (Evanston: Northwestern University Press, 1972), 67–69.

# FILMOGRAPHY

A listing of major, full-length theatrical features. The notation "Panavision" following the Photography credit indicates anamorphic ratio. Videotape versions do not reproduce the full width of the original frame.


## ARTHUR PENN

### 1958    THE LEFT-HANDED GUN

Script: Leslie Stevens, from the play by Gore Vidal.
Direction: Penn.
Photography (b&w): J. Peverell Marley.
Art direction: Art Loel.
Editing: Folmar Blangsted.
Music: Alexander Courage.
Ballad: William Goyen and Alexander Courage.
  Cast: Paul Newman (*William Bonney*), Lita Milan (*Celsa*), John Dehner (*Pat Garrett*), Hurd Hatfield (*Moultrie*), James Congdon (*Charlie Boudre*), James Best (*Tom Folliard*), Colin Keith-Johnston (*Tunstall*), John Dierkes (*McSween*), Bob Anderson (*Hill*), Wally Brown (*Moon*), Ainslie Pryor (*Joe Grant*), Marten Garralaga (*Saval*), Denver

Pyle (*Ollinger*), Paul Smith (*Bell*), Nestor Paiva (*Maxwell*), Jo Summers (*Mrs. Garrett*), Robert Foulk (*Brady*), Anne Barton (*Mrs. Hill*).

Produced by Fred Coe (Harroll Productions) for Warner Brothers. 102 min.

## 1962    THE MIRACLE WORKER

Script: William Gibson, from his play.
Direction: Penn.
Photography (b&w): Ernest Caparros.
Art direction: George Jenkins, Mel Bourne.
Editing: Aram Avakian.
Music: Laurence Rosenthal.

Cast: Anne Bancroft (*Annie Sullivan*), Patty Duke (*Helen Keller*), Victor Jory (*Captain Keller*), Inga Swenson (*Kate Keller*), Andrew Prine (*James Keller*), Kathleen Comegys (*Aunt Ev*), Beah Richards (*Viney*), Jack Hollender (*Mr. Anagnes*).

Produced by Fred Coe (Playfilms) for United Artists. 106 min.

## 1964    MICKEY ONE

Script: Alan Surgal.
Direction: Penn.
Photography (b&w): Ghislain Cloquet.
Production design: George Jenkins.
Editing: Aram Avakian.
Music: Eddie Sauter, improvisations by Stan Getz.

Cast: Warren Beatty (*Mickey*), Alexandra Stewart (*Jenny*), Hurd Hatfield (*Castle*), Franchot Tone (*Ruby Lapp*), Teddy Hart (*Breson*), Jeff Corey (*Fryer*), Kamatari Fujiwara (*the artist*), Donna Michell (*the girl*), Ralph Foody (*police captain*), Norman Gottschalk (*the evangelist*), Dick Lucas (*employment agent*), Benny Dunn (*nightclub comic*), Helen Witkowski (*landlady*), Mike Fish (*Italian restaurant owner*).

Produced by Arthur Penn (A Florin/Tatira Production) for Columbia. 93 min.

## 1966    THE CHASE

Script: Lillian Hellman, based on the novel and play by Horton Foote.
Direction: Penn.
Photography (Panavision): Joseph LaShelle and (uncredited) Robert Surtees.

Production design: Richard Day
Editing: Gene Milford.
Music: John Barry.

Cast: Marlon Brando (*Sheriff Calder*), Jane Fonda (*Anna Reeves*), Robert Redford (*Bubber Reeves*), E. G. Marshall (*Val Rogers*), Angie Dickinson (*Ruby Calder*), Janice Rule (*Emily Stewart*), Miriam Hopkins (*Mrs. Reeves*), Martha Hyer (*Mary Puller*), Richard Bradford (*Damon Puller*), Robert Duvall (*Edwin Stewart*), James Fox (*Jake Jason Rogers*), Diana Hyland (*Elizabeth Rogers*), Henry Hull (*Briggs*), Jocelyn Brando (*Mrs. Briggs*), Steve Ihnat (*Archie*).

Produced by Sam Spiegel (Lone Star/Horizon) for Columbia. 135 min.

## 1967    BONNIE AND CLYDE

Script: David Newman and Robert Benton.
Direction: Penn.
Photography: Burnett Guffey.
Art direction: Dean Tavoularis.
Editing: Dede Allen.
Music: Charles Strouse, Flatt and Scruggs.
Costumes: Theadora van Runkle.
Special consultant: Robert Towne.

Cast: Warren Beatty (*Clyde Barrow*), Faye Dunaway (*Bonnie Parker*), Michael J. Pollard (*C. W. Moss*), Gene Hackman (*Buck Barrow*), Estelle Parsons (*Blanche*), Denver Pyle (*Frank Hamer*), Dub Taylor (*Ivan Moss*), Evans Evans (*Velma Davis*), Gene Wilder (*Eugene Grizzard*).

Produced by Warren Beatty (A Tatira-Hiller Production) for Warner Brothers. 111 min.

## 1969    ALICE'S RESTAURANT

Script: Venable Herndon and Arthur Penn, based on the recording "The Alice's Restaurant Massacree" by Arlo Guthrie.
Direction: Penn.
Photography: Michael Nebbia.
Art direction: Warren Clymer.
Editing: Dede Allen.
Music: Arlo Guthrie, Woody Guthrie, Joni Mitchell, Gary Sherman.
Musical supervision: Gary Sherman.

Cast: Arlo Guthrie (*Arlo*), Pat Quinn (*Alice*), James Broderick (*Ray*), Michael McClanathan (*Shelly*), Geoff Outlaw (*Roger*), Tina Chen (*Mari-Chan*), Kathleen Dabney (*Karin*), Police Chief William Obanhein (*Officer Obie*), Seth Allen (*evangelist*), Monroe Arnold (*Blueglass*), Joseph Boley (*Woody*), Vinnette Carroll (*lady clerk*), M. Emmet Walsh (*group W sergeant*), Judge James Hannon (*himself*), Graham Jarvis (*music teacher*).

Produced by Hillard Elkins and Joe Manduke (A Florin Production) for United Artists. 111 min.

## 1970    LITTLE BIG MAN

Script: Calder Willingham, from the novel by Thomas Berger.
Direction: Penn.
Photography (Panavision): Harry Stradling, Jr.
Production design: Dean Tavoularis.
Editing: Dede Allen.
Music: John Hammond.

Cast: Dustin Hoffman (*Jack Crabb*), Faye Dunaway (*Mrs. Pendrake*), Martin Balsam (*Allardyce T. Merriweather*), Richard Mulligan (*General Custer*), Chief Dan George (*Old Lodge Skins*), Jeff Corey (*Wild Bill Hickok*), Amy Eccles (*Sunshine*), Kelly Jean Peters (*Olga*), Carol Androsky (*Caroline*), Robert Little Star (*Little Horse*), Cal Bellini (*Younger Bear*), Ruben Moreno (*Shadow That Comes in Sight*), Steve Shemayne (*Burns Red in the Sky*), William Hickey (*historian*), Thayer David (*Rev. Silas Pendrake*), Ray Dimas (*young Jack Crabb*), Alan Howard (*adolescent Jack Crabb*).

Produced by Stuart Millar (Hiller Productions, Stockbridge Productions) for Cinema Center Films/National General Pictures. 150 min.

## 1975    NIGHT MOVES

Script: Alan Sharp.
Direction: Penn.
Photography: Bruce Surtees.
Production design: George Jenkins.
Editing: Dede Allen, Stephen A. Rotter.
Music: Michael Small.

Cast: Gene Hackman (*Harry Moseby*), Jennifer Warren (*Paula*), Edward Binns (*Joey Ziegler*), Harris Yulin (*Marty Heller*), Kenneth Mars (*Nick*), Janet Ward (*Arlene Iverson*), James Woods (*Quentin*),

Anthony Costello (*Marv Ellman*), John Crawford (*Tom Iverson*), Melanie Griffith (*Delly Grastner*), Susan Clark (*Ellen Moseby*).

Produced by Robert M. Sherman (Hiller Productions/Layton) for Warner Brothers. 99 min.

## 1976    THE MISSOURI BREAKS

Script: Thomas McGuane.
Direction: Penn.
Photography: Michael Butler.
Production design: Albert Brenner.
Editing: Jerry Greenberg, Stephen Rotter, Dede Allen.
Music: John Williams.

Cast: Marlon Brando (*Lee Clayton*), Jack Nicholson (*Tom Logan*), Kathleen Lloyd (*Jane Braxton*), Randy Quaid (*Little Tod*), Frederick Forrest (*Cary*), Harry Dean Stanton (*Calvin*), John McLiam (*David Braxton*), John Ryan (*Si*), Sam Gilman (*Hank*).

Produced by Elliott Kastner and Robert M. Sherman for United Artists. 126 min.

## 1981    FOUR FRIENDS

Script: Steve Tesich.
Direction: Penn.
Photography: Ghislain Cloquet.
Production design: David Chapman.
Editing: Barry Malkin, Marc Laub.
Music: Elizabeth Swados.

Cast: Craig Wasson (*Danilo*), Jodi Thelen (*Georgia*), Michael Huddleston (*David Levine*), Jim Metzler (*Tom*), Reed Birney (*Louie*), Elizabeth Lawrence (*Mrs. Prozor*), Miklos Simon (*Mr. Prozor*), Lois Smith (*Mrs. Carnahan*), James Leo Herlihy (*Mr. Carnahan*), Julia Murray (*Adrienne*), David Graf (*Gergley*), Nga Bich Thi Duong (*Tom's Wife*).

Produced by Arthur Penn and Gene Lasko for Filmways. 115 min.

## 1985    TARGET

Script: Howard Berk and Don Petersen, from a story by Leonard Stern.
Direction: Penn.
Photography: Jean Tournier.
Production design: Willy Holt.
Editing: Stephen A. Rotter, Richard P. Cirincione.

Music: Michael Small.
Special consultant: Gene Lasko.

Cast: Gene Hackman (*Walter "Duke" Lloyd*), Matt Dillon (*Chris Lloyd*), Gayle Hunnicutt (*Donna Lloyd*), Josef Summer (*Taber*), Ilona Grubel (*Carla*), Victoria Fyodorova (*Lise*), Herbert Berghof (*Schroeder*), Guy Boyd (*Clay*), James Selby (*Ross*), Tomas Henvsa (*Henke*), Glasses (*Jean-Pol Dubois*), Ulrich Haupt (*older agent*), Robert Ground (*Marine Sargeant*), Ray Fry (*Mason*), Richard Munch (*the Colonel*), Catherine Rethi (*Nurse*), Jean-Pierre Stewart (*Ballard*).

Produced by Richard D. Zanuck and David Brown for Warner Brothers/CBS. 115 min.

### 1987    DEAD OF WINTER

Script: Marc Shmuger and Mark Malone.
Direction: Penn.
Photography: Jan Weincke.
Production design: Bill Brodie.
Editing: Rick Shaine.
Music: Richard Einhorn.

Cast: Mary Steenburgen (*Julie Rose, Katie McGovern, Evelyn*), Roddy McDowall (*Mr. Murray*), Jan Rubes (*Dr. Joseph Lewis*), William Russ (*Rob Sweeney*), Ken Pogue (*Officer Mullavy*), Wayne Robson (*Officer Huntley*).

Produced by John Bloomgarden and Marc Shmuger for MGM. 100 min.

## STANLEY KUBRICK

### 1953    FEAR AND DESIRE

Script: Howard G. Sackler.
Direction, photography (b&w), editing: Kubrick.

Cast: Frank Silvera (*Mac*), Kenneth Harp (*Corby*), Virginia Leith (*the girl*), Paul Mazursky (*Sidney*), Steve Coit (*Pletcher*).

Produced by Stanley Kubrick for Joseph Burstyn. 68 min.

### 1955    KILLER'S KISS

Script: Kubrick, Howard O. Sackler.
Direction, photography (b&w), editing: Kubrick.

Music: Gerald Fried.

Choreography: David Vaughan.

Cast: Frank Silvera (*Vincent Rapallo*), Jamie Smith (*Davy Gordon*), Irene Kane (*Gloria Price*), Jerry Jarret (*Albert*), Ruth Sobotka (*Iris*), Mike Dana, Felice Orlandi, Ralph Roberts, Phil Stevenson (*hoodlums*), Julius Adelman (*mannequin factory owner*), David Vaughan, Alec Rubin (*conventioneers*).

Produced by Stanley Kubrick and Morris Bousel (Minotaur) for United Artists. 61 min.

## 1956    THE KILLING

Script: Kubrick, based on the novel *Clean Break* by Lionel White.

Additional dialogue: Jim Thompson.

Direction: Kubrick.

Photography (b&w): Lucien Ballard.

Art direction: Ruth Sobotka Kubrick.

Editing: Betty Steinberg.

Music: Gerald Fried.

Cast: Sterling Hayden (*Johnny Clay*), Jay C. Flippen (*Marvin Unger*), Marie Windsor (*Sherry Peatty*), Elisha Cook (*George Peatty*), Coleen Gray (*Fay*), Vince Edwards (*Val Cannon*), Ted de Corsia (*Randy Kennan*), Joe Sawyer (*Mike O'Reilly*), Tim Carey (*Nikki*), Kola Kwariani (*Maurice*).

Produced by James B. Harris (Harris-Kubrick Productions) for United Artists. 83 min.

## 1957    PATHS OF GLORY

Script: Kubrick, Calder Willingham, Jim Thompson, based on the novel by Humphrey Cobb.

Direction: Kubrick.

Photography (b&w): George Krause.

Art direction: Ludwig Reiber.

Editing: Eva Kroll.

Music: Gerald Fried.

Cast: Kirk Douglas (*Colonel Dax*), Ralph Meeker *(Corporal Paris)*, Adolphe Menjou (*General Broulard*), George Macready (*General Mireau*), Wayne Morris (*Lieutenant Roget*), Richard Anderson (*Major Saint-Auban*), Joseph Turkel (*Private Arnaud*), Timothy Carey (*Private Ferol*), Peter Capell (*Colonel Judge*), Susanne Christian (*German girl*),

Bert Freed (*Sergeant Boulanger*), Emile Meyer (*priest*), John Stein (*Captain Rousseau*).

Produced by James B. Harris (Harris-Kubrick Productions) for United Artists. 86 min.


## 1960    SPARTACUS

Script: Dalton Trumbo, based on the novel by Howard Fast.
Direction: Kubrick.
Photography (Super Technirama-70): Russell Metty.
Additional photography: Clifford Stine.
Production design: Alexander Golitzen.
Editing: Robert Lawrence, Robert Schultz, Fred Chulack.
Music: Alex North.

Cast: Kirk Douglas (*Spartacus*), Laurence Olivier (*Marcus Crassus*), Jean Simmons (*Varinia*), Charles Laughton (*Gracchus*), Peter Ustinov (*Batiatus*), John Gavin (*Julius Caesar*), Tony Curtis (*Antoninus*), Nina Foch (*Helena*), Herbert Lom (*Tigranes*), John Ireland (*Crixus*), John Dall (*Glabrus*), Charles McGraw (*Marcellus*), Joanna Barnes (*Claudia*), Harold J. Stone (*David*), Woody Strode (*Draba*).

Produced by Kirk Douglas and Edward Lewis (Bryna) for Universal. 196 min.


## 1961    LOLITA

Script: Vladimir Nabokov, based on his novel.
Direction: Kubrick.
Photography (b&w): Oswald Morris.
Art direction: William Andrews.
Editing: Anthony Harvey.
Music: Nelson Riddle, Bob Harris.

Cast: James Mason (*Humbert Humbert*), Sue Lyon (*Lolita Haze*), Shelley Winters (*Charlotte Haze*), Peter Sellers (*Clare Quilty*), Diana Decker (*Jean Farlow*), Jerry Stovin (*John Farlow*), Suzanne Gibbs (*Mona Farlow*), Gary Cockrell (*Dick*), Marianne Stone (*Vivian Darkbloom*), Cec Linder (*physician*), Lois Maxwell (*Nurse Mary Lore*), William Greene (*Swine*).

Produced by James B. Harris (Seven Arts/Anya/Transworld) for MGM. 153 min.

## 1963    DR. STRANGELOVE, OR HOW I LEARNED TO STOP WORRYING AND LOVE THE BOMB

Script: Kubrick, Terry Southern, Peter George, based on George's novel *Red Alert*.
Direction: Kubrick.
Photography (b&w): Gilbert Taylor.
Production design: Ken Adam.
Special Effects: Wally Veevers.
Editing: Anthony Harvey.
Music: Laurie Johnson.

Cast: Peter Sellers (*Group Captain Lionel Mandrake, President Merkin Muffley, Dr. Strangelove*), George C. Scott (*General Buck Turgidson*), Sterling Hayden (*General Jack D. Ripper*), Keenan Wynn (*Colonel Bat Guano*), Slim Pickens (*Major Kong*), Peter Bull (*Ambassador de Sadesky*), Tracy Reed (*Miss Scott*), James Earl Jones (*Lieutenant Lothar Zogg, bombardier*), Jack Creley (*Mr. Staines*), Frank Berry (*Lieutenant H. R. Dietrich, D.S.O.*), Glenn Beck (*Lieutenant W. D. Kivel, navigator*), Shane Rimmer (*Captain Ace Owens, copilot*), Paul Tamarin (*Lieutenant B. Goldberg, radio operator*), Gordon Tanner (*General Faceman*).

Produced by Kubrick (Hawk Films) for Columbia. 94 min.

## 1968    2001: A SPACE ODYSSEY

Script: Kubrick, Arthur C. Clarke, based on Clarke's story "The Sentinel."
Direction: Kubrick.
Photography (Super Panavision): Geoffrey Unsworth.
Additional photography: John Alcott.
Production design: Tony Masters, Harry Lange, Ernie Archer.
Special photographic effects design and direction: Kubrick.
Special photographic effects supervision: Wally Veevers, Douglas Trumbull, Con Pederson, Tom Howard.
Editing: Ray Lovejoy.
Music: Richard Strauss, Johann Strauss, Aram Khachaturian, György Ligeti.
Costumes: Hardy Amies.

Cast: Keir Dullea (*David Bowman*), Gary Lockwood (*Frank Poole*), William Sylvester (*Dr. Heywood Floyd*), Daniel Richter (*moonwatcher*),

Douglas Rain (*voice of HAL 9000*), Leonard Rossiter (*Smyslov*), Margaret Tyzack (*Elena*), Robert Beatty (*Halvorsen*), Sean Sullivan (*Michaels*), Frank Miller (*Mission Control*), Penny Brahms (*stewardess*), Alan Gifford (*Poole's father*).

Produced by Kubrick for MGM. 141 min.

## 1971    A CLOCKWORK ORANGE

Script: Kubrick, from the novel by Anthony Burgess.
Direction: Kubrick.
Photography: John Alcott.
Production design: John Barry.
Editing: Bill Butler.
Music: Walter Carlos.

Cast: Malcolm McDowell (*Alex*), Patrick Magee (*Mr. Alexander*), Anthony Sharp (*Minister of the Interior*), Godfrey Quigley (*prison chaplain*), Warren Clarke (*Dim*), James Marcus (*Georgie*), Aubrey Morris (*Deltoid*), Miriam Karlin (*Cat Lady*), Sheila Raynor (*Mum*), Philip Stone (*Dad*), Carl Duering (*Dr. Brodsky*), Paul Farrell (*tramp*), Michael Gover (*prison governor*), Clive Francis (*lodger*), Madge Ryan (*Dr. Branom*), Pauline Taylor (*psychiatrist*), John Clive (*stage actor*), Michael Bates (*chief guard*).

Produced by Kubrick for Warner Brothers. 137 min.

## 1975    BARRY LYNDON

Script: Kubrick, from the novel by William Makepeace Thackeray.
Direction: Kubrick.
Photography: John Alcott.
Production design: Ken Adam.
Editing: Tony Lawson.
Music: J. S. Bach, Frederick the Great, Handel, Mozart, Paisiello, Schubert, Vivaldi, The Chieftains.
Music adaptation: Leonard Rosenman.
Costumes: Ulla-Britt Soderlund, Milena Canonero.

Cast: Ryan O'Neal (*Barry Lyndon*), Marisa Berenson (*Lady Lyndon*), Patrick Magee (*the Chevalier*), Hardy Kruger (*Captain Potzdorf*), Marie Kean (*Barry's mother*), Gay Hamilton (*Nora*), Murray Melvin (*Reverend Runt*), Godfrey Quigley (*Captain Grogan*), Leonard Rossiter

(*Captain Quinn*), Leon Vitali (*Lord Bullingdon*), Diana Koerner (*German girl*), Frank Middlemass (*Sir Charles Lyndon*), André Morell (*Lord Wendover*), Arthur O'Sullivan (*highwayman*), Philip Stone (*Graham*), Michael Hordern (*narrator*).

Produced by Kubrick and Jan Harlan for Warner Brothers. 185 min.

## 1980 THE SHINING

Script: Kubrick and Diane Johnson, from the novel by Stephen King.
Direction: Kubrick.
Photography: John Alcott.
Production design: Roy Walker.
Editing: Ray Lovejoy.
Music: Béla Bartók, Wendy Carlos, Rachel Elkin, György Ligeti, Krzysztof Penderecki.
Cast: Jack Nicholson (*Jack Torrance*), Shelley Duvall (*Wendy Torrance*), Danny Lloyd (*Danny Torrance*), Scatman Crothers (*Hallorann*), Barry Nelson (*Stuart Ullman*), Joe Turkel (*Lloyd*), Philip Stone (*Delbert Grady*), Anne Jackson (*Doctor*), Tony Burton (*Larry Durkin*), Lia Beldam (*young woman in bath*), Billie Gibson (*old woman in bath*), Lisa Burns, Louise Burns (*the Grady girls*).

Produced by Stanley Kubrick (Hawk Films) for Warner Brothers.. 145 min.

## 1987 FULL METAL JACKET

Script: Kubrick, Michael Herr, Gustav Hasford, based on Hasford's novel, *The Short-Timers*.
Direction: Kubrick.
Photography: Douglas Milsome.
Production design: Anton Furst
Editing: Martin Hunter.
Music: Abigail Mead.
Cast: Matthew Modine (*Private Joker*), Lee Ermey (*Gunnery Sergeant Hartman*), Vincent D'Onofrio (*Private Pyle*), Arliss Howard (*Cowboy*), Adam Baldwin (*Animal Mother*), Dorian Harewood (*Eightball*), Kevyn Major Howard (*Rafterman*), Ed O'Ross (*Lieutenant Touchdown*).

Produced by Kubrick (Puffin Films) for Warner Brothers. 118 min.

# MARTIN SCORSESE

## 1969    WHO'S THAT KNOCKING AT MY DOOR?

Script and direction: Scorsese (additional dialogue by Betzi Manoogian).
Photography (b&w): Michael Wadleigh, Richard Coll, Max Fisher.
Art direction: Victor Magnotta.
Editing: Thelma Schoonmaker.
   Cast: Zina Bethune (*the young girl*), Harvey Keitel (*J. R.*), Anne Collette (*young girl in dream*), Lennard Kuras (*Joey*), Michael Scala (*Sally Gaga*), Harry Northup (*Harry*), Bill Minkin (*Iggy*), Phil Carlson (*the guide*), Wendy Russell (*Gaga's small friend*), Robert Uricola (*the armed young man*), Susan Wood (*Susan*), Marissa Joffrey (*Rosie*), Catherine Scorsese (*J. R.'s mother*), Victor Magnotta and Paul De Bionde (*waiters*), Saskia Holleman, Tsuai Yu-Lan, Marieka (*dream girls*), Martin Scorsese (*gangster*), Thomas Aiello.
   Produced by Joseph Weill, Betzi Manoogian, and Haig Manoogian (Trimrod) for release by Joseph Brenner Associates. 90 min. Earlier versions known as *Bring on the Dancing Girls* (1965) and *I Call First* (1967). Also released as *J. R.*

## 1972    BOXCAR BERTHA

Script: Joyce H. Corrington, John William Corrington, from the book *Sister of the Road* by Boxcar Bertha Thompson as told to Ben L. Reitman.
Direction: Scorsese.
Photography: John Stephens.
Visual consultant: David Nichols.
Editing: Buzz Feitshans.
Music: Gib Guilbeau, Thad Maxwell.
   Cast: Barbara Hershey (*Bertha*), David Carradine (*Bill Shelley*), Barry Primus (*Rake Brown*), Bernie Casey (*Von Morton*), John Carradine (*H. Buckram Sartoris*), Victor Argo and David R. Osterhout (*The McIvers*), "Chicken" Holleman (*Michael Powell*), Grahame Pratt (*Emeric Pressburger*), Harry Northup (*Harvey Hall*), Ann Morell (*Tillie*), Marianne Dole (*Mrs. Mailer*), Joe Reynolds (*Joe*), Gayne Rescher and Martin Scorsese (*brothel clients*).
   Produced by Roger Corman for American International. 88 min.

## 1973    MEAN STREETS

Script: Scorsese, Mardik Martin.
Direction: Scorsese.
Photography: Kent Wakeford.
Visual consultant: David Nichols.
Editing: Sid Levin.

Cast: Harvey Keitel (*Charlie*), Robert De Niro (*Johnny Boy*), Amy Robinson (*Teresa*), David Proval (*Tony*), Richard Romanus (*Michael*), Cesare Danova (*Giovanni*), Victor Argo (*Mario*), George Memmoli (*Joey Catucci*), Lenny Scaletta (*Jimmy*), Jeannie Bell (*Diane*), Murray Mosten (*Oscar*), David Carradine (*drunk*), Robert Carradine (*young assassin*), Lois Walden (*Jewish girl*), Harry Northup (*Vietnam veteran*), Dino Seragusa (*old man*), D'Mitch Davis (*black cop*), Peter Fain (*George*), Julie Andelman (*girl at party*), Robert Wilder (*Benton*), Ken Sinclair (*Sammy*), Catherine Scorsese (*woman on the landing*), Martin Scorsese (*Shorty, the killer in the car*).

Produced by Jonathan T. Taplin (Taplin-Perry-Scorsese) for Warner Brothers. 110 min.

## 1974    ALICE DOESN'T LIVE HERE ANYMORE

Script: Robert Getchell.
Direction: Scorsese.
Photography: Kent Wakeford.
Production design: Toby Carr Rafelson.
Editing: Marcia Lucas.
Original music: Richard LaSalle.

Cast: Ellen Burstyn (*Alice Hyatt*), Kris Kristofferson (*David*), Alfred Lutter (*Tommy*), Billy Green Bush (*Donald*), Diane Ladd (*Flo*), Lelia Goldoni (*Bea*), Lane Bradbury (*Rita*), Vic Tayback (*Mel*), Jodie Foster (*Audrey*), Harvey Keitel (*Ben*), Valerie Curtin (*Vera*), Murray Moston (*Jacobs*), Harry Northup (*Joe and Jim's bartender*), Mia Bendixsen (*Alice aged 8*), Ola Moore (*old woman*), Martin Brinton (*Lenny*), Dean Casper (*Chicken*), Henry M. Kendrick (*shop assistant*), Martin Scorsese and Larry Cohen (*diners at Mel and Ruby's*), Mardik Martin (*customer in club during audition*).

Produced by David Susskind and Audrey Maas for Warner Brothers. 112 min.

1976     TAXI DRIVER

Script: Paul Schrader.
Direction: Scorsese.
Photography: Michael Chapman.
Art direction: Charles Rosen.
Visual consultant: David Nichols.
Editing: Marcia Lucas, Tom Rolf, Melvin Shapiro.
Music: Bernard Herrmann.
Creative consultant: Sandra Weintraub.

Cast: Robert De Niro (*Travis Bickle*), Cybill Shepherd (*Betsy*), Jodie Foster (*Iris*), Harvey Keitel (*Sport*), Peter Boyle (*Wizard*), Albert Brooks (*Tom*), Leonard Harris (*Charles Palantine*), Diahnne Abbott (*concession girl*), Frank Adu (*angry black man*), Vic Argo (*Melio*), Gino Ardito (*policeman at rally*), Garth Avery (*Iris's friend*), Harry Cohn (*cabbie in Belmore*), Copper Cunningham (*hooker in cab*), Brenda Dickson (*soap opera woman*), Harry Fischler (*dispatcher*), Nat Grant (*stick-up man*), Richard Higgs (*tall Secret Service man*), Beau Kayser (*soap opera man*), Vic Magnotta (*Secret Service photographer*), Robert Maroff (*mafioso*), Norman Matlock (*Charlie T.*), Bill Minkin (*Tom's assistant*), Murray Moston (*Iris's timekeeper*), Harry Northup (*doughboy*), Gene Palma (*street drummer*), Carey Poe (*campaign worker*), Steven Prince (*Andy, gun salesman*), Peter Savage (*the john*), Martin Scorsese (*passenger watching silhouette*), Robert Shields (*Palantine aide*), Ralph Singleton (*TV interviewer*), Joe Spinell (*personnel officer*), Maria Turner (*angry hooker on street*), Robin Utt (*campaignworker*).

Produced by Michael and Julia Phillips (Bill/Phillips production), for Columbia. 112 min.

1977     NEW YORK, NEW YORK

Script: Earl Mac Rauch, Mardik Martin, from a story by Rauch.
Direction: Scorsese.
Photography: Laszlo Kovacs.
Production design: Boris Leven.
Supervising film editors: Irving Lerner, Marcia Lucas.
Editing: Tom Rolf, B. Lovitt.
Original songs by John Kander and Fred Ebb ("Theme From *New York, New York*," "There Goes the Ball Game," "But the World Goes 'Round," "Happy Endings").
Saxophone solos and technical consultant: Georgie Auld.

Musical supervisor and conductor: Ralph Burns.

Choreography: Ron Field.

Costumes: Theadora van Runkle.

Cast: Liza Minnelli (*Francine Evans*), Robert De Niro (*Jimmy Doyle*), Lionel Stander (*Tony Harwell*), Barry Primus (*Paul Wilson*), Mary Kay Place (*Bernice*), Georgie Auld (*Frankie Harte*), George Memmoli (*Nicky*), Dick Miller (*Palm Club owner*), Murray Moston (*Horace Morris*), Lenny Gaines (*Artie Kirks*), Clarence Clemons (*Cecil Powell*), Kathi McGinnis (*Ellen Flannery*), Norman Palmer (*desk clerk*), Adam David Winkler (*Jimmy Doyle, Jr.*), Dimitri Logothetis (*desk clerk*), Frank Sivera (*Eddie di Muzio*), Diahnne Abbott (*Harlem club singer*), Margo Winkler (*argumentative woman*), Steven Prince (*record producer*), Don Calfa (*Gilbert*), Bernie Kuby (*justice of the peace*), Selma Archerd (*wife of justice of the peace*), Bill Baldwin (*announcer in Moonlit Terrace*), Mary Lindsay (*hatcheck girl in Meadows*), Jon Cutler (*musician in Frankie Hart's band*), Nicky Blair (*cab driver*), Casey Kasem (*D. J.*), Jay Salerno (*bus driver*), William Tole (*Tommy Dorsey*), Sydney Guilaroff (*hairdresser*), Peter Savage (*Horace Morris's assistant*), Gene Castle (*dancing sailor*), Louie Guss (*Fowler*), Shera Danese (*Doyle's girl in Major Chord*), Bill McMillan (*D. J.*), David Nichols (*Arnold Trench*), Harry Northup (*Alabama*), Marty Zagon (*manager of South Bend ballroom*), Timothy Blake (*nurse*), Betty Cole (*charwoman*), De Forest Covan (*porter*), Phil Gray (*trombone player in Doyle's band*), Roosevelt Smith (*bouncer in Major Chord*), Bruce L. Lucoff (*cab driver*), Bill Phillips Murry (*waiter in Harlem club*), Clint Arnold (*trombone player in Palm Club*), Richard Alan Berk (*drummer in Palm Club*), Jack R. Clinton (*bartender in Palm Club*), Wilfred R. Middlebrooks (*bass player in Palm Club*), Jake Vernon Porter (*trumpet player in Palm Club*), Nat Pierce (*piano player in Palm Club*), Manuel Escobosa (*fighter in Moonlit Terrace*), Susan Kay Hunt, Teryn Jenkins (*girls at Moonlit Terrace*), Mardik Martin (*well-wisher at Moonlit Terrace*), Leslie Summers (*woman in black at Moonlit Terrace*), Brock Michaels (*man at table in Moonlit Terrace*), Washington Rucker, Booty Reed (*musicians at hiring hall*), David Armstrong, Robert Buckingham, Eddie Garrett, Nico Stevens (*reporters*), Peter Fain (*greeter in Up Club*), Angelo Lamonea (*waiter in Up Club*), Charles A. Tamburro, Wallace McClesky (*bouncers in Up Club*), Ronald Prince (*dancer in Up Club*), Robert Petersen (*photographer*), Richard Raymond (*railroad conductor*), Hank Robinson (*Francine's bodyguard*), Harold Ross (*cab driver*), Eddie Smith (*man in bathroom at Harlem club*).

Produced by Irwin Winkler and Robert Chartoff for United Artists. 137 min.

## 1978  THE LAST WALTZ

Direction: Scorsese.

Photography: Michael Chapman, Laszlo Kovacs, Vilmos Zsigmond, David Myers, Bobby Byrne, Michael Watkins, Hiro Narita.

Production design: Boris Leven.

Editing: Yeu-Bun Yee, Jan Roblee.

Concert producer: Bill Graham.

Concert music production: John Simon. (Audio production: Rob Fraboni).

Music editor: Ken Wannberg.

Treatment and creative consultant: Mardik Martin.

The performers in order of appearance: Ronnie Hawkins, Dr. John, Neil Young, The Staples, Neil Diamond, Joni Mitchell, Paul Butterfield, Muddy Waters, Eric Clapton, Emmylou Harris, Van Morrison, Bob Dylan, Ringo Starr, Ron Wood.

Poems by Michael McClure, Sweet William Fritsch, Lawrence Ferlinghetti.

Interviewer: Scorsese.

The Band: Rick Danko (bass, violin, vocal), Levon Helm (drums, mandolin, vocal), Garth Hudson (organ, accordion, saxophone, synthesizers), Richard Manuel (piano, keyboards, drums, vocal), Robbie Robertson (lead guitar, vocal).

Produced by Robbie Robertson for United Artists. Executive producer: Jonathan Taplin. Filmed on location at Winterland Arena, San Francisco, November 1976, and MGM Studios, Culver City, and Shangri-La Studios, Malibu, thereafter. 119 min.

## 1980  RAGING BULL

Script: Paul Schrader and Mardik Martin, based upon *Raging Bull* by Jake La Motta, with Joseph Carter and Peter Savage.

Direction: Scorsese.

Photography (b&w): Michael Chapman.

Production design: Gene Rudolph.

Editing: Thelma Schoonmaker.

Music: Pietro Mascagni.

Cast: Robert De Niro (*Jake LaMotta*), Joe Pesci (*Joey*), Cathy Moriarity (*Vickie*), Frank Vincent (*Salvy*), Nicholas Colosanto (*Tommy Como*), Mario Gallo (*Mario*), Frank Adonis (*Patsy*), Joseph Bono (*Guido*), Frank Topham (*Toppy*), Theresa Saldano (*Lenore*), Lori Anne Flax (*Irma*), Bill Hanrahan (*Eddie Eagen*), James V. Christy (*Dr. Pinto*), Bernie Allen (*Comedian*), Don Dunphy (*himself*), Charles Scorsese (*Charlie*), Martin Scorsese (*man in dressing room*), Floyd Anderson (*Jimmy Reeves*), Johnny Barnes (*Sugar Ray Robinson*), Eddie Mustafa Mohammad (*Billy Fox*), Kevin Mahon (*Tony Janiro*), Louis Raftis (*Marcel Cerdan*), Johnny Turner (*Laurent Dauthuille*).

Produced by Robert Chartoff and Irwin Winkler for United Artists. 128 min.

## 1982    THE KING OF COMEDY

Script: Paul D. Zimmerman.
Direction: Scorsese.
Photography: Fred Schuler.
Production design: Boris Leven.
Editing: Thelma Schoonmaker.
Music production: Robbie Robertson.

Cast: Robert De Niro (*Rupert Pupkin*), Jerry Lewis (*Jerry Langford*), Sandra Bernhard (*Masha*), Diahnne Abbott (*Rita*), Shelley Hack (*Cathy Long*), Margo Winkler (*Receptionist*), Tony Boschetti (*Mr. Gangemi*), Ralph Monaco (*Raymond Wirtz*), Fred De Cordova (*Bert Thomas*), Edgar J. Scherick (*Wilson Crockett*), Thomas M. Tolan (*Gerrity*), Ray Dittrich (*Giardello*), Richard Dioguardi (*Capt. Burke*), Jay Julien (*Langford's lawyer*), Harry Ufland (*Langford's agent*), Kim Chan (*Jonno*), Audrey Dummett (*Cook*), Martin Scorsese (*T.V. director*), Thelma Lee (*woman in telephone booth*), Catherine Scorsese (*Rupert's mother*), Cathy Scorsese (*Dolores*), Charles Scorsese (*first man at bar*), Mardik Martin (*second man at bar*), Ed Herlihy, Victor Borge, Dr. Joyce Brothers., Tony Randall (*themselves*).

Produced by Arnon Milchan (Embassy International Pictures) for Twentieth Century-Fox. 109 min.

## 1985    AFTER HOURS

Script: Joseph Minion.
Direction: Scorsese.
Photography: Michael Ballhaus.
Production design: Jeffrey Townsend.

Editing: Thelma Schoonmaker.

Music: Howard Shore.

Cast: Griffin Dunne (*Paul Hackett*), Rosanna Arquette (*Marcy*), Verna Bloom (*June*), Teri Garr (*Julie*), John Heard (*Tom*), Linda Fiorentino (*Kiki*), Catherine O'Hara (*Gail*), Thomas Chong (*Pepe*), Cheech Marin (*Neil*), Will Patton (*Horst*), Robert Plunket (*Mark*), Bronson Pinchot (*Lloyd*).

Produced by Amy Robinson, Griffin Dunne, Robert F. Colesberry (Geffen Company) for Warner Brothers. 97 min.

## 1986    THE COLOR OF MONEY

Script: Richard Price, based on the novel by Walter Tevis.

Direction: Scorsese.

Photography: Michael Ballhaus.

Production Design: Boris Leven.

Editing: Thelma Schoonmaker.

Music: Robbie Robertson.

Cast: Paul Newman (*Eddie*), Tom Cruise (*Vincent*), Mary Elizabeth Mastrantonio (*Carmen*), Helen Shaver (*Janelle*), John Turturro (*Julien*), Bill Cobbs (*Orvis*), Keith McCready (*Grady Seasons*), Forest Whitaker (*Amos*), Bruce A. Young (*Moselle*).

Produced by Irving Axelrad and Barbara De Fina for Touchstone Pictures. 117 min.

# STEVEN SPIELBERG

Like Robert Altman before him, Spielberg directed a number of television shows before he began making features. In 1985 he returned to television as executive producer and sometime director of *Amazing Stories*. *Duel* was a made-for-television movie shown theatrically abroad and is considered his first major film. I have not included the sequence Spielberg directed for the 1983 film *Twilight Zone: The Movie*.

## 1971    DUEL

Script: Richard Matheson.

Direction: Spielberg.

Photography: Jack A. Marta.

Production design: Robert S. Smith.

Editing: Frank Morriss.

Music: Billy Goldenberg.

Cast: Dennis Weaver (*David Mann*), Tim Herbert (*station attendant*), Charles Seel (*old man*), Eddie Firestone (*cafe owner*), Shirley O'Hara (*waitress*), Gene Dynarski (*man in cafe*), Lucile Benson (*Snakorama lady*), Alexander Lockwood (*old man in car*), Amy Douglass (*lady*).

Produced by George Eckstein for Universal Television. 74 min./90 min., theatrical release.

## 1973    SUGARLAND EXPRESS

Script: Hal Barwood, Matthew Robbins, from a story by Spielberg.

Direction: Spielberg.

Photography (Panavision): Vilmos Zsigmond.

Production design: Joseph Alves.

Editing: Edward M. Abroms, Verna Fields.

Music: John Williams.

Cast: Goldie Hawn (*Lou Jean Poplin*), William Atherton (*Clovis Poplin*), Ben Johnson (*Capt. Tanner*), Michael Sacks (*Officer Slide*), Gregory Walcott (*Officer Mashburn*), Harrison Zanuck (*Baby Langston*), Steve Kanaly, Louise Latham, A. Hudgins, Buster Daniels.

Produced by Richard D. Zanuck and David Brown for Universal. 110 min.

## 1975    JAWS

Script: Peter Benchley, Carl Gottlieb, from Benchley's novel.

Direction: Spielberg.

Photography (Panavision): Bill Butler.

Underwater photography: Rexford Metz.

Production design: Joseph Alves.

Special effects: Robert A. Mattey.

Editing: Verna Fields.

Music: John Williams.

Cast: Roy Scheider (*Brody*), Richard Dreyfuss (*Hooper*), Robert Shaw (*Quint*), Lorraine Gary (*Ellen Brody*), Murray Hamilton (*Vaughn*), Carl Gottlieb (*Meadows*), Jeffrey C. Kramer (*Hendricks*), Susan Backlinie (*Chrissie*), Jonathan Filley (*Cassidy*), Chris Rebello (*Michael Brody*), Jay Mello (*Sean Brody*), Ted Grossman (*estuary victim*), Lee Fierro (*Mrs. Kintner*), Jeffrey Voorhees (*Alex Kintner*), Craig

Kingsbury (*Ben Gardner*), Dr. Robert Nevin (*medical examiner*), Peter Benchley (*interviewer*).

Produced by Richard D. Zanuck and David Brown for Universal. 124 min.

## 1977 CLOSE ENCOUNTERS OF THE THIRD KIND

Script and Direction: Spielberg.
Photography (Panavision): Vilmos Zsigmond.
Additional photography: William A. Fraker, Douglas Slocombe, John Alonzo, Laszlo Kovacs.
Production design: Joe Alves.
Special effects: Douglas Trumbull.
Editing: Michael Kahn.
Music: John Williams.

Cast: Richard Dreyfuss (*Roy Neary*), François Truffaut (*Claude Lacombe*), Teri Garr (*Ronnie Neary*), Melinda Dillon (*Jillian Guiler*), Cary Guffey (*Barry Guiler*), Bob Balaban (*David Laughlin*), J. Patrick McNamara (*project leader*), Warren Kemmerling (*Wild Bill*), Roberts Blossom (*farmer*), Philip Dodds (*Jean Claude*), Shawn Bishop (*Brad Neary*), Adrienne Campbell (*Silvia Neary*), Justin Dreyfuss (*Toby Neary*), Lance Hendricksen (*Robert*), Merrill Connally (*team leader*), George Dicenzo (*Major Benchley*).

Produced by Julia Phillips and Michael Phillips for Columbia/EMI. 135 min./"Special Edition" re-release 132 min.

## 1979 1941

Script: Robert Zemeckis, Bob Gale, from a story by Zemeckis, Gale, and John Milius.
Direction: Spielberg.
Photography (Panavision): William A. Fraker.
Production design: Dean Edward Mitzner.
Special effects: A. D. Flowers.
Visual effects supervisor: Larry Robinson.
Editing: Michael Kahn.
Music: John Williams.

Cast: Dan Aykroyd (*Sergeant Tree*), Ned Beatty (*Ward Douglas*), John Belushi (*Wild Bill Kelso*), Lorraine Gary (*Joan Douglas*), Murray Hamilton (*Claude*), Christopher Lee (*Von Kleinschmidt*), Tim Matheson (*Birkhead*), Toshiro Mifune (*Commander Mitamura*), Warren

Oates (*Maddox*), Robert Stack (*General Stilwell*), Treat Williams (*Sitarksi*), Nancy Allen (*Donna*), Eddie Deezen (*Herbie*), Bobby DiCicco (*Wally*), Dianne Kay (*Betty*), John Candy (*Foley*), Frank McRae (*Ogden Johnson Jones*), Perry Lang (*Dennis*), Slim Pickens (*Hollis Wood*), Wendie Jo Sperber (*Maxine*), Lionel Stander (*Scioli*), Ignatius Wolfington (*Meyer Mishkin*), Joseph P. Flaherty (*U.S.O. M.C.*)

Produced by Buzz Feitshans (A-Team) for Universal. Executive producer: John Milius. 118 min.

## 1981    RAIDERS OF THE LOST ARK

Script: Lawrence Kasdan, based on a story by George Lucas and Philip Kaufman.
Direction: Spielberg.
Photography (Panavision): Douglas Slocombe.
Production design: Norman Reynolds and Leslie Dilley.
Visual effects: Richard Edlund, Kit West, Bruce Nicholson, Joe Johnston.
Editing: Michael Kahn.
Music: John Williams.

Cast: Harrison Ford (*Indiana Jones*), Karen Allen (*Marion Ravenwood*), Wolf Kahler (*Dietrich*), Paul Freeman (*Belloq*), Ronald Lacey (*Toht*), John Rhys-Davies (*Sallah*), Denholm Elliott (*Brody*), Anthony Higgins (*Gobler*), Alfred Molina (*Satipo*), Vic Tablian (*Barranca*), George Harris (*Katanga*).

Produced by Frank Marshall (Lucasfilm) for Paramount. Executive producer: George Lucas. 118 min.

## 1982    E.T. THE EXTRA-TERRESTRIAL

Script: Melissa Mathison.
Direction: Spielberg.
Photography: Allan Daviau.
Effects photography: Mike McAlister.
Special visual effects: Industrial Light and Magic.
Production design: James. D. Bissell.
Editing: Carol Littleton.
Music: John Williams.

Cast: Henry Thomas (*Elliott*), Robert MacNaughton (*Michael*), Drew Barrymore (*Gertie*), Dee Wallace (*Mary*), Peter Coyote ("*Keys*"), K. C. Martel (*Greg*), Sean Frye (*Steve*), Tom Howell (*Tyler*), Erika Eleniak (*pretty girl*), David O'Dell (*schoolboy*), Richard Swingler (*science teacher*), Frank Toth (*policeman*), Carlo Rambaldi, Ben Burtt, Steve Townsend, Robert Short, Beverly Hoffman, Caprice Rothe, Robert Avila, Eugene Crum, Frank Schepler, Bob Townsend, Steve Willis, Richard Zarro, Ronald Zarro, Pat Billon, Tamara de Treaux, Matthew De Meritt, Tina Palmer, Nancy MacLean, Pam Ybarra (*E.T.*).

Produced by Spielberg and Kathleen Kennedy for Universal. 120 min.

## 1984    INDIANA JONES AND THE TEMPLE OF DOOM

Script: Willard Huyck and Gloria Katz, based on a story by George Lucas.
Direction: Spielberg.
Photography (Panavision): Douglas Slocombe.
Production design: Elliott Scott.
Visual effects: Dennis Muren.
Editing: Michael Kahn.
Music: John Williams.

Cast: Harrison Ford (*Indiana Jones*), Kate Capshaw (*Willie Scott*), Ke Huy Quan (*Short Round*), Amrish Puri (*Mola Ram*), Roshan Seth (*Chattar Lal*), Philip Stone (*Captain Blumburtt*), Roy Chiao (*Lao Che*), D. R. Nanayakkaru (*shaman*), Dharmadasa Kuruppu (*chieftain*), David Yip (*Wu Han*), Ric Young (*Kao Kan*), Raj Singh (*little maharaja*), Pat Roach (*chief guard*).

Produced by Robert Watts for Paramount. Executive producers: George Lucas and Frank Marshall. 118 min.

## 1985    THE COLOR PURPLE

Script: Menno Meyjes, based on the novel by Alice Walker.
Direction: Spielberg.
Photography: Allen Daviau.
Production design: J. Michael Riva.
Editing: Michael Kahn.
Music: Quincy Jones.

Cast: Whoopi Goldberg (*Celie*), Danny Glover (*Mr.* ), Margaret Avery (*Shug Avery*), Oprah Winfrey (*Sofia*), Willard Pugh (*Harpo*), Akosua Busia (*Nettie*), Adolph Caesar (*Mr.'s father*), Rae Dawn Chong (*Squeak*), Dana Ivey (*Miss Millie*), Desreta Jackson (*young Celie*).

Produced by Spielberg, Kathleen Kennedy, Frank Marshall, Quincy Jones (Guber-Peters and Amblin' Entertainment) for Warner Brothers. 152 min.


# ROBERT ALTMAN

### 1957    THE DELINQUENTS

Script and direction: Altman.
Photography (b&w): Charles Paddock (or Harry Birch).
Art direction: Chet Allen.
Editing: Helene Turner.
Music: Bill Nolan Quintet Minus Two.
Song: Bill Nolan, Ronnie Norman ("The Dirty Rock Boogie"), sung by Julia Lee.
Cast: Tom Laughlin (*Scotty*), Peter Miller (*Cholly*), Richard Bakalyn (*Eddy*), Rosemary Howard (*Janice*), Helene Hawley (*Mrs. White*), Leonard Belove (*Mr. White*), Lotus Corelli (*Mrs. Wilson*), James Lantz (*Mr. Wilson*), Christine Altman (*Sissy*), George Kuhn (*Jay*), Pat Stedman (*Meg*), Norman Zands (*Chizzy*), James Leria (*Steve*), Jet Pinkston (*Molly*), Kermit Echols (*barman*), Joe Adleman (*station attendant*).
Produced by Altman (Imperial Productions) for United Artists. 72 min.


### 1957    THE JAMES DEAN STORY

Script: Stewart Stern.
Direction: Altman, George W. George.
Photography (b&w): 29 various cameramen (stills: Camera Eye Pictures).
Production design: Louis Clyde Stoumen.
Music: Leith Stevens.
Song: Jay Livingston, Ray Evans.
Narrator: Martin Gabel.
Cast: Marcus, Ortense, and Markie Winslow (*Dean's aunt, uncle, and cousin*), Mr. and Mrs. Dean (*his grandparents*), Adeline Hall (*his drama teacher*), Big Traster, Mr. Carter, Jerry Luce, Louis de Liso, Arnie Langer, Arline Sax, Chris White, George Ross, Robert Jewett,

John Kalin, Lew Bracker, Glenn Kramer, Patsy d'Amore, Billy Karen, Lille Kardell (*his friends*), Officer Nelson (*highway patrolman*).

Produced by Altman and George W. George for Warner Brothers. 83 min.

## 1968    COUNTDOWN

Script: Loring Mandel, based on the novel *The Pilgrim Project* by Hank Searls.
Direction: Altman.
Photography (Panavision): William W. Spencer.
Art direction: Jack Poplin.
Editing: Gene Milford.
Music: Leonard Rosenman.

Cast: James Caan (*Lee*), Robert Duvall (*Chiz*), Joanna Moore (*Mickey*), Barbara Baxley (*Jean*), Charles Aidman (*Gus*), Steve Ihnat (*Ross*), Michael Murphy (*Rick*), Ted Knight (*Larson*), Stephen Coit (*Ehrman*), John Rayner (*Dunc*), Charles Irving (*Seidel*), Bobby Riha, Jr. (*Stevie*).

Produced by William Conrad (Productions) for Warner Brothers. 101 min.

## 1969    NIGHTMARE IN CHICAGO

Script: Donald Moessinger, from the novel *Killer on the Turnpike* by William P. McGivern.
Direction: Altman.
Photography: Bud Thackery.
Music: Johnny Williams.

Cast: Charles McGraw (*Georgie Porgie*), Ted Knight (*reporter*), Robert Ridgely, Philip Abbott, Barbara Turner, Charlene Lee, Arlene Kieta.

Produced by Altman for Roncom/Universal. 81 min. (Release version of the TV movie *Once Upon a Savage Night*, expanded with outtakes from an original 54 min. to 81 min. Shorter version first televised on 2 April 1964.)

## 1969    THAT COLD DAY IN THE PARK

Script: Gillian Freeman, from the novel by Richard Miles.
Direction: Altman.
Photography: Laszlo Kovacs.

Art Direction: Leon Erickson.
Editing: Danford Greene.
Music: Johnny Mandel.

Cast: Sandy Dennis (*Frances Austen*), Michael Burns (*the boy*), Susanne Benton (*Nina*), Luana Anders (*Sylvie*), John Garfield, Jr. (*Nick*), Michael Murphy (*the rounder*).

Produced by Donald Factor and Leon Mirell (Factor-Altman- Mirell Films) for Commonwealth United Entertainment, Inc. 115 min.

## 1970    M.A.S.H.

Script: Ring Lardner, Jr., from the novel by Richard Hooker.
Direction: Altman.
Photography (Panavision): Harold E. Stine.
Art direction: Jack Martin Smith, Arthur Lonergan.
Editing: Danford B. Greene.
Music: Johnny Mandel.
Song: Johnny Mandel and Mike Altman ("Suicide Is Painless").

Cast: Donald Sutherland (*Hawkeye Pierce*), Elliott Gould (*Trapper John McIntyre*), Tom Skerritt (*Duke Forrest*), Sally Kellerman (*Major Hot Lips*), Robert Duvall (*Major Frank Burns*), Jo Ann Pflug (*Lt. Dish*), René Auberjonois (*Dago Red*), Roger Bowen (*Col. Henry Blake*), Gary Burghoff (*Radar O'Reilly*), David Arkin (*Sgt. Major Vollmer*), Fred Williamson (*Spearchucker*), Michael Murphy (*Me Lay*), Kim Atwood (*Ho-Jon*), Tim Brown (*Corporal Judson*), Indus Arthur (*Lt. Leslie*), John Schuck (*Painless Pole*), Ken Prymus (*Pfc. Seidman*), Dawne Damon (*Capt. Scorch*), Carl Gottlieb (*Ugly John*), Tamara Horrocks (*Capt. Knocko*), G. Wood (*General Hammond*), Bobby Troup (*Sgt. Gorman*), Bud Cort (*Private Boone*), Danny Goldman (*Capt. Murrhardt*), Corey Fischer (*Capt. Bandini*), J. B. Douglas, Yoko Young.

Produced by Ingo Preminger for Aspen/Twentieth Century-Fox. Associate producer: Leon Ericksen. 116 min.

## 1970    BREWSTER McCLOUD

Script: Brian McKay (uncredited), Doran William Cannon.
Direction: Altman.
Assistant director: Tommy Thompson.
Photography (Panavision): Lamar Boren, Jordan Cronenweth.
Art direction: Preston Ames, George W. Davis.
Wings designed by Leon Ericksen.

Editing: Lou Lombardo.
Music: Gene Page.
Songs: Francis Scott Key, Rosamund Johnson and James Weldon Johnson, John Phillips, sung by Merry Clayton, John Phillips.

Cast: Bud Cort (*Brewster McCloud*), Sally Kellerman (*Louise*), Michael Murphy (*Frank Shaft*), William Windom (*Haskel Weeks*), Shelley Duvall (*Suzanne Davis*), René Auberjonois (*lecturer*), Stacy Keach (*Abraham Wright*), John Schuck (*Lt. Alvin Johnson*), Margaret Hamilton (*Daphne Heap*), Jennifer Salt (*Hope*), Corey Fischer (*Lt. Hines*), G. Wood (*Capt. Crandall*), Bert Remsen (*Douglas Breen*), Angelin Johnson (*Mrs. Breen*), William Baldwin (*Bernard*), William Henry Bennet (*band conductor*), Gary Wayne Chason (*camera shop clerk*), Ellis Gilbert (*butler*), Verdie Henshaw (*Feathered Nest Sanatorium manager*), Robert Warner (*camera shop assistant manager*), Dean Goss (*Eugene Ledbetter*), Keith V. Erickson (*Prof. Aggnout*), Thomas Danko (*color lab man*), W. E. Terry, Jr. (*police chaplain*), Ronnie Cammack (*Wendell*), Dixie M. Taylor (*nursing home manager*), Pearl Coffey Chason (*nursing home attendant*), Amelia Parker (*nursing home manageress*), David Welch (*Breen's son*).

Produced by Lou Adler (Adler-Phillips/Lion's Gate Films) for MGM. Associate producers: Robert Eggenweiler, James Margellos. 105 min.

## 1971    McCABE AND MRS. MILLER

Script: Altman, Brian McKay, from the novel *McCabe* by Edmund Naughton.
Direction: Altman.
Assistant director: Tommy Thompson.
Photography (Panavision): Vilmos Zsigmond.
Production design: Leon Ericksen.
Art direction: Phillip Thomas, Al Locatelli.
Editing: Lou Lombardo.
Music: Leonard Cohen.

Cast: Warren Beatty (*John McCabe*), Julie Christie (*Constance Miller*), René Auberjonois (*Sheehan*), Hugh Millais (*Butler*), Shelley Duvall (*Ida Coyle*), Michael Murphy (*Sears*), John Schuck (*Smalley*), Corey Fischer (*Mr. Elliott*), William Devane (*Clement Samuels*), Anthony Holland (*Ernie Hollander*), Bert Remsen (*Bart Coyle*), Keith Carradine (*cowboy*), Jace Vander Veen (*Breed*), Manfred Shulz (*Kid*), *Jackie Crossland* (*Lily*), Elizabeth Murphy (*Kate*), Linda Sorenson

(*Blanche*), Elizabeth Knight (*Birdie*), Maysie Hoy (*Maysie*), Linda
Kupecek (*Ruth*), Janet Wright (*Eunice*), Carey Lee McKenzie (*Alma*),
Rodney Gage (*Sumner Washington*), Lili Francks (*Mrs. Washington*).
Produced by David Foster and Mitchell Brower for Warner Brothers.
Associate producer: Robert Eggenweiler. 121 min.

## 1972   IMAGES

Script and direction: Altman (with passages from *In Search of Unicorns*
by Susannah York).
Photography (Panavision): Vilmos Zsigmond.
Art direction: Leon Ericksen.
Editing: Graeme Clifford.
Music: John Williams (with sounds by Stomu Yamash'ta).
Cast: Susannah York (*Cathryn*), René Auberjonois (*Hugh*), Marcel
Bozzuffi (*René*), Hugh Millais (*Marcel*), Cathryn Harrison (*Susannah*),
John Morley (*old man*).
Produced by Tommy Thompson for Lion's Gate Films/The Hem-
dale Group/Columbia. 101 min.

## 1973   THE LONG GOODBYE

Script: Leigh Brackett, from the novel by Raymond Chandler.
Direction: Altman.
Assistant director: Tommy Thompson.
Photography (Panavision): Vilmos Zsigmond.
Editing: Lou Lombardo.
Music: John Williams.
Cast: Elliott Gould (*Philip Marlowe*), Nina van Pallandt (*Eileen
Wade*), Sterling Hayden (*Roger Wade*), Mark Rydell (*Marty Augustine*),
Henry Gibson (*Dr. Verringer*), David Arkin (*Harry*), Jim Bouton (*Terry
Lennox*), Warren Berlinger (*Morgan*), Jo Ann Brody (*Jo Ann Eggen-
weiler*), Steve Coit (*Detective Farmer*), Jack Knight (*Mabel*), Pepe Cal-
lahan (*Pepe*), Vince Palmieri (*Vince*), Pancho Cordoba (*doctor*), Enrique
Lucero (*Jefe*), Rutanya Alda (*Rutanya Sweet*), Tammy Shaw (*dancer*),
Jack Riley (*piano player*), Ken Sansom (*colony guard*), Jerry Jones
(*Detective Green*), John Davies (*Detective Dayton*), Rodney Moss
(*supermarket clerk*), Sybil Scotford (*real estate lady*), Herb Kerns
(*Herbie*).
Produced by Jerry Bick and Elliot Kastner (Lion's Gate Films) for
United Artists. Associate producer: Robert Eggenweiler. 112 min.

## 1974    THIEVES LIKE US

Script: Calder Willingham, Joan Tewkesbury, Altman, from the novel
  by Edward Anderson.
Direction: Altman.
Photography: Jean Boffety.
Visual consultants: Jack DeGovia, Scott Bushnell.
Editing: Lou Lombardo.
Radio research: John Dunning.

  Cast: Keith Carradine (*Bowie*), Shelley Duvall (*Keechie*), John
Schuck (*Chicamaw*), Bert Remsen (*T-Dub*), Louise Fletcher (*Mattie*),
Ann Latham (*Lula*), Tom Skerritt (*Dee Mobley*), Al Scott (*Capt. Stam-
mers*), John Roper (*Jasbo*), Mary Waits (*Noel*), Rodney Lee, Jr. (*James
Mattingly*), William Watters (*Alvin*), Joan Tewkesbury (*lady in train
station*), Eleanor Matthews (*Mrs. Stammers*), Pam Warner (*woman in
accident*), Suzanne Majure (*Coca-Cola girl*), Walter Cooper and Lloyd
Jones (*sheriffs*).

  Produced by Jerry Bick and George Litto for United Artists. Associate producers: Robert Eggenweiler, Thomas Hal Phillips. 123 min.


## 1974    CALIFORNIA SPLIT

Script: Joseph Walsh.
Direction: Altman.
Assistant director: Tommy Thompson.
Photography (Panavision): Paul Lohmann.
Production design: Leon Ericksen.
Editing: Lou Lombardo, assisted by Tony Lombardo and Dennis Hill.

  Cast: Elliott Gould (*Charlie Waters*), George Segal (*Bill Denny*), Ann
Prentiss (*Barbara Miller*), Gwen Welles (*Susan Peters*), Edward Walsh
(*Lew*), Joseph Walsh (*Sparkie*), Bert Remsen ("*Helen Brown*"), Barbara
London (*lady on the bus*), Barbara Ruick (*Reno barmaid*), Jay Fletcher
(*robber*), Jeff Goldblum (*Lloyd Harris*), Barbara Colby (*receptionist*),
Vince Palmieri (*first bartender*), Alyce Passman (*go-go girl*), Joanne
Strauss (*mother*), Jack Riley (*second bartender*), Sierra Bandit (*woman
at bar*), John Considine (*man at bar*), Eugene Troobnick (*Harvey*),
Richard Kennedy (*used-car salesman*), John Winston (*tenor*), Bill Duffy
(*Kenny*), Mike Greene (*Reno dealer*), Tom Signorelli (*Nugie*), Sharon
Compton (*Nugie's wife*), Arnold Herzstein, Marc Cavell, Alvin Weiss-
man, Mickey Fox, Carolyn Lohmann (*California Club poker players*),

"Amarillo Slim" Preston, Winston Lee, Harry Drackett, Thomas Hal Phillips, Ted Say, A. J. Hood (*Reno poker players*).

Produced by Altman and Joseph Walsh (Won World/Persky Bright/ Reno) for Columbia. Associate producer: Robert Eggenweiler. 109 min.

## 1975 NASHVILLE

Script: Joan Tewkesbury.
Direction: Altman.
Assistant directors: Tommy Thompson, Alan Rudolph.
Photography (Panavision): Paul Lohmann.
Editing: Sidney Levin, Dennis Hill.
Political campaign: Thomas Hal Phillips.
Songs: "200 Years" (lyrics by Henry Gibson, music by Richard Baskin), "Yes, I Do" (lyrics and music by Richard Baskin and Lily Tomlin), "Down to the River" (lyrics and music by Ronee Blakley), "Let Me Be the One" (lyrics and music by Richard Baskin), "Sing a Song" (lyrics and music by Joe Raposo), "The Heart of a Gentle Woman" (lyrics and music by Dave Peel), "Bluebird" (lyrics and music by Ronee Blakley), "The Day I Looked Jesus in the Eye" (lyrics and music by Richard Baskin and Robert Altman), "Memphis" (lyrics and music by Karen Black), "I Don't Know If I Found It in You" (lyrics and music by Karen Black), "For the Sake of the Children" (lyrics and music by Richard Baskin and Richard Reicheg), "Keep a Goin'" (lyrics by Henry Gibson, music by Richard Baskin and Henry Gibson), "Swing Low Sweet Chariot" (arrangements by Millie Clements), "Rolling Stone" (lyrics and music by Karen Black), "Honey" (lyrics and music by Keith Carradine), "Tapedeck in His Tractor (The Cowboy Song)," (lyrics and music by Ronee Blakley), "Dues" (lyrics and music by Ronee Blakley), "I Never Get Enough" (lyrics and music by Richard Baskin and Ben Raleigh), "Rose's Cafe" (lyrics and music by Allan Nicholls), "Old Man Mississippi" (lyrics and music by Juan Grizzle), "My Baby's Cookin' in Another Man's Pan" (lyrics and music by Jonnie Barnett), "One, I Love You" (lyrics and music by Richard Baskin), "I'm Easy" (lyrics and music by Keith Carradine), "It Don't Worry Me" (lyrics and music by Keith Carradine), "Since You've Gone" (lyrics and music by Garry Busey), "Trouble in the U.S.A." (lyrics and music by Arlene Barnett), "My Idaho Home" (lyrics and music by Ronee Blakley).
Cast: David Arkin (*Norman*), Barbara Baxley (*Lady Pearl*), Ned Beatty (*Delbert Reese*), Karen Black (*Connie White*), Ronee Blakley

(*Barbara Jean*), Timothy Brown (*Tommy Brown*), Keith Carradine (*Tom Frank*), Geraldine Chaplin (*Opal*), Robert Doqui (*Wade*), Shelley Duvall (*L.A. Joan*), Allen Garfield (*Barnett*), Henry Gibson (*Haven Hamilton*), Scott Glenn (*Pfc. Glenn Kelly*), Jeff Goldblum (*tricycle man*), Barbara Harris (*Albuquerque*), David Hayward (*Kenny Fraiser*), Michael Murphy (*John Triplette*), Allan Nicholls (*Bill*), Dave Peel (*Bud Hamilton*), Cristina Raines (*Mary*), Bert Remsen (*Star*), Lily Tomlin (*Linnea Reese*), Gwen Welles (*Sueleen Gay*), Keenan Wynn (*Mr. Green*), James Dan Calvert (*Jimmy Reese*), Donna Denton (*Donna Reese*), Merle Kilgore (*Trout*), Carol McGinnis (*Jewel*), Sheila Bailey and Patti Bryant (*Smokey Mountain Laurel*), Richard Baskin (*Frog*), Jonnie Barnett, Vassar Clements, Misty Mountain Boys, Sue Barton, Elliott Gould, Julie Christie (*themselves*).

Produced by Altman (ABC Entertainment), for Paramount. Associate producers: Robert Eggenweiler, Scott Bushnell. 161 min.


## 1976 BUFFALO BILL AND THE INDIANS, OR SITTING BULL'S HISTORY LESSON

Story and script: Alan Rudolph, Altman, based on the play *Indians* by Arthur Kopit.
Direction: Altman.
Assistant director: Tommy Thompson.
Photography (Panavision): Paul Lohmnnn.
Production design: Tony Masters.
Music: Richard Baskin.
Editing: Peter Appleton, Dennis Hill.
Costumes: Anthony Powell.

Cast: Paul Newman (*the Star*), Joel Grey (*the Producer*), Kevin McCarthy (*the Publicist*), Harvey Keitel (*the Relative*), Allan Nicholls (*the Journalist*), Geraldine Chaplin (*the Sure Shot*), John Considine (*the Sure Shot's Manager*), Robert Doqui (*the Wrangler*), Mike Kaplan (*the Treasurer*), Bert Remsen (*the Bartender*), Bonnie Leaders (*the Mezzo-Contralto*), Noelle Rogers (*the Lyric Coloratura*), Evelyn Lear (*the Lyric Soprano*), Denver Pyle (*the Indian Agent*), Frank Kaquitts (*the Indian*), Will Sampson (*the Interpreter*), Ken Krossa (*the Arenic Director*), Fred N. Larsen (*the King of the Cowboys*), Jerry and Joy Duce (*the Cowboy Trick Riders*), Alex Green and Gary MacKenzie (*the Mexican Whip and Fast Draw Act*), Humphrey Gratz (*the Old Soldier*), Pat McCormick (*the President of the United States*), Shelley Duvall (*the First Lady*), Burt

Lancaster (*the Legend Maker*). With people from the Stoney Indian Reserve.

Produced by Robert Altman for Dino De Laurentiis Corporation/ Lion's Gate Films/Talent Associates Norton Simon, Inc./United Artists. Executive producer: David Susskind. Associate producers: Robert Eggenweiler, Scott Bushnell, Jac Cashin. 123 min.

## 1977    THREE WOMEN

Script and direction: Altman.
Photography (Panavision): Chuck Rosher.
Art direction: James D. Vance.
Visual consultant: J. Allen Highfill.
Murals: Bodhi Wind.
Editing: Dennis Hill.
Music: Gerald Busby.

Cast: Shelley Duvall (*Millie Lammoreaux*), Sissy Spacek (*Pinky Rose*), Janice Rule (*Willie Hart*), Robert Fortier (*Edgar Hart*), Ruth Nelson (*Mrs. Rose*), John Cromwell (*Mr. Rose*), Sierra Pecheur (*Ms. Bunweill*), Craig Richard Nelson (*Dr. Maas*), Maysie Hoy (*Doris*), Belita Moreno (*Alcira*), Leslie Ann Hudson (*Polly*), Patricia Ann Hudson (*Peggy*), Beverly Ross (*Deidre*), John Davey (*Dr. Norton*).

Produced by Robert Altman for Lion's Gate Films. Twentieth Century-Fox. Associate producers: Robert Eggenweiler and Scott Bushnell. 124 min.

## 1978    A WEDDING

Script: John Considine, Patricia Resnick, Allan Nicholls, Altman, from a story by Considine and Altman.
Direction: Altman.
Assistant director: Tommy Thompson.
Photography (Panavision): Charles Rosher.
Editing: Tony Lombardo.
Music: John Hotchkiss.
Song: "Bird on a Wire" by Leonard Cohen.
Bridal consultant: Carson, Pirie, Scott & Co., Chicago.

Cast: The Groom's Family: Lillian Gish (*Nettie Sloan*), Ruth Nelson (*Beatrice Sloan Cory*), Ann Ryerson (*Victoria Cory*), Desi Arnaz, Jr. (*Dino Corelli, the groom*), Belita Moreno (*Daphne Corelli*), Vittorio Gassman (*Luigi Corelli*), Nina van Pallandt (*Regina Corelli*), Virginia

Vestoff (*Clarice Sloan*), Dina Merrill (*Antoinette Sloan Goddard*), Pat McCormick (*Mackenzie Goddard*), Luigi Proietti (*Little Dino*).

The Bride's Family: Carol Burnett (*Tulip Brenner*), Paul Dooley (*Snooks Brenner*), Amy Stryker (*Muffin Brenner, the bride*), Mia Farrow (*Buffy Brenner*), Dennis Christopher (*Hughie Brenner*), Mary Seibel (*Aunt Marge Spar*), Margaret Ladd (*Ruby Spar*), Gerald Busby (*David Ruteledge*), Peggy Ann Garner (*Candice Ruteledge*), Mark R. Deming (*Matthew Ruteledge*), David Brand, Chris Brand, Amy Brand, Jenny Brand, Jeffrey Jones, Jay D. Jones, Courtney MacArthur, Paul D. Keller III (*the Ruteledge children*).

The Corelli House Staff: Cedric Scott (*Randolph*), Robert Fortier (*Jim Habor, gardener*), Maureen Steindler (*Libby Clinton, cook*).

The Wedding Staff: Geraldine Chaplin (*Rita Billingsley*), Mona Abboud (*Melba Lear*), Viveca Lindfors (*Ingrid Hellstrom*), Lauren Hutton (*Flo Farmer*), Allan Nicholls (*Jake Jacobs*), Maysie Hoy (*Casey*), John Considine (*Jeff Kuykendall*), Patricia Resnick (*Redford*), Margery Bond (*Lombardo*), Dennis Franz (*Koons*), Harold C. Johnson (*Oscar Edwards*), Alexander Sopenar (*Victor*).

The Friends and Guest: Howard Duff (*Dr. Jules Meecham*), John Cromwell (*Bishop Martin*), Bert Remsen (*William Williamson*), Pamela Dawber (*Tracy Parrell*), Gavan O'Hirlihy (*Wilson Briggs*), Craig Richard Nelson (*Capt. Reedley Roots*), Jeffry S. Perry (*Bunky Lemay*), Marta Heflin (*Shelby Munker*), Lesley Rogers (*Rosie Bean*), Timothy Thomerson (*Russell Bean*), Beverly Ross (*Nurse Janet Schulman*), David Fitzgerald (*Kevin Clinton*), Susan Kendall Newman (*Chris Clinton*).

The Musicians: Ellie Albers (*gypsy violinist*), Tony Llorens (*at the piano-bar*), Chuck Banks' Big Band with Chris La Kome (*in the ballroom*).

Produced by Robert Altman for Lion's Gate Films. Twentieth Century-Fox. Executive producer: Tommy Thompson. Associate producers: Robert Eggenweiler, Scott Bushnell. 124 min.

## 1979  QUINTET

Script: Altman, Frank Barhydt, Patricia Resnick, from a story by Altman, Resnick, Lionel Chetwynd.
Direction: Altman.
Assistant director: Tommy Thompson.
Photography: Jean Boffety.

Production design: Leon Erickson.
Editing: Dennis Hill.
Music: Tom Pierson.

Cast: Paul Newman (*Essex*), Fernando Rey (*Grigor*), Bibi Anderson (*Ambrosia*), Vittorio Gassman (*St. Christopher*), Nina van Pallandt (*Deuca*), Bridgette Fossey (*Vivia*), David Langton (*Redstone*), Craig Nelson (*Goldstar*), Tom Hill (*Francha*).

Produced by Altman for Lion's Gate Films. Twentieth Century Fox. Associate producer: Allan Nicholls. 118 min.

## 1979    A PERFECT COUPLE

Script: Robert Altman and Allan Nicholls.
Direction: Altman.
Assistant director: Tommy Thompson.
Photography: Edmond L. Koons.
Set decoration: Leon Erickson.
Editing: Tony Lombardo.
Music: Allan Nicholls, Tom Pierson.

Cast: Paul Dooley (*Alex Theodopoulos*), Marta Heflin (*Sheila Shea*), Titos Vandis (*Alex's father*), Belito Moreno (*Eleausa*), Henry Gibson (*Fred Batt*), Dimitra Arliss (*Athena*), Allan Nicholls (*Dana 115*), Ann Ryerson (*Skye 147*), Dennis Franz (*Costa*), Margery Bond (*Wilma*), Ted Neeley (*Teddy*), Fred Bier, Jette Sear (*the imperfect couple*).

Produced by Robert Altman, Tommy Thompson, Robert Eggenweiler, Scott Bushnell for Lion's Gate Films. Twentieth Century-Fox. 110 min.

## 1980    HEALTH

Script: Altman, Frank Barhydt, Paul Dooley.
Direction: Altman.
Assistant director: Tommy Thompson.
Production manager: Robert Eggenweiler.
Photography (Panavision): Edmond L. Koons.
Art direction: Robert Quinn.
Editing: Dennis Hill, Tom Benko.

Cast: Carol Burnett (*Gloria Burbank*), Lauren Bacall (*Esther Brill*), James Garner (*Harry Wolff*), Glenda Jackson (*Isabella Garnell*), Diane Stilwell (*Willow Wertz*), Henry Gibson (*Bobby Hammer*), Paul Dooley (*Dr. Gill Gainey*), Donald Moffat (*Col. Cody*), Alfre Woodard (*Sally

*Benbow*), Ann Ryerson (*Dr. Ruth Ann Jackie*), Robert Fortier (*Chief of Security*), Allan Nicholls (*Jake Jacobs*), MacIntyre Dixon (*Fred Munson*), Dick Cavett, Dinah Shore (*themselves*).

Produced by Altman, Tommy Thompson, Scott Bushnell, Wolf Kroeger for Lion's Gate Films. Twentieth Century-Fox. 96 min.

## 1980    POPEYE

Script: Jules Feiffer, based on the characters by E. C. Segar.
Direction: Altman.
Photography: Giuseppe Rotunno (Panavision).
Production design: Wolf Kroeger.
Location manager: Robert Eggenweiler.
Editing: John W. Holmes, Davie Simmons.
Supervising editor: Tony Lombardo.
Music and Lyrics: Harry Nilsson (additional score by Tom Pierson).

Cast: Robin Williams (*Popeye*), Shelley Duvall (*Olive Oyl*), Ray Walston (*Poopdeck Pappy*), Paul Dooley (*Wimpey*), Paul L. Smith (*Bluto*), Richard Libertini (*Geezil*), Donald Moffat (*taxman*), MacIntyre Dixon (*Cole Oyl*), Roberta Maxwell (*Nana Oyl*), Donovan Scott (*Caster Oyl*), Allan Nicholls (*Rough House*), Wesley Ivan Hurt (*Swee' Pea*), Bill Irwin (*Ham Gravy*), Robert Fortier (*Bill Barnacle*), Linda Hunt (*Mrs. Oxheart*), Carlo Pellegrini (*Swifty*), Dennis Franz (*Spike*), David Arkin (*mailman/policeman*).

Produced by Robert Evans for Paramount Pictures and Walt Disney Productions. Associate producer: Scott Bushnell. 111 min.

## 1982    COME BACK TO THE FIVE AND DIME, JIMMY DEAN, JIMMY DEAN

Script: Ed Graczyk, based on his play.
Direction: Altman.
Photography: Pierre Mignot.
Production design: David Cropman.
Editing: Jason Rosenfield.
Music: Allan Nicholls.

Cast: Sandy Dennis (*Mona*), Cher (*Sissy*), Karen Black (*Joanne*), Sudie Bond (*Juanita*), Marta Heflin (*Edna Louise*), Kathy Bates (*Stella Mae*), Mark Patton (*Joe*).

Produced by Scott Bushnell for Sandcastle 5 Productions/Mark Goodson/Viacom. 102 min.

## 1983    STREAMERS

Script: David Rabe, from his play.
Direction: Altman.
Assistant Director: Allan Nichols.
Photography: Pierre Mignot.
Art direction: Stephen Altman.
Editor: Norman C. Smith.

Cast: Mitchell Lichenstein (*Richie*), Matthew Modine (*Billy*), David Alan Grier (*Roger*), Michael Wright (*Carlyle*), Guy Boyd (*Rooney*), George Dzundza (*Cokes*), Albert Macklin (*Martin*).

Produced by Altman and Nick J. Mileti for Mileti Productions/ United Artists. Associate producer: Scott Bushnell. 118 min.

## 1984    O. C. AND STIGGS

Script: Donald Cantrell and Ted Mann.
Direction: Altman.
Photography: (Panavision): Pierre Mignot.
Production design: Scott Bushnell.
Editing: Elizabeth Kling.
Music: King Sunny Adé and his African Beats.

Cast: Daniel H. Jenkins (*O. C.*), Neill Barry (*Stiggs*), Paul Dooley (*Randall Schwab*), Jane Curtin (*Elinore Schwab*), Martin Mull (*Pat Col-etti*), Dennis Hopper (*Sponson*), Ray Walston (*Gramps*), Louis Nye (*Garth Sloan*), Melvin Van Peebles (*Wino Bob*), Tina Louise (*Florence Beaugereaux*), Cynthia Nixon (*Michelle*), Jon Cryer (*Randall Schwab Jr.*), Donald May (*Jack Stiggs*), Carla Borelli (*Stella Stiggs*).

Produced by Robert Altman and Peter Newman for MGM/UA. Associate Producer: Scott Bushnell. 109 min.

## 1984    SECRET HONOR

Script: Donald Freed and Arnold M. Stone.
Direction: Altman.
Assistant director: Allan Nicholls.
Photography: Pierre Mignot.
Art direction: Stephen Altman.
Editing: Juliet Weber.
Music: George Burt.

Cast: Philip Baker Hall (*Richard M. Nixon*).

Produced by Altman and Scott Bushnell in association with the University of Michigan Department of Communication and the Los Angeles Actors' Studio/Cinecom. 85 min.

## 1985    FOOL FOR LOVE

Script: Sam Shepard, based on his play.
Direction: Altman.
Photography (Panavision): Pierre Mignot.
Production design: Stephen Altman.
Unit production manager: Allan Nicholls.
Editing: Luce Grunenwaldt and Steve Dunn.
Music: George Burt.

Cast: Sam Shepard (*Eddie*), Kim Basinger (*May*), Harry Dean Stanton (*old man*), Randy Quaid (*Martin*), Martha Crawford (*May's mother*), Louise Egolf (*Eddie's mother*), Sura Cox (*teenage May*), Jonathan Skinner (*teenage Eddie*), April Russell (*young May*), Deborah McNaughton (*The Countess*), Lon Hill (*Mr. Valdes*).

Produced by Menahem Golan and Yoram Globus for Cannon Films. Associate producers: Scott Bushnell and Mati Raz. 105 min.

## 1987    BEYOND THERAPY

Script: Christopher Durang and Altman, based on the play by Durang.
Direction: Altman.
Photography: Pierre Mignot.
Production design: Stephen Altman.
Editing: Steve Dunn.
Music: Gabriel Yared.

Cast: Julie Hagerty (*Prudence*), Jeff Goldblum (*Bruce*), Glenda Jackson (*Charlotte*), Tom Conti (*Stuart*), Christopher Guest (*Bob*), Geneviève Page (*Zizi*), Cris Campion (*Andrew*), Sandrine Dumas (*Cindy*), Bertrand Bonvoisin (*Le Gérant*), Nicole Evans (*the cashier*), Louis-Marie Taillefer (*the chef*), Matthew Lesniak (*Mr. Bean*), Laure Killing (*Charlie*).

Produced by Steven M. Haft for New World Pictures. Associate producer: Scott Bushnell. 93 min.

# INDEX